AF251903

AUTOMOBILE CLUB · SOUTHERN CALIFORNIA
AAA

Desert Areas

- Resort Cities
- Joshua Tree
- Colorado River Area
- Imperial Valley
- Anza-Borrego
- East Mojave Area
- West Mojave Area
- Death Valley

Automobile Club of Southern California

For-sale edition distributed by authorized distributors only.

ISBN: 1-56413-295-1
Printed in the United States of America

Contents

CALIFORNIA DESERT AREAS

The California desert's great appeal lies in its diversity. Things to do range from bird watching at remote palm oases to shopping in ultra-chic resorts. Popular activities include such unlikely pastimes as snow skiing, surfing and even saltwater fishing. Festivals and sporting events abound. Yet many people still come to the desert to enjoy the peace and renewal that its sweeping landscapes and brooding mountains provide. For all the development that has occurred in recent years, much of this vast region remains wonderfully desolate, untouched by man's progress.

This book, a reference guide for visitors to the desert area, describes activities, points of interest, events, recreation and places to stay. For easy use of the publication, most information is divided into six geographical sections. (A key map on pages 10 and 11 indicates the section boundaries.) Each region has its own distinct character.

The **Resort Cities area** has all the amenities required of those wanting to take advantage of the desert climate without losing the sense of civilization. With over 80 golf courses, 10,000 swimming pools, 600 tennis courts, 300 hotels, numerous art galleries, shopping centers and exclusive boutiques, world-class restaurants, premiere night spots, casinos and a water park, this area is replete with things to do.

In contrast, the attraction of the **Joshua Tree area** lies in the unspoiled beauty of the low (Colorado) and high (Mojave) desert environments. Two paved roads provide easy access to more than a half million acres of mammoth rock formations, mountain ranges, flats of dramatic Joshua trees and creosote bushes. Joshua Tree National Park's off-road and hiking trails provide challenging, intimate views of this breathtaking environment.

The **Anza-Borrego area** offers secluded canyons and jagged mountains, as well as colorful wildflower displays and a diverse population of desert wildlife. The beauty of this region can be thoroughly enjoyed in Anza-Borrego Desert State Park.

The Cornelia White House at the Village Green Heritage Center offers a glimpse of early Palm Springs life.

Desert flowers are always pretty, and in the case of Jimsonweed, powerful too!

Imperial Sand Dunes Recreation Area has an almost cinematic quality with its rolling ranges of golden red sand dunes.

The sparsely settled **East Mojave area** preserves a vast, wild region of dry lakes, sand dunes, extinct volcanoes and lava beds. The center-piece of this region is the 1.4 million acre Mojave National Preserve. For nature lovers, this area is more than just "the way to Las Vegas."

The burgeoning communities of the more populated **West Mojave area** are supported by the aerospace industry and military installations, although it too has many parks and sanctuaries to preserve and protect this region's rugged beauty, flora and fauna.

The **Death Valley area** presents an awesome example of the forces of nature. Spectacular canyons, craters, sand dunes, salt flats, snow-capped mountains, badlands, ghost towns and ruins, and a unique collection of animal and plant life comprises much of Death Valley National Park, which attracts millions of visitors each year from around the world.

The **Colorado River area** provides water for agriculture, as well as being a source of recreation and tourism. The river meanders through mountain ranges, and across desert valleys and flatlands, creating a stark contrast to the surrounding barren landscape.

The potential of the desert as a booming agricultural economy and as a major source of water recreation is illustrated in the **Imperial Valley area**. The scale of the vast acreage of farmland coupled with the expanse of the Salton Sea gives new meaning to the word "oasis." Yet the

Mother Nature sure comes up with some amazing scenery— we have here the Trona Pinnacles in the West Mojave.

SOUTHERN CALIFORNIA DESERT AREAS

1. Resort Cities, page 38
2. Joshua Tree Area, page 66
3. Colorado River Area, page 82
4. Imperial Valley Area, page 100
5. Anza-Borrego Area, page 118
6. East Mojave Area, page 132
7. West Mojave Area, page 154
8. Death Valley Area, page 176

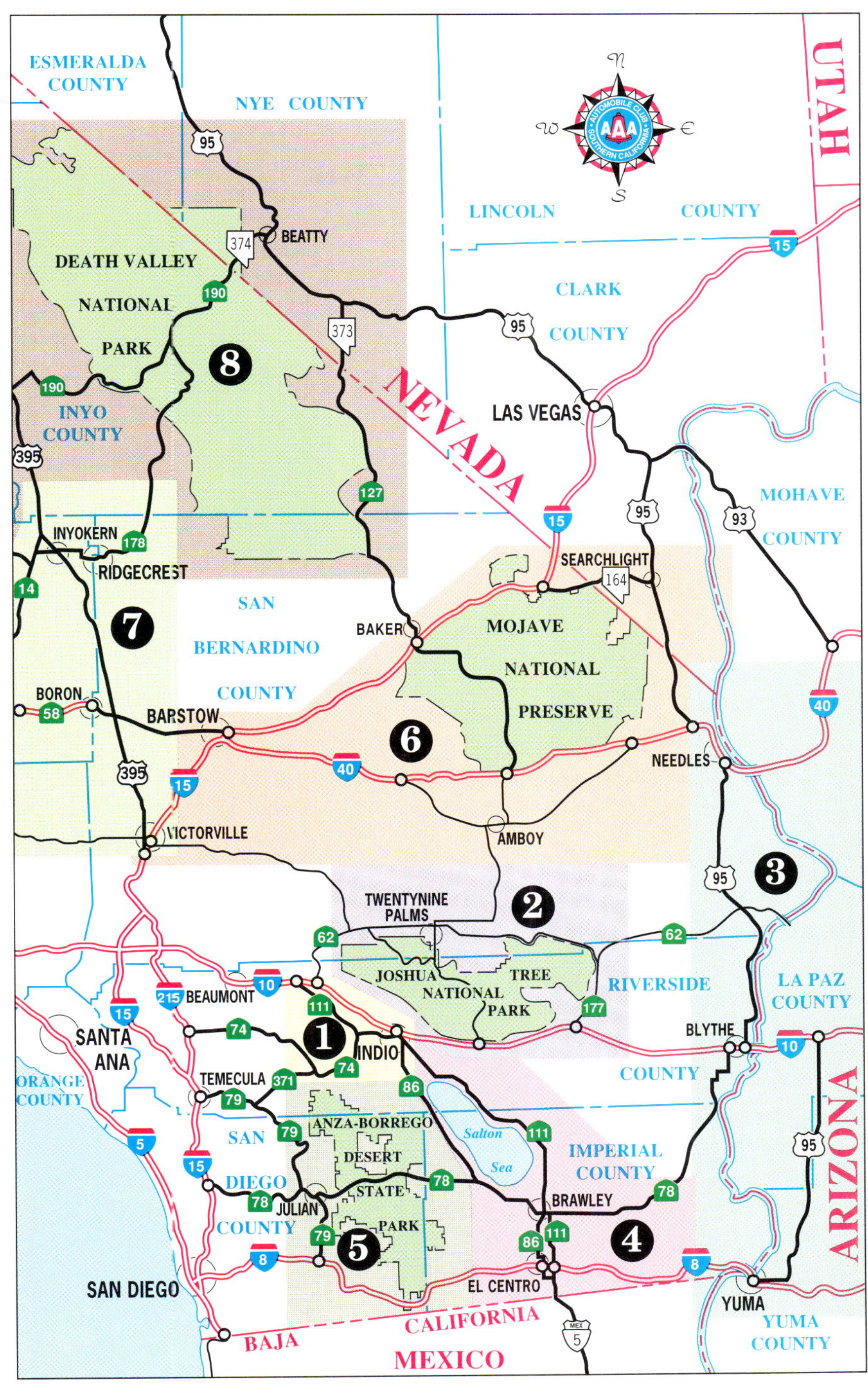

11
ESMERALDA COUNTY
NYE COUNTY
95
BEATTY
374
DEATH VALLEY
190
NATIONAL
PARK
8
190
INYO COUNTY
395
178
INYOKERN
RIDGECREST
14
7
SAN
BERNARDINO
COUNTY
BORON
58
BARSTOW
395
15
VICTORVILLE
127
NEVADA
LINCOLN COUNTY
CLARK COUNTY
95
LAS VEGAS
15
95
373
BAKER
MOJAVE
NATIONAL
PRESERVE
SEARCHLIGHT
164
93
MOHAVE COUNTY
6
40
AMBOY
NEEDLES
40
95
3
UTAH
15
TWENTYNINE PALMS
2
62
62
JOSHUA TREE
NATIONAL PARK
177
RIVERSIDE
LA PAZ COUNTY
BEAUMONT
10
215
111
74
1
INDIO
SANTA ANA
15
74
TEMECULA
371
79
ORANGE COUNTY
79
SAN
5
15
DIEGO
78
JULIAN
COUNTY
86
ANZA-BORREGO
DESERT
79
STATE
PARK
79
5
8
SAN DIEGO
Salton Sea
111
IMPERIAL COUNTY
78
BRAWLEY
78
BLYTHE
10
COUNTY
95
ARIZONA
86
111
4
8
EL CENTRO
YUMA
YUMA COUNTY
MEX 5
BAJA CALIFORNIA
MEXICO
N
W
E
S
AUTOMOBILE CLUB SOUTHERN CALIFORNIA
AAA

CALL
BOX

▼ *Showing The Way*

To help you find your way around the desert areas of Southern California, the Automobile Club of Southern California publishes a number of comprehensive maps, guides and books. For a statewide overview, the *California* map relates each of the counties that comprise the desert region: Imperial, Inyo, Kern, Los Angeles, Riverside, San Bernardino and San Diego. Detailed maps, most in the new *Explore!* format, are available for each of these counties except Inyo, which is covered on the *Guide to Death Valley National Park*. The California/Arizona border area is covered on the *Guide to the Colorado River*. The Auto Club *Lancaster-Palmdale*, *Victor Valley* and *Palm Springs-Indio* city maps provide additional coverage and are strongly recommended for locating attractions listed by street address. Apart from "conventional" accommodations listed in the AAA *California/Nevada TourBook*, the *Central and Southern California Camping Map* and *Bed & Breakfast Southern California* provide information about unique places to stay. With the exception of the AAA *California/Nevada TourBook*, which is available only to members through AAA offices, all of these handy references and guides are available in selected bookstores throughout Southern California, and are also available to Auto Club members at district offices.

Geography

The region was not always so arid. The desert landscape, molded over the centuries by earthquake and flood, at one time was pastureland. Thousands of years ago the northernmost portion of the area was covered by vast lakes. Volcanic activity further sculpted many of the region's most salient features. In the west, pressure from earthquake faults, most notably the San Andreas in the northeast near the base of the Little San Bernardino Mountains, formed mountain ranges that today comprise much of Anza-Borrego Desert State Park. Water from the Gulf of California flooded north as far as San Gorgonio Pass, then retreated—only to reappear and disappear again and again.

(Today evidence of ancient seas and lakes appears in several places: The waterline is evident on the mountains forming the eastern edge of Anza-Borrego Desert State Park. The floor of Death Valley is covered with large salt deposits left from the evaporated water. And seashells can still be found south of Split Mountain and in the Coyote Mountains, as well as in the Imperial Valley.) As the ancient faulting continued, the coastal and peninsular mountains grew higher and eventually blocked the cooling sea breezes and rain-bearing clouds, causing the region to become arid.

A major force in the desert's geography is the Colorado River. Its origins are in the mountains of Colorado, and it

Interstate 15 cuts across the East Mojave.

The Colorado River cuts a wide swath through the desert near Parker, Arizona.

works its way southwest across what is now Utah and northern Arizona, then cuts south toward the Gulf of California. Around 900 A.D., the Colorado River changed its course, forming a lake in the depression caused by the ancient seas. Known as Lake Cahuilla, it covered 2000 square miles at its fullest. About 500 years ago it evaporated, leaving salt flats known as the Salton Sink.

The Salton Sea, one of the region's most distinctive geographic features, was created in the Salton Sink between 1905 and 1907 when Colorado River water, brought in via canals to irrigate the Imperial Valley, broke through a levee. The salt accumulation from ancient Lake Cahuilla mixed with the river water and earned the Salton Sea its name. Irrigation runoff from surrounding farm lands continues to increase the salinity and further compound the mineral content of the sea's water. Today the lower Colorado River acts as the state boundary between Arizona and the states of Nevada and California. Three man-made lakes, Mead, Mohave and Havasu, have been created by the construction of dams to control water flow in the river.

Climate

The desert is notorious for its hot weather, but in fact, most months are comfortable. In the lower deserts, average daytime temperatures at midwinter fall in the 70-degree range with nights in the upper 30s; spring and autumn days are usually in the 80s with nights in the 50s. Summer is indeed hot, with daytime temperatures rising above 100 degrees and nights cooling to the 70s and 80s. Death Valley is one of the hottest places in the world—air temperature readings of over 120 degrees are common during the summer months, and ground temperatures are usually 50 percent higher. The higher desert may range from 5 to 15 degrees cooler throughout the year. Rainfall is sparse, generally only 3 to 10 inches annually, and a portion of that arrives in the form of summer thunderstorms. Death Valley's higher elevations are usually covered with snow from November to May. Humidity along the Colorado River is usually a few percent higher than in other parts of the desert due to evaporation of river water, but this seems to have no mitigating effect on the desert heat.

▼ *Desert Travel Tips*

The following suggestions will help you prepare for hiking or driving in remote desert areas.

1. Let someone know where you are going and when you expect to return. This can be a park ranger, the Bureau of Land Management office nearest your point of departure, or a friend who will notify the authorities if you fail to return when expected.

2. Check the weather and road or trail conditions before you leave. If flash floods are expected, stay out of dry washes—without warning a wall of water can come charging through. Sandy paved roads can cause a passenger-vehicle driver to lose control. Many dirt roads are impassable for passenger cars; some are too poor even for four-wheel-drive vehicles, particularly during and after rainstorms. It is not unwise to stop the car and walk through muddy or sandy spots to check for firmness prior to driving a vehicle through the suspect area.

3. Travel with a companion when going off the pavement.

4. Take enough water for both you and your vehicle on backcountry trips. On short hikes take a canteen. One gallon of water per person, per day, and five gallons for your vehicle are recommended. An extra day's supply of water per person is a wise precaution against emergencies.

5. Carry a detailed map of the area you are entering; a topograhic map is a good idea.

6. Layer your clothing and wear light colors. Take a hat to protect your head and face from the elements.

7. Use sunglasses and sunscreen.

8. When traveling to remote areas, take extra food, a first aid kit and a tarp or similar item for shade.

9. In case of emergency, stay with your vehicle. Desert search and rescue experience has shown that it is faster and easier to find a vehicle than an individual on foot.

10. Most domestic pets, including cats and dogs, do not easily survive desert travel. On a warm day, the temperature in a parked car can reach 160 degrees in a matter of minutes, even with partially opened windows. *Pets should not be left in a parked car!* Take plenty of water for your pet.

Colorful flowers are found in spring at the Cholla Cactus Garden in Joshua Tree National Park.

Desert Flora

One aspect of the desert that draws visitors to areas other than the resorts is the amazingly varied plant life. Many desert plants and cacti are slow-growing and can take 20 or more years to grow to an average size. To the casual observer the desert may appear to be a barren expanse of drifting sand, but in spring the desert can be a vast carpet of blooming flowers. When adequate rain has fallen during the previous autumn and winter (only a few inches are necessary), the desert floor erupts in color with purple sand verbena, white desert primrose and yellow desert sunflowers. This vibrant display at low elevations usually begins in February and extends into March. Flowers come to the mid-elevations in March; agave, brittlebush, mallow, creosote and ocotillo add a variety of color to the landscape. In the high desert, coreopsis, desert primrose and encelia brighten the landscape in spring. Cacti also offer colorful blooms throughout the spring. All varieties of cholla cactus produce vivid yellow flowers, while the flat cacti, such as beaver tail and hedgehog, sprout pink flowers. Prickly pear blooms range from pale yellow to orange, and the old-man cactus offers yellow blooms. Farther up the mountains, prickly poppy, chia, penstemon and buttercup bloom from April to June.

The Antelope Valley portion of the western Mojave Desert is known for its spring displays of the California Poppy and other colorful wildflowers. Several wildflower sanctuaries dot the area, most located east of Lancaster and Palmdale and south of Edwards Air Force Base.

At a distance the smoke tree, with its gray-green color and lacy foliage, gives the impression of wisps of smoke. In summer the tree is dotted with bright purple flowers. The palo verde tree is more bush-like, with yellow blooms somewhat resembling small sweet peas. Although typically seen as a landscaping element in the cities of the Southwest, the natural habitat of the California fan palm or *Washingtonia filifera* is remote desert oases.

Joshua trees, found primarily in the higher Mojave Desert, can grow to a height of 30 feet. Large Joshuas with many branches denote great age (they rarely grow more than one-half inch each year). A species of yucca, and therefore a member of the agave family, the Joshua displays creamy-white, bell-shaped blossoms from February to late April.

Nearly 1000 species of plants, including 21 species found nowhere else in the world, grow in the harsh environment preserved in Death Valley National Park. One of these unusual plants is the Desert Bearpoppy, which has large white flowers and leaves covered with long silvery hairs; it is found in the Panamint Mountains and southwest of the Ubehebe Crater. The Death Valley Sage, another endemic specie, is a shrub two to three feet high with clusters of small purple and blue flowers; it grows in Titus Canyon and the southern Funeral Mountains east of Furnace Creek. A member of the sunflower family, the Panamint Daisy's large, showy yellow flowers grow on stems of 12 inches or more in length; it is found on the approach to Wildrose from Panamint Valley. Mid-February to April typically sees these plants in bloom.

The creosote bush, also known as greasewood, is found throughout the desert, often with ocotillo, brittlebush, and any of a variety of chollas. Along drainage washes mesquite and cat's claw are quite common. In the northern desert the mountain tops are sometimes covered with a pygmy forest of piñon, California and Utah juniper, and scrub oak. In areas where there is a constant source of water, such as along Piute Creek and the Mojave River in Afton Canyon, cottonwood and willow trees grow.

The tumbleweed has become an example of typical desert flora. Also known as the Russian-Thistle, the plant is actually native to Eurasia. When ripe, the bush dries into a round form, breaks off at the root and, pushed by wind and water, tumbles across the desert floor. Another plant that was introduced to the desert is the tamarix. One variety was planted as windbreaks in the valleys, while another type is now commonly found near water. Various forms of mustard plants also were brought by priests in their early explorations and mission settlements.

Wildflowers and desert plants are for the enjoyment of all. The law prohibits picking flowers or removing plants from their native habitat. In order to avoid damaging fragile plantlife, hiking in areas without well-defined trails is not encouraged.

Wildlife

A surprising assortment of creatures call the desert home. Lizards are perhaps the most common species seen, inhabiting both the upper and lower deserts. The endangered fringe-toed lizard is native to the Coachella Valley, and the banded gecko makes its home in the Imperial Sand Dunes. Snakes are seldom seen, however the nonpoisonous bull snake is sometimes found near developed areas. On more remote

▼ *Rattled About Rattlesnakes?*

The deserts of California are home to the rattlesnake. Spring is rattlesnake season, so visitors to the desert areas should be aware of where they step and where they put their hands. During morning hours these poisonous reptiles can be found in dry rocky hills, sunning themselves on ledges or among rocks, and in transit along sand dunes. On summer nights they're out hunting, and on cool nights they look for a warm place—an animal burrow, a tangle of branches, a pile of rocks or wood, or even underneath a parked car.

Not all rattlesnake bites are the same. Because of chemicals in the venom, some rattlesnake bites cause swelling, pain, blisters and even bleeding under the skin. Others just leave fang puncture marks. *Regardless of the type of wound, all snake bites require immediate medical attention.* Treatment may consist of a simple procedure to prevent infection and tetanus. There is an antidote for rattlesnake bites and most people recover after treatment.

Symptoms of a rattlesnake bite include tingling of the lips, face, fingers and toes. In severe cases there may be shock, kidney failure, shortness of breath and partial paralysis. Often the severity of the symptoms depend on how much venom is injected by the snake. Adult rattlers may not inject venom when they bite, or only inject a portion of venom. Very young rattlesnakes frequently inject all of their venom. Baby rattlesnakes are born in the spring and their venom is full strength; they also lack control in injecting their venom.

Rattlesnakes are "pit vipers" because they have small openings between the nostrils and eyes.

Visitors to the desert areas can reduce the risk of rattlesnake attack and severe injury by doing the following:

- Wear heavy, knee-high socks with high-top shoes or boots and long pants tucked into the shoes.

- Avoid hiking alone or at night. Stay on clear paths. Be wary of tall grass and heavy underbrush.

- Do not step over a log or a large stone; walk around it.

- Look carefully before sitting down and do not lie near wood or rubbish piles.

- Camp on open ground after checking carefully for snakes and likely places where snakes can hide.

- Avoid gathering firewood at night.

Note that even if a rattlesnake is dead for up to an hour it can still bite with a reflex action. Even if the head is severed it can still bite. If a rattlesnake bite occurs please do the following:

- Get the victim away from the snake.

- ***Call 911 immediately*** to transport the victim to the hospital or take the victim to the nearest hospital (see *Quick Guide* boxes for emergency information).

- To keep circulation as slow as possible, keep the victim calm and still. Remove rings, watches or tight clothing if the bite is on the hands or arms. Make sure the fingers are straight.

Do not do the following:

- Do not give the victim alcohol, coffee or any medication.

- Do not apply a tourniquet.

- Do not put heat or ice on the wound.

- Do not try to suck out the venom.

- Do not cut into the bite area.

For more information contact the Los Angeles Regional Drug and Poison Center at (213) 222-3212 or (800) 777-6476; open 24 hours.

Clockwise from top left: kit fox, Gambel's quail, jack rabbit and desert tortoise.

trails it is possible to encounter a diamondback rattlesnake or sidewinder (both are poisonous—take a close look at any sticks lying near your path, one just might be a snake sunning itself). The desert tortoise is also found throughout the region, and several high-density areas have been designated as preserves to protect this threatened species. Several wildlife sanctuaries have been established in the Antelope Valley.

In a dry, desert environment one would not expect to find fish, but the minnow-like desert pupfish lives its whole life cycle in just a few days in pools left by rains and runoff. They live in saline waters at four different locations in Death Valley and can be seen at Anza-Borrego Desert State Park headquarters. Saltwater fish have been introduced to the Salton Sea (see separate listing, *Imperial Valley*). Freshwater fish, such as striped bass, largemouth bass, channel catfish, flathead catfish, crappie, bluegill and rainbow trout, are fairly common in the waters of the Colorado River. Trout are planted on a regular basis.

Desert bugs include several kinds of spiders, including some varieties that are poisonous. Furry, fuzzy tarantulas are infrequently seen and are more terrifying to look at than they are dangerous. Beetles' shells are sometimes surprisingly colorful. Large orange and black worms are plentiful in spring in the Yuha Desert.

All kinds of feathered friends fly the desert's skies, including the roadrunner, desert owl, mourning dove, raven, red-tailed hawk and golden eagle. Many migratory birds stop off in the Salton Sea area (see separate listing, *Imperial Valley Area*). Constant water supplies in Afton Canyon and Kelso also attract many birds.

Small animals, such as the kangaroo rat, cactus mouse, jack rabbit, cottontail and skunk are occasionally spotted by sharp-eyed observers. Larger animals, such as the bighorn sheep, mule deer, coyote, bobcat and fox, are almost never seen.

A few attractions offer exhibits of native wildlife (see *Wildlife* in Index).

Economy

The ancient seas once covering the Salton Sink left behind land well-suited to supporting the region's thriving, modern-day economy. Aided by extensive irrigation, fertile soils in the Imperial Valley and the eastern end of the Coachella Valley yield great quantities of produce, shipped throughout the United States. Military installations are part of the economy in the Yuma area as well as in San Bernardino County, where space exploration is also an economic factor. The Resort Cities cater to tourists with acres and acres of golf courses and accompanying resorts.

Historical aircraft, such as the SR-71 Blackbird, are included in the tour at NASA Dryden Flight Research Facility on Edwards Air Force Base.

Performing Arts

The Resort Cities area could easily be considered the center of theatrical and performing arts in the California desert. The **McCallum Theatre for the Performing Arts** at the Bob Hope Cultural Center in Palm Desert and the **Palm Springs Desert Museum**'s theater offer name and local entertainment ranging from musicals to concerts. These venues together with the **Fabulous Palm Springs Follies** comprise more than a start for engaging entertainment in the Coachella Valley. In the West Mojave's Antelope Valley, the **Lancaster Performing Arts Center** presents local performance groups as well as hosting regional talent. The **Amargosa Opera House** in Death Valley features performances from opera and pantomime in a unique converted movie theater.

Activities for Children

Enjoyable activities for children abound in the California Desert Areas. The wonders of the desert environment appeal to most young people.

With proper supervision and precautions—sun protection, enough drinking water, watching out for snakes and other predatory wildlife—desert recreation can be healthful and safe. Outdoor family activities that are wholesome and enjoyable to youngsters are described in the *Recreation* chapter, which elaborates on hiking, horseback riding and even select locations for boating, fishing and ice skating. All of the following attractions and activities are covered in the several area chapters of this book.

Animal parks and zoos are naturals for attracting children's interest. At the **Living Desert**, a wildlife and botanical park in Palm Desert, they can observe desert

The McCallum Theatre for the Performing Arts, part of the Bob Hope Cultural Center, hosts visiting and local performances and shows.

creatures from North America and other arid regions of the world, such as owls, reptiles, Mexican wolves and a golden eagle. Hikes on nature trails reveal vegetation from various American desert regions. At the **Sahati Camel Farm and Desert Animal Breeding Center** in Yuma, children can observe camels and other exotic desert animals, including ibex, oryx, caracals and fennec foxes. Rare and exotic cats, both tropical and midlatitude species, may be seen at the **Exotic Feline Breeding Compound** in Rosamond.

Children interested in the "Old West" will enjoy the exhibits on territorial and prison history at **Yuma Territorial State Historic Park** in Yuma. And **Calico Ghost Town**, near Barstow, offers the wonders of a historic silver-mining boom town. A train ride, a mine tour and a mystery shack provide educational fun. The **Hi-Desert Nature Museum** in Yucca Valley contains exhibits on flora, fauna and geology, and its "Kids' Korner" has hands-on activities. The **Victor Valley Museum** in Apple Valley has rocks and minerals, reptiles, Indian artifacts and antiques of pioneer settlers; it also has a children's room providing for hands-on experiences. Children interested in old western movies will enjoy the **Roy Rogers-Dale Evans Museum** in Victorville. The fort-style building is full of souvenirs and awards belonging to the famous couple. Budding scientists will pay attention to the marvels of aerospace at **NASA Dryden Flight Research Facility** on Edwards Air Force Base. A tour profiles the history of space flight and shows current aircraft. Also at Edwards, a memorable thrill in the life of a young person might be viewing a space **shuttle landing**. When this event occurs a remote viewing area is open to the public.

The Oasis Water Park in Palm Springs is a great place for cool fun in the hot sun.

The **Oasis Water Park** in Palm Springs delights children during the long hot season. This aquatic playground offers a wave pool for surfing, water slides, and a river for inner tubes. The **Palm Springs Aerial Tramway** provides thrills for children (and adults, too). The suspended cars climb about 6000 feet and whisk passengers from the desert floor up to high mountain woods. Mule-drawn **Covered Wagon Tours** through the Coachella Valley Preserve in Thousand Palms give youngsters a trip back in history and an education about the natural environment—the ecology of palms and other desert plants as well as wildlife.

Children may dissipate pent-up energy in the many parks, large and small, scattered over the desert areas.

Mojave Narrows Regional Park in Victorville has hiking, horseback riding and camping. The visitor centers of **Joshua Tree National Park** and **Anza-Borrego Desert State Park** offer educational exhibits appealing to persons of all ages, in addition to an assortment of recreational opportunities. The **Desert Tower**, west of Ocotillo on I-8, affords spectacular views of the Yuha Desert and Imperial Valley. Children also might be attracted to the adjacent caves and rock carvings of strange creatures.

Shopping

Shoppers find a nice variety of wares in the desert areas. The spectrum ranges from local souvenirs to exotic boutiques to the gamut of consumer goods found in two factory outlet centers and six major shopping malls. In general, concentrations of commercial districts and shopping centers correspond to the more densely populated regions.

The Resort Cities (Coachella Valley) have the most to offer, especially for tourists. Other shopping centers are found in the West Mojave (Antelope Valley), East Mojave (Victorville and Barstow) and the Imperial Valley.

In the Coachella Valley, upscale shops and boutiques and gourmet restaurants are sought after by discriminating shoppers in Palm Desert's **El Paseo** and in downtown Palm Springs along **Palm Canyon Drive**. Shopping in the Resort Cities really becomes a fresh-air happening with two regular street fairs, which include arts and crafts and farmers markets: **VillageFest** occurs each Thursday in Palm Springs and **Street Fair** is held each weekend in Palm Desert. Antique and second-hand shops are found in Cathedral City in the Coachella Valley and Lancaster in the Antelope Valley.

For eager lady shoppers (and some gentlemen, too) the outlet centers are a major magnet. The **Desert Hills Factory Stores** in Cabazon, 17 miles

Elegant restaurants and exclusive boutiques entice shoppers to El Paseo in Palm Desert.

Barstow's Factory Merchants Outlets Plaza is a great place to shop for bargains.

northwest of Palm Springs, and the **Factory Merchants Outlets Plaza** in Barstow carry a big variety of apparel, home furnishings, cosmetics and many more articles at reduced prices. Full-scale shopping malls are found in the major population centers: Palm Springs has the **Desert Fashion Plaza** and the **Palm Springs Mall**; in Palm Desert is the **Palm Desert Town Center**; El Centro has the **Valley Plaza** and **El Centro Center**; and Palmdale boasts the **Antelope Valley Mall**. (Antelope Valley Mall and Palm Desert Town Center are the two largest malls in the California Desert.)

Just across the border from the Imperial Valley, opposite Calexico, lies **Mexicali, Baja California**, a destination for American tourists seeking the crafts and flavor of Mexico. Mexicali, a city of about 750,000, has the whole spectrum from small stands and shops to large shopping malls. The biggest concentration of shops that sell typical Mexican arts and crafts and clothing items is located a short distance over the border and within walking distance of the crossing gate. The largest mall in the city is **Plaza Cachanilla**, located on Calzada López Mateos, 1$\frac{7}{10}$ miles southeast of the border.

History

Resort Cities

It is known that Yuman Indians lived along the shores of the ancient Lake Cahuilla (Ka-WEE-yah), a huge fresh-water body that once covered what we now call the Imperial Valley and much of the Coachella Valley. The lake, formed by water from the Colorado River, supplied abundant fish and plant life for the Yuman, especially along the northern shore near present-day Indio. When the Colorado River was rerouted over time, the lake gradually disappeared, and by the 14th or 15th century it was gone, leaving behind arid land. The Yumans also vanished around that time.

For at least the past 500 years, another people—the Agua Caliente, a sub-group of the Cahuilla—has lived in canyons in the Coachella Valley. Springs and streams in Tahquitz, Murray, Chino, Palm and Andreas canyons provided ample water for growing crops and drinking. They came to bathe in the hot mineral springs, now located on the grounds of the Palm Springs Spa Hotel, a practice that inspired the Spanish name *Agua Caliente* or "hot water." In 1876 the United States government deeded 32,000 acres of even-numbered sections of land to the Agua Caliente people for use as their reservation.

At the same time, odd-numbered sections—each one mile square—were given to Southern Pacific Railroad in return for building a rail line from Los Angeles across the California desert to Yuma, Arizona The railroad was able to sell its land, but until recently it was difficult for the Indians to do so.

The area's modern agricultural history began in 1884 when Judge John Guthrie McCallum moved from San Francisco to San Bernardino and then to Palm Springs, hoping the dry desert climate would improve his ailing son's health. McCallum planted fruit trees, irrigating them with water from Tahquitz Canyon. As his orchards expanded, he built a stone-lined ditch to bring water from the Whitewater River, 19 miles north of Palm Springs. Ten years after he'd arrived, the Whitewater River changed its channel, and there was a drought. The combined misfortunes made his farming endeavors impractical.

Another attempt at developing the Palm Springs area met with more success. Dr. Welwood Murray built the first small hotel and sanitarium in 1886 for people requiring the dry desert air for health reasons. In 1909 Nellie Coffman, daughter of a Santa Monica hotel man, opened the Desert Inn Hotel & Sanitarium. For many years, Palm Springs remained a tiny town catering to people who liked or needed the desert climate.

The town grew slowly until the 1930s, when actors Ralph Bellamy and Charles Farrell bought 200 acres of land in the sleepy village of Palm Springs. The two tennis courts they built subsequently grew into the Palm Springs Racquet Club. At that time, there were only two lodgings in town—Coffman's Desert Inn and the

---

Rock art is a major feature of the Maturango Museum in Ridgecrest.

El Mirador Hotel, built in 1928 and today part of the Desert Hospital. The Racquet Club grew as more Hollywood stars came to relax in Palm Springs and stay in the cottages that were soon built there.

World War II had an effect on the tiny community of Indio, whose 1942 population was just 1600 people. The train depot saw the arrival of thousands of men and equipment destined for the U.S. Armed Forces Desert Training Center, 30 miles east of town. Support facilities and families were based in Indio for more than two years.

In the years since the war, several factors have contributed to the area's phenomenal growth. The use of irrigation in the eastern end of the Coachella Valley has yielded a variety of agricultural products, including dates and citrus fruits. The health benefits of a warm, dry climate attracted many from around the country. Retirees began spending winters in the snow-free deserts, many becoming permanent residents. Hollywood's stars continued to retreat to the desert for rest and recreation. And, the popularity of golf drew those dedicated to the game as more and more courses were built for year-round play.

Today the resort communities in the upper Coachella Valley have approximately 80 AAA-approved hotels and resorts and a wide variety of restaurants. Many well-known personalities are permanent or seasonal residents, often becoming involved in local activities. Celebrities include entertainers Bob Hope and Andy Williams, entertainer-turned-politician Sonny Bono, former President Gerald Ford, *TV Guide* creator Walter Annenberg, singer Frank Sinatra, golf star Lee Trevino and actor William Devane.

Joshua Tree Area

The lush oases in the Joshua Tree area are thought to have been inhabited for the last 9000 years. The Serrano people formed the first of the known societies populating the northern portion of what is now Joshua Tree National Park. The Cahuilla lived in the southern portion, as well as many places throughout the Coachella Valley.

According to local legend, the Serrano originally lived in the San Bernardino Mountains. But because the women were not producing male children, their spiritual healer told them to travel east into the desert and settle in the first place they found water. He also told the group to plant a palm tree every time a male was born. During the first year after the Serrano found an oasis—the Oasis of Mara— 29 boys were born, and of course, 29 palms were planted.

Regardless of the legend's authenticity, palms were of great importance to these early peoples. Trunks provided poles for their houses, palm fronds were used as roofs and made into sandals, and stems of the fronds became cooking utensils. The palms had a spiritual significance for the Serrano, as they regularly burned vegetation within the oasis to purge the dead fronds of evil. This burning was materially beneficial because it cleared the undergrowth from around the trees and increased seed production.

The Serrano made use of other vegetation as those living near Mara or Twentynine Palms traveled regularly to the neighboring Fortynine Palms Oasis for such water-related plants as cattails and bulbs, which they used to vary a monotonous diet. Mesquite trees supplied bean pods, a source of nutrition that was ground, formed into cakes and dried. Mesquite bark was woven into a type of cloth, the thorns became needles, and the branches were made into bows for hunting.

In 1867 a band of Chemehuevi Indians came from the Colorado River to settle with the Serrano. The two peoples lived together peacefully, and eventually the Chemehuevi became assimilated by the more populous Serrano society. The Chemehuevi brought to the oasis their knowledge of irrigation and cultivation. These improvements were fairly short-lived, however, because by 1913 all the ancient inhabitants had either died from illnesses brought by Anglo settlers or were relocated out of Twentynine Palms to the nearby Morongo Reservation.

A dozen years before the Chemehuevi had come to the area, a U.S. government surveyor, Colonel Henry Washington, recorded the existence of Twentynine Palms Oasis. Not long after, gold was discovered (1873), and the Anaconda Mine opened south of Twentynine Palms. The Lost Horse, Desert Queen and Golden Bee also were soon producing gold from the area today known as Joshua Tree National Park.

As the gold supply dwindled, ranchers began running cattle. The upper desert at that time received more rainfall than it does today, so there were more springs and pools, and grass was abundant. One of the first ranches, the Desert Queen, was at one time owned by Bill Keys, who improved the ranch, raised his family in this remote area and started the first school.

The 1920s and '30s found settlers coming to the Twentynine Palms and Joshua Tree areas. Following World War I, veterans, including victims of wartime poison-gas attacks, settled there for the dry desert air. During the Depression, homesteaders were also drawn by free land. To save the region and its wildlife from overdevelopment, concerned citizens began a campaign to save the desert. In 1936, President Franklin Roosevelt acknowledged their efforts by designating Joshua Tree National Monument.

On October 31, 1994, the monument was elevated to national park status with the passage of the Desert Protection Act.

Colorado River Area

The prehistoric era is well represented in the Colorado River region on canyon walls, in caves and on desert flatlands. Petroglyphs, pictographs and intaglios are silent testimony of aboriginal Indian life that may date as far back as 10,000 years. The petroglyphs are carvings or inscriptions on a rock surface, while pictographs are drawings on a rock surface. Intaglios are the etchings of figures (human, coiled snake, etc.) in light-colored or white rock on a flat parcel of ground. They are best viewed from a higher elevation.

When the first Europeans arrived in the Colorado River region they found Mohave, Chemehuevi and Quechan Indians living along the banks of the river. These nomadic hunter-gatherers were adept at living on the sparse vegetation and wildlife of the desert.

Early European incursions into this area involved a Spanish attempt at a land route to the southern California coast. They were followed by American explorers, traders, miners and farmers/settlers. In 1858, the Butterfield Overland Stage Route traversed this area on its way from St. Louis, Missouri to San Francisco, California. This increase in population was bound to create tension and violence between the newcomers and the established Indian tribes. A U.S. military presence, based primarily in the Yuma area, was set up to protect American interests. The fort and supply depot was a vital base in the southwest until 1883.

By the late 1800s, miners, the railroads, limited agriculture and Indian reservations shared the use of this region. The 1940s saw the desert being utilized as a training area for combat in North Africa during World War II. Also at this time, the area around Poston, Arizona, was used as an internment camp for Japanese-American citizens.

Today the Colorado River region is traversed by three major Interstate highways and has become a major travel, recreation and tourist area. Other current enterprises include military installations, Indian reservations and agriculture.

Imperial Valley Area

As noted in the "Resort Cities" section of this chapter, Lake Cahuilla, an enormous inland freshwater lake, once covered most of the Coachella and Imperial valleys. The Yuman people lived along its shore, but when it began to dry up, they left. No humans could live in this barren land lying between the Colorado River on the east and the Vallecito and Santa Rosa mountains on the west.

This inhospitable terrain was crossed occasionally by a few daring explorers and priests in their efforts to reach the California coast. In 1774, Juan Bautista de Anza led the first European expedition through the area. The first site where gold was found in the present state of California was in the Cargo Muchacho Mountains in 1775. Lack of water meant the placer mining process couldn't be used to extract the gold, so it was another 100 years before lode mining developed in the district.

Old Plank Road, built in 1916, made it possible for motorists to cross shifting sand in the dune area of southeastern Imperial County (see listing).

In 1882 the Yuma Mining Company operated a stamp mill which crushed $167,000 dollars worth of gold from 14,000 tons of quartz. Other rich mines in the area included Ogilby, American Girl and Hedges, which in 1910 became known as Tumco (coined from The United Mines Company).

Records indicate that as early as 1849 a Dr. Oliver Wozencraft dreamed of bringing water to the Imperial Valley. He appealed to the California legislature and to the U.S. Congress for funds to channel water from the Colorado River. But it wasn't until after his death that the California Land and Development Company began diverting water. Canals were dug and irrigation from the Colorado River started in 1901, and for the next few years the valley saw rapid growth as settlers began farming the once-arid land. Barley was among the first and most successful crops planted. Because of the agricultural bounty— and the development of a dairy and hog industry as well—the Southern Pacific Railroad built a spur line to collect the commodities from Niland, Brawley, El Centro and as far south as Calexico.

Within three years the original canals were inadequate. A new larger and deeper channel was dug from the Colorado River to increase the water supply to the Imperial Valley. The following year the river rose and flood waters broke through the channel, causing the entire river to change its course and run north, creating the Salton Sea. Residents feared the entire valley would soon be one great lake, but levees were hastily built to save the larger towns of Imperial, El Centro and Brawley. Efforts to rechannel the wayward river finally succeeded in 1907. Still, Imperial Valley residents lived in constant fear that the Colorado would again flood and change its course. It wasn't until 1936, upon completion of Hoover Dam, that valley dwellers were assured of flood-free land.

In 1940 the All-American Canal, channeling water from the Imperial Dam on the Colorado River, opened to allow ample water for irrigation of more than 80,000 acres throughout the valley. Lettuce, fruits and vegetables, livestock feed, cotton and sugar beets are now the major crops grown in this fertile land.

Anza-Borrego Area

Evidence of several prehistoric peoples living in the Anza-Borrego area dates back about 10,000 years. The earliest-known inhabitants—the San Dieguitos —fished and hunted along ancient lakes and streams that existed at that time. The next two groups, both seed-gatherers, left remnants of culture in the form of bedrock mortars and pestles. The later prehistoric people left petroglyphs and pottery fragments, located in the southern area of Anza-Borrego Desert State Park around what is now called Indian Hill.

Next the Yuman and Shoshonean peoples settled in small family units in the area around what is now County Road S22. They were skilled at living off the land, gathering seeds and hunting with bows and arrows. Plants such as agave and yucca provided food, as well as fiber for clothing, bow strings and rope snares. The plants' roots were used for soap, its thorns for awls and its spines for needles.

In more recent history, the Cahuilla, a subgroup of Shoshonean people, lived in the mountains and desert of the Anza-Borrego area. In the years following the first white man's entry in 1772, the Cahuilla population began to decline and many moved to the mission at Santa Ysabel. After a small-pox epidemic in 1870, others left the desert, and the remaining Cahuilla were sent to Los Coyotes Reservation after an Indian uprising in 1891.

Although Indians were the first inhabitants, Anza-Borrego was named in part after Juan Bautista de Anza, leader of the first European expedition through the area. In 1774 Anza set out from Sonora, Mexico, for Monterey, California, accompanied by a contingent of 21 soldiers, a translator, two natives and a pair of priests. They successfully navigated the desert, arrived at the San Gabriel Mission and then proceeded to Monterey. Their route took them through Imperial County to Borrego Springs, and on into the San Jacinto Valley. Two years later Anza again led a party, this one of 240 settlers and 800 animals, through the Anza-Borrego area north to San Francisco. When the Sonora Road was established as a regular route for travelers in 1824, it closely followed the route used by Anza.

During the California gold rush in the mid-1800s, the same route was renamed the Southern Emigrant Trail and used for travel from Mexico to the gold fields. Still later, in 1858, this trail became part of the Butterfield Overland Mail Route, which ran from St. Louis, Missouri, to San Francisco. No thought was given to settling the desert during these early treks. The vast, dry expanse loomed as a barrier to cross before reaching the green and fertile areas of "the promised land," California.

East Mojave Area

A prehistoric tool site near present-day Barstow indicates that humans lived in the region possibly as long ago as 200,000 years. Petroglyphs, cave dwellings, arrowheads and other clues tell of aboriginal Indian life during the last 11,000 years. Artifacts representative of other cultures throughout the west have also been found, suggesting trade between the various ancient societies.

By the late 1700s the Mojaves, Piutes and Chemehuevi inhabited the area we call the East Mojave Desert. Guides from the Mojave people led Friar Francisco Garcés and other explorers who followed him across the desert as the Spanish empire rose and fell and the United States spread west. Garcés' account of his travels in 1775-76 is the first recorded crossing of the East Mojave.

Fur trappers from northern states began exploring the region in the early 1800s, including such figures as Jedediah Strong Smith and Kit Carson. By the middle of the century most New Mexican and Anglo traffic occurred over the Santa Fe Trail, later known as the Salt Lake route, which forked northward from the Mojave Road near Barstow's present location. Early travelers included mission escapees, slave traders, fur trappers, soldiers, explorers, stockmen, merchants, guides, gold seekers and immigrants. The geography and hydrology of the Mojave River dictated future developments, which were slow due to costly freight charges, crude mineral recovery methods, scarcity of water and lack of local subsistence.

Westward expansion created the need for a rail route to the Pacific Coast, and in 1854 the War Department sent Lieutenant A. W. Whipple to survey the area. His travels took him along the 35th Parallel, although it was more than 30 years before a rail line was completed. In 1857 Beale's famous Camel Caravan crossed the region

In the early 1880s a railroad spur linked Manvel to Goffs. Manvel got a post office in 1893, then in 1907 the town name was changed to Barnwell. A few ruins are still visible at the Barnwell site in the East Mojave.

while traveling from Camp Verde, Texas, to Ft. Tejon, California, searching for a wagon route. This path became known as the Government Road, later called the Mojave Road. In the 1860s military posts were established along this route to protect U.S. mail deliveries from troublesome Indian attacks. By 1868 the mail route was moved to the safer southern La Paz route and the Mojave Road outposts were abandoned.

The geologically rich East Mojave held in store precious minerals, and by 1870 mining explorations had begun. Gold, silver, copper, iron, lead, zinc, tin and tungsten were recovered from places with exotic names like Trojan, Orange Blossom, Vanderbilt, Exchequer, Enterprise, Old Dad, Onyx, Carbonate King, Golden Fleece, Wanamingo and Bagdad. Supplies for these isolated mines were brought in from San

Francisco through San Bernardino, then carried by freight wagons over the Government Road; burros carried supplies into areas inaccessible by wagon. Most outgoing ore was shipped to the British Isles for smelting. With freight charges costing hundreds of dollars per ton and supplies and travel so expensive, only the richest deposits were mined. Mining activity peaked between 1900 and the end of World War I, with movement of supplies and ore aided by the rail lines. During the Great Depression high gold prices and low mining costs prompted more exploration. The Second World War also increased the demand for minerals, although production never reached earlier levels. Modern mining techniques have resulted in fewer but more productive mines in the East Mojave.

In 1883 the main line of the Southern Pacific Railroad (now Santa Fe) was completed to Needles, where it connected with the Atlantic and Pacific line. Ten years later a branch line was completed from Goffs through Lanfair Valley to Barnwell, serving area mines. The central East Mojave saw construction of a Union Pacific rail line in 1905, establishing the communities of Kelso, Cima and Ivanpah. Another branch line, completed a few years later, ran from Searchlight, Nevada through Barnwell and the New York Mountains into Ivanpah Valley.

By the end of the last century, miners, the railroad and area ranchers shared the land without conflict. Cattlemen grazed thousands of head over more than a million acres. In 1910, however, homesteading and dry farming were attempted in Lanfair Valley, and conflicts over water rights developed between the farmers and the cattlemen. That, combined with a drought in 1925 and other poor conditions, caused the homesteaders to abandon their efforts in the East Mojave.

During World War II, the military established the Desert Training Center to prepare troops for combat in North Africa. The California-Arizona Maneuver Area included 11 camps, two of which, Camps Ibis and Clipper, were in the southeastern portion of the East Mojave. After 50 years, little evidence remains of most of these camps, although it is possible to find rock-lined walkways, insignias, outdoor chapels and tank tracks.

West Mojave Area

The geological forces that shaped the west Mojave area are visible everywhere. The San Andreas Fault runs along the base of the mountains on the southern end of the Antelope Valley. Faulting over millions of years has turned, twisted, lifted, dropped and compressed the land, and due to its various compositions it resulted in dramatic and unusual features such as those preserved in Devil's Punchbowl County Park. Evidence of ancient animal life at the park indicates that the area was inhabited by two species of the three-toed horse, an ancient skunk-like animal, a primitive camel and a small antelope. In the upper portion of the Mojave Desert, ancient Owens Lake was the uppermost of a series of lakes, remains of which are evidenced by the dry lakes dotting the desert terrain. Geothermal conditions contributed to what we call the Trona Pinnacles, tufa spires jutting out of the desert floor near a dry lake bed.

Prehistoric peoples left some evidence of their presence near Fossil Falls, at Red Rock Canyon and in Little Petroglyph Canyon. These small groups were nomadic in lifestyle.

Many of the communities in the West Mojave were mining settlements, such as Willow Springs, Randsburg and Boron. Mojave was established as a townsite when the railroad came through in 1876. German Lutherans settled the town of Palmenthal in 1886, which became Palmdale in 1908.

Placer gold was found in the Red Rock area in 1893, where surface diggings yielded $2,500,000 of the ore. Silver was mined in the same area 25 years later. Ezra Hamilton, a Los Angeles pottery and brick manufacturer, mined clay in the Willow Springs area and in 1894 found gold in the fire clay. Two years later he found the lode he called the Lida Mine. Not a healthy man, Hamilton was impressed with the curative powers of the desert and in 1911 established Willow Springs as a health resort. Remnants of the town and mine are today part of Tropico, near Rosamond. The Yellow Aster Mine, in the Rand Mining District, gave up more than $6,000,000 in gold between 1895 and World War I, when production dwindled due to the war and a flu epidemic. The area never again regained its affluence and population.

Borax was mined from Searles Lake and Death Valley and freighted to Mojave for processing. (Those who watched television in the 1950s may remember the show *Death Valley Days*, which featured wagons full of borax being pulled by a 20-mule team.) By 1927 borates were being mined from the world's richest deposit near the town of Boron. The product has thousands of applications and is shipped to users throughout the world.

The clear air, dry climate, dry lake beds and low population made the West Mojave attractive to the military for testing purposes. Muroc Bombing and Gunnery range was established in 1933 as a temporary facility. By 1937 it had become the Muroc Army Air Field, a semipermanent tent camp. Fighters and bombers trained during World War II at Muroc, taking aim at the *Muroc Maru*, a full-scale wooden mock-up of a Japanese Mogami-class heavy cruiser built on the dry lake bed (it later became a distraction to desert drivers who thought they were seeing a mirage; it was dismantled in 1950). Secret testing of a jet-powered aircraft, the Bell XP-59A "Airacomet," took place at Muroc in 1942. Within the next few years Muroc became a full-fledged flight test base, trying out hundreds of military, commercial and experimental aircraft. The sound barrier was first broken at Muroc on October of 1947 by Captain Charles B. Yeager flying the Bell

X-1. That craft and other historic flying machines are on display at the base. Testing of rockets and missiles also took place here, which in 1950 was renamed Edwards Air Force Base in memory of Captain Glen W. Edwards, a test pilot who was killed while flying the YB-49, an experimental aircraft called the Flying Wing. Numerous related industries have installations at Edwards, including NASA, which uses Rogers Dry Lake Bed as a landing site for the space shuttles. The U.S. Naval Weapons Center at China Lake, a remote site ideal for testing and experimenting with ballistic weapons, was established during World War II.

Death Valley Area

Four seperate native Indian cultures have existed in Death Valley during different periods. The Nevares Spring People, a group of primitive hunters and seed gatherers, arrived on the scene perhaps 9000 years ago. Lakes still existed in the basin then, the climate was mild and game was plentiful. Four thousand years later the culturally similar Mesquite Flat People replaced the original inhabitants. The third group, the Saratoga Spring People, arrived about 2000 years ago in what had probably by then become a dry, hot desert. These more advanced hunters and gatherers created handcrafts and left mysterious, meticulously created stone patterns in the valley. The Desert Shoshone moved into the desolate area 1000 years ago. They were nomads, living on game, mesquite beans and piñon nuts. They camped in the valley near water sources during the winter and moved into the cooler mountains in summer.

The first white people to enter the valley were two groups of emigrants on their way to the California gold fields. Perhaps 100 people wandered down Furnace Creek Wash in late 1849 while looking for a shortcut to the Mother Lode country. Lost and out of food, the two seperate groups were forced to endure severe hardships before they could escape from the desert. Their experience provided the valley with its morbid name.

One of these unfortunate travelers fashioned a gunsight out of a piece of rubble. The rock was later found to be silver. As a result of this pleasant accident, Death Valley was subjected to a series of mining booms that lasted for nearly a century. Instant wealth in the forms of gold, silver, copper and lead provided the impetus; instant towns such as Panamint City, Ballarat, Chloride City, Rhyolite, Harrisburg, Greenwater, Skidoo and Leadfield were the result. Few remained active for long, and most people who invested money or work found little to repay their hopes.

The most profitable and longest-sustained mining activities in the region centered on borates. Discovered in 1873, the borax deposits were first successfully exploited by W.T. Coleman. He built the Harmony Borax Works and developed the famous system of 20-mule-team wagons that hauled the processed mineral 165 miles across the desert to the railroad at Mojave. Borax mining was carried out later near the site of Ryan.

The first tourist facilities in Death Valley were some tent houses built in the 1920s at the site of today's Stovepipe Wells. In 1927, a borax company turned its crew quarters at Furnace Creek Ranch into a resort and built the Furnace Creek Inn. The valley

"Shorty" Harris (center), for whom Harrisburg was named, was a famous "single-blanket jackass prospector" of the Death Valley region. The photo is undated, but the car puts this scene as pre-World War I.

quickly became popular as a winter destination, and in 1933 an area of almost 3000 square miles was established as a national monument under the administration of the National Park Service. As a result of the Desert Protection Act, signed into law in 1994 by President Bill Clinton, about 1.3 million acres were added to Death Valley and the monument became a national park—the largest national park in the contiguous United States.

RESORT CITIES

The Coachella Valley sits at the base of imposing Mt. San Jacinto, stretches southeast along the foothills of the Santa Rosa Mountains to the Salton Sea, and butts up against the Mecca Hills to the east and the Indio Hills to the north. The cities of the Coachella Valley offer the finest in resort amenities— golf, tennis, swimming, boutique shopping, gourmet dining, name entertainment and luxurious accommodations. Yet each city has its own distinctive ambiance, its own "place" in the balance of tourism, commerce, wealth, recreation, politics and dreams for the future.

Clusters of dates hang high in the date palms.

Largely residential, **Cathedral City** is primarily known for its retail stores, many of which offer products for the home. In **Desert Hot Springs** thermal waters have long attracted those interested in its healing effects. Exclusive homes and resorts are repre-

A drive on Seven Level Hill provides spectacular views of the Resort Cities.

sentative of **Indian Wells**, while **Indio** is has long been an agricultural center, with citrus and dates grown here. The National Date Festival is held on the grounds of the Desert ExpoCentre in Indio.

Art comes to mind when referring to **La Quinta**, which hosts an annual art festival and is home to several long-established resorts. In **Palm Desert**, a relatively young city, the Living Desert's exotic wild animals and El Paseo's fashion boutiques attract locals as well as visitors.

Perhaps the best-known of Coachella Valley's cities, **Palm Springs** became famous as a get-away for stars in the movie industry, and remains note-worthy on many counts. Major resorts and shopping areas are located here, as well as the valley's only commercial airport.

Golf courses, resorts and shopping comprise the attractions in **Rancho Mirage**, which is also home to the esteemed Eisenhower Medical Center. The small community of **Thousand Palms** abuts the Coachella Valley

Preserve, a protected area of palms, springs and wildlife.

History and culture are the focus of the Palm Springs Desert Museum.

Thousand Palms Oasis is a haven for plants, animals and humans.

Resort Cities

Although communities fancy and plain sprawl the length of the Coachella Valley, the natural environment still impacts everyday life. Palm oases provide a sanctuary for indigenous plants and animals. On the western end of the valley, windmills cover the hills to capture the rather constant light breezes for electrical power. Occasionally, strong winds whip sand from the valley floor into blinding dust storms, or thunderstorms bring rainfall sufficient to flood low-lying areas. Searing hot in summer, days the rest of the year are balmy and perfect for enjoying the beautiful outdoors.

Effective March 22, 1997, area code (619) will change to (760).

Cathedral City

The city was named—depending upon whom you talk to—either for a nearby rock formation or a canyon in the adjacent San Jacinto Mountains. Supporting a population of 34,000, the town has several golf courses (see *Recreation*). The community's business and retail district is known locally for building supplies, home furnishings, general mercantile stores and auto sales, plus antique and second-hand shops. Noticeably absent, however, is a cathedral. (See *Palm Springs/ Cathedral City Area Map* under Palm Springs.)

▼ *A Quick Guide to Cathedral City*

See also A Quick Guide to The Resort Cities *in this chapter.*
Effective March 22, 1997, area code (619) will change to (760).

Police (nonemergency)
(619/760) 321-0111

Visitor Services
Cathedral City Chamber of
　　Commerce
68-845 Perez Rd., Ste. 6
Cathedral City 92234
Phone: (619) 328-1213

Desert Hot Springs

Although Indians had long enjoyed the local soothing natural springs, no one settled here until 1913 when Cabot Yerxa, a world traveler, homesteaded in the Coachella Valley. He initially visited Palm Springs, but at the time there were 107 residents,

---

Palm trees at dusk in Palm Desert.

▼ *A Quick Guide to the Resort Cities*

See also Quick Guide *boxes under Cathedral City, Desert Hot Springs, Indian Wells, Indio, La Quinta, Palm Desert, Palm Springs, Rancho Mirage and Thousand Palms. Effective March 22, 1997, area code (619) will change to (760).*

Population   243,642

Elevation   22 ft. below sea level to 466 ft. above

Emergency   911

Emergency Road Service for AAA Members

(800) AAA-HELP (in the USA and Canada)

(800) 955-4TDD (for the hearing impaired)

Highway Conditions
(619/760) 345-2767

Time   (619/760) 853-1212

Weather   (619/760) 345-3711

Newspapers

Major daily newspapers serving the Coachella Valley are the *The Desert Sun,* the *Los Angeles Times (Inland Empire Edition)* and *The Press-Enterprise.* The monthly *Inland Empire Business Journal* covers the valley's business environment.

Radio Stations

Classical: KPSC (88.5 FM); **Classic Rock:** KCMJ (92.7 FM); **Contemporary Rock:** KPSI (100.5 FM); **Country:** KCMJ (92.7 FM); **Hispanic:** KUNA (1400 FM), KCLB (970 AM); **News (Public Radio):** KCRW (89.3 and 90.0 FM); **Talk:** KPSI (1450 AM), KPSL (1010 AM). For a complete list of radio programs, consult the daily newspapers.

TV Stations

The area's major television stations include channels 2 (CBS), 11 (FOX), 3 and 42 (ABC), 8 (PBS) and 6 and 36 (NBC). For a complete list of television programs, consult the daily newspapers.

24-hour Activity Hotline
(619/760) 770-1992

Bus

SunBus operates throughout the Coachella Valley. (619/760) 343-3451 (from Desert Hot Springs, 323-4010). Cash fare is 75¢ plus 25¢ per transfer; exact fare required. Monthly passes are available. Service from Desert Hot Springs to Coachella, with occasional service to Mecca. Wheelchair lifts and bike racks available.

Train

Amtrak pickup point only, Jackson and Railroad Ave., Indio. Call (800) USA-RAIL for information and fares. The "Sunset Limited" stops in Indio on its cross-country route between Los Angeles and Miami.

Taxi

Two companies serve the Coachella Valley, A Valley Cabousine (619/760-340-5845) and Checker Cab (619/760-325-2868). Rates are regulated; the flag rate is $3 plus $2.16 per mile. Refer to the local yellow pages of the telephone directory under "Taxi" for phone numbers and information.

Visitor Services

Palm Springs Desert Resorts
    Convention & Visitors Bureau
69-930 Hwy. 111 in The Atrium
Rancho Mirage 92270
Phone: (619/760) 770-9000

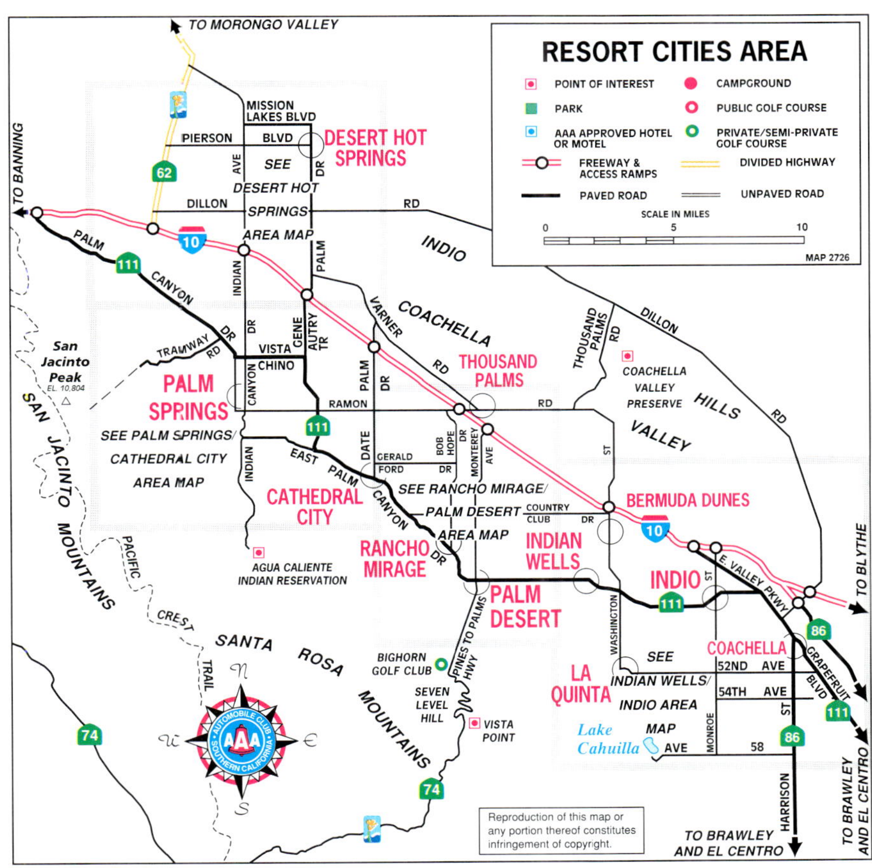

far too crowded for him. Yerxa moved on to what is now Desert Hot Springs, where he homesteaded 160 acres, ultimately constructing a unique pueblo-style residence. Because there was no surface water on his property, he walked 14 miles round trip every day to the railroad water tank. The following year he dug a well by hand and discovered the hot mineral water that has since made the town famous. In 1939, the Mayo Clinic analyzed the spring water and found it to be of very high quality. A secluded resort was established at Two Bunch Palms, where in the 1930s Chicago gangster Al Capone is reputed to have hidden from authorities.

Desert Hot Springs was first promoted for its health benefits by a Mr. L. W. Coffee in July 1941. He brought to the area a busload of Japanese-Americans who were interested in the investment potential of the curative waters. Since most of the prospective investors were relocated to intern-ment camps during World War II, little development occurred. After the war, the town began to grow steadily. Today, with a population of around 14,500, it is a quiet resort offering relaxation to many visitors who come

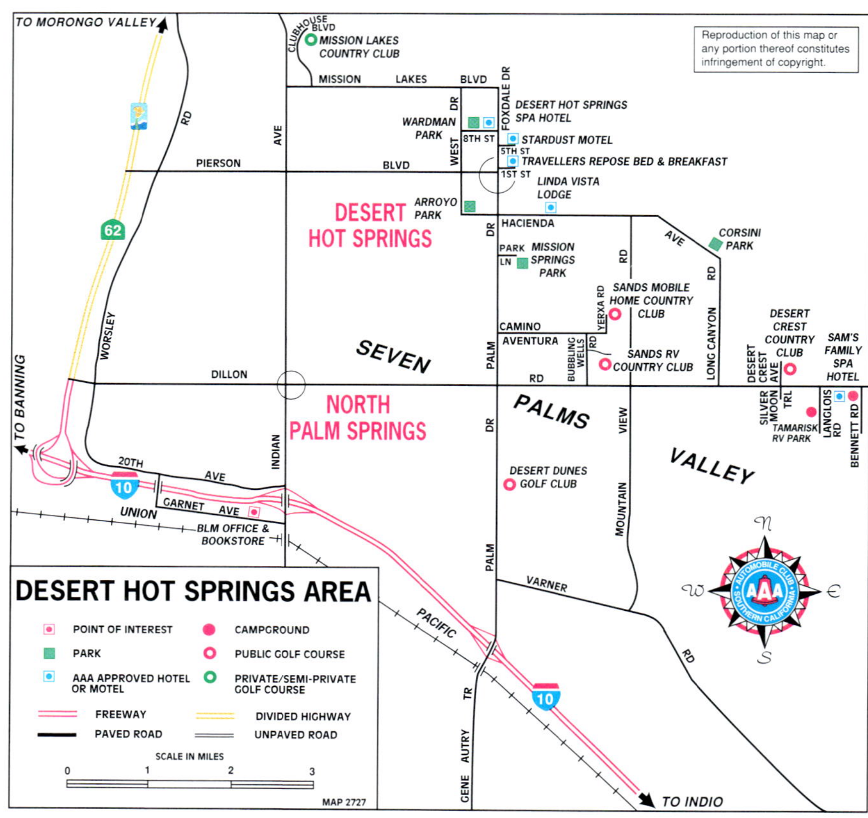

▼ *A Quick Guide to Desert Hot Springs*

See also A Quick Guide to The Resort Cities *in this chapter.*
Effective March 22, 1997, area code (619) will change to (760).

Police Nonemergency

(619/760) 329-2904, after hours (800) 950-2444

Visitor Services

Desert Hot Springs Chamber of Commerce
11-711 West Dr., Ste. A
Desert Hot Springs 92240
Phone: (619/760) 329-6403

to enjoy the desert air and the hot mineral waters.

Indian Wells

As the name implies, this was once a well site used by the Cahuilla Indians. The town was created in the 1950s to sell residential lots adjoining the Indian Wells Country Club. Today the city's established population is 3119, which nearly doubles in winter. Indian Wells has the reputation of being one of the highest income-per-capita communities in the nation. It is home to several major resort hotels and golf courses.

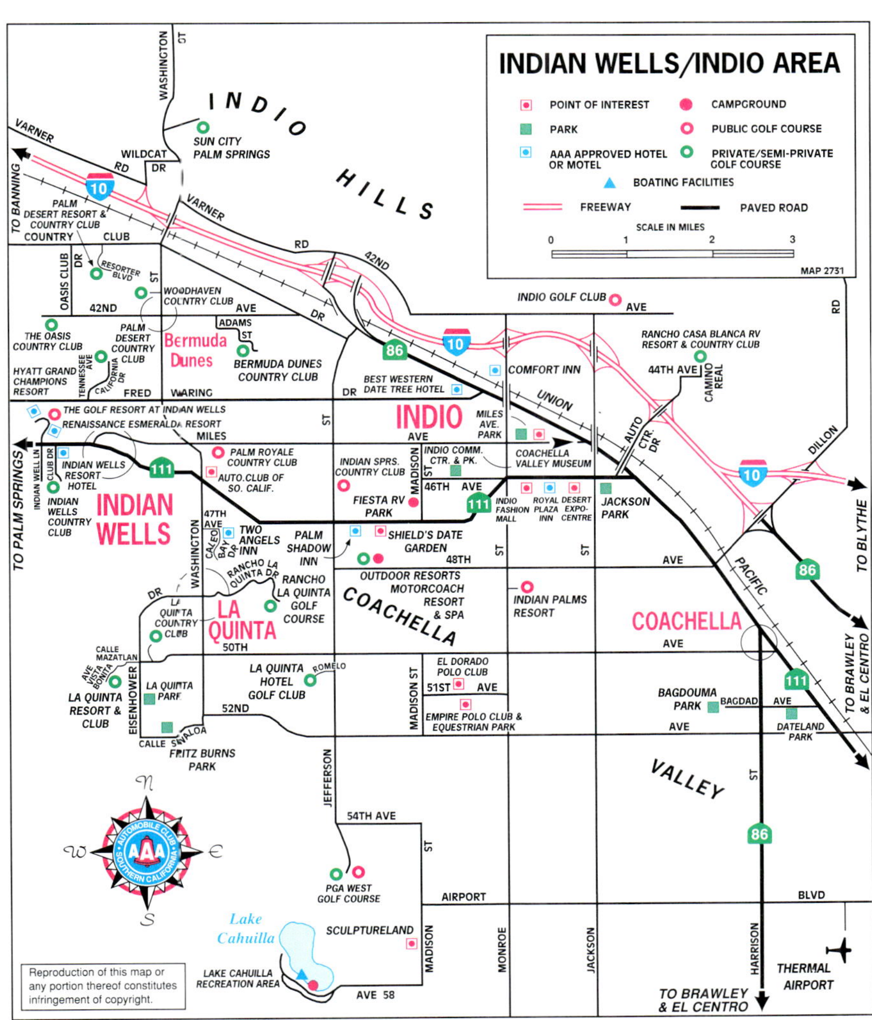

Reproduction of this map or any portion thereof constitutes infringement of copyright.

See also A Quick Guide to The Resort Cities *in this chapter.*

▼ *A Quick Guide to Indian Wells*

Effective March 22, 1997, area code (619) will change to (760).

Police Nonemergency
(800) 950-2444

Indio

Indio was originally known as Indian Wells, but the name was changed in 1876. Indio was a construction camp during building of the Southern Pacific Railroad, and afterward it was the site of railway yards, repair shops and a roundhouse. In 1894 a businessman, A.C. Tingman, laid out a township and

▼ *A Quick Guide to Indio*

See also A Quick Guide to The Resort Cities *in this chapter.*
Effective March 22, 1997, area code (619) will change to (760).

Police Nonemergency
(619/760) 347-8522

Hospitals

John F. Kennedy Memorial Hospital
47-111 Monroe St.
Indio 92201
Phone: (619/760) 347-6191

Visitor Services

Indio Chamber of Commerce
82-503 Hwy. 111
Indio 92234
Phone: (619/760) 347-0676

began selling lots. The town became an agricultural center when homesteaders settled and cultivated the land. By 1920 the city had become the "Date Capital" of the United States, and the center of valley commerce. With a population of 42,578, Indio today is a center for both tourism and agriculture. Two polo clubs provide exciting, celebrity-studded entertainment from November through May. The Indio Fashion Mall, an enclosed shopping center, is one of the largest malls in the Coachella Valley.

COACHELLA VALLEY MUSEUM AND CULTURAL CENTER *82-616 Miles Ave., 92202. (619/760) 342-6651. From Oct. through May, the museum is open Wed. through Sat. from 10 a.m. to 4 p.m. and Sun. from 1 to 4 p.m.; in Jun. and Sept. it is open Fri. through Sun. Closed Jul. and Aug. Adults $1; ages 12 and under, and 60 and over, 50¢.* The former home and medical office of Dr. Harry Smiley, a long-time resident of the area, houses the museum and cultural center. The structure was built in 1926 and now contains displays of Indian artifacts, old farm equipment, household antiques, a blacksmith shop

Interesting glimpses into the area's history are found at the Coachella Valley Museum in Indio.

▼ *Water, Water Everywhere*

Desert life is dependent on water. Artesian wells were discovered in the Coachella Valley around 1855, and in 1949 additional water from the Colorado River was brought in for irrigating farmlands—the southern portion of the valley, from Indio to the Salton Sea, is primarily devoted to agriculture, producing dates, citrus and vegetable crops. Today, water flows freely from underground aquifers, and estimates expect that source to last for at least another 200 years.

and an art museum; there is also a small gift shop.

DATE PALMS from Algeria were introduced in 1890 as an experimental agricultural crop. Dates have since become the major fruit of the Coachella Valley, supplying close to 90 percent of the total consumed in the United States. The Deglet Noor was the most common variety, but is quickly being replaced by the larger Medjool date, which is highly prized for its flavor.

An eight-year-old palm can produce as much as 300 pounds of dates in a year. From September through January, dates are picked by hand three or four times. Date palms require water twice each month, a considerable amount for a desert plant.

A number of date retailers are located along SR 111 between Thermal and Indian Wells; a few are listed.

Indian Wells Date Gardens and Chocolatier *74-774 Highway 111, Indian Wells 92210. (619/760) 346-2914.*

Oasis Date Gardens *59-111 Highway 111, Thermal 92274. (619/760) 399-5665.*

Shields Date Gardens *80-255 Highway 111, Indio 92201. (619/760) 347-0996.*

ELDORADO POLO CLUB *50-950 Madison St., 92202. (619/760) 342-2223. The club sponsors polo games from Nov. through mid-Apr. on Sat. and Sun. at 10 a.m., noon and 2 p.m. Admission is free on*

Date palms stand in stately rows in Indio.

every tournament day except Sun. (admission is $6); children under 14 are admitted free. Clubhouse day membership is $25.

EMPIRE POLO CLUB AND EQUESTRIAN PARK *81-800 Ave. 51, 92201. (619/760) 342-2762. Call for events schedule. A $5 fee is charged for Grand Prix events held in Jan., Feb. and Mar.* This lush, 176-acre park has five polo fields, an amphitheater that seats 14,000 people, a rose garden and croquet pavilion, and two small lakes surrounded by grass, trees, sculpture and benches. Nearly 100 equestrian events are held annually, including international competitions ranging from World Cup qualifiers in the hunter/jumper class to Arabian, Tennessee Walker, Morgan, Peruvian Paso and dressage horses. The park also has a western town with a complete rodeo facility.

NATIONAL DATE FESTIVAL *Desert ExpoCentre, 46-350 Arabia St., 92202. (619/760) 863-8247. Begins mid- or late Feb.* The date takes center stage at this 10-day festival, which features daily camel and ostrich races, and each night an Arabian Nights Pageant on an open-air stage. Of course, sampling dates is one of the more popular activities at the festival. In addition to varieties of dried and fresh dates, hundreds of foods using the exotic fruit are on display and available for purchase. Other exhibits include citrus fruit, livestock, gems and minerals, industrial arts, photography and fine arts. There also are concerts by top-name performers and carnival rides and games.

La Quinta

La Quinta, whose name means "country estate," is the home of the well-known

---

▼ A Quick Guide to La Quinta

See also A Quick Guide to The Resort Cities *in this chapter.*
Effective March 22, 1997, area code (619) will change to (760).

Police Nonemergency
(619/760) 863-8990

Visitor Services

La Quinta Chamber of Commerce
51-351 Avenida Bermudas
La Quinta 92253
Phone: (619/760) 564-3199

Automobile Club of Southern California

La Quinta District Office
46-050 Washington St.
Mailing address: P.O. Box 1658
La Quinta 92253
Phone: (619/760) 771-1162
Office hours: Mon. through Fri. 9 a.m. to 5 p.m.

La Quinta Hotel Golf & Tennis Resort, built in the 1920s. The community's village atmosphere attracts tourists, new residents and businesses. The city's permanent population is 16,634, with a seasonal influx of some 8,000 temporary residents. According to a local publication, La Quinta has "...more golf courses on a per capita basis than any city in the world." Noteworthy annual events include major golf tournaments and the La Quinta Arts Festival. (See *Annual Events*.)

LAKE CAHUILLA RECREATION AREA *5 miles southeast of La Quinta off Madison St. and Ave. 58; administrative office at 58-075 Jefferson St. (mailing address: P.O. Box 3507, Riverside 92519.)*

Open Oct. through May; open selected days Jun. through Sept. (especially weekends); swimming pool open weekends May through Oct. Fishing is $5 for adults, $4 for ages 6 to 15. Call for current prices and hours. This 710-acre recreation area, featuring a 135-acre lake, provides camping, fishing and picnicking areas. Campsites provide electric, sewer and water hookups, and shaded picnic facilities are available. (See also *Recreation*.)

SCULPTURELAND *57-325 Madison St. (mailing address: P.O. Box 1566, 92253). (619/760) 564-6464; FAX (619/760) 564-1166. Open Tues. through Sun. 9 a.m. to 5 p.m. Closed Mon. Admission $5; ages 62 and over, $4; children ages 3-15, $3.* More than 200 pieces of large sculpture are displayed at this 20-acre park. Painter Bernardo Gouthier, founder and owner of the park, presents work by over 100 artists from 14 countries, with emphasis on American artists. Visitors may walk or ride a golf cart for self-guided tours of the park, following paved walkways leading past the park's creations, each of which is available for lease or purchase. The grounds also include picnic areas and a three-acre lake. Sculptureland sponsors an annual Fine Arts Festival, a three-day art show held in February (see *Annual Events*), and serves as a venue for other events.

Palm Desert

Palm Desert was created as a real estate development in 1946. Today, with a population of about 35,000, the community boasts a sizable shopping and commercial district along SR 111 and Monterey Avenue. Palm Desert Town Center, Coachella Valley's largest shopping mall, houses an ice rink, movie

---

theaters, five department stores and numerous smaller shops. El Paseo shopping area offers dozens of boutiques and specialty stores ranging from antiques and brass to tennis clothes and swimwear, plus a variety of art galleries, restaurants and cafes. Palm Desert also is the home of College of the Desert community college and the Bob Hope Cultural Center. The Pines-to-Palms Highway (SR 74) provides a scenic and convenient route from Palm Desert to the resort and wilderness areas of the San Jacinto Mountains.

COLLEGE OF THE DESERT *43-500 Monterey Ave., 92260. (619/760) 346-8041.* Established in 1958, this community college is an educational, artistic and athletic center for the resort cities area. Offering associate of arts degrees, curricula includes nursing, business, golf management, hospitality management, athletics, and fine and performing arts. California State University San Bernardino offers upper division courses on this campus.

The McCallum Theatre for the Performing Arts *On campus at 73-000*

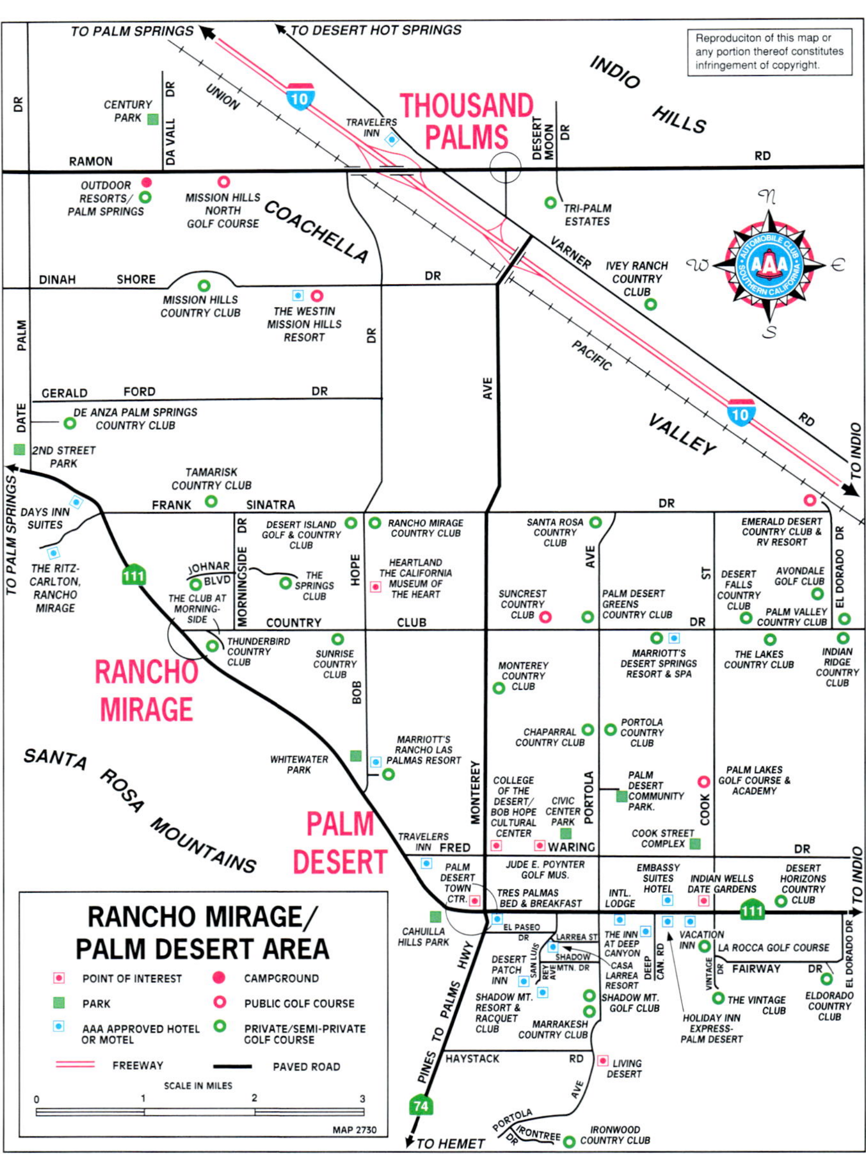

Fred Waring Drive, 92260. (619/760) 346-6505. Tours of the center are offered from Sept. through Jun., Mon. through Fri. at 9:45 a.m. Allow 45 minutes for the tour. The Bob Hope Cultural Center, completed in 1988, is the location of the 1131-seat McCallum Theatre for the Performing Arts. The theater features popular entertainment and is a home for community-based performing arts groups.

Street Fair *(619/760) 568-9921 or 773-2567. Held each weekend from 7 a.m. to 2 p.m. (during summer months the fair* *closes at noon on weekends; the fair is not held on holidays). Free admission and parking.* This event, sponsored by the alumni association, is filled with bargains from 340 vendors offering antiques, arts and crafts, furniture and used items. There is also entertainment, and a farmers market sells locally grown produce.

JUDE E. POYNTER GOLF MUSEUM *At the Institute of Golf Management, on Fred Waring Dr. between Monterey and San Pablo aves. (mailing address: 43-500 Monterey Ave., 92260). (619/760) 341-2491. From Oct. to mid-Jun., open daily 8 a.m. to 9 p.m; from mid-Jun. through Sept. the hours are Mon. through Fri., 4 to 9 p.m.; Sat. and Sun. 7 a.m. to 9 p.m. Free admission.* This small museum exhibits a variety of antique and collectible golf prints and equipment. Displays include clubs dating from the late 1800s, and

balls and golf tee molds, most of which were donated by Mr. Jude E. Poynter, a former chairman of the Senior Masters Golf Association. Also shown are a collection of clubs belonging to former President Gerald R. Ford and team photos of the biannual Ryder Cup Matches.

LIVING DESERT *4 miles south of SR 111 at 47-900 Portola Ave., Palm Desert 92260. (619/760) 346-5694. Open daily; Oct. 1 through June 15, 9 a.m. to 5 p.m.; June 16 through July 31 and Sept. 1 through 30, 8 a.m. to noon. Closed Aug. General admission is $7 for adults, $6 for ages 62 and over, and $3.50 for ages 3 to 12. A 50-minute guided tour on a shaded electric cart is available for an additional $4.* This desert wildlife and botanical park offers a rare view of the flora and fauna from around the world. More than 130 animal species are presented, including mountain lions, Mexican

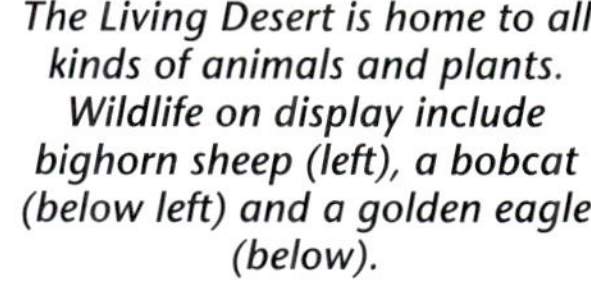

The Living Desert is home to all kinds of animals and plants. Wildlife on display include bighorn sheep (left), a bobcat (below left) and a golden eagle (below).

wolves, golden eagles, meerkats, zebras, oryx and bighorn sheep. Nocturnal creatures such as owls and bats, reptiles and desert insects are also on exhibit. The Indian Ethno-botanical Garden, one of the interpretive gardens representing 10 North American desert regions, displays many of the edible and medicinal plants used by the Cahuilla Indians. A wide variety of desert plants and other souvenir items may be purchased in the plant nursery and gift shop. The park has a system of paved and graded nature trails with signage and an observation deck, a hands-on discovery room for children, picnic areas, a cafe and snack bar.

PINES-TO-PALMS HIGHWAY (SR 74) climbs from Palm Desert into the San Bernardino National Forest and on to Idyllwild (off SR 243). It takes about an hour to travel from the warm, dry desert to the cooler pine forest of Idyllwild, a mountain community with galleries, hiking trails, restaurants and shops at an elevation of 5303 feet in the San Jacinto Mountains. On the way to Idyllwild, Vista Point, an overlook at the top of Seven Level Hill, reveals spectacular views of the valley far below and the highway's striking steep and winding course.

Palm Springs

Sun-seekers congregate here from October through May, students prefer

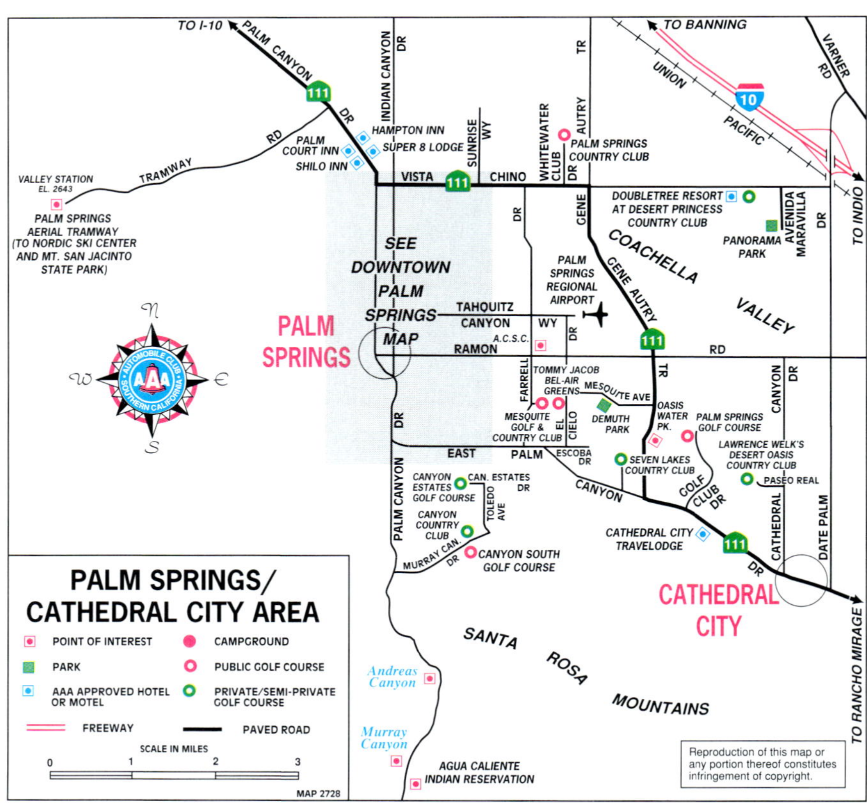

spring break, and golfers tee off year-round in Palm Springs, most famous of California's desert resort cities. Incorporated in 1938, it is one of the major cities in the lower desert, with permanent residents numbering 40,200 and the population more than doubling during the high (winter) season.

Palm Springs is something of a vacationer's paradise. Stores of all description line Palm Canyon and Indian Canyon drives, the main streets through town. Numerous art galleries display works of contemporary artists, and apparel stores sell the latest in resort wear. Luxury items fill the Desert Fashion Plaza, in the heart of town, with its two upscale department stores and many smaller specialty shops. Pedestrians stroll along the palm-lined thoroughfare, stopping at one of many outdoor restaurants for a meal or afternoon refreshments.

AGUA CALIENTE INDIAN RESERVATION *Entrance 4 miles south of Palm Springs on S. Palm Canyon Dr. (mailing address: 960 E. Tahquitz Canyon Wy., Ste. 106, 92262). (619/760) 325-5673. The reservation entrance is open daily from 8 a.m. to 5 p.m. Entrance fees are $5 for adults, $1 for ages 6 to 12, $3.50 for students and military with identification, and $2.50 for ages 62 and over. Group rates and seasonal passes are available. Equestrians pay a $6 entrance fee.* Comprised of 32,000 acres in and around Palm Springs, much of the reservation has been left in its natural state, with modern homes and commercial buildings on some parcels of land. One local landmark, the Spa Hotel, is built on the site of the mineral springs to which the Indians once attributed curative powers. The Cahuilla Tribal Council has reserved

▼ *A Quick Guide to Palm Springs*

See also A Quick Guide to The Resort Cities *in this chapter.*
Effective March 22, 1997, area code (619) will change to (760).

Police Nonemergency
(619/760) 323-8116

Hospitals

Desert Hospital
1150 N. Indian Canyon Dr.
Palm Springs 92262
Phone: (619/760) 323-6511

Visitor Services

Palm Springs Visitors Information
　Center
2781 N. Palm Canyon Dr.
Palm Springs
Phone: (619/760) 778-8418,
(800) 347-7746

Palm Springs Chamber of Commerce
190 W. Amado Rd.
Palm Springs 92262
Phone: (619/760) 325-1577

Automobile Club of Southern California

Palms Springs District Office
300 S. Farrell Dr.
Mailing address: P.O. Box 1590
Palm Springs 92263-1587
Phone: (619/760) 320-1121
Office hours: Mon. through Fri.
9 a.m. to 5 p.m.

several parts of the reservation for the enjoyment of visitors; brief descriptions of these places follow.

Andreas Canyon is a lush oasis along a cool stream leading from the mountains. Some of the canyon's features are giant Indian grinding stones, unusual rock formations, caves once used by the Agua Caliente and numbers of Washingtonia palms.

Murray Canyon is smaller and less accessible than the other canyons, but it contains spectacular rock formations, mortar holes and caves. It is an ideal spot for picnicking and hiking.

Palm Canyon is 15 miles long and has an abundance of Washingtonia palms, the only palms native to California. This is the largest grove of Washingtonias in the United States. The canyon and its lush oasis can be viewed from vantage points on the rim or by hiking. The last half mile of the road to the rim is narrow and winding. A trading post at the parking area offers souvenirs and refreshments.

BLM BOOKSTORE *Located in the Bureau of Land Management Office at 63-500 Garnet Ave. (mailing address: P.O. Box 2000, North Palm Springs 92258-2000). Open Mon. through Fri. from 7:45 a.m. to 4:30 p.m..* This bookstore, sponsored by the Southwest Natural and Cultural Heritage Association, offers a variety of area maps and books on subjects ranging from flora and fauna to archaeology and physical geography.

FABULOUS PALM SPRINGS FOLLIES *The Historic Plaza Theatre, 128 S. Palm Canyon Dr. (mailing address: 113 S. Indian Canyon Dr., 92262). (619/760) 327-0225. The show runs from Nov. through May with up to 10 performances a week; the museum is available to the audience one hour prior to show time. Show prices range from $25 to $39, except on New Years Eve when the show is $65.*

Only minutes from sophisticated downtown Palm Springs is the beautiful natural oasis of Palm Canyon.

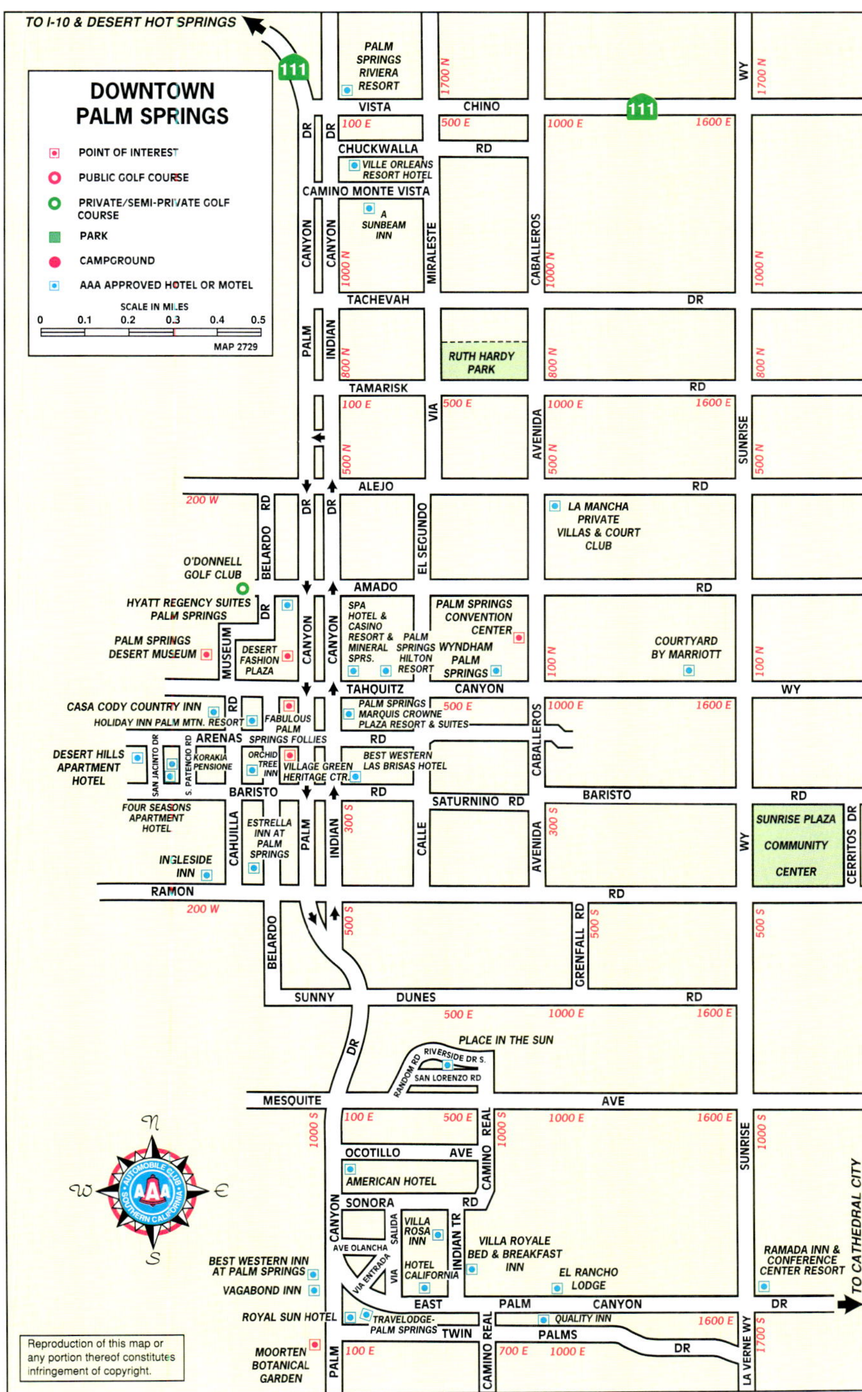

Reproduction of this map or any portion thereof constitutes infringement of copyright.

Call for current performance schedule. The Palm Springs Follies revue features talented and lively performers age 50 and above in a production recalling the 1930s Ziegfeld Follies. The show is presented in The Historic Plaza Theatre, which opened in 1936 and was recognized for its Spanish colonial architecture. What is most notable is the design of the auditorium itself which, by lighting effects and detailed paintings, places the audience amid an idealized Spanish village on a starry night.

The theater's roster of performers has included such names as Frank Sinatra, Doris Day, Bing Crosby, Pearl Bailey, Jack Benny and Don Ameche. **Palm Springs Star Walk**, at the theater's entrance, is paved with golden palm stars honoring celebrities with connections to the city, including William Powell, Bob Hope, Ginger Rogers and Ruby Keeler. Audience members receive complimentary admission to the **Palm Springs Hollywood Museum**, which presents the Helen Rose collection of gowns worn by legendary movie stars; exhibits of memorabilia from famous stars Bob Hope, Kirk Douglas, Ginger Rogers, Charlie Farrell, Ruby Keeler, William Powell and Gene Autry; and a photo gallery of stars and personalities dating back to the 1930s.

MOORTEN BOTANICAL GARDEN
1701 S. Palm Canyon Dr., 92262. (619/760) 327-6555. Open Mon. through Sat. from 9 a.m. to 4:30 p.m. and Sun. from 10 a.m. to 4 p.m. Admission is $2 for adults, 75¢ for ages 5 to 15. This historic landmark, established in 1938 by Chester "Cactus Slim" and Patricia Moorten, features 3000 varieties of

Some of the biggest names in show biz have appeared at the Plaza Theatre in Palm Springs.

desert plants from throughout the world.

OASIS WATER PARK *1500
Gene Autry Tr., 92264.
(619/760) 325-7873, (800)
247-4664. From mid-Mar.
through Jun. the park is open
daily from 11 a.m. to 5:30
p.m.; from Jun. to Labor Day
the park is open daily from 11
a.m. to 7:00 p.m.; from Labor
Day through Oct. the park is
open weekends only from 11
a.m. to 5:30 p.m. The park is
closed Nov. through mid-Mar.
The health club is open all
year. Admission is $17.95 for
adults, $11.50 for seniors and
children 40 to 60 inches tall;
children under 40 inches free.
Belly boards must be rented
from the park at $2 per hour
or $5 per day.* The 21-acre
aquatic park features a wave
pool producing up to four-
foot waves for surfing and
belly-boarding and the
Black Widow double-rider
water slide. Also offered are
12 additional water slides
(including five minislides for small
children), a river for inner tubes,
heated spas, a fitness center, outdoor
pavilion and three cafes.

*Moorten Botanical Garden has thousands of cacti
on display.*

PALM SPRINGS AERIAL TRAMWAY
*6 miles northwest of Palm Springs off SR
111 and Tramway Rd. (mailing address:
1 Tramway Rd., 92262). (619/760)
325-1391. The Tramway operates Mon.
through Fri. from 10 a.m.; Sat., Sun. and
holidays from 8 a.m. during daylight-
saving time; the last car up the mountain
leaves at 9 p.m. and returns at 10:45 p.m.
The rest of the year, the last car travels up
at 8 p.m. and returns at 9:45 p.m. During
Aug. the tram closes for equipment maintenance. Round-trip fares are $16.95 for
adults, $13.95 for seniors and $10.95 for
ages 5 to 12. Parking is free. A special
ride-and-dine combination, in effect daily
after 4 p.m., includes the round-trip tram
ride and dinner at the Alpine Restaurant
at the Mountain Station. The combination
is $20.95 for adults and $13.95 for ages
5 to 12.* Passengers are carried from
the Valley Station (2643 feet) in Chino
Canyon to the Mountain Station (8516
feet) at the eastern edge of Long Valley
in the San Jacinto Mountains. The 80-
passenger tram cars travel 13,800 feet
in 14 minutes up the jagged face of
the range, affording spectacular views
of the desert below. Each station has

Traveling from the desert floor to a forested peak in the San Jacinto Mountains, the Palm Springs Aerial Tramway carries passengers 13,800 feet in about 14 minutes.

modern" architecture, adjoins the Wyndham Palm Springs Hotel and offers facilities for conventions, trade shows, consumer exhibits and concerts.

PALM SPRINGS DESERT MUSEUM *101 Museum Dr., 92262. (619/760) 325-0189. Open Tues. through Thurs., Sat. and Sun. 10 a.m. to 4 p.m.; Friday 10 a.m. to 8 pm., closed Mondays and major holidays. Admission is $5 for adults, $2 for ages 6 to 17 and military personnel, and $4 for ages 62 and over; free admission on the first Fri. of each month. Parking is free.* Exhibits of paintings, sculpture, American Indian artifacts and the natural sciences are housed in this excellent museum. The museum is complemented by fountains and desert landscaping, and the facility also contains the Annenberg Theater, a 450-seat auditorium for the performing arts.

a cocktail lounge, snack bar, gift shop, observation deck and picnic area. Mountain Station also has a restaurant and banquet facilities. It offers access to Mount San Jacinto State Park, which includes 54 miles of hiking trails, winter sports areas, backcountry campgrounds, mule-train rides and picnic sites (see *Recreation*).

PALM SPRINGS CONVENTION CENTER *277 Avenida Caballeros, 92262. (619/760) 325-6611.* This 150,000-square-foot center houses Spring Theater, exhibit halls and breakout rooms. The building, with its "desert

VILLAGEFEST *S. Palm Canyon Dr. between Baristo and Amado rds. (619/760) 320-3781. Thurs.; Oct. through Jun. from 6 to 10 p.m.; during Sept. from 7 to 10 p.m. Not held on major holidays and may close from mid-Jul. through Aug. due to hot weather.* The street is closed to traffic and is filled with 150 booths offering gourmet coffees, barbecued ribs, ethnic foods, art works, handcrafts and jewelry. A farmer's market sells produce, and live entertainment adds to the festive atmosphere.

VILLAGE GREEN HERITAGE CENTER *221 S. Palm Canyon Dr.* This museum complex presents aspects of the diverse

Windmills generate electricity in the Coachella Valley.

▼ *An Answer Blowing in the Wind?*

At the western end of the valley, hundreds of windmills dot the hills and desert floor. Low-maintenance sources of renewable energy, these commercially owned wind turbine generators capture ocean air coming into the desert through San Gorgonio Pass. Still in an experimental phase, turbines may have two or more blades and can be set for upwind or downwind drafts of 8 to 50 mph, although most operate at wind speeds of 10 to 11 mph. Winds generate power 30 to 40 percent of the time, with a typical wind turbine generator producing 195,000 kilowatt hours of electricity per year, or enough to supply 30 to 35 houses.

ethnic and cultural influences that are part of Palm Springs' history and development.

Agua Caliente Cultural Museum *(619/760) 323-0151. Open Fri. and Sat. 10 a.m. to 4 p.m. and Sun. from noon to 3 p.m. Donations accepted.* This museum houses artifacts and photos in displays profiling the Cahuilla Tribe's cultural heritage and history. Included are histories and descriptions of pre-Columbian North American societies and their interrelations with each other and the European cultures that settled on the continent.

McCallum Adobe and Cornelia White House *(619/760) 323-8297. Open Wed. and Sun. from noon to 3 p.m. and Thurs. through Sat. from 10 a.m. to 4 p.m. General admission is 50¢ per home; children admitted free if accompanied by an adult.* Both museums, located in two historical buildings in the Village Green, are operated by the Palm Springs Historical Society. The McCallum Adobe built by pioneer John G. McCallum in 1884 is the oldest remaining building in Palm Springs. It contains an extensive collection of historical photographs, paintings, clothes, tools, books and

▼ *Tours*

Tours listed are for information and convenience. The Automobile Club of Southern California does not recommend one tour company over another and cannot guarantee the services offered.

BUS *Both sightseeing companies pick up passengers at most major Palm Springs hotels.*

Celebrity Tours *4751C E. Palm Canyon Dr., Palm Springs 92264. (619/760) 770-2700. Reservations are necessary.* One- and two-hour sightseeing tours view celebrities' homes in the Palm Springs area.

Gray Line Tours *15501 Little Morongo Rd., Desert Hot Springs 92240. (619/760) 325-0974. Reservations should be made at least one hour in advance.* Provides a 1½ hour drive-by tour of celebrity homes in the Palm Springs area.

HELICOPTER *Helicopter rides over the area vary in time and price depending on length of the tour and what the customer wishes to see.*

Landells Aviation *69-873 Silvermoon Tr., Desert Hot Springs 92241. (619/760) 329-6468.* Half-hour tours in winter; charters are available.

HOT AIR BALLOON *Soaring over the Coachella Valley in a hot air balloon offers an unusual perspective on the desert's natural and human environments. All companies listed fly only from October through May; it is too hot for balloons in the summer. Flights are usually in the early morning or in the evening. Prices range from $100 to $150 for about a one-hour flight. Reservations are required.*

American Balloon Charters *P.O. Box 2173, Palm Springs, 92263. (800) 359-6837; (619/760) 327-8544.*

Desert Balloon Charters *Palm Desert, Thermal. (619/760) 398-8575.*

Dream Flights Hot Air Balloon Adventures *69-640 20th Ave., Desert Hot Springs, 92241. (619/760) 321-5154, (800) 933-5628.*

Fantasy Balloon Flights *83-701 Ave. 54, Thermal 92274. (619/760) 398-6322; (800) 462-2683.*

OFF-ROAD *Many off-road tours involve considerable hiking. The company listed below provides professional guides that are very knowledgeable in the nature of the local area and safety.*

Desert Adventures *38225 S. Palm Canyon Dr., Palm Springs (mailing address: 611 S. Palm Canyon Dr., Ste. 7445, 92264). (619/760) 864-6530. Prices are from $65 to $99. Reservations required.* In the fall and spring Desert Adventures offers guided sunrise and sunset tours in four-wheel-drive vehicles equipped with water misting jets. Tours include treks into the Santa Rosa Mountains National Scenic area. Short hikes are offered on selected tours.

Ruddy's 1930s General Store Museum is quite a contrast to shops found in Palm Springs today.

Indian ware. Miss Cornelia's "Little House," built by Dr. Welwood Murray in 1893, was the first hotel in Palm Springs. Restored to reflect the accommodations of the 19th century, it is a showcase of antique furniture.

Ruddy's 1930s General Store Museum *(619/760) 327-2156. Open Oct. through Jun., Fri. through Sun. from 10 a.m. to 4 p.m.; rest of the year open Sat. and Sun. from 10 a.m. to 4 p.m. Adult admission is 50¢, children under age 12 admitted free.* This museum offers a look at a general store of the 1930s and early 1940s. Groceries, beauty aids, soap, notions and tobacco from this era are on display in their original containers. More than 6000 separate items are arranged in old showcases.

Rancho Mirage

Rancho Mirage, with a population of about 10,000, is located at the base of the San Jacinto Mountains. A quiet residential community, the city is also home to internationally known institutions and events, including the

---

▼ *A Quick Guide to Rancho Mirage*

See also A Quick Guide to The Resort Cities *in this chapter.*
Effective March 22, 1997, area code (619) will change to (760).

Police Nonemergency
(619/760) 341-1600

Hospitals

Eisenhower Medical Center
39-000 Bob Hope Dr.
Rancho Mirage 92270
Phone: (619/760) 340-3911

Visitor Services
Rancho Mirage Chamber of
    Commerce
42-464 Rancho Mirage Ln.
Rancho Mirage 92270
Phone: (619/760) 568-9351

Some of the displays at Heartland, the California Museum of the Heart will make your heart skip a beat.

Eisenhower Medical Center, the Betty Ford Clinic and the Nabisco Dinah Shore LPGA Invitational. Forty years ago it was known mainly for the now closed Desert Air Hotel, which was patronized by private pilots—many of them Hollywood celebrities—who flew directly to the hotel to dine, swim and relax. The city now boasts some of Coachella Valley's finest resort hotels. (See *Rancho Mirage/Palm Desert Area Map* under Palm Desert.)

HEARTLAND, THE CALIFORNIA MUSEUM OF THE HEART *39-600 Bob Hope Dr., 92270. (619/760) 324-3278. Open Mon. through Fri. from 8:30 a.m. to 6:30 p.m.; Sept. through May, Sat. from 8 a.m. to noon. Heartbeat Cafe; call for current hours. Donation $2.50 adults; $2 age 62 and older; 50¢ ages 6 through 17*

and students and military with I.D.; under age 6, free. Enter the museum through a giant tricuspid heart valve and see the colorful and unique interactive exhibits which educate visitors to the functions of the heart and the cardiovascular system. Examine a "wall of blood cells," interact with a self-testing circulatory diagram, learn about the dangers of smoking from three giant smoking cigarette butts, hear sounds of your own heart and hearts with arrhythmias and murmurs, and walk inside a giant tactile coronary artery to learn the process of atherosclerosis. Take your blood pressure and test your risk factors for cardiac disease. The neon-illuminated Heart Beat Cafe offers heart-healthy, low fat, low cholesterol foods.

Thousand Palms

A small community north of I-10, Thousand Palms is home to a couple of golf courses and several subdivisions. Close to 6000 people reside in this midvalley city.

▼ A Quick Guide to Thousand Palms

See also A Quick Guide to The Resort Cities *in this chapter.*
Effective March 22, 1997, area code (619) will change to (760).

Police Nonemergency
(800) 950-2444

Visitor Services

Thousand Palms Chamber of
    Commerce
72-715 La Canada Wy.
Thousand Palms 92276
Phone: (619/760) 343-1988

▼ *A Bright Future for the Resort Cities*

In a rush of enthusiasm, the news coming out of the Resort Cites area sounds like, "If we can get these bureaucrats to stop putting up roadblocks, we can declare the recession over, roll up our sleeves and get things done!" As the cities of Palm Springs, Desert Hot Springs, Cathedral City, Rancho Mirage, Palm Desert, Indian Wells, La Quinta, Indio and Coachella look toward their economic future, the "roadblocks" are at times quite literal but not impassable. Rancho Mirage, for example, recently wrested a portion of SR 111 from CalTrans so it can be relandscaped to meet the city's high aesthetic standards. In a give-and-take game of Sacramento politics, Cathedral City Mayor Pro Tem J. Velasquez is also securing his community's portion of SR 111 while the city receives state funds for a new library.

Other issues remain unresolved. Palm Springs voters will decide the fate of Palm Springs City Council's proposed expansion of its regional airport. The Referendum, Measure M, will either initiate or hinder a three-stage expansion project slated to be completed in 2015. According to Civil Servant Allen Smoot, the first stage of the project addresses the issue of safety: "The runway [of Palm Springs Regional Airport] is 8500 feet long. The primary aircraft that come to Palm Springs are the McDonnell MD-80s; that's what American and Alaska Airlines use. The MD-80 has a very quiet engine, but it does not perform well in hot climates. The hotter the climate, the longer the time the aircraft needs to get off the ground." Some local residents are concerned that runway expansion will increase noise levels and congestion, and the safety issue could be used as a smoke screen by developers aggressively seeking to increase tourism revenue.

If air traffic does not increase over Palm Springs, then perhaps personal travel by rail will be more common. After more than two years, the proposal for building a passenger train platform in Palm Springs is still unsettled. Both Amtrak and Metrolink are being courted by Palm Springs officials to help things along. So far Amtrak looks like the more responsive of the two. Amtrak trains already stop in Indio six mornings a week between 1 and 3 a.m. on the "Sunset Limited" route between Los Angeles and Miami.

Indio itself has a project in limbo. Under the auspices of Midland Properties of Kansas City, the planned Gateway North Marketplace and Desert Cities Automall promises to be a revenue generator for Indio. Mayor Tom Hunt did not hold back when he talked about Indio's past economic woes: "This is the first year [1995] in several that we have adopted a balanced budget with no service cuts or takebacks." If the project gets free of its legal tangle, then Indio can join resort cities like La Quinta, which openly welcomes mass merchandising interests. Palm Desert, on the other hand, can afford to be choosy. As Coachella Valley's second largest generator of hotel sales (in 1994 the city received $4.8 million in bed taxes), Palm Desert hosts a full merchandising cross section. Acting City Manager Ray Diaz said, "We try to keep from over-emphasizing any one segment." With that idea in mind, the City of Palm Desert is behind the El Paseo project, a proposed 200,000-square-foot expansion of its Saks Fifth Avenue location.

Palm Springs, of course, is not short on elegance. Rose Narva, a notable hotelier, is quite eager to own and operate The Givenchy Spa Resort. Tentatively scheduled to open on its Palm Springs site in 1996, it would be the sister spa of the Trianon Palace in Versailles, which opened in 1992. Rose's counterpart would be the fashion icon Hubert de Givenchy, a prominent name in international beauty products. Agua Caliente architect David Christian is putting his good name behind yet another Palm Springs expansion project, the Palm Springs International Speedway. The 50,000-seat raceway will cover 605 acres and cost an estimated $40 million. Groundbreaking should take place once funding is arranged.

Not to be outdone by the new kids on the block, existing Palm Springs attractions have their own future growth in mind. The Steve Chase Wing of The Palm Springs Desert Museum will be a 15,000-square-foot addition to the museum. Construction of the wing, which will contain new galleries and an educational center, should be completed by November 1996.

Future growth seems to be on a very grand scale in Coachella, a town that is 97 percent Mexican American. Inspired by the NAFTA treaty and its location near the U.S.-Mexico border, this town is poised to reap the benefits of free trade. City Manager Bruce Daniels observes that "All the commercial and tourist traffic from Mexico will pass right by us…" For the immediate future Coachella envisions developing an entertainment district. There is talk of expanding on the Indian gaming casinos already in the area as an initial push towards this goal.

Bureaucrats or no, the future will bring a lot of new attractions to the Resort Cities area. Both residents and investors in the economic future of the desert communities are making sure that there will be many new exciting and entertaining places to visit.

COACHELLA VALLEY PRESERVE
Approximately 6 miles north of Thousand Palms off Thousand Palms Rd. (mailing address: P.O. Box 188, 92276). (619/760) 343-1234. The preserve is open daily 8 a.m. to sunset. Groups of 12 or more should call for special arrangements. Hiking and horseback riding (where specified) are permitted in the preserve (no horse rentals are available at the sanctuary). Picnicking near the visitors center is allowed. Motorized vehicles and bicycles are not permitted on trails or dirt roads within the preserve. Pets, firearms, overnight camping and smoking are prohibited. Hikers must pack out all trash.

This building at Thousand Palms Oasis serves as the visitor center for the Coachella Valley Preserve.

Created to protect the endangered Coachella Valley fringe-toed lizard, this 21,000-acre preserve system also contains one of the largest groves of Washingtonia palms in California at the Thousand Palms Oasis. Near the oasis, sand dunes provide a critical habitat for the flat-tailed horned lizard and rare round-tailed ground squirrels, as well as the fringe-toed lizard. The preserve also hosts a number of resident and migratory birds, adding to a total assemblage of more than 180 species that thrive here. Brochures describing the area and its trails may be obtained at the visitor information area at the Thousand Palms Oasis.

COVERED WAGON TOURS *P.O. Box 1106, La Quinta. 92253. (619/760) 347-2161, (800) 367-2161. Call for directions and schedule; subject to cancellation in adverse weather conditions. Refreshments and a cowboy dinner (optional) follow the ride. Adult dinner tour, $55; tour only, $30; ages 7 through 16, half price; ages 6 and under, no charge. Reservations are required.* Mule-drawn covered wagons travel approximately seven miles through the Coachella Valley Preserve, passing Hidden and Horseshoe oases to an overlook of Pushawalla Oasis, all of which are on the San Andreas Fault. Wildlife are often spotted, including coyotes, desert tortoises, lizards, snakes and many varieties of birds. During the ride a naturalist describes local plants, their uses in the native culture and contemporary applications, and area geology; tales of Indian adventures and cowboy songs help recreate an atmosphere of the "Old West."

JOSHUA TREE AREA

The Joshua Tree area spans both the upper (Mojave) and lower (Colorado) deserts. Dramatic scenery presents itself at every turn—huge piles of gigantic boulders, intriguing Joshua trees reaching skyward, windswept mountains seemingly devoid of vegetation, dense forests of cholla cacti, old mining sites, lush tropical oases. Both rest and recreation bring their rewards here. Travelers find warm weather, clear blue skies, dry desert air and captivating scenery.

Spring wildflowers add splashes of color to the desert.

The small outpost of **Chiriaco Summit** served for decades primarily as a roadside stopping place for travelers on I-10 and before that on US 60. During World War II the U.S. Army's Desert Training Center was headquartered near here and hundreds of thousands of soldiers used the rugged terrain to train for combat. That era is memorialized in the General Patton Memorial Museum in Chiriaco.

Joshua Tree National Park preserves thousands of square miles of both upper and lower deserts, much of it rugged wilderness. Although the park has a few historical and mining sites, its primary attraction is recreation—rock climbing, bicycling and camping. Each year, thousands

"Old blood and guts" left a lasting impression on the desert.

Rock formations common to Joshua Tree National Park entice climbers, campers and photographers.

of visitors come here looking to "get back to nature."

On the northern edge of Joshua Tree National Park sit the small high-desert cities of the **Morongo Basin**—Morongo Valley, Yucca Valley, Joshua Tree and Twentynine Palms. Strung out along SR 62, each of these communities has its own identity and contributions to the balance of life and culture in the High Desert. Indeed, the dry desert air and a slower-paced way of life are what attracted many to settle here.

These fanciful owl carvings greet visitors at the Hi-Desert Nature Museum.

Joshua Tree Area

The majority of this harsh, vast, desolate region will remain largely uninhabited, protected from further human development and exploitation. Even so, past human activities have left marks on the landscape that even time will not erase—mine ruins, tailings and shafts; roads carved into the earth; hooks and bolts imbedded in rock walls by climbers. The strange-looking Joshua trees, the piles of boulders, the purplish mountains, the stands of cactus—they'll be there for a long time to come.

Effective March 22, 1997, area code (619) will change to (760).

Chiriaco Summit

The dry and desolate area around Chiriaco Summit has, with one exception, seen little settlement. Early inhabitants included Chemehuevi and Cahuilla peoples, explorers and miners. Modern civilization left its mark on the region in 1933, when construction began on an aqueduct to bring much-needed water from the Colorado River to the burgeoning coastal cities of Southern California. Completed in 1941, the Colorado River Aqueduct has five pumping stations along its 242-mile course. Four miles east of Chiriaco Summit on I-10, Hinds Pumping Station is visible on the mountainside north of the highway.

Originally known as Shaver's Summit, its present name came from Joseph Chiriaco, a former surveyor who worked on the aqueduct.

The area's population boomed during a two-year period when more than one million soldiers came to the U.S. Armed Forces Desert Training Center to prepare for World War II combat. Roads at the abandoned camp are still visible on the desert floor.

CAMP YOUNG MEMORIAL *¼ mile north of I-10 on Cottonwood Spring Rd., ⅝ mile east.* The memorial marker commemorates the site of Camp Young, headquarters of the U.S. Armed Forces Desert Training Center during World War II. Camp Young was one of 11 divisional training camps established by General George S. Patton in the deserts of California, Arizona and Nevada. He felt the terrain and climate provided ideal training conditions for combat in North Africa. An information kiosk gives details of the camp's 25-month training operation.

GENERAL PATTON MEMORIAL MUSEUM *30 miles east of Indio off I-10 at Chiriaco Summit; 92201. (619/ 760) 227-3483. Open daily from 9 a.m. to 5 p.m. Closed Thanksgiving and Dec. 25. Admission is $4 for adults; $3.50 for seniors; ages 12 and under admitted free.*

The distinctive-looking Joshua tree is found in the Mojave Desert.

▼ *Commanding History*

Between April 30, 1942, and April 30, 1944, with our country involved in World War II, one million soldiers received combat training at the Desert Training Center. One of them was my father.

In December 1942, Army Lieutenant Jacob G. Miller left Camp White, Oregon, with the 355th Engineer General Service Regiment for Camp Young, in the desert 30 miles east of Indio, California. In addition to training, their mission included building roads, bridges, landing strips, railroad sidings and spurs, as well as temporary buildings for the troops at the Desert Training Center. During his tenure at Camp Young, Dad was transferred to the 605th Engineer Camouflage Battalion. Wearing the prescribed uniform of green combat fatigues, the soldiers practiced concealing themselves and their equipment using camouflage techniques, including the use of trees, shrubs and camouflage paint on their vehicles.

Military life at Camp Young was as good as desert camps went, according to my father, but nonetheless it was not easy. Men lived usually four to a tent, each of which had an open light bulb hanging down in the middle, and the tent floor was wood. This was not the most secure housing, and in one storm more than 400 tents were blown away. Tent furnishings consisted of each man's cot and footlocker. Air conditioning and running water were nonexistent, but there was a field phone which could be used to contact headquarters— personal phone calls had to be made from pay phones. Rest room facilities—latrines—were pits dug into the ground and enclosed by small tents. Water for the camp came from the Los Angeles Aqueduct, which ran nearby. Soldiers had a choice in where they could purchase personal supplies—there were 115 post exchange units throughout the camp, most housed in tents.

Troops stationed at the Desert Training Center generally worked six days a week, with some men receiving passes to go into town for their day off. Field duty usually lasted for a week or two, sometimes longer. The days were long. Breakfast was very early, lunch was midday and dinner was prob-

Wall of the Fallen honors those who have given their lives in military service to the United States.

ably around 6 p.m. Each unit took meals in its own mess hall, a long wooden building with refrigerators and storage units at one end. In the early days of the camp fresh produce was available, kept cool by 300-lb. blocks of ice brought in from San Bernardino or Indio. But before long the meals consisted of desert rations; Dad recalls that the camp cooks worked wonders with artificial eggs and powdered milk, and that the meals often included cookies.

Communication with headquarters was maintained through the regular use of field phones, plus each unit had its own messenger. Classification of materials and messages often was Top Secret, Secret or Restricted, even in the American desert, so far from the actual battlefields in Europe, Africa and the Pacific.

Despite temperatures sometimes approaching 130 degrees, soldiers wore regulation fatigues made from a heavy, denim-like fabric; in those days long sleeves were standard year round. Each man carried his rifle and canteen throughout the day, and on field exercises wore a complete pack as well. On especially hot days, soldiers could fry eggs on the tailgate of a truck. Tarps had to be placed over the motor pool, otherwise the metal parts were too hot to handle. In this extreme heat the tents were shady and relatively cooler, which also made them appealing to rattlesnakes.

The men were preparing for the eventuality of mortal combat overseas, but that reality sometimes made itself present at Camp Young. Prior to practicing on the infiltration course, men would walk the course shoulder to shoulder to clear it of poisonous snakes. Then the soldiers would crawl the course while a steady stream of machine gun fire was leveled just inches over their heads. In one exercise a soldier came face to face with a sidewinder and in panic rose to his feet, right into the line of deadly fire.

The torture of life at the Desert Training Center was eased by mail from home, which usually arrived daily in camp and twice a week in the field. Chaplains held services almost daily, both in camp chapels and in the field. The men had to have some recreation, too—Dad recalls they cleared some desert and made themselves a baseball diamond. For entertainment, USO shows were put on at the camp, and occasionally some troops were able to attend shows put on in Palm Springs at the Plaza Theatre (Dad remembers seeing Jack Benny and Dennis Day, big stars in those days). The harsh conditions of military service often fostered friendships which lasted throughout the remainder of the men's lives—Dad is still in contact with Colonel William Mohr, his commanding officer in the 605th, as well as many other old "Army buddies."

In December of 1943, Dad and the rest of the 605th Engineer Camouflage Battalion were transferred to Camp Van Dorn, Mississippi. In the summer of 1944 Lieutenant Miller became part of the staff of the newly organized 1158th Engineer Combat Group. The next December they shipped out to Europe—but that's another story.

— by Kristine Miller

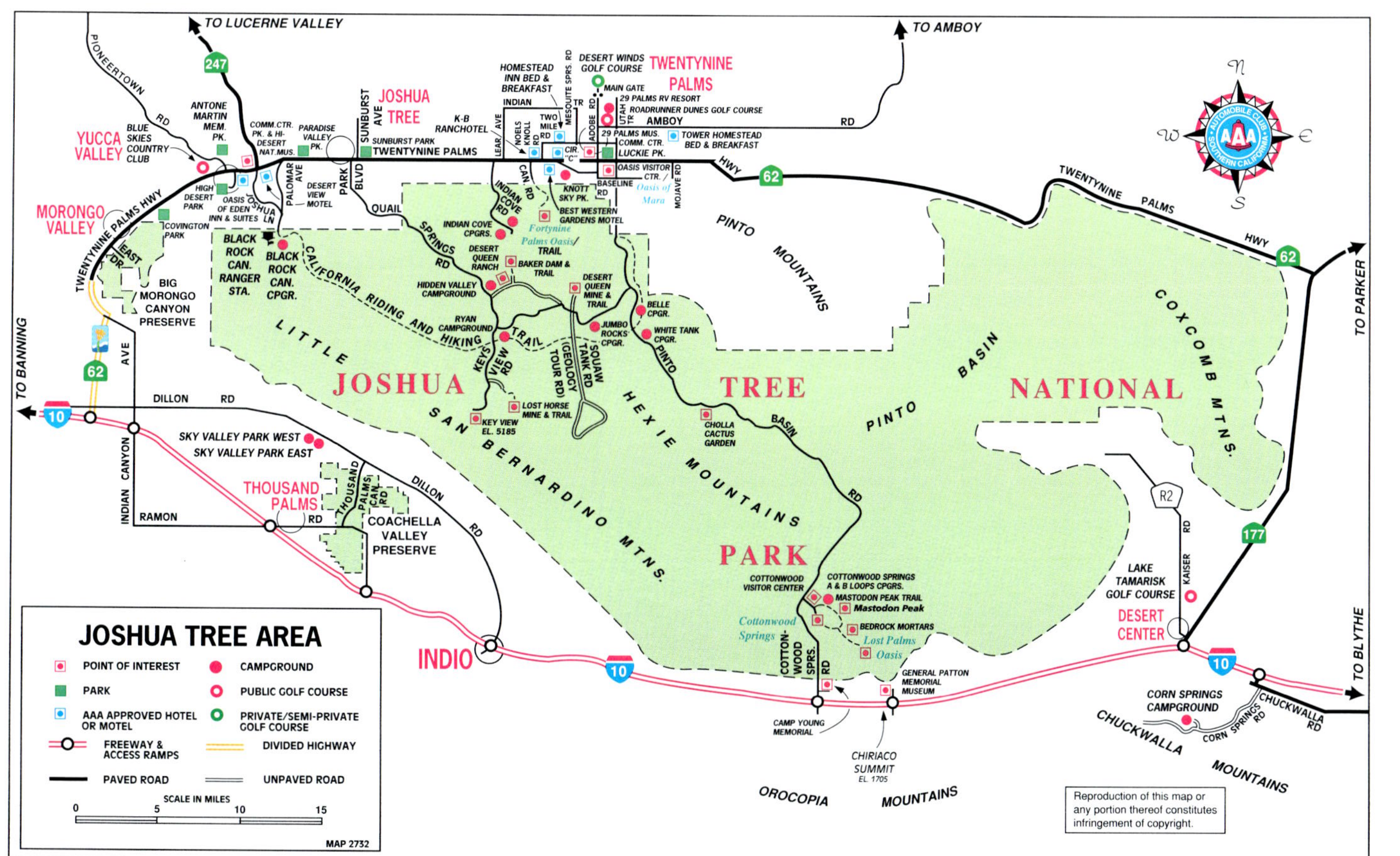
TO LUCERNE VALLEY
TO AMBOY
247
PIONEERTOWN RD
ANTONE MARTIN MEM. PK.
BLUE SKIES COUNTRY CLUB
YUCCA VALLEY
COMM. CTR. PK. & HI-DESERT NAT. MUS.
PARADISE VALLEY PK.
SUNBURST AVE
SUNBURST PARK
JOSHUA TREE
TWENTYNINE PALMS
K-B RANCHOTEL
HOMESTEAD INN BED & BREAKFAST
DESERT WINDS GOLF COURSE
TWENTYNINE PALMS
MAIN GATE
29 PALMS RV RESORT
ROADRUNNER DUNES GOLF COURSE
AMBOY
29 PALMS MUS. COMM. CTR.
TOWER HOMESTEAD BED & BREAKFAST
RD
MORONGO VALLEY
HIGH DESERT PARK
OASIS OF EDEN INN & SUITES LN
JOSHUA LN
COVINGTON PARK
PALOMAR AVE
DESERT VIEW MOTEL
PARK BLVD
QUAIL
INDIAN
NOELS KNOLL RD
TWO MILE RD
MESQUITE SPRS. RD
CIR. "C"
ADOBE RD
UTAH TR
LEAR AVE
CAN. RD
INDIAN COVE RD
KNOTT SKY PK.
BEST WESTERN GARDENS MOTEL
Fortynine Palms Oasis TRAIL
OASIS VISITOR CTR.
Oasis of Mara
BASELINE RD
MOJAVE RD
HWY 62
PINTO MOUNTAINS
TWENTYNINE PALMS HWY
COXCOMB MTNS.
TO PARKER
HWY 62
TWENTYNINE PALMS HWY
EAST DR
BIG MORONGO CANYON PRESERVE
BLACK ROCK CAN. RANGER STA.
BLACK ROCK CAN. CPGR.
SPRINGS RD
INDIAN COVE CPGRS.
DESERT QUEEN RANCH
HIDDEN VALLEY CAMPGROUND
BAKER DAM & TRAIL
DESERT QUEEN MINE & TRAIL
RYAN CAMPGROUND
CALIFORNIA RIDING AND HIKING TRAIL
KEYS VIEW RD
GEOLOGY TOUR RD
SQUAW TANK RD
JUMBO ROCKS CPGR.
BELLE CPGR.
WHITE TANK CPGR.
PINTO
LITTLE
JOSHUA
HEXIE MOUNTAINS
TREE
PINTO BASIN
NATIONAL
LOST HORSE MINE & TRAIL
KEY VIEW EL. 5185
SAN BERNARDINO MTNS.
CHOLLA CACTUS GARDEN
BASIN
TO BANNING
AVE
10
62
DILLON RD
INDIAN CANYON
RAMON
SKY VALLEY PARK WEST
SKY VALLEY PARK EAST
THOUSAND PALMS
THOUSAND PALMS CAN RD
DILLON RD
COACHELLA VALLEY PRESERVE
PARK
RD
PARK
COTTONWOOD VISITOR CENTER
COTTONWOOD SPRINGS A & B LOOPS CPGRS.
MASTODON PEAK TRAIL
Mastodon Peak
BEDROCK MORTARS
Cottonwood Springs
COTTON-WOOD SPRS. RD
Lost Palms Oasis
GENERAL PATTON MEMORIAL MUSEUM
CAMP YOUNG MEMORIAL
CHIRIACO SUMMIT EL. 1705
OROCOPIA MOUNTAINS
INDIO
10
LAKE TAMARISK GOLF COURSE
R2
177
KAISER RD
DESERT CENTER
10
TO BLYTHE
CORN SPRINGS CAMPGROUND
CHUCKWALLA
CORN SPRINGS RD
CHUCKWALLA RD
CHUCKWALLA MOUNTAINS
Chiriaco Summit

JOSHUA TREE AREA
POINT OF INTEREST
CAMPGROUND
PARK
PUBLIC GOLF COURSE
AAA APPROVED HOTEL OR MOTEL
PRIVATE/SEMI-PRIVATE GOLF COURSE
FREEWAY & ACCESS RAMPS
DIVIDED HIGHWAY
PAVED ROAD
UNPAVED ROAD
SCALE IN MILES
0   5   10   15
MAP 2732
Reproduction of this map or any portion thereof constitutes infringement of copyright.

Built on the site of General George S. Patton's Desert Training Center, the museum contains an assortment of memorabilia from World War II and other periods of military history, with special displays of tanks and artillery. A 26-minute video presentation provides insight into the general's career. In the entry hall is a five-ton relief map detailing the development of Southern California's water system.

Joshua Tree National Park

HEADQUARTERS—Oasis Visitor Center *1 block south of SR 62 on Utah Tr., north of the park (mailing address: Joshua Tree National Park, 74485 National Park Dr., Twentynine Palms 92277-3597). (619/760) 367-7511. The visitor center is open daily 8 a.m. to 6 p.m. Closed Dec. 25.* Rangers can answer questions and provide information on weather, road conditions and places of interest. The center has displays about desert ecology and sells books, maps and pamphlets.

Black Rock Canyon Ranger Station *Just inside the park boundary, reached by following SR 247 (Joshua Ln.) from the center of Yucca Valley.* Set among Joshua trees on a scenic hillside, the station offers information, assistance, educational displays, books and maps.

Cottonwood Visitor Center *5 miles north of the park's southern entrance on Pinto Basin Rd. Open daily 8 a.m. to 4 p.m.* Rangers are on hand to assist visitors, exhibits explain the Colorado Desert, and various books and maps are for sale.

Admission to Joshua Tree National Park is $5 per vehicle. Pedestrians, bicyclists and bus passengers are charged $3 each. An annual pass to the park is $15. Visitors planning to see several national parks or monuments throughout the

Mormon pioneers are the ones who gave the Joshua tree its name.

▼ *A Quick Guide to Joshua Tree Area*

See also Quick Guide *boxes under Resort Cities.*
Effective March 22, 1997, area code (619) will change to (760).

Population   60,000

Elevation   2000 ft.

Emergency   911

Police Nonemergency
(619/760) 366-3707

**Emergency Road Service for
AAA Members**

(800) AAA-HELP (in the USA and
Canada)

(800) 955-4TDD (for the hearing
impaired)

Highway Conditions
(800) 427-7623

Time   (619/760) 853-1212

Weather   (805) 988-6610

Newspapers

Major daily newspapers serving the
Morongo Basin are the *Desert Trail*
and the *High Desert Star.*

Radio Stations

Contemporary Rock: KQYN (1250
AM); **Country:** KDHI (95.7 FM);
Adult Contemporary/News: KCDZ
(107.7 FM); **Talk/News:** KNWZ
(106.9 FM). For a complete list of
radio programs, consult the daily
newspapers.

24-hour Activity Hotline
(619/760) 770-1992

Bus

The Morongo Basin Transportation
Authority operates in Twentynine
Palms, Joshua Tree, Yucca Valley,
Morongo Valley, Landers and
Wonder Valley. It also provides
intercity transportation to the Palm
Springs resort areas; phone (800) 794-
6282. Intra-city cash fare is $1; dial-a-
ride service is $1.50 (24-hour advance
notice required); call for current
intercity rates; exact fare required.
Monthly punch passes are $17 for
adults, $15 for students and $8.50 for
seniors. Wheelchair lifts available.

Train

The nearest **Amtrak** passenger rail
stations are located in Indio (see *Resort
Cities*) and in San Bernardino at 1170
West 3rd Street; phone (909) 884-
1307. The "Desert Wind," "Southwest
Chief" and "Sunset Limited" lines
serve the California desert areas (with
bus connections on selected routes).
Call (800) USA-RAIL for complete
information and fares.

Taxi

Alpha Yellow Cab provides service for
the entire Morongo Basin. Rates are
regulated; the flag rate is $1.75 plus
$1.75 per mile. Wheelchair vans avail-
able. Refer to the local yellow pages of
the telephone directory under "Taxi"
for phone numbers and information.

Hospitals

Hi-Desert Medical Center
6601 White Feather Rd.
Joshua Tree 92252
(619/760) 366-3711, (800) 464-8055

Avalon Urgent Care Center
58471 Twentynine Palms Hwy.
Yucca Valley 92284
(619/760) 365-0851

year should purchase a Golden Eagle Passport ($25), which provides admission to all federal fee areas for a 12-month period. Persons age 62 years and older are eligible for the Golden Age Passport, available for a one-time fee of $10; it waives entrance fees to federal areas and provides discounts on camping. Disabled persons may receive a free Golden Access Pass; it brings the same benefits as the Golden Age Passport.

In 1936 a region representative of Southwestern desert environments was preserved for future generations with the establishment of Joshua Tree National Monument. The monument's name came from the presence of thousands of Joshua trees throughout much of the protected area; the giant yucca tree's name came from Mormon pioneers who thought it resembled the Biblical prophet Joshua beckoning the weary traveler to the Promised Land. In 1994 the monument was elevated to national park status and its land area was increased.

The park bridges a transition zone between two distinct desert ecosystems: the northern portion of the park lies within the Mojave or "high" desert, ranging in elevation roughly from 3000 to 6000 feet; to the south and east, the landscape descends to the Colorado or "lower" desert, where elevations approach sea level. Five mountain ranges mold both desert regions into broad valleys and secluded canyons. The Little San Bernardino Mountains define the western edge of the park. To the north, separating the park from the Morongo Basin, are the harsh Pinto and Queen mountain ranges. The barren Hexie Mountains rise from the central part of the park, and along the southeast boundary stand the low-lying Eagle Mountains.

The Coxcomb Mountains border the eastern edge of the national park.

Rainfall in the Colorado and lower Mojave deserts barely exceeds three inches annually on average. The upper Mojave Desert gets a little more precipitation—six to eight inches each year. Though very limited, this rainfall, coupled with cooler temperatures in the northern, higher section, permits a surprising variety of desert vegetation to thrive. Joshua trees and various cacti cover rocky mountainsides, oases support groves of palms in shaded canyons, and after winter and spring showers waves of brilliant wildflowers appear.

At first glance, a desert landscape may appear devoid of wildlife. A closer look, however, reveals a wide variety of mammals, birds, reptiles and insects, ranging from the coyote to the pungent stink bug. Soaring above the park, golden eagles scour the desert floor for food, while in the rugged mountains,

The spindly ocotillo is very hardy.

JOSHUA TREE AREA

elusive bighorn sheep survey the panorama from lofty perches. As testimony to their environmental adaptation, many animals, such as the tarantula and the yucca night lizard, shun the heat of day and prefer to set out after sunset to hunt—and be hunted.

Visitors may pursue a variety of interests and activities in the park. Spectacular and ever-changing scenery await both car and foot travelers. Mine and ranch sites attract history buffs, while Joshua trees, cactus gardens and a wide variety of flora appeal to plant lovers. Hikers may explore on trails through the desert, and rock climbers can choose from a dizzying assortment of ascents.

There are no dining facilities, accommodations, or gas stations within Joshua Tree National Park. The *only* water available is at four locations: Oasis Visitors Center, Indian Cove Ranger Station, Cottonwood Springs and Black Rock Canyon Campground. All visitors hiking into the backcountry must register at a backcountry board.

BARKER DAM TRAIL *Begins 2 miles northeast of Hidden Valley Campground, just off Quail Springs Rd.* This half-mile path passes an area known as Wonderland of Rocks, ending at a pool of water behind a dam built by cattlemen around 1900. Cattle no longer graze in the park, but the rain-fed pool provides a valuable source of water for wildlife.

CALIFORNIA RIDING AND HIKING TRAIL *Runs through the park for 35 miles.* The trail provides excellent viewing of the park's varied scenery for those on foot or horseback. The western terminus is off Joshua Lane near Black Rock Canyon; the eastern trailhead is off Utah Trail at the park boundary. Intermediate access points are Covington Flats, and Keys View and Geology Tour roads (see listings).

CHOLLA CACTUS GARDEN *Northeast of the Hexie Mountains on Pinto Basin Rd.* This easily accessible preserve gives visitors an opportunity to observe a mix of plants and animals typical of

The Cholla Cactus Garden is representative of the plant life found in the Colorado Desert.

the Colorado Desert. A short trail winds through an unusually dense concentration of cholla cacti. The cholla is often called "teddy bear" cactus because of the deceptively soft, fluffy appearance of its sharp spines. (The cholla's spines can puncture skin with only the slightest touch.)

COTTONWOOD SPRING *5 miles north of the south entrance to the park and 1 mile east of the visitor center.* Set in a grove of palms and cottonwood trees, this inviting oasis is a haven for desert birds. Nearby, off Lost Palms Trail, are mortar holes that were worn in stone by Cahuilla women who once ground seeds and grain here.

DESERT QUEEN MINE TRAIL *Begins off a dirt road running north opposite Geology Tour Rd.* A ¾-mile trail leads east to the mine site where high-grade ore was mined and processed by the McHaney brothers in the 1890s. Do not enter dangerous tunnels and mine shafts in the area.

DESERT QUEEN RANCH *Open only to ranger-guided tours originating at the ranch gate, reached from a 2-mile dirt road leading from Hidden Valley Campground (watch for signs). Tours are held in spring and fall on Sat. and Sun. More information can be obtained at park entrance stations and visitor centers.* Gold, discovered near the ranch about 1890, quickly enticed owners Bill and Jim McHaney away from ranching. They developed and operated the Desert Queen Mine until its high-grade ore was exhausted. In the early 1900s, Bill Keys took over the mine and 160 acres of the old ranch. He built a house, raised a family with his wife, ran cattle and mined what was left of the gold. He lived there until his death in 1969.

FORTYNINE PALMS OASIS TRAIL *Begins off Canyon Rd. 4 miles west of Twentynine Palms off SR 62.* This moderately strenuous trail extends 1½ miles to the oasis where water-loving plants thrive and animals come to drink from the pool created by the spring.

GEOLOGY TOUR ROAD *Begins in Queen Valley, heading south from the main park road (Quail Springs Rd.). In wet weather motorists should limit their explorations to the first 5½ miles of the road. Before beginning the tour, check with rangers about current road conditions. A brochure discussing the area's natural phenomena is available at the road entrance or can be purchased at the visitor centers for 25¢.* Signed "Squaw Tank," the rough dirt road reaches 18 miles into the heart of the national park, permitting motorists in four-wheel-drive vehicles to enter a desert realm rarely accessible by automobile. Centuries of erosion have resulted in the formation of great alluvial fans that spill toward the roadway from the surrounding mountains. Scattered across the valley floor are monzogranite rock piles (igneous rock formed by the solidification of molten magma), massive heaps of boulders that rise above stands of Joshua trees; also visible is the smooth, parched surface of a desert playa, or dry lake bed. Motorists can drive to Squaw Tank, an early concrete dam, and those who venture away from the road on foot can find Indian petroglyphs and abandoned mines (do not enter tunnels or mine shafts).

KEYS VIEW *20 miles south of the town of Joshua Tree off Quail Springs and Keys View rds.* This windy overlook at the crest of the Little San Bernardino Mountains stands at 5185 feet. The impressive view from the summit encompasses the Coachella Valley with

Snow-capped Mount Jacinto and the western Coachella Valley are part of the panorama visible from Keys View.

third variation credits the McHaney brothers, cattle ranchers (and possibly cattle rustlers), as stealing Johnny's horse so that they could stake the claim first. In any case, gold worth more than $270,000 was taken from the mine in its first 10 years. Ore-crushing machinery and various foundations are still visible at the site.

MASTODON PEAK TRAIL *Climbs from Cottonwood Campground to 3371-foot Mastodon Peak.* In four miles, this moderately strenuous trek takes hikers past the abandoned Mastodon Mine and on to the summit, where the Hexie Mountains, Pinto Basin and Salton Sea dominate the vista.

the San Jacinto Range beyond, the Salton Sea far below and Mount San Gorgonio (11,499 feet) to the west.

LOST HORSE MINE TRAIL *Begins 1⅛ miles east of Keys View Rd. on the old mine road. This four-mile round-trip hike should be made in cool weather because the trail lacks shade and water.* The mine has a colorful history. One story states that a cowboy, Johnny Lang, found gold here while searching for his lost horse. Another version says that Lang bought the claim from a man who discovered gold while searching for *his* lost horse. And a

OASIS OF MARA *Just south of SR 62 off Pinto Basin Rd.* This is the historic "Twentynine Palms Oasis" first recorded in an 1855 survey under the charge of Colonel Henry Washington, but referred to as *Marrah* (or *Mara*, which means land of little water) by the Chemehuevi people. This ancient oasis is arguably the most important factor in the foundation of modern Twentynine Palms. A self-guided, half-mile loop tour begins west of the Oasis Visitor Center. A natural spring once sustained a pool of fresh water here, but years of overuse have lowered the

A short stroll from the Oasis Visitor Center leads to the Oasis of Mara.

water table to the point where surface water seldom appears.

Morongo Basin

Stretching across the desert north of Joshua Tree National Park is Morongo Basin, extending 40 miles from the community of Morongo Valley on the western end to the abandoned mining town of Old Dale on the east end. Settlement in the basin has spread along SR 62, the basin's primary east/west transportation corridor. On the east side is Twentynine Palms, with the towns of Joshua Tree, Yucca Valley and Morongo Valley to the west.

Permanent settlement of the Morongo Basin didn't occur until a small contingent of homesteaders arrived in the 1870s. Chuck Warren, one of the first ranchers in the region, settled Morongo Valley in 1874. His ranch was one of the few stopping places for travelers bound for the Colorado River and mines scattered across the desert. In 1881, Warren's son Mark dug a well in Yucca Valley that became known as "Warren's Well," a gathering place for settlers and site of meetings, square dances and barbecues for many years.

With the subdivision of the basin's four towns in the 1930s, the pace of development accelerated. Even with the influx of new residents, however, the basin remained rural. Few telephones were installed before 1940, and it wasn't until after World War II that electricity reached the area.

The valley's largest town, **Yucca Valley,** is located toward the western end of the Morongo Basin at an elevation of 3256 feet. This community is centered around the crossroads of SR 62, which runs to the western end of the Coachella Valley, and SR 247, which connects to the Barstow area. Yucca Valley's population totals nearly 18,800.

The city of **Twentynine Palms** spreads across a 2000-foot-high valley toward the eastern end of the Morongo Basin. This city is the region's service center for Joshua Tree National Park and the nearby Marine Corps Air Ground Combat Center. Twentynine Palms' population is around 15,000, with the Marine base adding another 10,000 area residents.

Just north of a primary entrance to Joshua Tree National Park is the town of **Joshua Tree**, home to nearly 4000 residents. Copper Mountain Campus, an extension of the College of the Desert in Palm Desert, offers Joshua Tree and neighboring communities classes in art, business administration, liberal studies and natural resources.

At the western edge of the basin is **Morongo Valley**, a community of nearly 3600 desert dwellers. Residents of these high desert communities are similar in that they cherish the quiet desert lifestyle and small-town atmosphere.

ANTONE MARTIN MEMORIAL PARK

½ mile north of SR 62 on Sunnyslope Dr., off Mohawk Tr. in Yucca Valley (mailing address: P.O. Box 1537, 92286). (619/760) 365-3868. Free admission. Located on a sloping, sandy hill, this park, also known as Desert Christ Park, contains concrete statuary depicting Biblical scenes. The white, larger-than-life-size statues were created between 1950 and 1961 by sculptor Antone Martin.

BIG MORONGO CANYON PRESERVE

½ mile southeast of the town of Morongo Valley off SR 62 and East Dr. (mailing address: P.O. Box 780, Morongo Valley 92256). (619/760) 363-7190. Open Fri. through Wed. from 7:30 a.m. to sunset for hiking, bird watching and nature

A wooden path leads visitors through the marshes of the Big Morongo Canyon Preserve.

study. Groups of 12 or more people need to schedule their visits in advance with the manager. Camping, firearms and collecting of any kind are prohibited in the preserve, and pets are not permitted. Bicycles not allowed past the parking lot. Visitors are asked to limit their excursions to designated trails. This 4500-acre preserve was established in 1968 to protect indigenous flora and fauna. Year-round surface water supports a surprisingly lush streamside forest, which can be viewed from a network of trails. The preserve is well known for its wide variety of birds and is a favorite stop for birdwatchers. Other animals include raccoons, kangaroo rats and a wide assortment of reptiles.

HI-DESERT NATURE MUSEUM *Located at the Community Center Complex, 57116 Twentynine Palms Hwy., Yucca Valley 92284. (619/760) 369-7212. Open Tues. through Sun. from 10 a.m. to 5 p.m. Closed Jan. 1, Thanksgiving and Dec. 25. Donations.* Founded in 1964, this small museum has a wide variety of note-worthy exhibits on Southern California flora, fauna, history and geology. Special displays include a spring wildflower exhibit and live small desert animals and reptiles. The "Kids' Korner" has a hands-on activity area.

TWENTYNINE PALMS MUSEUM COMMUNITY CENTER *6136 Adobe Rd., Twentynine Palms (mailing address: Twentynine Palms Historical Society, P.O. Box 1926, 92277). Open Wed. through Sun. from 1 to 4 p.m. Donations.* The museum contains a small rotating exhibit of Indian artifacts, old mining implements and cattlemen's and home-steader's items. Museum visitors also can browse through a collection of ref-erence books pertaining to the desert.

COLORADO RIVER AREA

The Colorado River winds its way through the stark landscape, a shimmering ribbon of water that seems totally out of place in the middle of the desert. Originating high in the mountains of the state of Colorado, the river cuts through the canyons and deserts of the Colorado Plateau—crossing southeastern Utah to Lake Powell, dropping through the Grand Canyon in northern Arizona, into man-made Lake Mead in Nevada—finally reaching the the Mojave and Sonoran deserts. As the river flows south towards the Gulf of California, the land on both sides of the Colorado River offers vast expanses of level desert punctuated by numerous small mountain ranges. The river itself meanders lazily towards the Mexican border and eventually empties out into the Gulf of California.

Immense intaglios were etched onto the surface of the desert by ancient Indians.

The **California side** of the Colorado River includes portions of San Bernardino, Riverside and Imperial counties. Water recreation is the area's major attraction, and visitors come year round for boating, fishing, water-skiing, jet-skiing and swimming. But the desert also draws those wishing to explore the

I-40 traverses the Colorado River at Topock Gorge.

Recreation is a major economic factor in the region; Senator Wash offers primitive facilities.

back roads, rugged hills and abandoned mines. Adjacent to the river are the communities of Needles, on I-40, and Blythe, on I-10. These towns serve as staging areas for those who wish to enjoy the area's vast recreational offerings.

On the **Arizona side** of the river lie Mohave, La Paz and Yuma counties. The city of Lake Havasu City developed around the famous London Bridge, moved stone by stone from England and reassembled here, connecting the Arizona shore with an island in the river. The town of Parker developed south of the dam by the same name. Both these towns are popular destinations for river recreation enthusiasts. Further south, near the Mexico border, the rapidly growing city of Yuma straddles I-8. Yuma began in the 1800s as a river-crossing for travelers heading west. Today it is a center for agriculture and tourism, as well as a popular destination among winter visitors.

By the time the mighty Colorado River nears the Gulf of California it is quite shallow, having been tamed by a series of dams and lakes which provide power for the cities of the Southwest and water for agriculture and recreation.

Massive turbines inside Parker Dam generate electrical power.

Colorado River Area

This lower portion of the Colorado River was originally peopled by American Indians of the Mojave, Chemehuevi and Quechan tribes. The first Europeans in the area were the Spanish who were seeking a land route from central Mexico to their colonies along the southern California coast. They were followed in the 1800s by explorers, miners, U.S. soldiers and a handful of American settlers. Today much of the area is still sparsely settled.

Effective March 22, 1997, area code (619) will change to (760).

THE CALIFORNIA SIDE

The sparse and rugged California side of the Colorado River is still largely undeveloped. The Palo Verde Valley is a vast agricultural area specializing in alfalfa, Sudan grass, lettuce and all kinds of melons. Two larger population centers have developed along two transcontinental highways: Needles along I-40 and Blythe along I-10. Other smaller communities include Parker Dam, Earp, Palo Verde and Winterhaven (see *Campgrounds & Trailer Parks*). These smaller towns provide minimal services for the traveler and are usually associated with agriculture, hydrologic projects or an Indian Reservation.

Blythe

The community of Blythe was named in honor of Thomas H. Blythe, an English pioneer who had settled in the area in 1877. Even though the center of town is a few miles west of the Colorado River, early farmers were still plagued by seasonal flooding until the completion of Hoover Dam in 1935. Today it is a thriving agricultural community of more than 21,000.

CIBOLA NATIONAL WILDLIFE REFUGE *20 miles south; P.O. Box AP, 92226. (520) 857-3253. Open daily during daylight hours. Free.* More than 16,000 acres of protected river and marsh lands are home to numerous wildlife species, including at least 200 species of bird. Among the many endangered bird species which visit or nest at the refuge during the year are bald eagles, brown pelicans, peregrine falcons and Yuma clapper rails. Strictly controlled hunting of legal species is allowed with a valid hunting license and appropriate stamps for the state in which you will be hunting.

INDIAN INTAGLIOS *15 miles north off of US 95. Open daily. Free.* Six giant white rock intaglios (figures incised on the surface) were carefully laid out on two adjoining mesas by ancient Indians. The figures represent both

---

Scenic Buckskin Mountain looms over a state park and the Colorado River.

COLORADO RIVER AREA

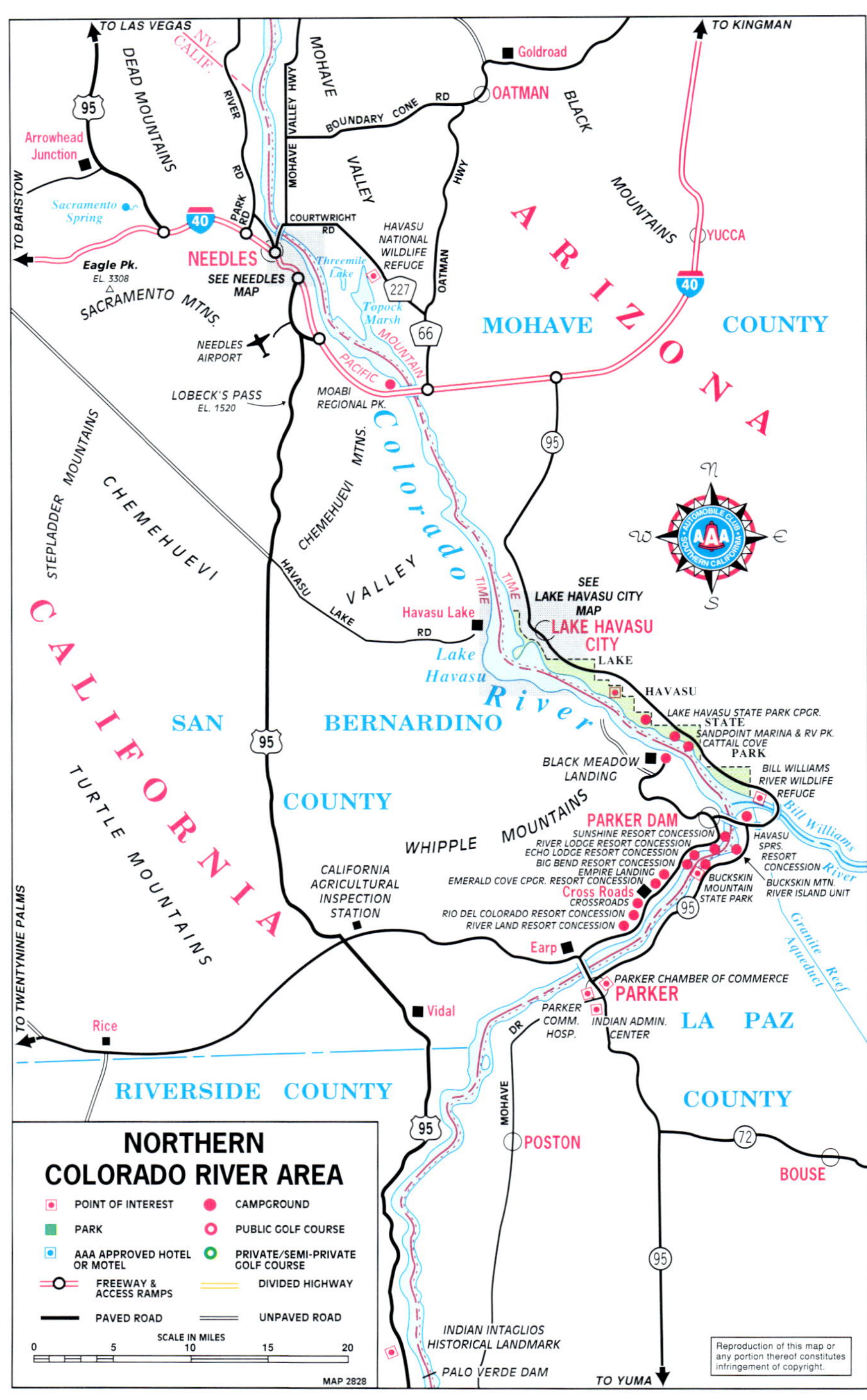

NORTHERN COLORADO RIVER AREA

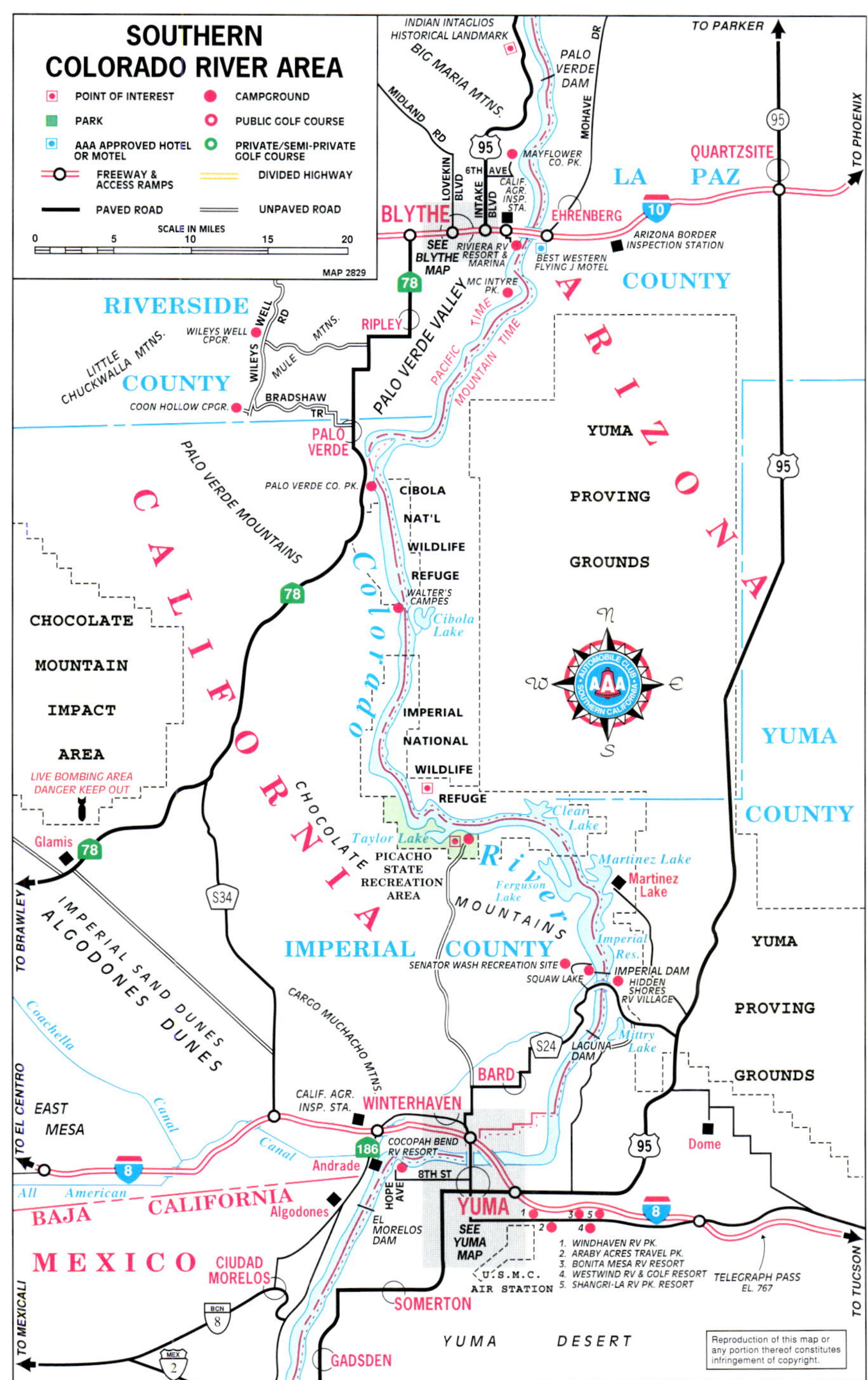
SOUTHERN
COLORADO RIVER AREA

POINT OF INTEREST
PARK
AAA APPROVED HOTEL OR MOTEL
FREEWAY & ACCESS RAMPS
PAVED ROAD
CAMPGROUND
PUBLIC GOLF COURSE
PRIVATE/SEMI-PRIVATE GOLF COURSE
DIVIDED HIGHWAY
UNPAVED ROAD

SCALE IN MILES
0   5   10   15   20
MAP 2829

INDIAN INTAGLIOS HISTORICAL LANDMARK
BIG MARIA MTNS.
PALO VERDE DAM
MOHAVE DR
TO PARKER
95
TO PHOENIX
MAYFLOWER CO. PK.
QUARTZSITE
MIDLAND RD
LOVEKIN BLVD
6TH AVE
INTAKE BLVD
CALIF. AGR. INSP. STA.
LA PAZ
BLYTHE
EHRENBERG
10
COUNTY
SEE BLYTHE MAP
RIVIERA RV RESORT & MARINA
BEST WESTERN FLYING J MOTEL
ARIZONA BORDER INSPECTION STATION
78
MC INTYRE PK.
RIVERSIDE
RIPLEY
WILEYS WELL CPGR.
WELL RD
MULE MTNS.
PALO VERDE VALLEY
Pacific Time
Mountain Time
A R I Z O N A
LITTLE CHUCKWALLA MTNS.
COUNTY
WILEYS
BRADSHAW TR
COON HOLLOW CPGR.
PALO VERDE
YUMA
PROVING
GROUNDS
95
PALO VERDE MOUNTAINS
PALO VERDE CO. PK.
CIBOLA NAT'L WILDLIFE REFUGE
78
WALTER'S CAMPES
Cibola Lake
Colorado
C A L I F O R N I A
CHOCOLATE
MOUNTAIN
IMPACT
AREA
LIVE BOMBING AREA DANGER KEEP OUT
IMPERIAL
NATIONAL
WILDLIFE
REFUGE
N
W   E
S
YUMA
Glamis
78
CHOCOLATE
Clear Lake
Taylor Lake
PICACHO STATE RECREATION AREA
River
Martinez Lake
COUNTY
TO BRAWLEY
IMPERIAL SAND DUNES
ALGODONES DUNES
S34
Ferguson Lake
Martinez Lake
M O U N T A I N S
YUMA
CARGO MUCHACHO MTNS
IMPERIAL   COUNTY
Imperial Res.
SENATOR WASH RECREATION SITE
SQUAW LAKE
IMPERIAL DAM
HIDDEN SHORES RV VILLAGE
PROVING
Coachella
Canal
S24
LAGUNA DAM
Mittry Lake
GROUNDS
TO EL CENTRO
EAST MESA
Canal
BARD
95
CALIF. AGR. INSP. STA.
WINTERHAVEN
Dome
8
Canal
186
COCOPAH BEND RV RESORT
8TH ST
All American
Andrade
BAJA CALIFORNIA
Algodones
HOPE AVE
YUMA
SEE YUMA MAP
8
M E X I C O
CIUDAD MORELOS
EL MORELOS DAM
U.S.M.C. AIR STATION
1. WINDHAVEN RV PK.
2. ARABY ACRES TRAVEL PK.
3. BONITA MESA RV RESORT
4. WESTWIND RV & GOLF RESORT
5. SHANGRI-LA RV PK. RESORT
TELEGRAPH PASS EL. 767
TO TUCSON
BCN 8
MEX 2
SOMERTON
TO MEXICALI
Y U M A   D E S E R T
GADSDEN
Reproduction of this map or any portion thereof constitutes infringement of copyright.

COLORADO RIVER AREA

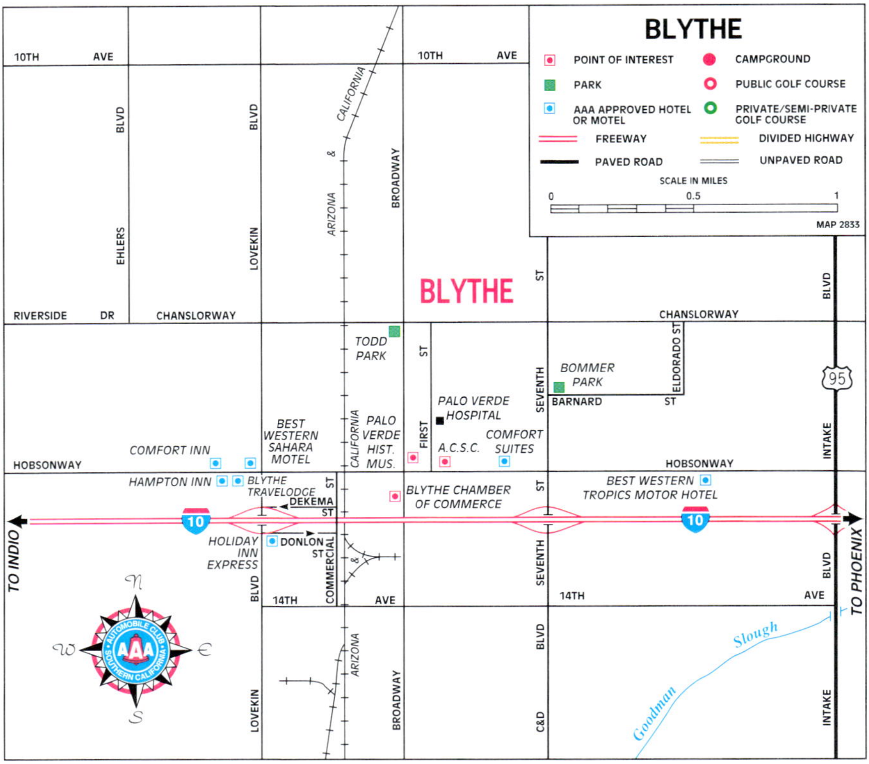

COLORADO RIVER AREA

BLYTHE

- ◉ POINT OF INTEREST
- ■ PARK
- ◉ AAA APPROVED HOTEL OR MOTEL
- ● CAMPGROUND
- ◉ PUBLIC GOLF COURSE
- ◉ PRIVATE/SEMI-PRIVATE GOLF COURSE
- FREEWAY
- DIVIDED HIGHWAY
- PAVED ROAD
- UNPAVED ROAD

SCALE IN MILES
0   0.5   1

MAP 2833

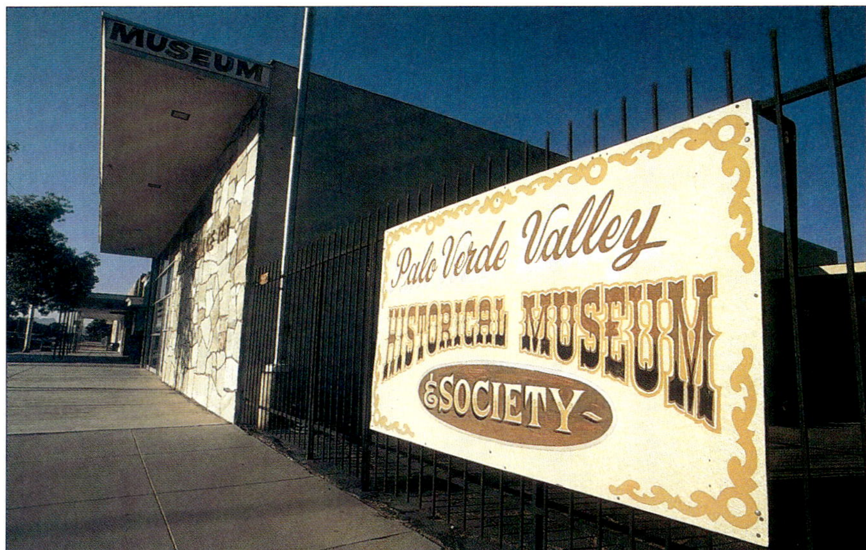

The Palo Verde Historical Museum provides insight into the region's pioneer era.

RESORT CITIES

▼ *A Quick Guide to Blythe*

Effective March 22, 1997, area code (619) will change to (760).

Police Nonemergency
(619/760) 922-5111

Weather   (619/760) 922-5173

Radio Stations
Top 40: KJMB (100.3 FM)

Taxi
Morelocks Taxi (619/760) 922-4039

Hospitals
Palo Verde Hospital
250 N. First St.
Blythe, CA 92226
(619/760) 922-4115

Visitor Services
Blythe Chamber of Commerce
201 S. Broadway
Blythe, CA 92225
(619/760) 922-8166

Automobile Club of Southern California
Blythe District Office
221 E. Hobsonway
Blythe, CA 92225
(619/760) 922-3194

---

animals and humans, the largest being human-shaped and measuring 171 feet in length. Today three intaglios are within fenced enclosures and can be viewed from the perimeter, although they are best seen from higher elevations.

PALO VERDE HISTORICAL MUSEUM
150 N. Broadway, 92225. (619/760) 922-8770. Open Nov. through Apr., Tue. through Fri. 10 a.m. to 4 p.m., Sat. 9 a.m. to noon. Closed holidays and during the summer. Free. This museum displays home furnishings, implements and old photographs of pioneer families of the Palo Verde Valley. The wagons and farm equipment of these early farmers are also on display, and there are also exhibits highlighting the history of the Blythe area. A desert garden of local flora is located behind the museum.

Needles

Needles, with a population of around 6000, is situated on the west bank of

---

▼ *A Quick Guide to Needles*

Effective March 22, 1997, area code (619) will change to (760).

Police Nonemergency
(619/760) 326-9200

Weather   (619/760) 922-5173

Radio Stations
Talk: KTOX (1340 AM)

Taxi
Big LJ's Taxi (619/760) 326-6200

Hospitals
Needles Desert Communities
   Hospital
1401 Bailey Ave.
Needles, CA 92363
(619/760) 326-4531

Visitor Services
Needles Chamber of Commerce
100 G St.
Needles, CA 92363
(619/760) 326-2050

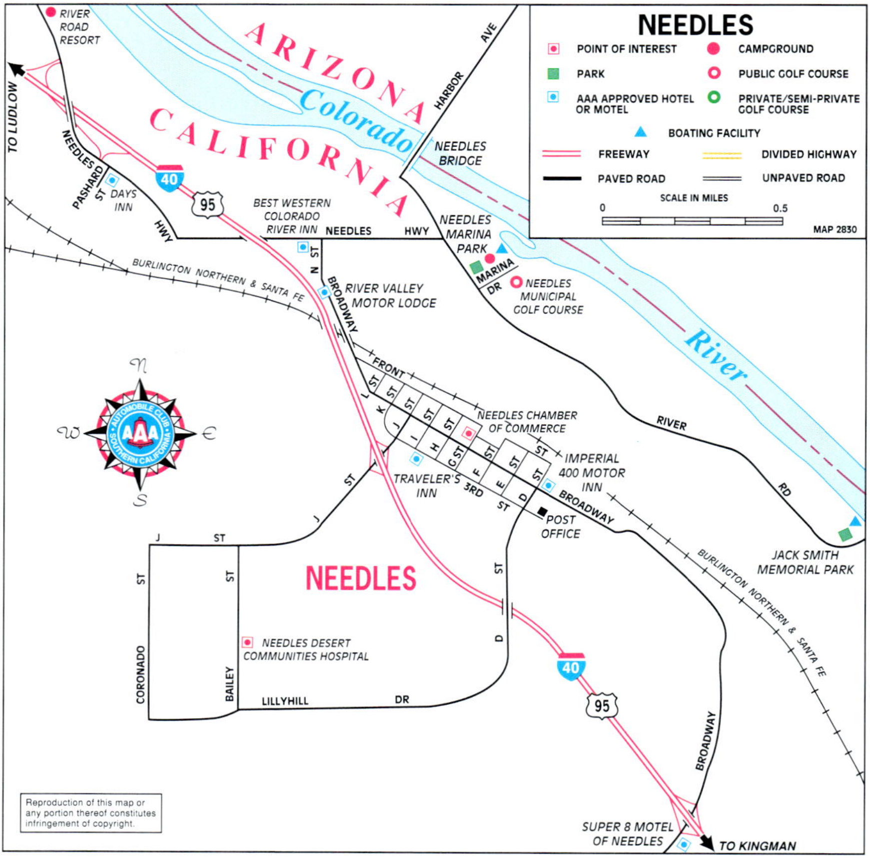

COLORADO RIVER AREA

The Needles mountain range creates an imposing background for the Colorado River.

the Colorado River. The city was named for the needle-like mountain peaks that can be seen across the river south of I-40. Founded in 1883 as an important railroading center, it is still a depot for the Burlington Northern Santa Fe Railroad. The major industries today are agriculture, tourism and recreation. Fishing, boating, water-skiing and jet-skiing are all very popular along this stretch of the river.

Winterhaven

Winterhaven is located across the Colorado River from Yuma, Arizona, along I-8. Situated within the Fort Yuma Reservation of the Quechan Indian tribe, this community of more than 3500 is the largest on the reservation. It is the commercial and administrative center of the Fort Yuma Reservation. Agriculture is an economic staple and the area is known for dates, melons, lettuce and cauliflower.

PICACHO STATE RECREATION AREA *26 miles north via an unpaved road; P.O. Box 848, 92283. (619/760) 393-3052. Open all year. Free.* Access road conditions are rough and best-suited for high-clearance, off-road vehicles. Picacho S.R.A. preserves a section of the Colorado River in near-perfect natural condition. There are several camping areas, some accessible by car while others are boat-in or hike-in only. Other activities include boating, fishing, rafting, water-skiing, hiking, bird watching and visiting Indian petroglyph sites.

QUECHAN MUSEUM *Indian Hill; P.O. Box 11352, Yuma, AZ 85366. (619/760) 572-0661. Open Mon. through Fri. 8 a.m. to 5 p.m., Sat. 10 a.m. to 4 p.m. Closed holidays. Adults $1; children ages 11 and under, free.* The museum is comprised of three rooms: the Spanish room, the U.S. military room and the Quechan room. Two rooms contain artifacts and documents relating to Spanish and U.S. military actions and as well as their relationships to the Quechan Indian tribe. The Quechan room contains historic tribal artifacts such as pottery, weapons, clothing, cradles and old photographs.

THE ARIZONA SIDE

While large sections of the Arizona shoreline are Indian reservation, state park, military reservation or national wildlife refuge, the Arizona side still boasts a much higher population density than its California counterpart. The larger urban centers include Lake Havasu City, Parker and Yuma. The smaller community of Ehrenberg is situated across the Colorado River from Blythe, just a few miles north of I-10 (see *Lodging & Restaurants* and *Campgrounds & Trailer Parks*).

Lake Havasu City

On the east bank of Lake Havasu is Lake Havasu City, a planned resort community with a population of over 24,000. It is home to famous London Bridge, which was taken apart stone by stone, transported from London and reassembled here. The bridge spans a man-made channel that separates the main part of the city from a recreational island. The island is home to a resort, marina, campground and a golf course. The Lake Havasu section of the river is popular with boaters, fishermen and jet skiers.

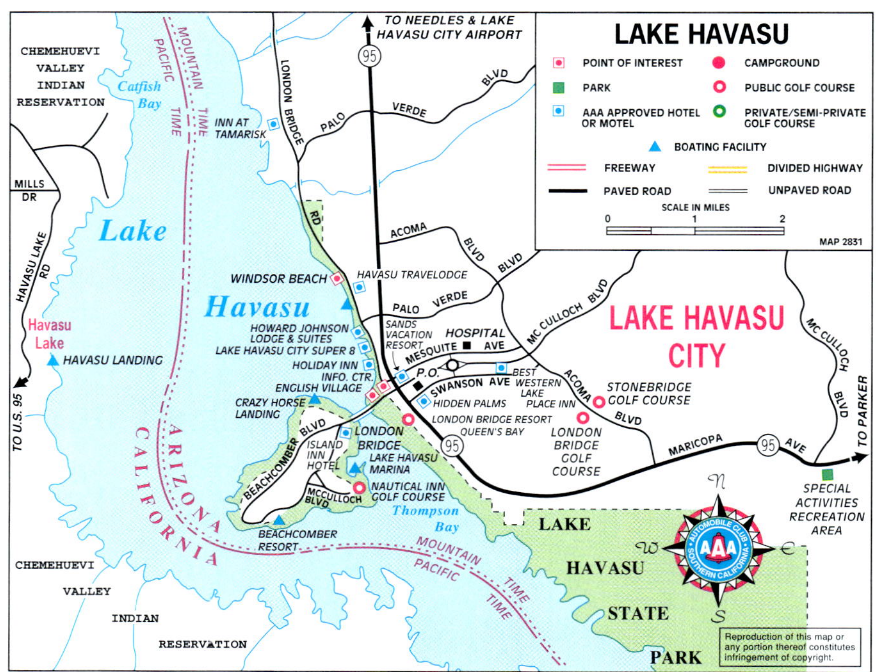

CATTAIL COVE STATE PARK *15 miles south along SR 95. (520) 855-1223. Open daily; May through Sept. 8 a.m. to 6 p.m., rest of year to 5 p.m. Admission $7 per vehicle.* The park was named for the numerous cattails growing in the marshland along the Colorado River. The park has a boat launch ramp, boat rentals, a marina, general store and restaurant, and offers opportunities for boating, fishing, hiking, camping and picnicking.

HAVASU NATIONAL WILDLIFE REFUGE *North and south of I-40. (619/760) 326-3853. Open daily 8 a.m. to 4 p.m. Free.* The refuge consists of more than 37,000 acres of river and marsh lands. Species inhabiting the refuge range from beaver, deer, rabbit, coyote and bighorn sheep to a wide assortment of birds, including the rare Yuma clapper rail. The greater section of the refuge, south of I-40, is accessible only by boat or on foot.

LAKE CRUISES *Depart from the English Village, 1 block west of SR 95 on McCulloch Blvd.*

Blue Water Charters *501 English Village, 86403. (520) 855-7171. Tours depart daily at 2:30 p.m. (MST); schedule may vary and passenger minimum must be met. Adults $19.80; ages 6-12, $10.70; ages 5 and under, free.* Ancient Indian petroglyphs, geological sites, wildlife and American Indian legends relating to the area are the subjects of this fully narrated, 3-hour, round-trip scenic cruise to Topock Gorge. There is also a shuttle service across Lake Havasu to the resort casino at Havasu Landing.

Dixie Bell Cruises *North of London Bridge along the seawall, English Village, 86403. (520) 453-6776. Tours depart three times daily (departure times vary). Adults $12; ages 6-12, $5; ages 5 and under, free.* Fully narrated 60-minute

---

▼ *A Quick Guide to Lake Havasu City*

Police Nonemergency
(520) 855-4884

Radio

40s, 50s & 60s: (98 AM); **Top 40:** KZUL (105.1 FM).

Newspapers

Today's Havasu Herald is published daily except Monday and Friday.

Taxi

Cab service is provided by Mohave Cab at (520) 453-1666 and City Cab at (520) 680-0664. In addition, City Transit provides local service between any two points for $3 per person; (520) 453-7600.

Hospitals

Havasu Samaritan Regional Hospital
101 Civic Center Ln.
Lake Havasu City, AZ 86403
(520) 855-8185

Visitor Services

Arizona Tourist Information Center
420 English Village
Lake Havasu City, AZ 86403
(520) 855-5655

---

tours around Pittsburg Point highlight The Needles, local geological sites, regional history and the story of the formation of Lake Havasu. A full-service cocktail lounge is available during the cruise.

LAKE HAVASU STATE PARK *Off McCulloch Blvd. and south along the river to Cattail Cove State Park. (520) 855-2784. Open daily; May through Sept. 8 a.m. to 6 p.m., rest of year to 5 p.m.*

Admission $7 per vehicle. The park has a boat launch ramp and offers opportunities for fishing, boating, camping, hiking and picnicking.

LONDON BRIDGE *1 block west of SR 95 on McCulloch Blvd., 86403. (520) 855-0888. Open daily. Free. Parking $2.* Originally built in 1828, this bridge served Londoners crossing the Thames River for 140 years. Purchased in 1968 for $7 million by developer Robert McCulloch, the bridge was transported from London, England, stone by stone and then reassembled here as a focal point for his new Lake Havasu City. The bridge was dedicated in 1971 and opened to vehicular traffic crossing over to an island in the river.

London Bridge was shipped stone by stone from its original site on the River Thames in England.

A jolly good time can be had at the English Village in Lake Havasu City.

English Village *At the foot of the bridge. Shops open daily, most from 9 a.m. to 6 p.m.* Carrying on with the British theme, this collection of shops features Tudor-style architecture, lamp posts, call boxes and neatly trimmed hedges. More than 60 gift shops offer British-themed arts, crafts and souvenirs, as well as general merchandise such as sunglasses, jewelry, women's apparel, candles and kites. Several restaurants and lounges provide sustenance, and a number of candy stores satisfy those shoppers with a sweet tooth. Boat cruises depart from here, and there are boat rentals and other activities for the entire family.

Parker

The community of Parker may seem small in size with a resident population of 4000, but it is important as the administrative center for the Colorado River Indian Reservation and as the La Paz County seat. Founded in 1908,

---

▼ *A Quick Guide to Parker*

Police Nonemergency
(520) 669-6141

Radio
Country: KLPZ (1380 AM)

Hospitals

Parker Community Hospital
1200 Mohave Rd.
Parker, AZ 85344
(520) 669-9201

Visitor Services

Parker Chamber of Commerce
1217 California Ave.
Parker, AZ 85344
(520) 669-2174

its early history was as a railroad town for the Santa Fe line. Today it is the site of the headquarters for the Arizona and California Railroad. Parker is also a major staging area for river recreation enthusiasts.

BILL WILLIAMS RIVER NATIONAL WILDLIFE REFUGE *60911 SR 95, 85344. (520) 667-4144. Open daily during daylight hours. Free.* Most of the region's remaining stands of cottonwood and willow trees are located within this refuge. It is also home to a wide range of other flora and wildlife, including over 275 species of bird. Among these is the endangered Yuma clapper rail, which nests in the refuge during the spring.

BUCKSKIN MOUNTAIN STATE PARK *11 miles north on SR 95. (520) 667-3231. Open daily; May through Sept. 8 a.m. to 6 p.m., rest of year to 5 p.m. Admission $7 per vehicle.* Rising bluffs serve as a backdrop to the Colorado River in this state park. Facilities include a boat launch ramp, general store, restaurant and snack bar. Recreational activities available are boating, fishing, camping, hiking and picnicking.

INDIAN ADMINISTRATION CENTER *At the intersection of Mojave Rd. and 2nd Ave., 85344. (520) 669-9211. Open Mon. through Fri. 8 a.m. to noon and 1 p.m. to 5 p.m. (MST). Closed Sat., Sun. and major holidays. Donation.* The center includes a library and a museum featuring displays of artifacts and handicrafts by the four Colorado River tribes—Mojave, Chemehuevi, Navajo and Hopi. Displays include models of traditional homes, pottery, jewelry, beadwork and a large collection of Chemehuevi baskets.

PARKER DAM *15 miles north of Parker via SR 95. (619/760) 663-3712. Self-guided tours of the power plant are offered daily; May through Oct. 8 a.m. to 4 p.m.; Nov. through Apr. 8:30 a.m. to 4:30 p.m.*

Parker Dam is the point of origin for the Colorado River Aqueduct and the Central Arizona Project.

COLORADO RIVER AREA

Free. The dam was built between 1934 and 1938 and is the world's deepest dam. Seventy-three percent (or 235 feet) of the structural height of the dam is below the original bed of the Colorado River. It provides reservoir storage of water for both the Colorado River Aqueduct and The Central Arizona Project. Southern California metropolitan areas receive water from the Colorado River Aqueduct, whereas the Central Arizona Project provides water for the central and southern part of that state.

Yuma

Yuma is a major metropolitan area situated along I-8 in the southwestern corner of Arizona. The population of over 62,000 nearly doubles during the winter months as tourists arrive from the colder climes in search of sun and warmth. Founded as a military post and a river-crossing station during the California Gold Rush in the mid-1800s, Yuma is now a major agricultural center and tourist mecca. Tourists find an abundance of historical landmarks as well as other points of interest to visit. The economy is also bolstered by a large U.S. military presence.

CENTURY HOUSE MUSEUM AND GARDENS *240 Madison Ave., 85364. (520) 782-1841. Open Tue. through Sat. 10 a.m. to 4 p.m. (MST). Free.* Once the home of pioneer merchant E.F. Sanguinetti, the museum preserves the flavor of Yuma's territorial era with period furnishings in three rooms and exhibits detailing the history of the region. The grounds feature an aviary with a large assortment of tropical birds and a garden of Mediterranean plants. There is also a library and

The Century House Museum uses period furnishings and costumes to transport visitors to a simpler time.

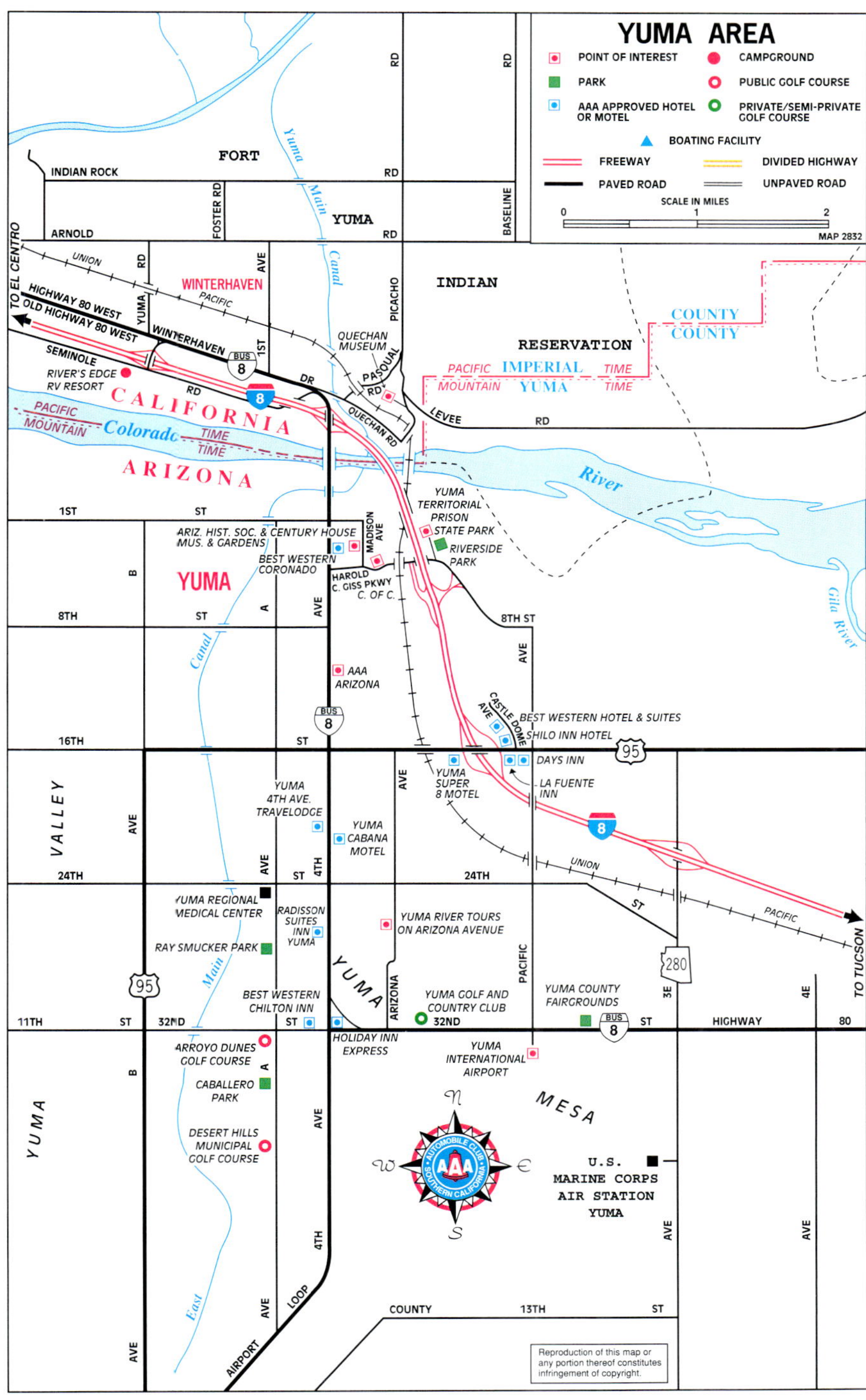
YUMA AREA
POINT OF INTEREST
CAMPGROUND
PARK
PUBLIC GOLF COURSE
AAA APPROVED HOTEL OR MOTEL
PRIVATE/SEMI-PRIVATE GOLF COURSE
BOATING FACILITY
FREEWAY
DIVIDED HIGHWAY
PAVED ROAD
UNPAVED ROAD
SCALE IN MILES
0   1   2
MAP 2832
FORT
INDIAN ROCK
RD
YUMA
RD
BASELINE
ARNOLD
UNION
FOSTER RD
YUMA AVE
Yuma Main Canal
WINTERHAVEN
PACIFIC
INDIAN
PICACHO
COUNTY
COUNTY
HIGHWAY 80 WEST
OLD HIGHWAY 80 WEST
TO EL CENTRO
WINTERHAVEN
1ST
BUS 8
QUECHAN MUSEUM
PASQUAL RD
RESERVATION
PACIFIC MOUNTAIN
IMPERIAL YUMA
TIME
TIME
SEMINOLE
RIVER'S EDGE RV RESORT
CALIFORNIA
RD
DR
QUECHAN RD
LEVEE
RD
PACIFIC MOUNTAIN
Colorado
TIME
TIME
ARIZONA
River
1ST
ST
MADISON AVE
YUMA TERRITORIAL PRISON STATE PARK
ARIZ. HIST. SOC. & CENTURY HOUSE MUS. & GARDENS
BEST WESTERN CORONADO
RIVERSIDE PARK
Gila River
YUMA
B
A
AVE
HAROLD C. GISS PKWY
C. OF C.
8TH ST
8TH
ST
Canal
AVE
AAA ARIZONA
BUS 8
CASTLE DOME AVE
BEST WESTERN HOTEL & SUITES
SHILO INN HOTEL
95
16TH
ST
DAYS INN
VALLEY
AVE
AVE
YUMA SUPER 8 MOTEL
LA FUENTE INN
8
YUMA 4TH AVE. TRAVELODGE
YUMA CABANA MOTEL
24TH
ST
4TH AVE
24TH
UNION
ST
PACIFIC
TO TUCSON
YUMA REGIONAL MEDICAL CENTER
RADISSON SUITES INN YUMA
YUMA RIVER TOURS ON ARIZONA AVENUE
RAY SMUCKER PARK
Main
YUMA
ARIZONA
PACIFIC
280
3E
4E
95
BEST WESTERN CHILTON INN
YUMA GOLF AND COUNTRY CLUB
YUMA COUNTY FAIRGROUNDS
11TH
ST
32ND
ST
32ND
BUS 8 ST
HIGHWAY
80
ARROYO DUNES GOLF COURSE
B
A
HOLIDAY INN EXPRESS
YUMA INTERNATIONAL AIRPORT
YUMA
CABALLERO PARK
MESA
DESERT HILLS MUNICIPAL GOLF COURSE
N
W E
S
AUTOMOBILE CLUB SOUTHERN CALIFORNIA
U.S. MARINE CORPS AIR STATION YUMA
YUMA
AVE
AVE
East
LOOP
4TH AVE
AIRPORT AVE
COUNTY
13TH
ST
Reproduction of this map or any portion thereof constitutes infringement of copyright.

▼ *A Quick Guide to Yuma*

Police Nonemergency
(520) 783-4421

Radio

Country: KTTI (95.1 FM); **Top 40:** KJDK (93.1 FM); **Easy Listening:** KECZ (1400 AM); **Rock & Roll:** KYJI (100.9 FM); **National Public Radio:** KAWC (88.9 FM and 1320 AM); **Country/50's Rock:** KBLU (560 AM).

TV Stations

The city of Yuma has two local network affiliates, channels 2 (CBS) and 3 (NBC); channel 10 (ABC) is received from Phoenix.

Newspapers

Yuma's major daily newspaper is the *Yuma Daily Sun.*

Taxi

Two companies offer taxi service in Yuma: Friendly Taxi Service at (520) 783-1000 and City Cab and Limousine Service at (520) 782-0111.

Hospitals

Yuma Regional Medical Center
2400 Ave. A
Yuma, AZ 85364
(520) 344-2000

Visitor Services

Yuma Convention & Visitors Bureau
377 S. Main St.
Yuma, AZ 85364
(520) 783-0071

AAA Arizona

1045 S. 4th Ave.
Yuma, AZ 85364
(520) 783-3339

archive on the premises for historical and genealogical research.

IMPERIAL NATIONAL WILDLIFE REFUGE *3 miles north of Martinez Lake; P.O. Box 72217, Martinez Lake 85365. (520) 783-3371. Open daily during daylight hours. Free.* The refuge is home to a variety of wetland wildlife and vegetation, including deer, coyote, rabbit and large numbers of ducks, geese and other waterfowl. An observation tower and four lookout points provide excellent views and limited access to backwater lakes. There is also a one-mile hiking trail.

SAHATI CAMEL FARM AND DESERT WILDLIFE BREEDING CENTER *15672 S. Ave. 1E, 85365. (520) 627-2553. Guided tours offered Oct. through May, Mon. through Sat. at 10 a.m. and 2 p.m. (MST), Sun. at 2 p.m. (MST). Closed Thanksgiving and Dec. 25. Adults $3, children ages 2 and under, free. Reservations recommended.* This privately owned farm specializes in the breeding of desert wildlife for both sale and conservation purposes. Arabian camels (with a single large hump on their backs), Nubian ibex, Arabian oryx, caracals, wild goats and fennec foxes are among the exotic animals that can be seen at the center.

YUMA RIVER TOURS *1920 Arizona Ave., 85364. (520) 783-4400. Tours include lunch: all day, $49; 3 hours, $25. Call for schedule.* Two fully narrated history tours are offered. The day tour, which lasts five hours, makes stops at ancient Indian petroglyph sites, Picacho State Recreation Area and an old miner's cabin, and cruises the Imperial National Wildlife Refuge. The three-hour tour to Imperial Dam highlights the history of the Colorado River and the natural history of the area.

Yuma Territorial Prison State Park served the territory until 1909. The cell doorways are still intact: enter if you dare!

YUMA TERRITORIAL PRISON STATE PARK *Off of I-8 via Giss Pkwy. at 1 Prison Hill Rd., 85364. (520) 783-4771. Open daily 8 a.m. to 5 p.m. (MST). Closed Dec. 25. Adults $3; ages 12-17, $2; children ages 11 and under, free.* Built in 1876, this structure served as the territorial prison until 1909. During the prison's 33 years of operation more than 3000 prisoners were incarcerated here, including 29 women. While many buildings were destroyed over the years, the state park still encloses the main guard tower, main gate, main cell block, the dark cell and the prison cemetery. The park also has a river viewpoint and a museum depicting territorial and prison history.

IMPERIAL VALLEY AREA

In the southeastern portion of the Colorado Desert (California's low desert), the Imperial Valley and part of the lower Coachella Valley encompass extremely diverse landscapes. Recognized as one of the richest farming areas in the world, its winter produce (such as lettuce) is shipped all over the United States, and cattle feed and

Agriculture is the economic mainstay in Imperial County.

a variety of vegetables are grown on this former desert land. A vast saltwater sea provides recreation for humans and sanctuary for waterfowl. Sahara-like sand dunes attract off-road-vehicle enthusiasts as well as preserve unique indigenous plant and animal life. The region's variety has done much to shape its economy and recreational interests.

One of the valley's primary agricultural towns is **Brawley**, home of the Brawley Cattle Call. **Calexico** is another important farming community. Its location on the U.S.-Mexico border, right across from its sister city, Mexicali, means that international commerce is very visible at the local level. A high-flying flagpole puts the small, agriculturally based town of **Calipatria** on the map.

Imperial Valley's largest city, **El Centro**, serves as the

This cowboy statue in Brawley's Plaza Park pays tribute to the annual Cattle Call.

The Algodones Dunes are the subject of the Hugh Osborne Overlook.

valley's main agricultural center and offers tourists some variety in accommodations and restaurants. **Holtville** is known for its Carrot Festival, but some of the local economy is based on geothermal energy recovery. The Midwinter Fair is held in **Imperial** each March.

In the **Imperial Sand Dunes Recreation Area**, massive, sweeping sand hills rise from the flatlands to heights reaching 300 feet. With their constantly changing contours and steep faces, the dunes offer a great challenge to off-road-vehicle enthusiasts. **Ocotillo** sits at a crossroads on the southwest end of the valley, where Interstate 8 leads west to San Diego and County Road S2 veers northwest into Anza-Borrego State Park.

In the northern part of this region lies the **Salton Sea**, a shallow body of water 35 miles long and, at its widest, 15 miles across. Here recreation reigns, with many types of water sports available. Fishing predominates, but for the nonfisherman, there is also boating, bird watching and camping.

Waterfowl and migratory birds like the Salton Sea.

Imperial Valley Area

So much of California's desert areas is a study in contrasts, and the Imperial Valley is no exception. Extensive, barren sand dunes are just a few short miles from lush, green fields under cultivation. Thousands of acres of crops on irrigated lands belie the scant annual rainfall. In the middle of a dry, hot desert is a sea, the saltwater home to dozens of species of fish and waterfowl. Imperial Valley residents and visitors alike are here because of the land's diverse offerings.

Effective March 22, 1997, area code (619) will change to (760).

Brawley

With a population of nearly 20,000, Brawley lies 113 feet below sea level. It is located in north-central Imperial Valley and is intersected by state routes 78, 86 and 111. The town was originally settled by homesteaders about 1901. Today in all directions from Brawley the land is devoted to agriculture; permanent crops, along with field and garden crops, total more than 340,000 irrigated acres.

BRAWLEY CATTLE CALL *Cattle Call Park and other locations. (619/760) 344-3160. Celebrated in early Nov. over a 10-day period.* A PRCA-sanctioned rodeo, parades, a cook-off and mariachi and bluegrass music are the main attractions of the event. About 30,000 attend each year.

WIEST LAKE *5 miles northeast of Brawley off SR 111 and County Rd. S26 (Rutherford Rd.; mailing address: Imperial County Parks & Recreation Department, 155 S. 11th St., Ste. C, El Centro 92243). (619/760) 344-3712. Day use fee is $2; camping fees range from $7 to $12.* This small, brush-lined lake is available for swimming (summer only), water-skiing, use of personal watercraft and fishing for bass, bluegill, catfish and trout. There are a free paved ramp, a picnic area and a small campground. (Also see *Recreation*.)

Calexico

The name "Calexico" was derived from the combination of "California" and "Mexico." Likewise, Calexico's sister city across the international border became "Mexicali." In 1900 Calexico was a tent city populated by engineers working on the first canal to be built from the Colorado River in Mexico to the Imperial Valley. The first adobe building was erected in 1901 and became the town post office. Today, Calexico's population of around 24,600 has strong ties to Mexicali. Residents of both towns often cross the border in order to work, shop or attend school.

Sunset is a particularly awesome time to visit the sand dunes.

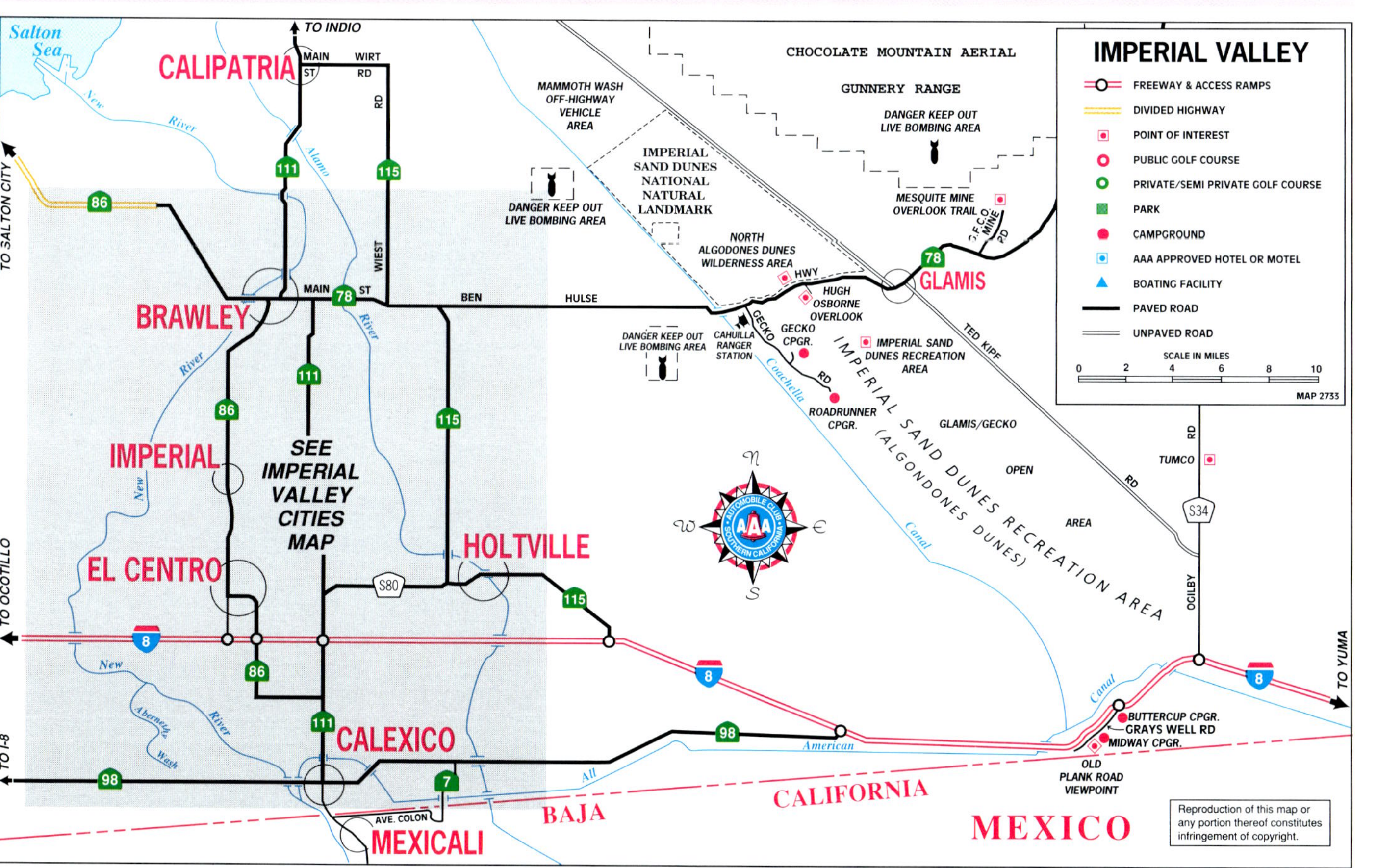
IMPERIAL VALLEY
FREEWAY & ACCESS RAMPS
DIVIDED HIGHWAY
POINT OF INTEREST
PUBLIC GOLF COURSE
PRIVATE/SEMI PRIVATE GOLF COURSE
PARK
CAMPGROUND
AAA APPROVED HOTEL OR MOTEL
BOATING FACILITY
PAVED ROAD
UNPAVED ROAD
SCALE IN MILES
0 2 4 6 8 10
MAP 2733
TO INDIO
CALIPATRIA
MAIN ST
WIRT RD
RD
111
115
86
Salton Sea
New River
Alamo
TO SALTON CITY
MAMMOTH WASH OFF-HIGHWAY VEHICLE AREA
CHOCOLATE MOUNTAIN AERIAL
GUNNERY RANGE
DANGER KEEP OUT LIVE BOMBING AREA
IMPERIAL SAND DUNES NATIONAL NATURAL LANDMARK
DANGER KEEP OUT LIVE BOMBING AREA
MESQUITE MINE OVERLOOK TRAIL
C.F.C.O. MINE RD
78
GLAMIS
NORTH ALGODONES DUNES WILDERNESS AREA
HWY
HUGH OSBORNE OVERLOOK
TED KIPF
BRAWLEY
MAIN ST
78
BEN
HULSE
River
GECKO
GECKO CPGR.
CAHUILLA RANGER STATION
DANGER KEEP OUT LIVE BOMBING AREA
Coachella
IMPERIAL SAND DUNES RECREATION AREA
RD
ROADRUNNER CPGR.
GLAMIS/GECKO
IMPERIAL SAND DUNES RECREATION AREA (ALGODONES DUNES)
OPEN AREA
WIEST
IMPERIAL
86
111
115
SEE IMPERIAL VALLEY CITIES MAP
New
HOLTVILLE
EL CENTRO
S80
115
TO OCOTILLO
8
86
98
New River
Abernethy Wash
111
CALEXICO
7
AVE. COLON
MEXICALI
BAJA
All
American
98
8
CALIFORNIA
MEXICO
TUMCO
RD
S34
OGILBY RD
TO YUMA
8
Canal
BUTTERCUP CPGR.
GRAYS WELL RD
MIDWAY CPGR.
OLD PLANK ROAD VIEWPOINT
Reproduction of this map or any portion thereof constitutes infringement of copyright.
TO I-8
AAA AUTOMOBILE CLUB OF SOUTHERN CALIFORNIA
N S E W

▼ *A Quick Guide to Imperial Valley*

Effective March 22, 1997, area code (619) will change to (760).

Population 96,800

Elevation
230 ft. below sea level to 2500 ft.

Emergency 911

Police Nonemergency

(619/760) 344-2111 (Brawley)
(619/760) 352-2111 (El Centro)
(619/760) 356-2991 (Holtville)

**Emergency Road Service for
AAA Members**

(800) AAA-HELP (in the USA and
Canada)

(800) 955-4TDD (for the hearing
impaired)

Highway Conditions
(800) 427-7623 (statewide service);
(619/760) 352-6136 (local service)

Time (619/760) 853-1212

Weather (805) 988-6610

Newspapers

Major daily newspapers serving the
Imperial Valley area are the *Calexico
Chronicle, The Holtville Tribune* and
The Imperial Valley Press.

Radio Stations

Contemporary Rock: KSIQ (96 FM);
Country: KROP (1300 AM); **Hispanic:**
KQVO (97.7 FM); **Oldies/Adult
Contemporary:** KXO (1230 AM/107.5
FM); **Talk (Religious):** KGBA (100.1
FM). For a complete list of radio pro-
grams, consult the daily newspapers.

24-hour Activity Hotline
(619/760) 770-1992

Bus

Imperial County Transit operates
throughout Imperial County from
Niland to Holtville; (619/760) 352-
4680. Cash fare for intracommunity
transportation is 50¢; intercommunity
fares start at $1; exact fare required.
Monthly passes are available at
Imperial Valley College. Wheelchair
lifts available.

Taxi

City Cab Company serves El Centro,
Imperial, Holtville, Mexicali and
other communities in Imperial
Valley; (619/760) 352-6141. Rates
are regulated; the flat flag rate is
$3.50 for intracity travel. Refer to the
local yellow pages of the telephone
directory under "Taxi" for phone
numbers and information.

Hospitals

El Centro Regional Medical Center
1415 Ross Ave.
El Centro 92244
(619/760) 339-7100

Pioneer's Memorial Hospital
207 W. Legion Rd.
Brawley 92227
(619/760) 351-3333

**Automobile Club of Southern
California**

El Centro District Office
300 S. Imperial Ave., Ste. 12
P.O. Box 3007
El Centro 92244-3007
(619/760) 352-6731
Office hours: Mon. through Sat.
9 a.m. to 5 p.m.

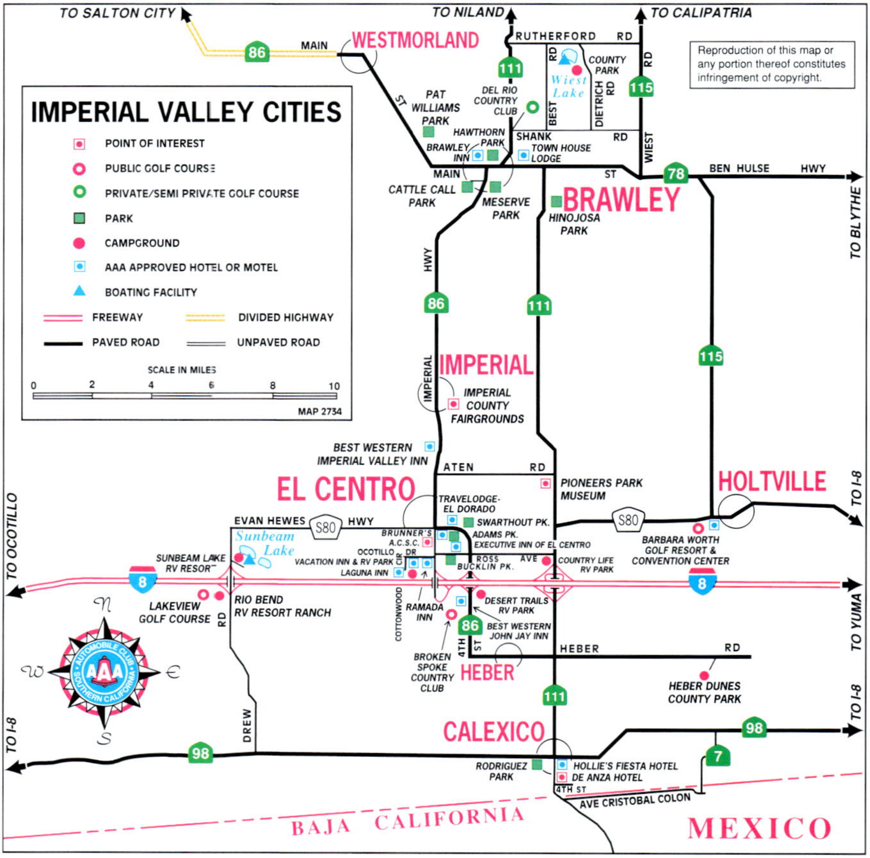

IMPERIAL VALLEY AREA

The De Anza Hotel is a historic landmark in Calexico.

DE ANZA HOTEL *233 E. 4th St., 92231. (619/760) 357-1112.* This landmark hotel, built in 1931, became a center of social activities for the Imperial Valley. During the Prohibition era, many Hollywood stars and wealthy business people rented accommodations in Calexico and visited Mexicali, where drinking and gambling were legal. The De Anza Hotel, with its custom-made furniture and air conditioning, was popular with these visitors. But when Prohibition was repealed in 1932 and gambling was banned in Mexico, hotel accommodations in Calexico were no longer in demand. Over the years the hotel became neglected and run-down. In 1956 Harold H. Johnson, an Imperial Valley rancher, purchased the property and began restoration. Many of the original furnishings, murals and gaslight chandeliers are in use today, adding historic charm to this old landmark.

Calipatria's flagpole is the highest point in town.

Calipatria

Located in the northern portion of the Imperial Valley at the intersection of state routes 111 and 115, Calipatria was known as Date City when it was founded in 1914 by the Imperial Valley Farm Lands Association. As few dates were grown in this area, however, the name was changed. The town of 3000 people is perhaps best known today for its 184-foot flagpole whose flag flies at sea level.

Another industry important to the Imperial Valley is geothermal energy recovery. Several plants, many on the southeast shore of Salton Sea off Sinclair and Gentry roads, produce electrical energy using steam generated by hot water deep below the earth's surface. Other geothermal operations are found nearby as well as in the areas around Holtville and Heber.

El Centro

Largest of the Imperial Valley towns (with a population of nearly 40,000), El Centro is located slightly south of midvalley on SR 86, SR 111 and I-8. It was founded in 1905 by W. F. Holt, a pioneer developer, and became a stop on the Southern Pacific rail line. El Centro is the seasonal home for members of the Navy's Blue Angels precision flying team because of the area's excellent winter flying weather. They can often be seen practicing their intricate maneuvers directly overhead.

El Centro serves as the market center for the Imperial Valley, one of the

The Imperial Country Courthouse is an El Centro landmark.

richest farming areas in the world. Tomatoes, cotton, sugar beets, melons and lettuce are a few of the crops raised here. The city contains the only three shopping malls in the county. El Centro has a number of AAA-approved accommodations and is a convenient overnight stop for travelers heading to Arizona or across the country.

SUNBEAM LAKE *7 miles west via I-8 and Drew Rd. (mailing address: Imperial County Parks & Recreation Dept., 155 S. 11th St., Ste. C, 92243). (619/760) 352-3308. Open all year. Day-use fee $2 per vehicle (up to four persons); 50¢ per additional person.* Two narrow, reed-lined lakes offer swimming (summer only), water-skiing, sailboarding, use of personal watercraft and fishing for bass, bluegill, trout, catfish and crappie. There are a paved ramp and a picnic area. (Also see *Recreation*.)

Holtville

The town that developer W. F. Holt founded and named after himself was incorporated in 1908. Located 10 miles east of El Centro on SR 115, this town of 5000 residents is known for its agriculture. Its substantial carrot crop covers more than 4000 acres. Holtville also offers neat, irrigated fields of watermelon, lettuce, cantaloupe, alfalfa, wheat, asparagus, cauliflower and broccoli. Several vegetable processing and packing plants are located within the city limits.

CARROT FESTIVAL *(619/760) 356-2923.* Activities related to the winter festival take place at various locations throughout the town. A cook-off features carrots (a recipe must contain at least two cups of carrots to qualify).

Other events include a horse show, a 4-H and Future Farmers of America livestock show, a carnival, parade, an arts and crafts show and a rib cook-off.

Imperial

The town was started by the California Land Development Company to house workers digging the canal from the Colorado River. The first store, bank and frame house in the valley were established here about 1900. It was expected to become the area's major city because of its location in the center of the valley, but El Centro, 3½ miles to the south, grew faster and now holds that distinction. Today the population of Imperial, located on SR 86, is approximately 4200.

Imperial serves an important role as headquarters for the Imperial Irrigation District, which dispenses all power and water to the Imperial Valley. Approximately 2.6 million acre-feet per year of Colorado River water is distributed to nine cities and 500,000 acres of agricultural lands. (An acre-foot is enough water to cover one acre of land with one foot of water.) The water is channeled to various farms and distribution points by the 82-mile-long All American Canal and 1675 miles of branch canals. Ninety-eight percent of this water is used by the agricultural industry.

The irrigation district also supplies electricity to approximately 70,000 customers. The residential power consumption in the Imperial Valley is one of the highest in the nation: because of the long, hot summers, virtually all homes and businesses are equipped with air conditioning. With construction of the All American Canal, the district built five hydroelectric falling water drops along the canal. Today these five drops—plus three built later—supply nearly 20 percent of the county's power. The remainder is supplied by steam and diesel plants and purchased from outside sources.

Irrigation is vital to agriculture in the Imperial Valley.

Pioneers Park Museum has an impressive collection of local memorabilia.

PIONEERS PARK MUSEUM *Across from Imperial Valley College at Hwy. 111 and 373 E. Aten Rd. (92251). (619/760) 352-1165. Open daily 10 a.m. to 4 p.m. Donations.* The county historical society's museum displays artifacts from early Imperial County farm and community life, as well as Indian pottery. Most of the permanent exhibits are a multicultural showcase profiling the ethnic groups that settled in and contributed to the development of the Imperial Valley; display items range from photos and clothing styles to toys, books and furniture. Names of veterans from the World Wars and the Vietnam War, and military artifacts are also shown in large outdoor displays.

Imperial Sand Dunes Recreation Area

Located along 40 miles of the eastern edge of the Imperial Valley, the dunes of Imperial Sand Dunes Recreation Area (formerly Algodones Dunes or Imperial Sand Hills) were formed by windblown beach sand from ancient Lake Cahuilla. Some sand crests reach heights of more than 300 feet. Picturesque scenery, opportunities for solitude and a chance to view rare plants and animals are all found in the dunes, 80 percent of which are now open to off-highway-vehicle use. This recreation area is a favorite among OHV enthusiasts. No water is available.

CAHUILLA RANGER STATION *½ mile south of SR 78 on Gecko Rd. (619/760) 344-3919. Call for current hours of operation. No water is available.* The center provides emergency first aid and visitor information about Imperial Sand Dunes Recreation Area.

GLAMIS/GECKO OPEN AREA *Imperial Sand Dunes State Recreation Area between I-8 and SR 78.* The dunes are highest and most beautiful off SR 78, especially near Glamis. Sand dunes are formed from blowing sand creating ridges generally running north and south. Because the wind in this area blows from west to east, the west side of a dune is called the windward side, while the other side, the leeward slope or slipface, is the steeper side. Dunes are at their best just after a sizable windstorm. They move eastward at a rate of about a foot a year. Many animals, including rats, lizards, kit foxes and snakes, live in or near these dunes but are difficult to see because they hide during the day and forage mainly at night.

The sand dunes are an exciting and popular area for off-highway vehicles. On holiday weekends thousands of people camp in the dunes off SR 78 and take off-highway vehicles south across the sandy terrain.

HUGH OSBORNE OVERLOOK *3 miles east of Gecko Rd. off SR 78. Parking allowed for 15 to 30 minutes. No water is available.* This high point, a paved parking area south of SR 78, in the Imperial Sand Dunes Recreation Area provides panoramic views of the sweeping dunes and is popular with off-highway-vehicle users. The protected area of the Imperial Sand Hills National Natural Landmark can be seen as well (see below).

IMPERIAL SAND DUNES NATIONAL NATURAL LANDMARK *North of SR 78 between the Coachella Canal and Glamis. Closed to vehicle travel, it is possible to walk into this wilderness study area.* This area was established to preserve the sand dunes and to protect sensitive plant and animal species, including the silver-leafed dune sunflower, Pierson's milkvetch, Giant Spanish needle, Couch's spadefoot toad, Andrew's dune scarab beetle and the banded gecko.

MESQUITE MINE OVERLOOK TRAIL *3 miles north of SR 78 on G.F.O.C. Mine Rd. (619/760) 352-6541. The trail is open daily from 8 a.m. to 4 p.m.* Gold Fields Mining Corporation began mining gold on this site in 1986. A one-mile trail climbs nearly 100 feet in elevation,

Mesquite Overlook Trail leads past plants, rocks and sometimes animals to a view of a gold mine.

providing an overview of the second-largest gold mine in California. A brochure available at the trailhead describes the geology, flora and fauna visible at numbered stops on the trail.

OLD PLANK ROAD *Visible from Grays Well Rd., east of Gordons Well Rd. off I-8 in Imperial Sand Dunes Recreation Area.* In 1914 motorists traveling to Yuma, Arizona, found it impossible to cross the sand dunes, so an "auto railroad" was built by the State of California. It was constructed of two 3- by 12-inch wooden planks laid parallel to another plank and bound with cross ties. Not only was it difficult for motorists to navigate, but the "auto railroad" soon wore out. In 1916 an improved wood roadway was constructed, consisting of four-inch-thick planks attached to cross ties and bound with steel straps. This "road" was constructed in sections that could be moved by a team of mules when the sand shifted. Double sections were placed at intervals for passing vehicles. The road was used for 10 years until a new highway was built. Along with the half-mile section on display at this location, there are a few remnants on display elsewhere. One section is exhibited at Pioneers Park Museum (see listing under Imperial). Another section is on display in the northwest corner of the courtyard at the Automobile Club of Southern California headquarters office in Los Angeles.

Ocotillo

DESERT VIEW TOWER *14 miles west of Ocotillo on I-8; In-Ko-Pah exit, 1 mile north; (619/760) 766-4612. Open daily 8:30 a.m. to 5 p.m. Adults, $1; ages 6 through 12, 50¢; ages five and under free.* This state historical monument affords spectacular views of the Yuha Desert and Imperial Valley. Construction began in the 1920s and continued

Remains of the Old Plank Road, a portable highway across the sand dunes, are on display just off I-8.

Stone creatures watch over the Desert Tower, which provides spectacular vistas of the Imperial Valley.

intermittently until 1950, when it was opened to the public. A four-level museum with gift shop displays antiques; the top floor is an observation deck. In the adjacent Boulder Park Caves are rock carvings of various actual and mythological creatures, carved in the 1920s.

Salton Sea

The Salton Sea is 35 miles long and up to 15 miles wide, with an average depth of 20 feet. It was formed by accident between 1905 and 1907 when a cut was made in the banks of the Colorado River to irrigate the Imperial Valley. Flood waters broke through the cut, causing the river to flow north into the Salton Sink, an ancient sea bed. The lake's surface is 228 feet below sea level, with no outlet.

Over the years three rivers—the New, the Alamo and the Whitewater—plus innumerable washes and canals have flushed saline agricultural runoff into this inland lake. Evaporation has caused a further concentration of salts. The lake is now slightly more salty than the ocean; seawater has 35,000 parts salt per million and the Salton Sea contains approximately 44,000 parts per million, with salinity increasing yearly.

Winter temperatures at the sea stay in the 70- to 80-degree range during the day, with the mercury falling into the 40s at night. Spring and fall are warmer and provide good weather for all types of water activities. Summer temperatures exceed 100 degrees daily, and the high humidity, caused by increased farming over the last 40 years, adds to the discomfort. Annual rainfall averages only 2½ inches.

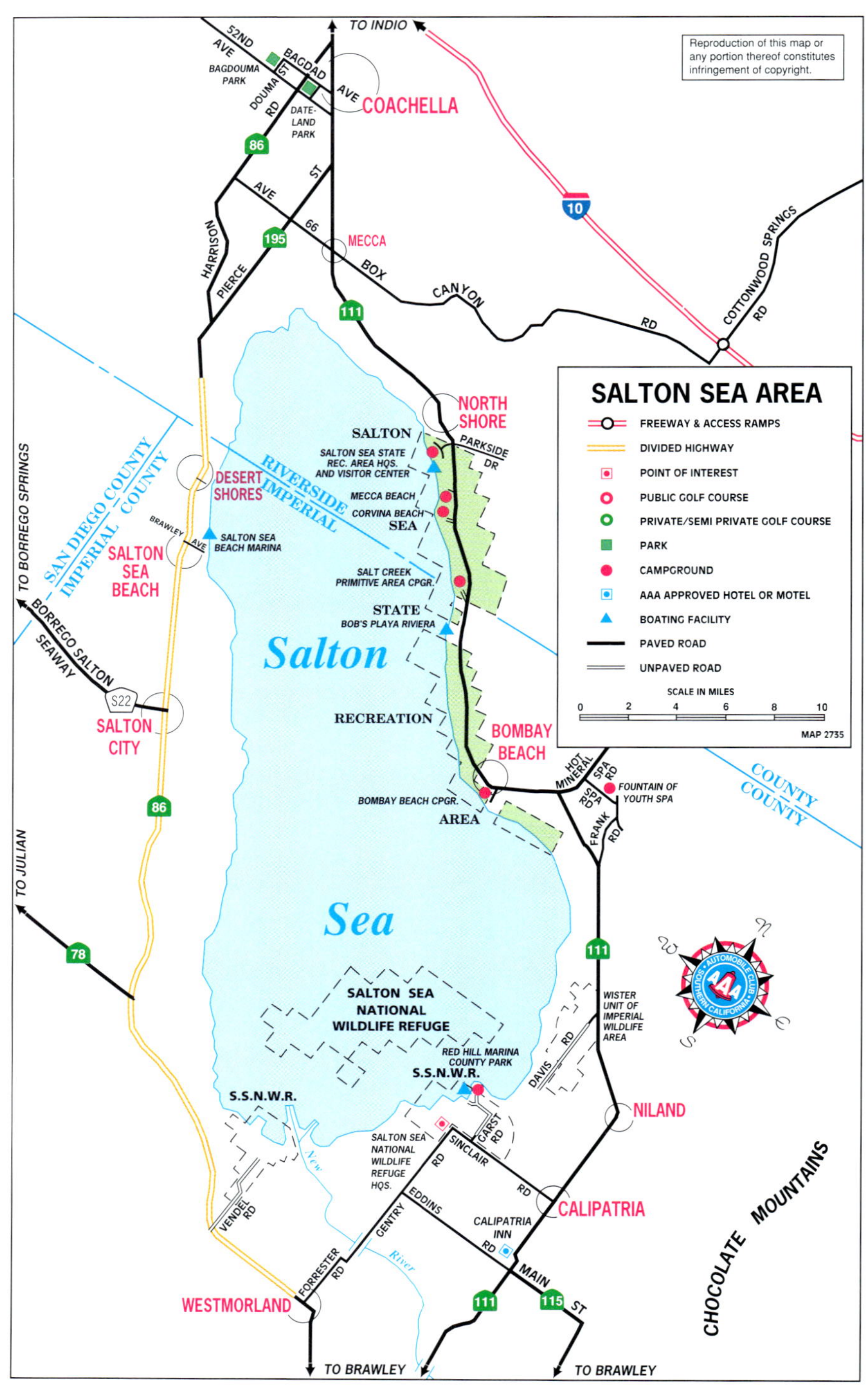
IMPERIAL VALLEY AREA
TO INDIO
52ND AVE
BAGDAD
ST
DOUMA RD
BAGDOUMA PARK
DATE-LAND PARK
AVE
66 ST
COACHELLA
86
HARRISON
PIERCE
195
MECCA
BOX
CANYON
RD
10
COTTONWOOD SPRINGS
COTTONWOOD SPRINGS RD
111
NORTH SHORE
PARKSIDE DR
SALTON
SALTON SEA STATE REC. AREA HQS. AND VISITOR CENTER
MECCA BEACH
CORVINA BEACH
SEA
SALT CREEK PRIMITIVE AREA CPGR.
STATE
BOB'S PLAYA RIVIERA
TO BORREGO SPRINGS
SAN DIEGO COUNTY
RIVERSIDE
IMPERIAL COUNTY
IMPERIAL
DESERT SHORES
BRAWLEY AVE
SALTON SEA BEACH MARINA
SALTON SEA BEACH
Salton
RECREATION
BOMBAY BEACH
HOT MINERAL SPA RD
SPA RD
FOUNTAIN OF YOUTH SPA
BORREGO SALTON SEAWAY
S22
SALTON CITY
BOMBAY BEACH CPGR.
AREA
FRANK RD
COUNTY
COUNTY
86
Sea
TO JULIAN
78
SALTON SEA NATIONAL WILDLIFE REFUGE
111
WISTER UNIT OF IMPERIAL WILDLIFE AREA
RED HILL MARINA COUNTY PARK
S.S.N.W.R.
DAVIS RD
S.S.N.W.R.
New
SALTON SEA NATIONAL WILDLIFE REFUGE HQS.
GARST RD
SINCLAIR RD
NILAND
CHOCOLATE MOUNTAINS
VENDEL RD
EDDINS
GENTRY RD
CALIPATRIA INN
RD
CALIPATRIA
FORRESTER RD
River
WESTMORLAND
111
115
MAIN ST
TO BRAWLEY
TO BRAWLEY

SALTON SEA AREA
FREEWAY & ACCESS RAMPS
DIVIDED HIGHWAY
POINT OF INTEREST
PUBLIC GOLF COURSE
PRIVATE/SEMI PRIVATE GOLF COURSE
PARK
CAMPGROUND
AAA APPROVED HOTEL OR MOTEL
BOATING FACILITY
PAVED ROAD
UNPAVED ROAD
SCALE IN MILES
0 2 4 6 8 10
MAP 2735

Reproduction of this map or any portion thereof constitutes infringement of copyright.

AUTOMOBILE CLUB OF SOUTHERN CALIFORNIA
AAA
N S E W

Sunset is made more beautiful by its reflection on the Salton Sea.

Fishing is the most popular sport at the Salton Sea. Eighteen miles of shoreline in Salton Sea State Recreation Area are available for anglers, as well as several boat rental agencies and ramps for launching (see *Recreation*). The Salton Sea is one of the most productive fisheries in California. According to the Department of Fish and Game, anglers catch an average of 1½ pounds of fish per hour, based on year-round statistics. In June and July the catch is even greater, when orangemouth corvina range in size from 15 to 20 pounds. During the fall and spring they average 4 to 10 pounds.

Sailboarding and water-skiing are popular sports, as are boating and sunbathing. Because of pollution, swimming is not recommended at the south end of the lake near the mouth of the New and Alamo rivers, but there are beaches for swimmers in the state recreation area and other areas to the north.

Birdwatching is particularly rewarding. Migratory birds such as Canadian and snow geese, and mallard, pintail and green-winged ducks use this inland sea as their winter home. Blue heron, egrets and about 350 other species have been spotted at or near the lake. The marshy areas at the south end of the lake are best for viewing all types of birds.

Five public campgrounds lie along the east side in Salton Sea State Recreation Area, and another, operated by Imperial County, is located south of the recreation area at Red Hill Marina (see *Recreation*). Private campgrounds operate on the west side of the Salton Sea in Salton City and Desert Shores.

SALTON SEA NATIONAL WILDLIFE REFUGE *(mailing address: P.O. Box 120, Calipatria 92233). (619/760) 348-5278. The refuge consists of two areas: headquarters is 6 miles west of SR 111 at Sinclair and Gentry rds. near Niland and*

Several geothermal plants are located near the Salton Sea National Wildlife Refuge.

that visit the area in winter. A wide variety of shore-birds and other species may be seen at the refuge; birds using the refuge change with the seasons. Endangered species, including the brown pelican, bald eagle, peregrine falcon and the Yuma clapper rail, visit the refuge along with other rare birds.

SALTON SEA STATE RECREATION AREA VISITOR CENTER *1½ miles south of North Shore off SR 111 at State Park Rd. (mailing address: P.O. Box 3166, North Shore 92254). (619/760) 393-3052. Open Oct. through May, daily 9 a.m. to 5 p.m. Closed Jun through Sept.* Volunteers can answer questions and provide information on the sea and surrounding area. A 20-minute video presentation covers the history of the sea from its formation to the present. Publications about the desert, bird watching, fishing, local American Indians and other topics are for sale.

Calipatria. The second area lies about 9 miles northwest of Westmorland off SR 86 and Vendel Rd. The refuge is open sunrise to sunset; headquarters office hours are Mon. through Fri. from 7 a.m. to 3:30 p.m. A designated trail is open all year; most roads within the refuge are closed to vehicles. Camping is not allowed within the area, and pets must be kept on a leash. The primary purpose of the refuge is to provide habitat for migrating and wintering waterfowl and other migratory birds. Refuge lands, including croplands and wetlands, are actively managed to provide a suitable food supply for the thousands of ducks and geese

WISTER UNIT OF IMPERIAL WILDLIFE AREA *4½ miles northwest of Niland off SR 111 on Davis Rd. (mailing address: HCO 1, Box 6, Niland 92257). (619/760) 359-0577. From Sept. through Jun., office hours are Mon. through Fri. 7 a.m. to 3:30 p.m.; in Jul. and Aug. the hours are Mon. through Fri. 6 a.m. to 2:30 p.m. Ages 16 and over are charged a $2.50 daily fee; a valid hunting, fishing or trapping license or a Wildlife Area Annual Pass also allows entry to the area. Controlled hunting of waterfowl and* *dove is allowed in season with the proper licenses and permits.* As many as 40,000 ducks and 20,000 geese use this area, administered by the California Department of Fish and Game. More than 400 species of birds have been identified here, including swans, herons, pelicans, ibises, song birds, quail and doves. In addition, it is estimated that half of the existing population of the endangered Yuma clapper rail live in the reserve. Shoreline birds are plentiful in the winter, with marsh birds predominant during the summer. Within the wildlife area there are approximately 4200 acres of man-made ponds and marshlands. An additional 1000 acres of cereal grains are seeded to provide a food source and resting area for the birds.

ANZA-BORREGO AREA

Rugged. Wild. Desolate. Sizzling hot. Each of these words represents extremes, and each can be applied to the Anza-Borrego area. The terrain is rugged, with sharp peaks, rocky alluvial fans and sandy badlands. The area is mostly undeveloped, so wildflowers and wild animals still reign. Human inhabitants are few and clustered mainly in one community. Summer temperatures in Anza-Borrego occasionally rival those recorded anywhere else in North America.

Anza-Borrego Desert State Park preserves some of the Southwest's most rugged wilderness.

Most of the area covered in this chapter is under the jurisdiction of **Anza-Borrego Desert State Park,** the largest state park in California. Encompassing 600,000 acres of wildly rugged mountain and desert terrain, it is

The environmentally sensitive Anza-Borrego Desert State Park Visitor Center was designed to blend into the natural desert terrain.

Yaqui Pass affords a spectacular view of Anza-Borrego.

a haven for the seldom-seen bighorn sheep. Vegetation ranges from the expected to the exotic, and in spring colorful wildflowers dot the hills and mountains. The park's visitor center is built partly underground and blends with the environment.

The town of **Borrego Springs**—not within but completely surrounded by the state park—offers a quiet retreat from the fast pace of big-city life. For visitors to the state park, the town provides a convenient place to shop, eat or spend the night. Much of the valley is devoted to agriculture—its ruby red grapefruit is famous. Emerald green golf courses add yet more contrast to the surrounding desert landscape.

Ocotillo Wells State Vehicular Recreation Area contains more than 46,000 acres adjacent to the eastern border of Anza-Borrego Desert State Park. Off-highway-vehicle travel is unrestricted here, and on weekends throughout most of the year all kinds

of dune buggies and motorcycles roam the sandy hills. Camping areas are also found within the recreation area.

Lush palm oases belie the barrenness of the desert.

Anza-Borrego Area

Anyone who takes time to become acquainted with the Anza-Borrego Area will be enchanted by its stark beauty, calmed by the quiet, relaxed by the unhurried pace, warmed by the brilliant sun, and challenged through its recreational opportunities. This is a world all its own.

Effective March 22, 1997, area code (619) will change to (760).

Anza-Borrego Desert State Park

In 1933, 185,000 acres of desert land in this area was made into a state park to preserve and protect it. The park was later expanded and divided into two parks—Anza and Borrego. Finally in 1957, it was further enlarged and restructured as one unit containing 600,000 acres of rugged, varied landscape ranging in elevation from 40 to 6000 feet.

Anza-Borrego Desert State Park is more than a popular stop for travelers escaping the harsh winters of the north and east. It is also an excellent place for those who are inspired by the beauty of wildflowers. Following good winter rains, the desert floor is a carpet of yellow desert dandelions, magenta sand verbena, desert sunflower and dune primrose. Brilliant red blossoms of the spindly ocotillo—the most prominent of the desert flora here—are found along with a profusion of intensely colored cactus flowers. For hikers the park offers trails ranging from short nature walks through palm oases to strenuous mountain pathways providing fantastic views of the sweeping desert far below.

Some of the park's canyons contain enough water to support cottonwood, willows and carrizo grass, as well as a variety of animals, such as bobcat, coyote, bighorn sheep and kit fox. The park also includes evidence of human history: reminders of bygone eras are apparent at the Vallecito County Park (Stage Station) and in Box Canyon. The Borrego Badlands constitute a striking landscape of stark gullies and washes created by centuries of flash floodwaters rushing from the badlands to Clark's Dry Lake.

A majority of roads within the park are unpaved. Contact the Visitor Center for information on vehicle accessibility and current conditions.

ANZA-BORREGO DESERT STATE PARK VISITOR CENTER *Palm Canyon Dr. just west of Co. Rd. S22, Borrego Springs 92004. (619/760) 767-4205; wildflower hotline (619/760) 767-4684. From Oct. through May the visitor center is open daily 9 a.m. to 5 p.m.; on holidays and Jun. through Sept. open Sat. and Sun., 9 a.m. to 5 p.m. The center offers information and exhibits pertaining to the park and the surrounding area. Exhibits focus on desert life—both plant and animal—as well as geology*

Ocotillo Wells State Vehicular Recreation Area has its very own "Pumpkin Patch."

ANZA-BORREGO AREA

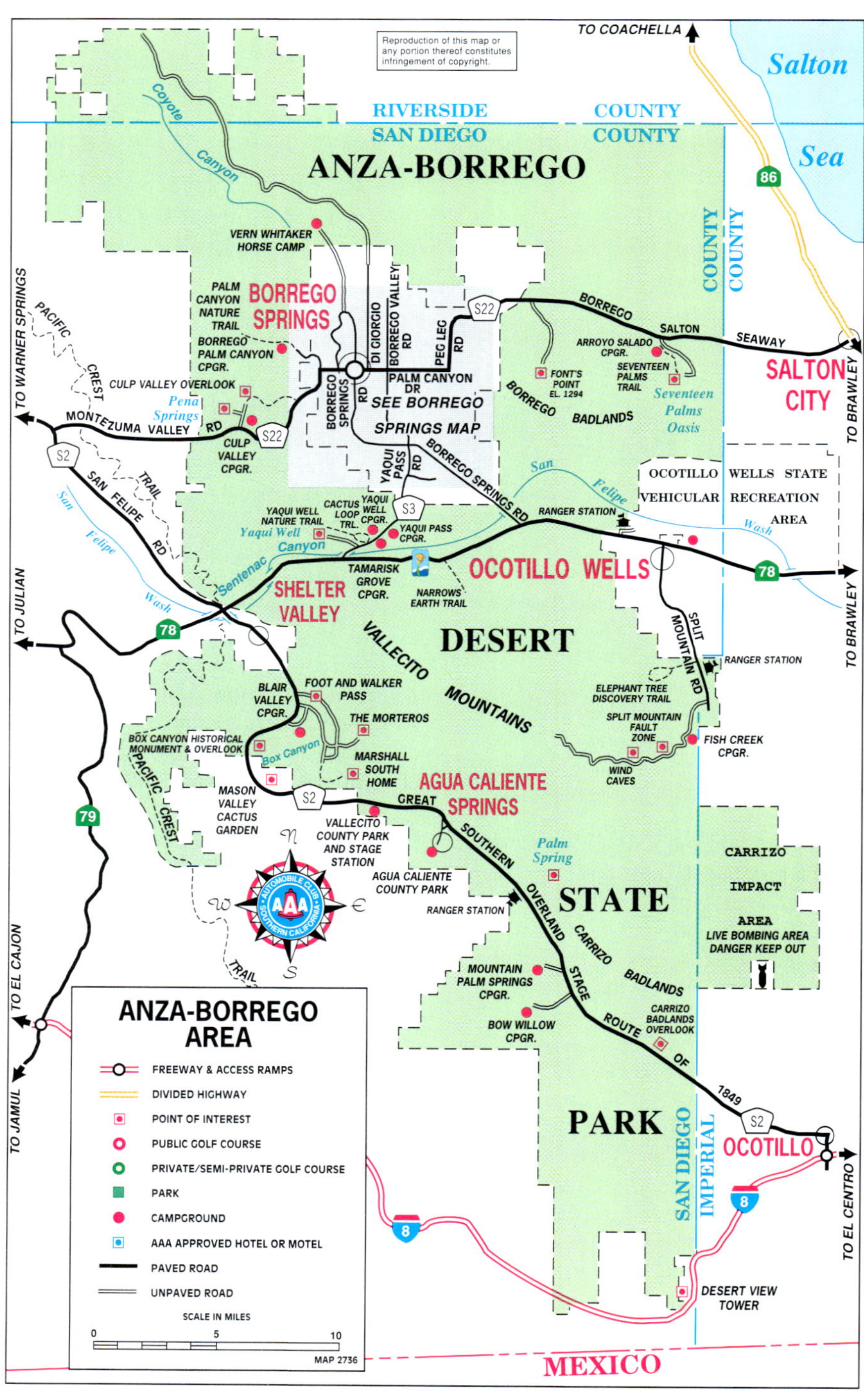

▼ *A Quick Guide to the Anza-Borrego Area*

See also Quick Guide *box under Borrego Springs.*
Effective March 22, 1997, area code (619) will change to (760).

Emergency   911

Emergency Road Service for AAA Members

(800) AAA-HELP (in the USA and Canada)

(800) 955-4TDD (for the hearing impaired)

Highway Conditions
(800) 427-7623

Time   (619/760) 853-1212

Weather   (619) 289-1212

Bus

Fares vary depending on distance traveled. Transfers to other MTS (Metropolitan Transit Service) and NCTD (North County Transit District) buses are free. Call (619/760) 765-0145 or 233-3004 for information.

The **Northeast Rural Bus** services Borrego Springs, Julian, Oak Grove, Ocotillo Wells, Agua Caliente and Ramona with Escondido, El Cajon and Grossmont. From Grossmont, connections can be made to the San Diego Trolley and the San Diego Transit.

The **Southeast Rural Bus** services Jacumba, Campo, Jamul, Pine Valley, Alpine Creek and Crest with El Cajon and Grossmont. From Grossmont, connections can be made to the San Diego Trolley and San Diego Transit.

Hospitals

Pioneer's Memorial Hospital
207 W. Legion Rd.
Brawley 92227
(619/760) 351-3333

Pomerado Hospital
15615 Pomerado Rd.
Poway 92064
(619) 485-6511

and American Indian history. A colorful slide show every half hour explores Anza-Borrego's beautiful wildflower population, from Desert Velvet to Loco Weed (*Astralagus*). More than 50 varieties of wildflowers have been found at the park, and each type is sorted by color and listed at the center. A video on bighorn sheep is also shown. Books, maps and posters may be purchased at the center. The building is unusual as it was built partly underground and designed to blend with its desert environment. The gardens surrounding the visitor center display labeled plants and trees native to the area. A pond contains the nearly extinct desert pupfish.

BIG T's DESERT TOURS *7572 Great Southern Overland Stage Rte., Julian 92036. (619) 765-1309. ½-day tour: $40 per person; call for group rates. Reservations required. Hotel pick-up.* This tour company offers personalized treks across the Anza-Borrego Desert in an air conditioned, CB-equipped four-wheel-drive vehicle.

BORREGO BADLANDS *South of Co. Rd. S22 between Font's Wash and the park's eastern boundary.* Floodwaters carved deep valleys, gullies, washes and sharp ridges into a dramatic, intimidating landscape. Iron deposits in the soil create brilliant pink, red, yellow and green hues. Motorists can view the Badlands from County Road S22, but only rough dirt roads enter this forbidding region.

BOX CANYON HISTORICAL MONU-MENT *31 miles southwest of the visitor center on Co. Rd. S2.* On January 19, 1847, Lt. Col. Philip St. G. Cooke and his Mormon Battalion, using only hand tools, completed a narrow road bypassing a dead-end canyon. This was one of the first roads leading into Southern California. The highest trail to the monument leads to an overlook where visitors can view the canyon, read a historical summary and see the remains of the road, which was used by gold seekers, immigrants and the Butterfield Overland Mail stagecoaches on their way to Northern California.

CARRIZO BADLANDS OVERLOOK *On Co. Rd. S2, a few yards off the paved road.* Two to 3 million years ago, mastodons, sabertooths, llamas, camels and zebras roamed this region. Paleontologists studying the fossils have found the Carrizo Badlands to contain one of the richest deposits of its kind on Earth. Once rich with water and herds of animals, the landscape in the last 20,000 years has become a desert. The view from the overlook is of the eroded and twisted sediments that remain.

COYOTE CANYON *8 miles north of S22 via DiGiorgio Rd. Closed from Jun. 16 through Sept. 15 to allow bighorn sheep undisturbed use of the water.* Known for its lush plant life and the only year-round stream in the park, Coyote Canyon is popular with hikers, horse-back riders and four-wheel-drive enthusiasts. The entire route is also suitable for mountain bicyclists. Ocotillo Flat and Lower Willows are both popular birding spots. A historic section of the

Anza Trail, Coyote Canyon traverses rugged backcountry and provides glimpses of isolated palm canyons. Three campsites of Anza's expedition are marked along the trail: El Vado, near the horse camp on the west side of Coyote Creek; Santa Catarina, north of Lower Willows; and First Child, located between Middle and Upper Willows.

CULP VALLEY OVERLOOK *Off Co. Rd. S22, 8 miles southwest of the visitor center.* From the Culp Valley Primitive Campground at an elevation of 3400 feet, a ¼-mile trail leads to dramatic views of the Borrego Valley, Coyote Mountain and the distant Santa Rosa Mountains.

ELEPHANT TREE DISCOVERY TRAIL *6 miles south of SR 78 via Split Mountain Rd. and turnoff to the Elephant Tree area.* Three rare elephant trees, characterized by a short, fat trunk and tapering twig-like branches, can be seen on this one-mile trail. Set on an alluvial fan, the trail also features plants representative of the area—creosote bush, barrel cactus, ocotillo, cholla and smoke tree. A brochure describing plants along the trail is available at the visitor center.

FONT'S POINT *3½ miles south of Co. Rd. S22.* The point was named after Father Font, a priest in Juan Bautista de Anza's second expedition through this region. Sightseers at the end of this road look down 300 to 400 feet into the Badlands' stark gorges and jagged hills leading to Salton Sea in one direction and to Mexico in another. Toward the west, the Peninsular Mountain range can be seen behind the San Jacinto, Santa Rosa and Jacumba ranges. Responsible for the desert climate, the Peninsular range creates a "rain shadow" by removing the moisture from the prevailing winds of the Pacific Ocean during most of

Over time the elements have created the forbidding Borrego Badlands (seen here from Font's Point).

the year. When the weather is wet, the graded road to the point is not always passable for either passenger or off-road vehicles. Drivers should check at the visitor center before attempting this unpaved road.

FOOT AND WALKER PASS *Off the ½-mile dirt road (usually accessible to passenger vehicles) that leads from Blair Valley Campground off Co. Rd. S2.* Signs along the 150-foot walk to the top of the pass and a monument tell of the difficult climb made here by the Old Butterfield Overland Stage. Passengers on the stagecoach were required to walk—and often had to help push the coach—up the steep grade.

MARSHAL SOUTH HOME (GHOST MOUNTAIN OR YAQUITEPEC) *3 miles south of Foot and Walker Pass off the Blair Valley Campground Rd.* A steep one-mile climb to the top of the hill reveals the remains of a homestead, built in 1932 by Marshal South and his wife. They and their three children lived a primitive lifestyle with no piped water and no electricity and ate primarily food native to the area.

MASON VALLEY CACTUS GARDEN *1 mile south of Box Canyon Monument on Co. Rd. S2.* This large, natural cactus patch features teddybear cholla, prickly pear, hedgehog, fishhook, barrel and buckhorn cacti. These spiny plants, usually in bloom from mid-April to late May, display a remarkable variety of colors and shapes. Visitors can walk among these wild plants, but care should be taken not to touch or brush against them.

▼ *Desert Bighorn Sheep*

Visitors to Anza-Borrego always hope to get a glimpse of the desert bighorn sheep, the most celebrated animal of the park. These elusive animals usually keep to the remote wilderness regions; they do, however, become bolder during mating season (August to November) and are occasionally seen by motorists on Yaqui Pass Road or near Montezuma Grade. For hikers, back-country water holes are the most likely places to spot a bighorn. Coyote Creek in the vicinity of Middle Willows, Palm Canyon and Rattlesnake Spring sometimes yield views of the handsome animals (park rangers can supply maps and directions to these remote areas).

The sheep average from 120 to 200 pounds, about the size of a small deer, and are tan or light brown with a creamy white stomach and rump. Horns, their most distinctive feature, on a mature ram curl around the ears and back up to the eyes. A female or ewe's horns are about eight to ten inches long. These rare creatures have been protected since 1873, and a continual effort is made to maintain their wilderness habitat.

The elusive bighorn sheep usually keep to the remote wilderness highcountry.

THE MORTEROS *Less than ½ mile to the left past the dirt road turnoff from Ghost Mountain.* An easy ¼-mile trail takes hikers to a collection of *morteros* (Indian grinding holes) which were used to grind grain, seeds and pods.

NARROWS EARTH TRAIL *Off SR 78, 4½ miles east of Tamarisk Grove.* The trail, a ½-mile easy loop, displays several of the park's interesting geological features. An alluvial fan joins 100-million-year-old granitic rocks and a visible earthquake fault line. A brochure explaining these features and others in the area is available at the visitor center or from a dispenser at the trailhead.

PALM CANYON NATURE TRAIL *Begins at the west end of the Borrego-Palm Canyon Campground and extends 1½ miles up the canyon.* Signs on the self-guided trail provide information about desert plants and the lives of American Indians who once lived here. The Borrego bighorn sheep can occasionally be seen in this area. At the end of a moderate uphill hike is a palm grove and, in season, a small stream and waterfall. Hikers can continue up the canyon to view the more than 200 palms; however, this second section is more difficult, with dense undergrowth and large boulders to navigate.

PALM SPRING *Off Co. Rd. S2, on the Southern Emigrant Trail.* This palm oasis was the first recorded in California, discovered in 1782 by Pedro Fages. It was a popular rest stop and watering hole for Mexican pioneers, mountain men, the Army of The West, the Mormon Battalion and the passengers of the Butterfield Stageline. The place is marked by a historical marker.

PEGLEG SMITH HISTORICAL MARKER *Near the junction of Pegleg Rd. and Co. Rd. S22.* This monument is a pile of rocks sporting a sign stating, "Let him who seeks Pegleg Smith's gold add 10 rocks to this monument." It was created to honor Thomas Long "Pegleg" Smith, a mountain man, fur trader, Indian fighter, adventurer—and very possibly a horse thief and liar. The story is that in 1829 Pegleg, while traveling from Utah to California, picked up some black rocks in the area of Anza-Borrego. In Los Angeles he "discovered" these rocks were almost pure gold. Strangely, however, it wasn't until the 1850s that Pegleg began telling of his discovery. He made a few trips to Anza-Borrego, but never could locate the area where he allegedly found the black rocks. He spent his remaining years telling of his discovery—and probably embellishing his story greatly in exchange for a few drinks.

Harry Oliver, a resident of Borrego Springs, formed the first Pegleg Club in 1916. Members met regularly on Oliver's birthday to tell stories about Pegleg and his gold. It was on his property that the monument was built. Today the Pegleg Liars Contest is held the first Saturday of April at the monument. Anyone may tell a story as long as it is no more than five minutes long, pertains to gold in the Southwest and is absolutely untrue.

The pile of rocks and historical marker honor the tall tales of Peg Leg Smith.

ANZA-BORREGO AREA

PENA SPRING *9 miles southwest of the visitor center off Co. Rd. S22 in Culp Valley.* This natural spring attracts all manner of wildlife. A variety of birds frequent the spring, as do coyote, deer and other smaller animals. Although less commonly seen, bobcats and mountain lions can sometimes be spotted in this area as well. The spring water is not recommended for human consumption.

SEVENTEEN PALMS TRAIL *Begins at Co. Rd. S22 and Arroyo Salado Campground.* Most of the 3½-mile trip southeast along the wash can be made in a four-wheel-drive vehicle, but the last ⁷⁄₁₀ mile must be traveled on foot. Seventeen Palms Oasis is the only year-round watering hole within miles, and though the water is drinkable, it is highly alkaline and may cause stomach disorders. The water should only be used in an extreme emergency. Early miners left messages and fresh water here for others passing through. Many animals use this watering spot, mainly at night. For this reason, overnight camping is prohibited near the oasis. The trail continues east for more than 16 miles, eventually joining SR 86 south of Salton City.

SPLIT MOUNTAIN FAULT ZONE *Off Split Mountain Rd., south of Fish Creek Campground.* The mountain, characterized by high red walls and layered cobbles, gets its name from being literally split apart along a fault. Ancient flood waters cut through the layered rock, forming Fish Creek. Flash floods brought thousands of tons of debris through the mountain, scouring out the deep gorge. Passenger cars can make the journey here if weather and road conditions permit; otherwise high-clearance vehicles are recommended.

VALLECITO STAGE STATION *On Co. Rd. S2, 18 miles south of SR 78. Open Sept. through May, daily from 9:30 a.m. to 6 p.m. $1 parking fee.* Not actually in Anza-Borrego Desert State Park, Vallecito Stage Station lies on the western boundary in San Diego County's

After crossing the desert in a stagecoach, Vallecito Stage Station was no doubt a welcome sight.

A stroll on the Yaqui Nature Trail (right) is a wonderful way to see desert flora (above).

Vallecito Park. The station, built in 1857, was a well-known watering place on the stage route between Los Angeles and San Antonio, Texas, where travelers found relief after crossing the scorching desert from Yuma, Arizona. Today the stage station is an empty, reconstructed sod house. Camping is allowed (see *Campgrounds & Trailer Parks*).

WIND CAVES *From Split Mountain travel 3 miles south along a dirt road.* A four-wheel-drive vehicle is recommended for travel to this site. Thousands of years of wind erosion created the smooth, round wind caves which were used by Indians. The mythological figures sculpted in the rock were created many years ago by an engineer who devoted hundreds of hours to the project.

YAQUI WELL NATURE TRAIL *Just southwest of Tamarisk Grove Campground.* The moderate, two-mile trail passes stands of ocotillo, mesquite and a variety of cacti on its way to Yaqui Well, where many types of birds abound. From Yaqui Well, the trail follows the poleline road four miles to Grapevine Canyon.

Borrego Springs

Established in the northern area of what is now Anza-Borrego State Park, Borrego Springs serves as an island of civilization among the 600,000 acres of dry lake beds, springs, sandstone canyons and palm groves.

The first homesteading residents of the area were cattlemen and farmers. People like John McCain and "Doc" Beaty called Borego Springs (with one 'r') home from the late 1800s to the early 1900s. By the mid-1920s the

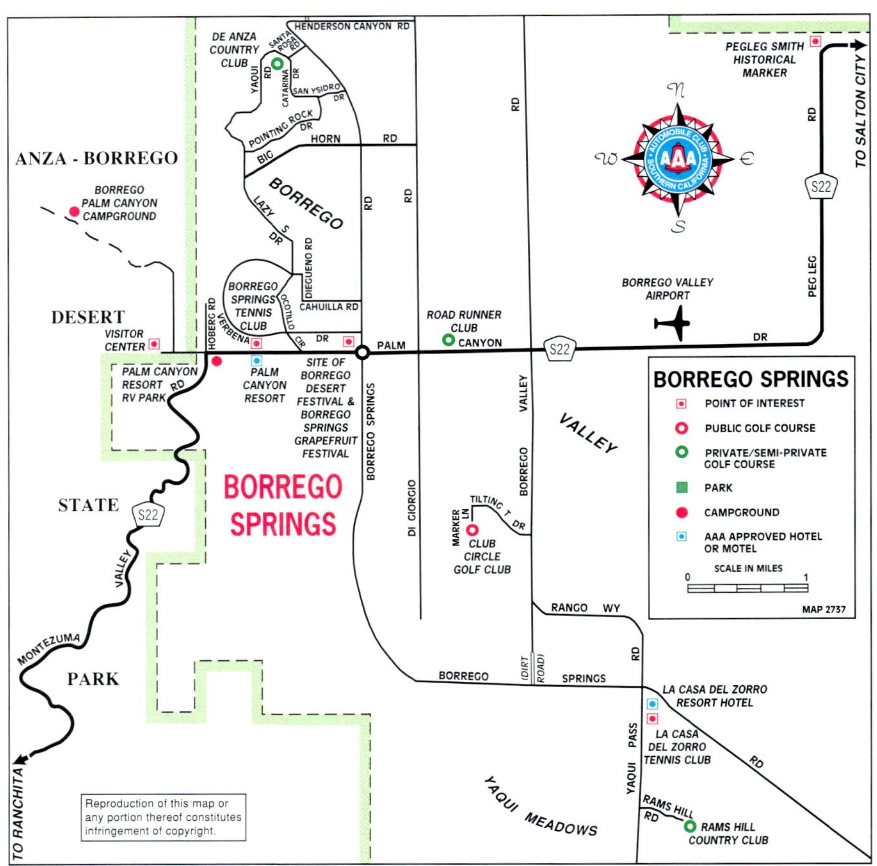

▼ *A Quick Guide to Borrego Springs*

See also A Quick Guide to Anza-Borrego Area *at the beginning of this chapter.*
Effective March 22, 1997, area code (619) will change to (760).

Visitor Services

Borrego Springs Chamber of
    Commerce
622 Palm Canyon Dr.
Mailing address: P.O. Box 66
Borrego Springs 92004
(619/760) 767-5555

town contained a small store, an auto repair shop and a post office. A well, bringing up good water, was discovered in 1926 and large-scale irrigation farming quickly resulted. After World War II developers subdivided the area in hopes of developing a resort community. Growth has been slow but steady through the years, and today the permanent population of Borrego Springs is about 3000. Additionally, during the winter months, snowbirds (escapees from the northern winter) temporarily double the population. The town offers a number of specialty shops and eating establishments, as well as several AAA-approved motels, privately operated campgrounds and resort complexes.

Ocotillo Wells State Vehicular Recreation Area

Ocotillo Wells SVRA offers more than 40,000 acres of dunes, dry washes and hills for all types of off-highway vehicles; access to adjacent BLM lands provides nearly 100,000 acres for recreation. Campers are advised to set up in areas safely away from vehicle traffic.

OCOTILLO WELLS STATE VEHICULAR RECREATION AREA *North of SR 78 on the eastern edge of Anza-Borrego Desert State Park (mailing address: P.O. Box 360, Borrego Springs 92004). (619/760) 767-5391. Camping is permitted throughout the area, but NO WATER IS AVAILABLE.* Vehicle repair shops, fuel, telephones and groceries can be obtained in the nearby town of Ocotillo Wells. (See Off-Highway-Vehicle Areas in *Recreation*.)

EAST MOJAVE AREA

The East Mojave is a land of extremes—vast dry lake beds and lush oases, pygmy forests and booming sand dunes, abandoned mines and deep-space tracking stations, soaring golden eagles and plodding desert tortoises, freezing winters and scorching summers, volcanic mountain ranges and rugged lava beds. This sparsely settled area is sometimes described as "The Lonesome Triangle," bounded on the south by Interstate 40, on the east by US 95 and on the north and west by Interstate 15.

The **Barstow Area** is one of the region's two major commercial centers. Long a crossroads for travelers across the desert, rail lines and interstate highways still converge here. Evidence of even earlier habitation by

Lava craters make an imposing backdrop to colorful wildflowers along Kelbaker Road.

ancient Indians has been found nearby at the Calico Early Man Archaeological Site. Dramatic and colorful land formations can be viewed up close and personal at Rainbow Basin National Natural Landmark.

Few paved highways pass through the **Mojave National Preserve**'s 1.4 million acres, so to

This house made entirely of bottles is an intriguing stop for visitors to Calico Ghost Town.

Hiking is one of many activities available in the Providence Mountains State Recreation Area.

as bedroom communities for the metropolitan Los Angeles area. The Roy Rogers and Dale Evans Museum is located in Victorville, as well as the San Bernardino County Fairgrounds and Victor Valley Community College. All sorts of recreational activities take place at Mojave Narrows Regional Park, and Class A professional baseball is played in nearby Adelanto.

really explore the desert means traveling into remote areas. A number of unpaved roads lead to old mines and interesting geological features. Some hardy souls still reside in the desert, attempting limited farming, ranching and mining. The only town of any size is Baker, and a handful of other settlements, such as Goffs, Essex, Ludlow and Kelso, generally number fewer than 50 residents and are scattered across the region. During World War II the military established several camps as part of the Desert Training Center's California-Arizona Maneuver Area, although little visible evidence remains of these installations after 50 years.

The **Victor Valley Area** functions as the region's other major commercial district, and its sprawled-together cities also double

Mojave Narrows Regional Park is a fun place for a day of play.

East Mojave Area

The East Mojave will remain largely wilderness, attractive only to those few willing and able to conquer the elements in order to enjoy the rugged, inhospitable terrain. Human habitation in the East Mojave has always been limited and will continue to be, not only by political boundaries but also due to the fact that the fragile, harsh desert cannot support much of what we call "modern civilization."

Effective March 22, 1997, area code (619) will change to (760).

Barstow Area

Barstow's crossroads location at the junction of three major highways—I-15, I-40 and SR 58—seems logical enough to today's travelers. In the 1860s the community developed as a way station and commercial center for stage lines, freight travelers and local miners, farmers and ranchers. By 1886 the full operation of the Barstow-San Bernardino rail line linked Kansas City with the Pacific Ocean. The influence of the railroad in the area's development resulted in the town being named for Santa Fe Railroad President William Barstow Strong. Santa Fe's continued rail developments, employment and services are indirectly responsible for the present highway locations and later establishment of the nearby military reservations in the 1940s. Barstow's population is currently 23,983, and with the surrounding communities and military installations the count reaches 60,000.

CALICO EARLY MAN ARCHAEO-LOGICAL SITE *15 miles northeast of Barstow off I-15 (mailing address: P.O. Box 535, Yermo 92398). (619/760) 255-8760. Open for tours Wed. at 1:30 and 3:30 p.m., and Thur. through Sun. at 9:30 and 11:30 a.m., and 1:30 and 3:30 p.m. Closed on Mon., Tues. and major holidays. Donations accepted.* Commercial mining excavations from 1963 revealed artifacts dating to the Pleistocene era, approximately 200,000 years ago. This is the oldest prehistoric tool site yet discovered in North America. Dr. Louis S.B. Leakey, the renowned archaeologist and paleontologist, visited the site in 1963; he continued as the site project director until his death in 1972. Excavations since 1964 have yielded thousands of stone tools and technically significant flakes, although no human skeletal evidence has been recovered at the site.

CALICO GHOST TOWN REGIONAL PARK *11 miles northeast off I-15 (mailing address: P.O. Box 638, Yermo 92398). (619/760) 254-2122. Open daily from 9 a.m. to 5 p.m. Closed Dec. 25. Admission to Calico is $5 per person; ages 6 through*

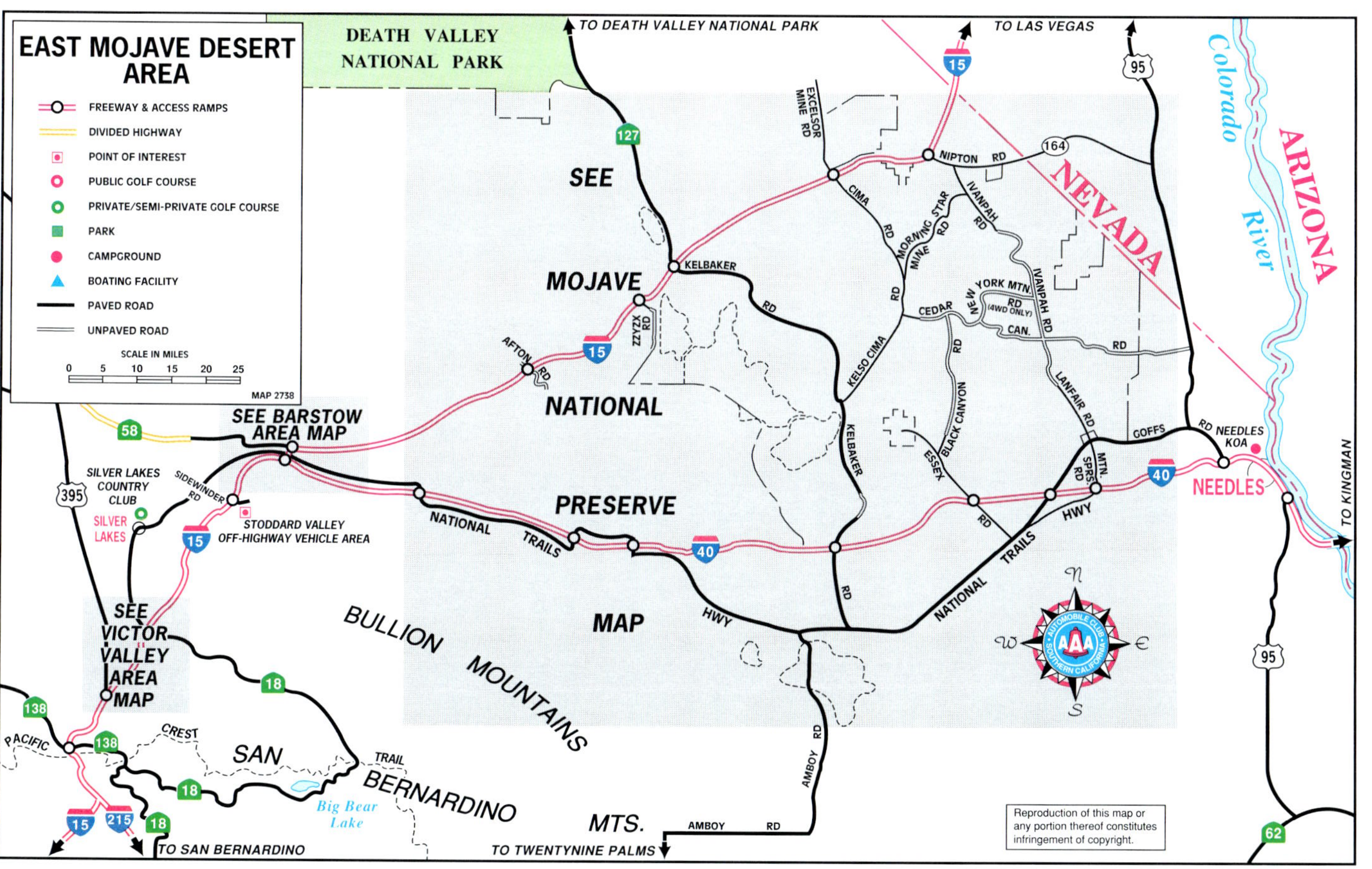
EAST MOJAVE DESERT AREA
FREEWAY & ACCESS RAMPS
DIVIDED HIGHWAY
POINT OF INTEREST
PUBLIC GOLF COURSE
PRIVATE/SEMI-PRIVATE GOLF COURSE
PARK
CAMPGROUND
BOATING FACILITY
PAVED ROAD
UNPAVED ROAD
SCALE IN MILES
0 5 10 15 20 25
MAP 2738
DEATH VALLEY NATIONAL PARK
TO DEATH VALLEY NATIONAL PARK
TO LAS VEGAS
NEVADA
ARIZONA
Colorado River
95
164
15
127
NIPTON RD
CIMA
CIMA RD
EXCELSOR MINE RD
MORNING STAR MINE RD
IVANPAH RD
IVANPAH RD
NEW YORK MTN RD (4WD ONLY)
CEDAR
CAN.
RD
RD
KELSO CIMA RD
KELBAKER
KELBAKER RD
BLACK CANYON
ESSEX
RD
LANFAIR RD
MTN. SPRS. RD
GOFFS
RD
RD NEEDLES KOA
NEEDLES
40
TO KINGMAN
SEE MOJAVE NATIONAL PRESERVE MAP
ZZYZX RD
AFTON RD
15
SEE BARSTOW AREA MAP
58
SILVER LAKES COUNTRY CLUB
SILVER LAKES
395
SIDEWINDER RD
STODDARD VALLEY OFF-HIGHWAY VEHICLE AREA
15
NATIONAL TRAILS
HWY
40
NATIONAL TRAILS HWY
RD
AMBOY RD
AMBOY RD
SEE VICTOR VALLEY AREA MAP
BULLION MOUNTAINS
PACIFIC
CREST
TRAIL
SAN BERNARDINO MTS.
Big Bear Lake
138
138
18
18
15
215
18
62
95
TO SAN BERNARDINO
TO TWENTYNINE PALMS
N E S W
AUTOMOBILE CLUB · SOUTHERN CALIFORNIA · AAA
Reproduction of this map or any portion thereof constitutes infringement of copyright.

15, $2. Parking is free. Additional fees for the Playhouse Theatre, shooting gallery, mine tour, mystery shack and train ride. Dramatic gunfights on Main Street and

guided, historical tours are also available. A hundred years ago this town had a population of 4000 people, supported by the nearby silver mine which pro-

▼ *A Quick Guide to the East Mojave Area*

See also Quick Guide *box under Victor Valley Area.*
Effective March 22, 1997, area code (619) will change to (760).

Elevation   Barstow, 2106

Emergency   911

Police Nonemergency
(619) 256-2211

Emergency Road Service for AAA Members

(800) AAA-HELP (in the USA and Canada)
(800) 955-4TDD (for the hearing impaired)

Highway Conditions
(800) 427-7623 (statewide); (619) 255-8760 (local)

Time   (619/760) 853-1212

Weather

National Weather Service
(805) 988-6610
California Desert Information Center
(619/760) 255-8760

Newspapers

Major daily newspapers serving the East Mojave Area are the *Desert Dispatch* and the *Apple Valley News*.

Radio Stations

Contemporary Rock: KDUC (94.3 FM); **Country:** KIXW (107.3 FM); **Hispanic:** KAPL (1550 AM); **Talk (Religious):** KHMS (88.7 FM). For a complete list of radio programs, consult the daily newspapers.

24-hour Activity Hotline
(619/760) 770-1992

Bus

Dial-A-Ride in the Barstow Area serves most of the major communities of the East Mojave; (619/760) 256-0315. Call for intercommunity rates. Wheelchair lifts available.

Train

The Desert Wind, Southwest Chief and Sunset Limited **Amtrak** lines serve the California desert areas (with bus connections on selected routes). Call (800) USA-RAIL for complete information and fares.

Taxi

Yellow Cab Company operates from Barstow; (619/760) 256-6868. Rates are regulated; the flag rate is $2 plus $2 per mile. Refer to the local yellow pages of the telephone directory under "Taxi" for phone numbers and information.

Hospitals

Barstow Community Hospital
555 South 7th Ave.
Barstow 92311
(619/760) 256-1761, ext. 124

Visitor Services

California Desert Information Center
831 Barstow Rd.
Barstow 92311
(619/760) 255-8760

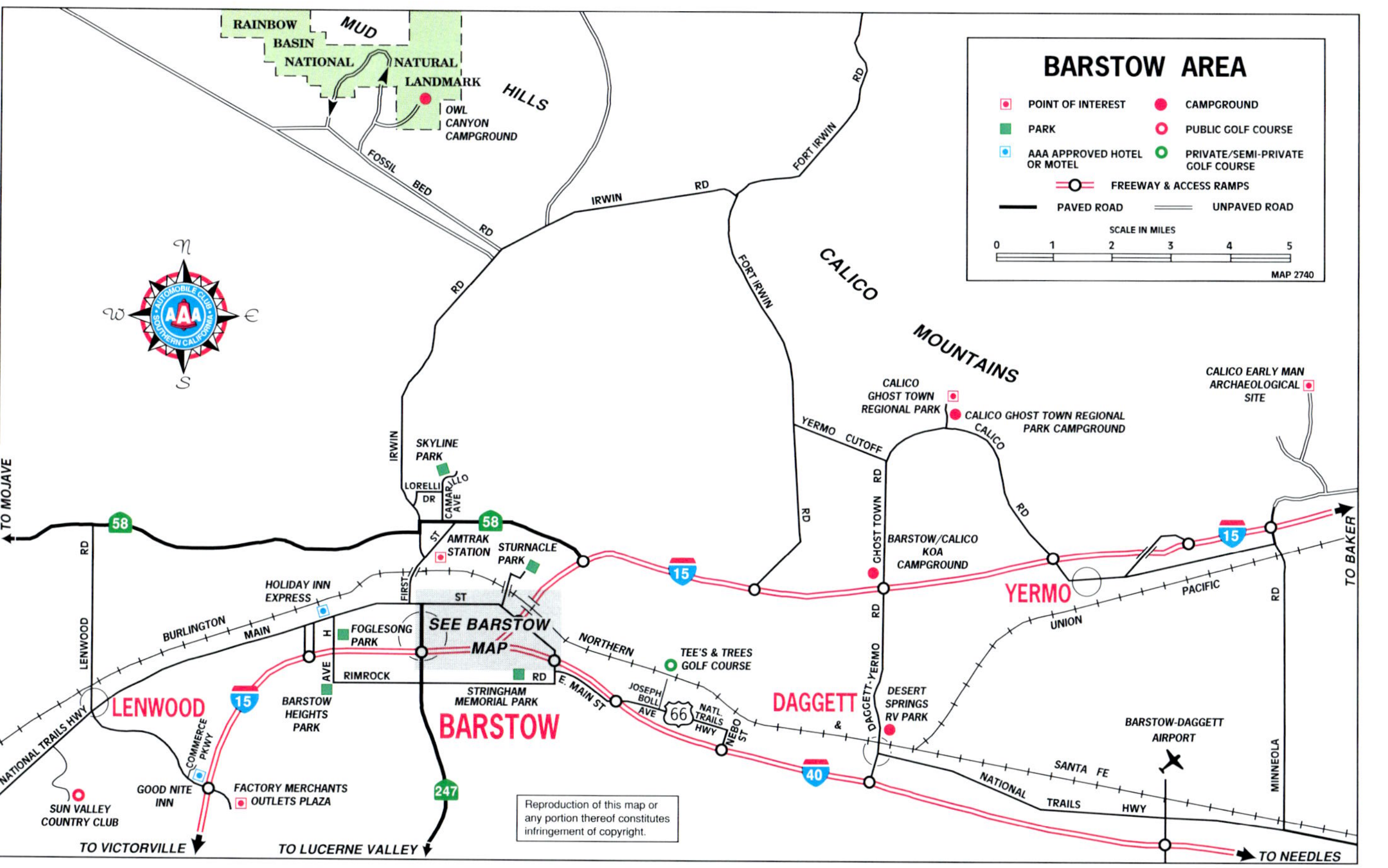
BARSTOW AREA
POINT OF INTEREST
PARK
AAA APPROVED HOTEL OR MOTEL
CAMPGROUND
PUBLIC GOLF COURSE
PRIVATE/SEMI-PRIVATE GOLF COURSE
FREEWAY & ACCESS RAMPS
PAVED ROAD
UNPAVED ROAD
SCALE IN MILES
0 1 2 3 4 5
MAP 2740
RAINBOW BASIN NATIONAL NATURAL LANDMARK
MUD HILLS
OWL CANYON CAMPGROUND
FOSSIL BED RD
IRWIN RD
FORT IRWIN RD
FORT IRWIN
CALICO MOUNTAINS
CALICO GHOST TOWN REGIONAL PARK
CALICO GHOST TOWN REGIONAL PARK CAMPGROUND
CALICO EARLY MAN ARCHAEOLOGICAL SITE
YERMO CUTOFF
RD
CALICO RD
GHOST TOWN RD
N W E S
AUTOMOBILE CLUB OF SOUTHERN CALIFORNIA
TO MOJAVE
IRWIN
SKYLINE PARK
LORELLI DR
CAMARILLO AVE
58
58
AMTRAK STATION
STURNACLE PARK
FIRST ST
ST
SEE BARSTOW MAP
15
BARSTOW/CALICO KOA CAMPGROUND
GHOST TOWN RD
YERMO
PACIFIC
UNION
HOLIDAY INN EXPRESS
BURLINGTON
MAIN
H AVE
FOGLESONG PARK
RIMROCK
NORTHERN
TEE'S & TREES GOLF COURSE
DAGGETT-YERMO RD
DESERT SPRINGS RV PARK
LENWOOD RD
15
BARSTOW HEIGHTS PARK
STRINGHAM MEMORIAL PARK
RD
E. MAIN ST
BARSTOW
JOSEPH BOLL AVE
66
NATL. TRAILS HWY
NEBO ST
DAGGETT
&
40
BARSTOW-DAGGETT AIRPORT
SANTA FE
NATIONAL TRAILS HWY
MINNEOLA RD
NATIONAL TRAILS HWY
LENWOOD
COMMERCE PKWY
GOOD NITE INN
FACTORY MERCHANTS OUTLETS PLAZA
SUN VALLEY COUNTRY CLUB
247
Reproduction of this map or any portion thereof constitutes infringement of copyright.
TO VICTORVILLE
TO LUCERNE VALLEY
TO BAKER
TO NEEDLES

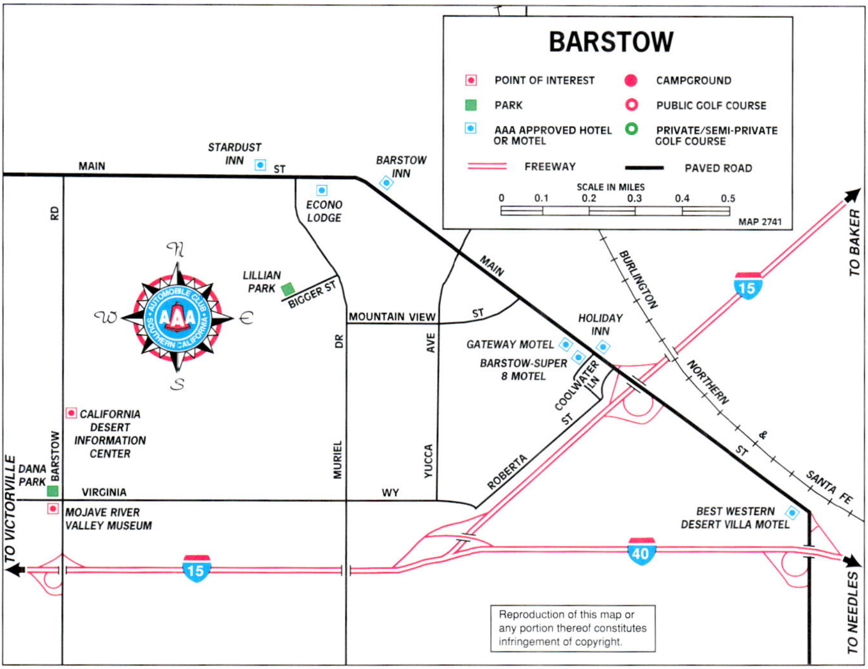

duced more than $13 million in ore.
The mines operated from 1881 to
1896; the price of silver dropped in
1895, signaling the beginning of the
end of Calico as a thriving community.
Brought back from ruin in 1951 by
Walter Knott (founder of Knott's
Berry Farm in Buena Park, California),
Calico Ghost Town is now a county
regional park. Visitors to Calico can
tour a mine, the Playhouse Theatre,
a museum, a mystery shack and ride
a working train.

CALIFORNIA DESERT INFORMATION
CENTER *831 Barstow Rd., Barstow
92311. (619/760) 255-8760. Managed
by the Bureau of Land Management. Open
daily 9 a.m. to 5 p.m. Closed Jan. 1 and
Dec. 25.* Exhibits depict the natural
history and environment of the major
California desert regions. Information
on recreational opportunities and road
and weather conditions is also available.

*Calico helps preserve the "Old West"
the way it was.*

Rainbow Basin National Natural Landmark gives an up-close look at badlands formations.

FACTORY MERCHANTS OUTLETS PLAZA *I-15 at Lenwood Rd. (619/760) 253-7342. Open daily 9 a.m. to 8 p.m. Closed Thanksgiving and Dec. 25.* More than 95 manufacturer-owned stores offer savings of 20 to 70 percent off department and specialty store prices. First-quality name brand merchandise ranges from shoes, accessories and apparel to housewares, linens and toys.

MOJAVE RIVER VALLEY MUSEUM *Corner of Barstow Rd. and Virginia Wy. (mailing address: P.O. Box 1282, Barstow 92311). (619/760) 256-5452. Open daily 11 a.m. to 4 p.m. Admission free.* Established in 1964, the museum is dedicated to preserving and interpreting the heritage of the Mojave River Valley. Displays include archaeological artifacts from the Calico Early Man site (see separate listing), mining equipment, railway cars and minerals and gemstones found in the area. More

recent human history is chronicled beginning with Father Garces' arrival in 1776 and progressing to space explorations based in the nearby military installations. A touch display for children features a slide show, a lesson in grinding corn, copper ore samples, reptile skin and several animal pelts.

RAINBOW BASIN NATIONAL NATURAL LANDMARK *10 miles north of Barstow via Irwin and Fossil Bed rds.* In what was a lake bed 10 to 30 million years ago, fossilized remains of saber-toothed tigers, mastodons, camels, three-toed horses and rhinoceros have been found. Minerals in the sedimentary layers create astonishing variations in color, and erosion has sculpted spectacular land formations. Follow a signed, four-mile one-way loop drive (this narrow, graded dirt road is impassable for vehicles larger than campers, and may be impassable to all vehicles following heavy rains; check locally for current conditions).

RASOR OFF-HIGHWAY-VEHICLE AREA *South of I-15 off Rasor Rd. (west of East Mojave National Preserve).* This area has diverse terrain for off-road recreation, ranging from level, sandy areas on the west and south to dunes and steep hills on the east and north. Camping is permitted in any open area safely away from traffic, but is limited to 14 days (for more details see Off-Highway-Vehicle Areas in *Recreation*).

STODDARD VALLEY OFF-HIGHWAY-VEHICLE AREA *8 miles south of Barstow via I-15 and Sidewinder Rd. (619/760) 255-8760 (Bureau of Land Management).* Off-road adventurers can find this territory located a short distance south of Barstow between I-15 and SR 247, offering rolling hills and open valley. Camping is allowed in much of the area (for more details see Off-Highway-Vehicle Areas in *Recreation*).

Mojave National Preserve

In the late 1700s Spanish priests first recorded crossing the Mojave Desert, and by the 1800s there were isolated military outposts, mining activity and some attempts to farm and raise livestock. The completion of rail lines through the region created a number of communities in the East Mojave, a few of which are still populated today.

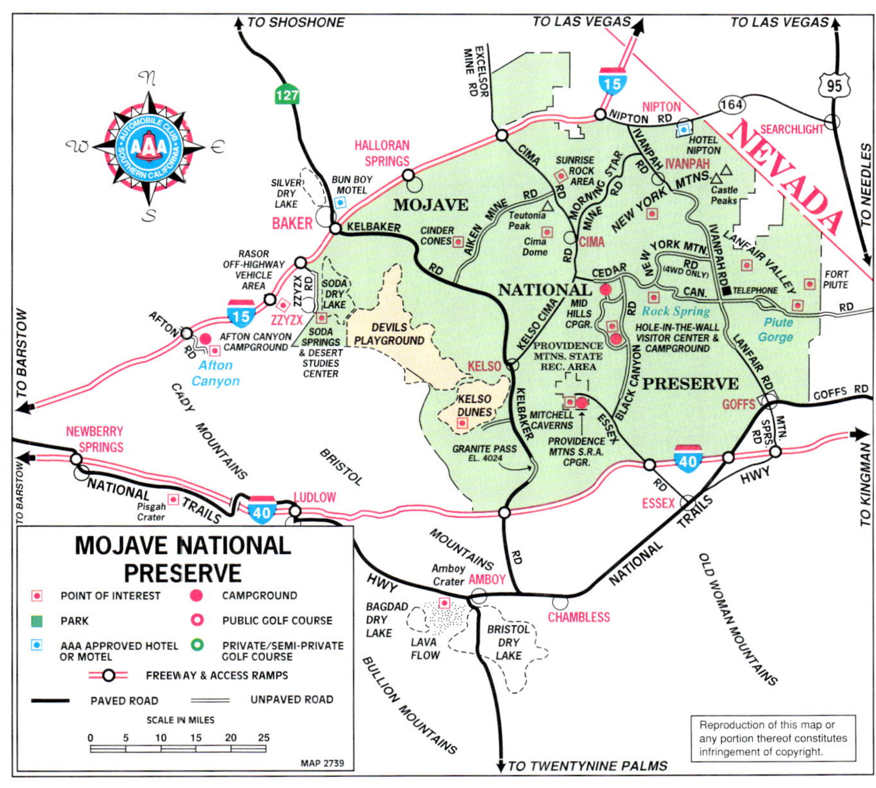

With the California Desert Protection Act signed into law on October 31, 1994, the East Mojave National Scenic Area was upgraded to the Mojave National Preserve, a status similar to national park status but with hunting and certain commercial uses allowed. A few mining and ranching ventures operate within the 1.4 million-acre preserve, but permanent human habitation is limited to a few villages whose roots date back to the days of early exploration and settlement. The attraction is in the seeming endlessness of the land, the dramatic geological formations, the contact with some of nature's most intriguing creatures, and the solitude found in escaping from civilization.

I-40 is the only major highway crossing Essex Road at the southern areas of the preserve. Most of the notable points of interest are accessible from Essex Road. In sequence, **Essex Road** leads to **Black Canyon Road** and further north, Black Canyon Road intersects **Cedar Canyon Road**. **Cima Road** crosses Cedar Canyon Road and runs generally in north-south directions. **I-15** east provides easy access to the preserve from the north.

It is important to carefully plan a route with high regard for fuel economy, as the nearest reliable sources for fuel are far to the west. Ludlow and Baker are both more than 20 miles away from the campgrounds mentioned below. **Some of these roads are unpaved and current conditions should be verified with the Bureau of Land Management prior to driving on them.** For information about the preserve, visit or call the California Desert Information Center in Barstow, (619/760) 255-8760 (see description under Barstow Area).

Along Black Canyon Road

The two developed campgrounds within the national preserve, Hole-in-the-Wall and Mid Hills, are located on or near this road (see *Campgrounds & Trailer Parks*). Mid Hills is a short distance north of Hole-in-the-Wall on a spur that branches west off Black Canyon Road.

HOLE-IN-THE-WALL VISITOR CENTER *On Black Canyon Rd., (619/760) 928-2572. Open Fri. through Sun.* Situated among interesting volcanic rock formations, Hole-in-the-Wall has a visitor center staffed by national park personnel (see listing). Two rugged hiking trails begin at the campgrounds. A trail from the picnic area leads westward through a very challenging patch of volcanic rock with several boulders to scramble over. The other trail connects the two campgrounds, winding seven miles down Wild Horse Canyon Road.

Along Cedar Canyon Road

In 1866, **Camp Rock Spring** was one of the most isolated and comfortless Army posts in the West. With area mining decreasing, the outpost was established to provide escort riders for the U.S. Mail and also to protect travelers. The natural spring provided water for Indians and others crossing the desert on the Mojave Trail. A rock house near the spring was built by Bert Smith, a victim of a World War I gas attack, who lived there until his death in 1954.

Along Cima Road

The small community of **Cima** originally developed as a railroad siding and commercial center for area ranchers

▼ *The Mojave Trail*

There was a time when the Mojave Trail was one of the most important land routes joining Southern California with areas of Sonora, Mexico, and the United States' New Mexico. In fact, this trail has been an important trade route since before the arrival of the Spanish to the New World. From the northern slopes of the San Bernardino Mountains it radiated in three major directions, leading to Tehachapi Pass in the northwest, Las Vegas in the northeast and Needles in the east. In many respects, our modern Route 66 and interstates 15 and 40 share the legacy of these ancient veins of commerce.

The early developers of the Mojave Trail were the Mohave Indians, a Hokan-speaking people concentrated along the Colorado River, in what is now the eastern edge of San Bernardino County, California, and Mohave County, Arizona. Their allies were the Yuma, from areas farther south in what is now Arizona. Both tribes distinguished themselves among neighboring societies with their extensive agricultural and commercial endeavors. Together they dominated the Colorado River until they were taken by the United States Army in 1859.

California was so abundant with wild edible plants and animals, few Californian Indian societies found a need to work the land. The Mohave people were probably the only California community who extensively cultivated the land, utilizing the fertile soil in the washes and lagoons of the Colorado River to grow an abundance of fruits and vegetables. Their vast and intricate network of trade, stretching from Mexico to Santa Barbara, shows their commitment to free commerce. Mohave business people were quite shrewd; they often systematically reinvested products gained from one transaction to use them in another. Mohave people also engaged in Indian slave trading with other tribes.

It should be no surprise to find that Mohave Indians guided Europeans through the supposed "wasteland" of the Mojave Desert. Capt. Juan Bautista de Anza had crossed the more southern Colorado Desert via the difficult Sonora-California route (see *History* and "Font's Point" in *Anza-Borrego Area*), but in 1776 Father Francisco Tomás Hermenegildo Garcés, who had been a member of de Anza's 34-man expedition, "discovered" an east-west route farther north—the Mojave Trail. With the help of a Mohave Indian guide named Sebastián Taraval, a mission runaway, Garcés and three other Mohave traveled from the present-day location of Fort Mohave (south of Laughlin) to the Mission at San Gabriel, a trek that lasted 21 days.

Spanish knowledge of the Mojave Trail brought much promise of power and wealth. There was even discussion about Spanish galleons stopping at Monterey or San Francisco with goods from China, which could then be carried via the Mojave Trail all the way to Sonora and New Mexico. But

Mohave, Yuma and Apache resistance to Spanish domination, and the turmoil of Mexican independence, brought an end to such dreams of empire. As far as Europeans were concerned, the Mojave Trail was "unsecured" or "closed" to government-regulated commerce.

By 1821 Mexico was independent from Spain and the Mojave Desert was under Mexican jurisdiction. But like the Spanish before them, Mexican authorities had little control over the Indian peoples of the desert areas, or the Americans trickling in from the northeast. Many of these Americans were fur trappers, like William Sublette, David E. Jackson, Jedediah Strong Smith and Thomas Long "Pegleg" Smith (a horse thief as well as a participant in the Gold Rush of the late 1840s; see "Pegleg Smith Historical Marker" listing under *Anza-Borrego Area*). With the exception of Pegleg Smith, all of these Americans had a stake in the Rocky Mountain Fur Company and in 1827 ended up traveling—via the Mojave Trail—to the San Joaquin Valley to trap beaver, becoming the first white men to cross the Sierra. Again, Mohave Indian guides led that first crossing from east to west.

Hostile Indians and the rugged terrain discouraged much travel across the Mojave, and with the notable exception of the New Mexican mule (and slave) trading in the 1830s, it wasn't until the Gold Rush of the 1840s and '50s that the Mojave Trail saw large-scale, non-Indian commerce and settlement. Pioneers were willing to endure the desert climate to take advantage of the opportunities for mining and commerce, and by the 1850s, hundreds of settlers began to claim the lands which were once the domain of the Paiute, Chemehuevi, Serrano and Mohave Indians. Soon there were gold mines in Salt Springs, a silver mine in Barstow, a Borax crusher and roaster at Marion (a settlement that no longer exists) and many other mineral operations sprinkled along the Mojave Trail. Roads and rail lines were later developed to connect these settlements with the outside world.

During the Civil War and for decades afterward, the U.S. governmental topological surveys spearheading road and rail development efforts precipitated clashes with the desert's Indians.

The government's solution, of course, was to establish United States Army posts in the area. Between 1859 and 1880, supplies and civilian assistance were urgently needed to support military posts such as Camp Cady, Fort Mohave and Fort Piute. Ranches and farms were established nearby to provide the much-needed barley, hay, cattle, sheep and produce—precursors to the modern ranching and agricultural developments present in the Mojave today.

As for the people of the old Mojave Desert, only the Chemehuevi and the Mohave still live in some semblance of their ancestral lands. They are confined to reservations along the Colorado River—back where the story of the Mojave Trail began.

Teutonia Peak is an obvious and interesting landmark along Cima Road.

and miners. By 1920 the town had grown to include a boarding house constructed of railroad ties, a store and a post office. In 1962 most of the original buildings were replaced by the structures you now see.

CIMA DOME *Best seen from a distance, driving along Cima Rd. (south of Cima from Mid-Hills) or from Teutonia Peak (two-hour hike from the Sunrise Rock area, 6 miles north of Cima).* This almost perfect, symmetrically rounded landform rises 1500 feet above the surrounding desert. A relatively small batholith (a molten mass of rock that stopped rising well below the surface), it is approximately 75 square miles in size and was once covered by volcanic material. Geologic uplifting and erosion created its present form, now covered by a large, dense forest of Joshua trees.

Along Essex Road

Essex Road crosses I-40 about 80 miles east of Ludlow. This paved road travels north about 12 miles towards Providence Mountains.

PROVIDENCE MOUNTAINS STATE RECREATION AREA *17 miles north of I-40 on Essex Rd. (mailing address: P.O. Box 1, Essex 92332-0001). (805) 942-0662 or (619/760) 928-2586.* Situated on the eastern slope of the Providence Mountains, the environment in the recreation area ranges from the desert floor's lowland creosote bush and burroweed scrub to a pygmy forest of piñon pines capping dramatic, craggy mountains. Colorful Fountain Peak (6996 feet) and Edgar Peak (7171 feet) are among the highest in the East Mojave. Mining activity in the area dates to the 1880s, when the Bonanza King Mine produced over $60 million in silver; during World War II the Vulcan mine produced iron ore. A paved road leads to the visitor center, which is at an elevation of 4300 feet. The 5900-acre recreation area offers a variety of activities including camping,

Colorful Mitchell Caverns were once used by area Indians to store food and other items.

picnicking, hiking and cavern tours. (See *Recreation*.)

Mitchell Caverns *From Labor Day weekend through Memorial Day weekend, tours Mon. through Fri. at 1:30 p.m., Sat., Sun. and state holidays at 10 a.m. and 1:30 and 3 p.m.; rest of year call for tour times. The caverns can be visited only by guided tour, each lasting approximately 90 minutes and involving a 1½-mile hike over sometimes uneven ground; there are also some stairs. Cavern temperature varies from the low 50s to the high 70s. Adults, $4; ages 6-12, $2. Tours of 10 or more should make reservations at least two weeks in advance.* The heated and compressed remains of marine life from an ancient shallow ocean formed limestone blocks that later were lifted and tilted on their sides by seismic and volcanic activity. Surface water dissolved the limestone along faults and fissures, creating the cavernous rooms seen today. The process of creating the beautifully sculptured stalactites, stalagmites, helictites, flowstone, cave shields and rare coral pipes took place over a period of 12 million years. Chemehuevi Indians used the caves for nearly 500 years, possibly for seasonal shelter, storage and ceremonies; anthropologists and archaeologists have found Chemehuevi pottery sherds, arrowheads and food caches. In the early 1930s, Jack and Ida Mitchell filed a silver claim on the property and then built a small resort, giving visitors guided tours of the caves. Two of the chambers, "El Pakiva" (The Sacred Pools) and "Tecopa" (named for a Chemehuevi chieftain), were named by Jack Mitchell.

Along I-15

This major freeway connects Barstow with Las Vegas, passing along the northern edge of the Mojave National Preserve.

AFTON CANYON *South of I-15 on Afton Rd.* Called the "Grand Canyon of the Mojave," Afton Canyon's multicolored

The Mojave River flows above ground in Afton Canyon, creating a lush, marshy area.

rock layers (stratigraphy) were sculpted by erosion caused by drainage from Lake Manix. The narrow, 600-foot-deep canyon with gullies was carved into the landscape over a period of about 19,000 years. In Afton Canyon the Mojave River flows above ground all year round, one of only three places where this occurs. Nearly 200 species of birds and other desert wildlife can be found in the area, attracted to the constant water supply. Indians are known to have lived in the canyon, and Jedediah Smith and Kit Carson traveled through the area in the early 1800s on a route later known as the Mojave Road. Camping, horseback riding (no rentals) and hiking areas are available (See *Recreation*).

BAKER *North of I-15 and SR 127. (619/760) 733-4469.* Boasting "the world's tallest thermometer," this small desert community offers gas, food, accommodations and last-minute supplies to travelers on I-15. Baker is frequently used as a base of operations

Baker boasts the world's largest thermometer.

for shooting music videos, commercials and motion pictures on location, and road testing for automobile manufacturers. SR 127 north provides access to Death Valley National Park. Kelbaker Road, a major route into the East Mojave, heads south from Baker.

SODA SPRINGS/ZZYZX *4⅛ miles south of I-15 on Zzyzx Rd.* The springs were a water source for travelers on the Mojave Road in the mid-1800s. The surrounding area has also been an Indian campsite, a military outpost, a wagon station, a siding on the Tonapah and Tidewater Railroad, and in the mid-1940s, a health resort and broadcast headquarters for radio evangelist Dr. Curtis Springer. Today the facilities are operated by the California State University system for their Desert Teaching and Research Facility. An unmanned visitor center provides more insight into varied history of the area.

Along Ivanpah/ Mountain Springs Road

This predominantly north-south route connects I-40 to Mountain Springs Road, which becomes Ivanpah Road just before Lanfair Valley.

GOFFS *6⅛ miles north of I-40 off Mountain Springs Rd.* In the 1880s, steam locomotives stopped for water at this important railroad siding on the Atlantic and Pacific Railroad. The siding also provided a turntable for the helper engines needed to pull the trains up the long grade from Needles. Named for an official with the railroad, the population fluctuated with area mining and railroad activities. Today a few homes, a cafe and a gas station comprise the settlement.

LANFAIR VALLEY *12 miles north of Goffs.* First called Paradise Valley, the area takes its present name from

Visitors to Zzyzx can stroll past the springs to the edge of Soda Dry Lake.

E.L. Lanfair, who settled in the valley in 1910 and organized local home-steaders. By 1917 the ranching and agricultural community had 130 registered voters, a store and a post office. Rainfall proved insufficient for the farmers, and water rights became a constant source of conflict between the ranchers, big cattlemen and the farmers. In 1923 the Nevada Southern Railroad abandoned its spur due to declining mining activity in the area. A deadly shoot-out in 1925 between a homesteader (who was a convicted train robber) and a local foreman (known for his shady past) contributed to the demise of the settlement. The store and post office closed in 1926 and most of the homesteaders left the area. Today much of the valley is still privately owned.

NEW YORK MOUNTAINS *North of Lanfair Valley.* Rising 7500 feet above sea level, these mountains are composed primarily of granite. Erosion has cut several canyons on the southern edge of the range, providing habitat for plants such as oak and white fir, which are not usually associated with the desert. In the northern portion of the range are red-hued Castle Peaks, jagged "andesitic" spires of volcanic origin formed by general uplifting of the area through faulting and further eroded by wind and water.

A number of good hiking areas can be found along New York Mountain Road. The seven- to eight-mile road, recommended for high-clearance vehicles only, provides access near the peaks, as well as opportunities for hiking and horseback riding (no rentals).

NIPTON *6⅜ miles east of Ivanpah Rd. off Nipton Rd., or 10 miles east of I-15 off Nipton Rd. Nipton Station 92364.*

Nipton still boasts an old-time trading post.

(619/760) 856-2335. The Los Angeles and Salt Lake Railroad had a cattle loading station here in 1905. The town's motto, "Where the past is present," reflects the community's 1900s mining-town atmosphere. The heart of the community, surrounded by a few small homes, features the renovated Hotel Nipton, a bed and breakfast inn furnished with antique furniture, and the Nipton Trading Post.

PIUTE GORGE *10 miles east of Lanfair Valley off Cedar Canyon Rd.* Spectacularly colored badlands are being eroded by water draining out of Lanfair Valley through the Piute Canyon fault zone. The gorge, which is nearly 200 feet deep, is on the east side of Lanfair Valley and is not easily detected until you reach the edge. An unmaintained trail allows access to the bottom of the gorge.

Along Kelbaker Road

This mostly paved major north-south route through the East Mojave leaves I-15 at Baker and heads south through Kelso. It crosses Granite Pass (elevation 4024 feet) before it intersects with I-40. Near the town of Amboy, Kelbaker Road reaches its southern terminus at National Trails Highway (formerly US 66).

AMBOY CRATER *10 miles south of I-40, west of Amboy.* This volcanic cinder cone is approximately 6000 years old and is one of the Mojave Desert's best examples of this type of geologic formation. The 285-foot-high crater lies on the northeastern edge of a 24-square-mile lava field. An ancient eruption poured lava onto Bristol Lake, separating it into today's Bristol and Bagdad lake beds. The last eruption was probably 500 years ago. Wildflowers provide color from late January through March. On the north side a steep hiking trail leads to the top of the crater, affording good views of the lava field and surrounding area. Allow two to three hours for the hike.

CINDER CONES *20 miles east of Baker.* More than 30 volcanic cones are clustered together on lava beds, providing excellent examples of relatively recent volcanic activity in the Mojave Desert—the cones range in age from 1000 to several million years old. Aiken Mine Road provides an interesting side trip through the heart of this region.

KELSO *18 miles north of I-40.* Kelso was developed in 1905-6, primarily to serve the railroad line between Los Angeles and Salt Lake City. Boiler water was easily obtainable at Kelso, a necessity for the steam locomotives pulling trains up the 18-mile, 2000-foot grade to Cima. The line was later sold to

Kelso Depot was once an important railroad stop in the East Mojave.

Union Pacific Railroad, which in 1924 built a Spanish-style depot to provide food and lodging for their workers. The historic depot functioned as a local community center and on occasion even served food to the public. Kelso also had railroad maintenance facilities and a roundhouse for the "helper engines" needed to pull the trains up the long grades. During World War II the community was home to nearly 2000 people, primarily employees and families of both Union Pacific and the Vulcan Iron Ore Mine in the nearby Providence Mountains, which supplied ore to the Kaiser steel mill at Fontana. The population of Kelso dwindled following the war with the closure of the mine in 1947, the use of diesel train engines that eliminated the need for water stops, and the decline of passenger rail service. Use of the depot dropped until its closure in 1985. A group of interested citizens saved the structure from destruction; plans call for the building to become a visitor center for the Mojave National Preserve. Due to the presence of water, the area is also known as a sanctuary for local and migratory birds.

KELSO DUNES *7½ miles south of Kelso, 4 miles west via graded road.* Rising more than 600 feet above the desert floor, this unique and isolated dune system was created by southeasterly winds blowing finely grained residual sand from the Mojave River sink, which lies to the northwest. The unusual color results from many golden rose quartz particles which are part of the dunes' composition. Another interesting feature of Kelso Dunes is the occasional "booming" sound, produced when dry sand grains slide down the steep lee side slip faces. In some years the dunes offer a nice display of spring wildflowers. The dunes can be explored on foot;

a hike to the top and back takes approximately two hours. The area is closed to all vehicles.

Victor Valley Area

Victor Valley's 2400 square miles range in elevation from 2500 to 4000 feet. The largest city, Victorville, is home to 41,000 people. Other valley communities include Apple Valley, Hesperia, Lucerne Valley and Adelanto. The High Desert Mavericks, a class A professional baseball team with a winning record,

▼ *A Quick Guide to Victor Valley Area*

See also A Quick Guide to The East Mojave Area *under Barstow Area. Effective March 22, 1997, area code (619) will change to (760).*

Population   250,000

Elevation   2175 ft.

Police Nonemergency
(619/760) 245-4211

Hospitals

Desert Valley Hospital
16850 Bear Valley Rd.
Victorville 92392
(619/760) 241-8000

Automobile Club of Southern California

Victorville District Office
12490 Amargosa Rd.
P.O. Box 1478
Victorville 92393-1478
(619/760) 246-6666
Office hours: Mon. through Fri.
9 a.m. to 5 p.m.

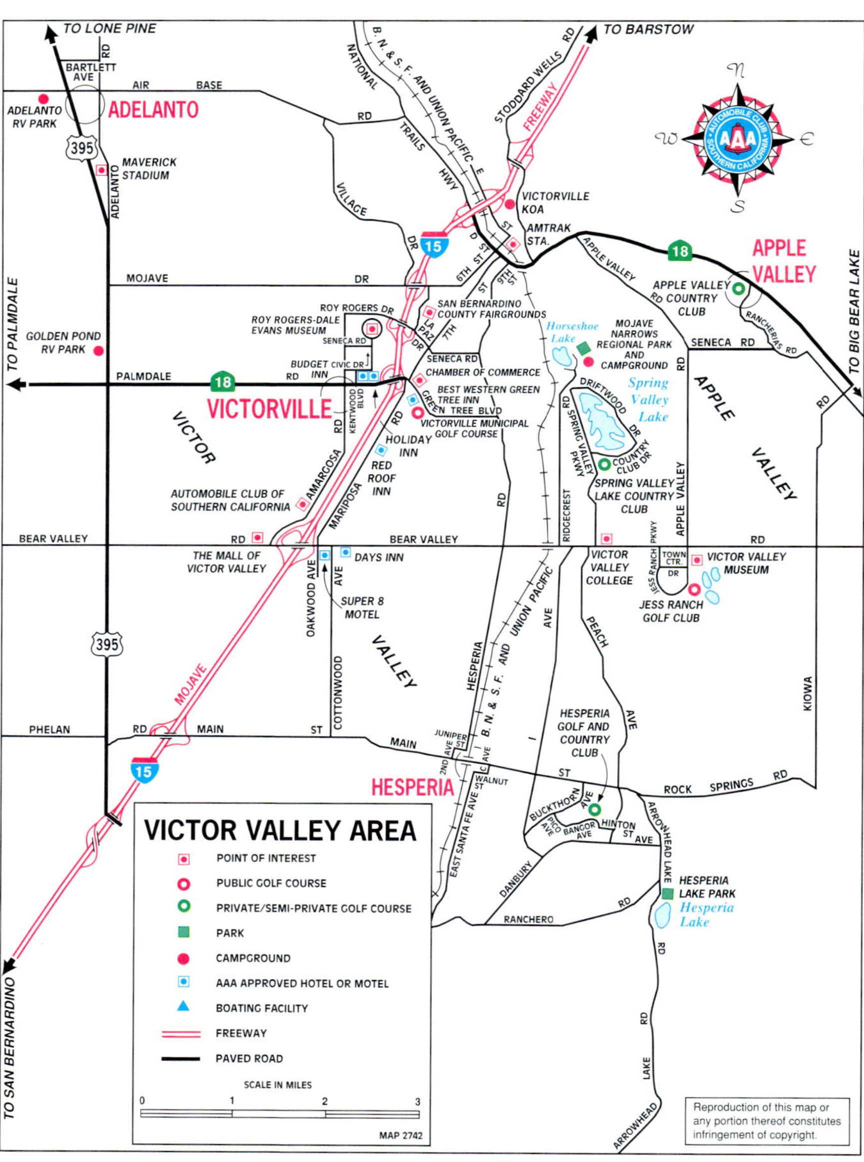

play at their stadium in Adelanto. San Bernardino County Fairgrounds and Victor Valley Community College are both located in Victorville. The Mall of Victor Valley, also in Victorville at I-15 and Bear Valley Road, offers major department stores in addition to a number of specialty shops and restaurants.

MOJAVE NARROWS REGIONAL PARK *4 miles east of I-15 on Bear Valley Rd., 2½ miles north on Ridgecrest and Yates rds. (619/760) 245-2226;*

*Equestrian Center, (619/760) 244-1644.
$5 day-use fee per vehicle.* Impressive
stands of cottonwoods and willows,
and broad meadows line riverbeds
creating an idyll of lush flora. Acres
of waterways provide for fishing and
pedal boat rides. Activities include picnicking, camping, hiking and equestrian trails, nature trails (one paved for
handicap accessibility), open turf areas
for baseball or frisbee, horseback riding
and hayrides, an archery range and
birdwatching. Annual events include
the Huck Finn Jubilee on Father's Day
weekend in June. (For camping and
fishing information see *Recreation*.)

ROY ROGERS-DALE EVANS MUSEUM
*15650 Seneca Rd., I-15 exit Roy Rogers
Dr., Victorville. (619/760) 243-4547.
Open daily 9 a.m to 5 p.m. Adults, $5;
ages 65 and older and 13 through 16,
$4; children ages 6 through 12, $3.*
Thousands of items from Roy and
Dale's personal and professional lives
are displayed in this fort-style building.
Roy's famous Palomino horse, Trigger,
plus Dale's horse Buttermilk and the
couple's dog Bullet, are preserved for
fans to see. Photos, props and gifts
from fans profile the Western stars'
acting and musical careers. Letters
and awards from political and entertainment leaders honor the couple's
humanitarian activities and professional achievements. Family heirlooms
and souvenirs of their world travels are
also exhibited. A gift shop is adjacent
to the lobby.

VICTOR VALLEY MUSEUM *11873
Apple Valley Rd., Apple Valley 92308.*

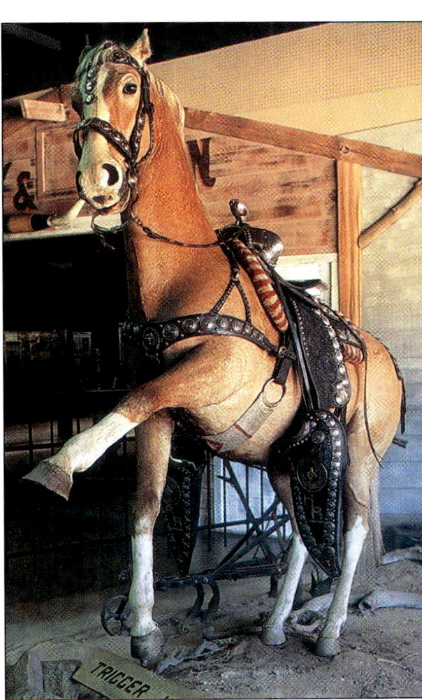

*Trigger Jr. is one of several of Roy and Dale's
famous animals preserved for posterity at the
Roy Rogers-Dale Evans Museum.*

*(619/760) 240-2111. Open Wed. through
Sun. 10 a.m. to 4 p.m. Closed major holidays. Adults, $3; seniors and ages 12 and
over, $2; ages 11 and under admitted free
with adult.* The museum's new building
is set on grounds landscaped with plants
native to the Mojave Desert. Indoors,
displays range from agates, minerals and
rocks to bugs and reptiles, American
Indian artifacts to period and area
antiques. There is an interesting collection of barbed wire, as well as various
agricultural implements. A children's
room provides for hands-on experiences.

WEST MOJAVE AREA

Red rock canyons and colorful fields of flowers, historic old mining towns and burgeoning modern cities, tortoises and racetracks, lions and tigers (alas, no bears), unearthly looking landscapes and identified flying objects— these represent the various and very assorted assets of the West Mojave Area. The broad expanses of tan desert are broken by reddish or purplish mountains and broad white dry lake beds, as well as flown over by all kinds of birds, planes and super men.

Most of the West Mojave's population resides in the **Antelope Valley**. Lancaster and Palmdale function as bedroom communities for the metropolitan Los Angeles area as well as being sizable cities in their own right. In spring the Antelope Valley California Poppy Preserve attracts thousands of visitors to view the blooming flowers.

Devil's Punchbowl offers dramatic scenery.

One of the nation's most recognized military installations is found in the **Edwards Air Force Base Area**. The climate lends itself to excellent year-round flying conditions, and Edwards Air Force Base has a long history of flight testing, pilot train-

Experimental and historic aircraft are included in the tour at NASA Dryden Flight Research Facility on Edwards Air Force Base.

ing and aircraft development, as well as serving as a landing site for the space shuttle. A breeding center for exotic cats, a tortoise preserve, a race track and the Twenty Mule Team Museum attract even more visitors to the area.

Boron's one-time railroad depot is now part of the Twenty Mule Team Museum.

The **Upper Mojave Desert**'s spooky-looking landscape has been used effectively by sci-fi filmmakers for location shooting. Fossil Falls and Red Rock Canyon provide more glimpses into the geologic wonders of the earth, whereas several old mining towns prove that the earth's treasures attracted people here for other reasons. A lunar landing module is on display at the China Lake Exhibit Center in Ridgecrest, and the Maturango Museum's historic rock art is of particular note.

Dry lakes such as Searles make for impressive landscapes.

West Mojave Area

The West Mojave is truly a land of contrasts. The area's one-time residents, a few small Indian tribal groups and miners seeking their fortunes, left their marks upon the land as surely as will the modern cities which now are home to thousands of people. One of the Earth's most startling natural environments serves as a colorful backdrop to some of the mankind's most technologically advanced aerospace endeavors. In the world of the West Mojave, much of it is truly out of this world.

Effective March 22, 1997, area code (619) will change to (760).

Antelope Valley

Antelope Valley got its name from the large herds that roamed the area in the mid-1800s. The animals are still seen occasionally. Now the largest city in the area, Lancaster began in 1876 as a supply depot and railhead for Chinese laborers working on the Southern Pacific Railroad's line between San Francisco and Los Angeles. Origins of the town's name are obscure—it might be from the birthplace (Lancaster, Pennsylvania) of M.L. Wicks, who established a Scottish colony in the area in 1882; possibly it was named by a Mr. Purnell, an employee of the Southern Pacific, whose job it was to name towns. Palmdale was founded in 1886 by German Lutherans who settled in the area and misidentified the Joshua trees as palms, giving the town its name.

Agriculture played a major role in Lancaster's early development, and mining was of some importance.

Events in the 1930s began changing the area's economic base to businesses that evolved into what is now known collectively as the aerospace industry. Lockheed Aircraft Company, Rockwell International, Northrop Aircraft Corporation and NASA (see Edwards Air Force Base) all have major installations in the area.

The relatively low cost of housing has made Lancaster and Palmdale popular bedroom communities for those willing to commute to work in metropolitan Los Angeles. The Lancaster Performing Arts Center is host to the valley's cultural endeavors and visiting artists. On the sidewalk in front of the hall is the Aerospace Walk of Honor, monuments recognizing test pilots associated with nearby Edwards Air Force Base.

Lancaster and Palmdale combine to make this the most densely populated part of the West Mojave Area. The two cities have numerous antique stores and markets. Antelope Valley Mall in Palmdale has several major department stores and dozens of specialty shops.

Wild West bad guys once hung out in what is now Vasquez Rocks County Park.

WEST MOJAVE AREA

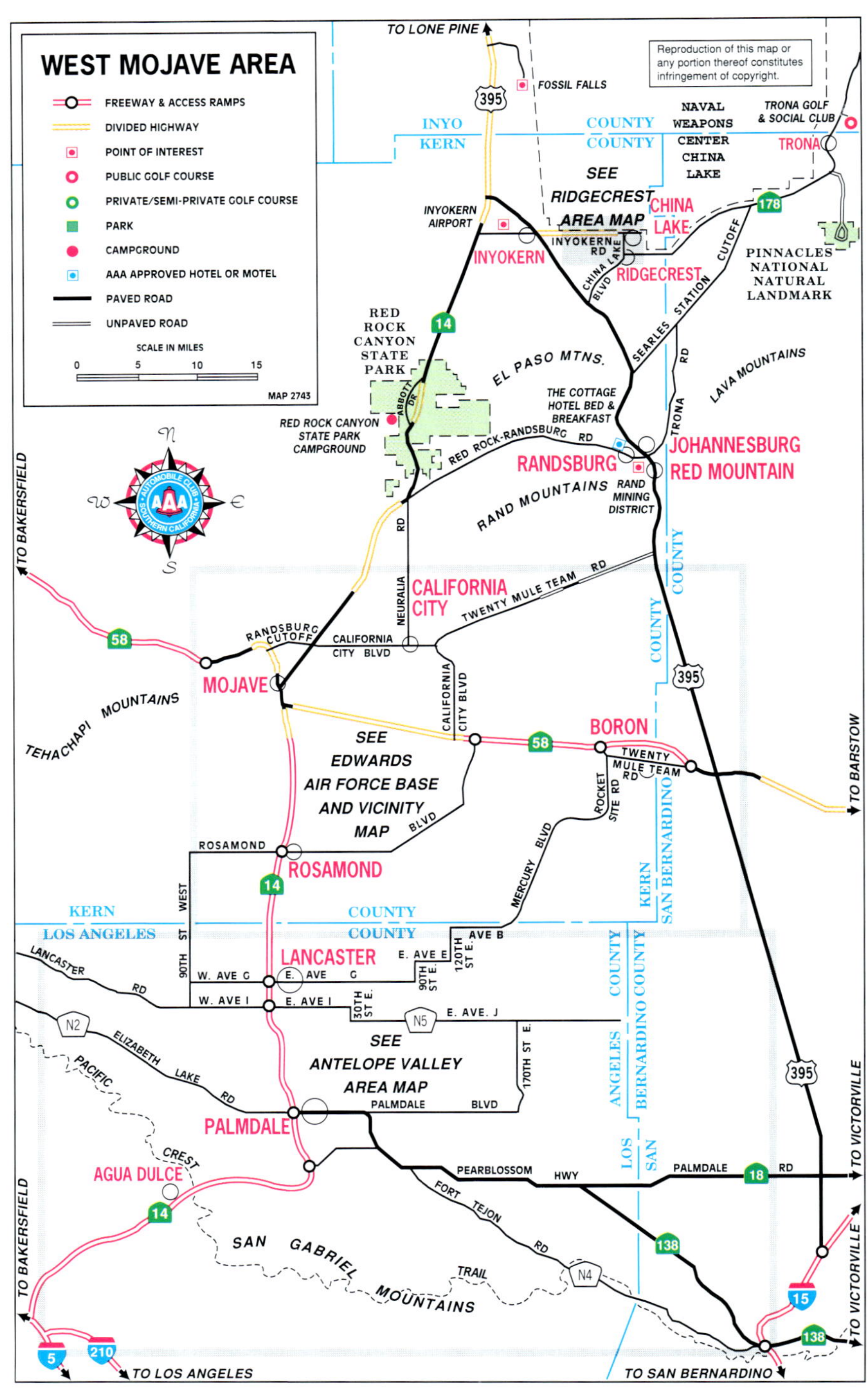

▼ *A Quick Guide to the West Mojave Area*

See also Quick Guide *box under Upper Mojave Desert.*
Effective March 22, 1997, area code (619) will change to (760).

Population   228,000

Elevation   2355

Emergency   911

Police Nonemergency
(805) 948-8541 (Antelope Valley)
(805) 824-2408 (Mojave)

Emergency Road Service for AAA Members

(800) AAA-HELP (in the USA and Canada)
(800) 955-4TDD (for the hearing impaired)

Highway Conditions
(800) 427-7623

Time   (805) 948-6611

Weather   805) 988-6610

Newspapers

Major daily newspapers serving the West Mojave Area are the *Los Angeles Times* and the *Mojave Desert News*.

Radio Stations

Adult Contemporary: KRAJ (103.9 FM); **Country:** KCNQ (102.5 FM); **News/Oldies/Sports:** KLOA (1240 AM). For a complete list of radio programs, consult the daily newspaper.

24-hour Activity Hotline
(619/760) 770-1992

Train

The Desert Wind, Southwest Chief and Sunset Limited **Amtrak** lines serve the California desert areas (with bus connections on selected routes). Call (800) USA-RAIL for complete information and fares.

Taxi

Refer to the local yellow pages of the telephone directory under "Taxi" for phone numbers and information.

Hospitals

Antelope Valley Hospital Medical
   Center
1600 W. Avenue J
Lancaster 93534
(805) 949-5000

Lancaster Community Hospital
43830 10th St.
Lancaster 93534
(805) 948-4781

Visitor Services

Lancaster Chamber of Commerce
554 W. Lancaster Blvd.
Lancaster 93534
(805) 948-4518

Palmdale Chamber of Commerce
38260 10th St. E., Ste. A
Palmdale 93550
(805) 273-3232

Automobile Club of Southern California

Lancaster District Office
1055 W. Avenue J
P.O. Box 1899
Lancaster 93539-1899
(805) 948-7661; FAX (805) 940-9199
Office hours: Mon. through Fri.
9 a.m. to 5 p.m.

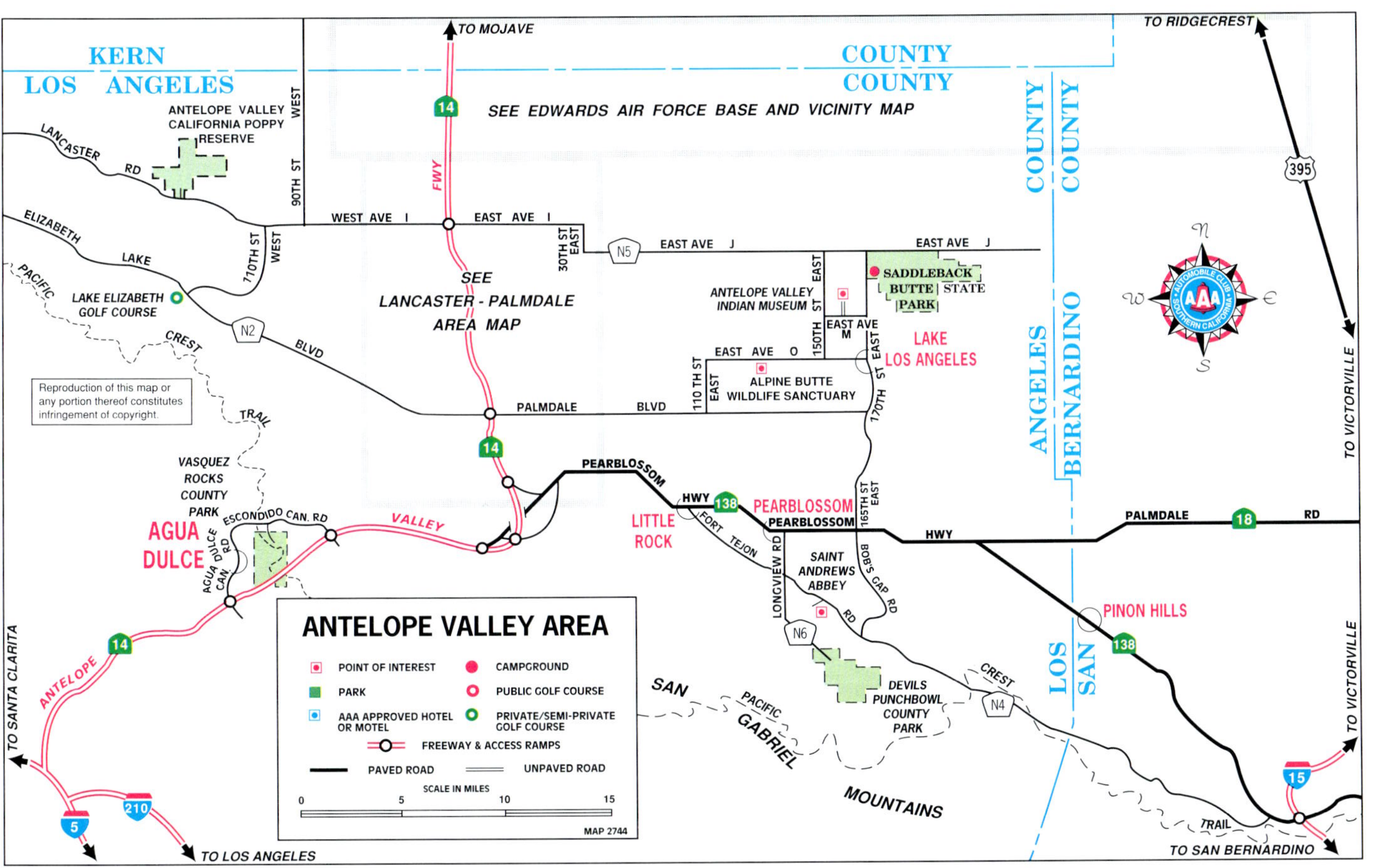
TO MOJAVE
TO RIDGECREST
KERN COUNTY
LOS ANGELES COUNTY
COUNTY
COUNTY
ANGELES COUNTY
BERNARDINO COUNTY
ANTELOPE VALLEY CALIFORNIA POPPY RESERVE
SEE EDWARDS AIR FORCE BASE AND VICINITY MAP
14
FWY
LANCASTER RD
90TH ST WEST
110TH ST WEST
WEST AVE I
EAST AVE I
30TH ST EAST
N5
EAST AVE J
EAST AVE J
ELIZABETH LAKE
PACIFIC
LAKE ELIZABETH GOLF COURSE
CREST
N2
BLVD
SEE LANCASTER - PALMDALE AREA MAP
SADDLEBACK BUTTE STATE PARK
ANTELOPE VALLEY INDIAN MUSEUM
150TH ST EAST
EAST AVE M
170TH ST EAST
LAKE LOS ANGELES
EAST AVE O
110TH ST EAST
ALPINE BUTTE WILDLIFE SANCTUARY
Reproduction of this map or any portion thereof constitutes infringement of copyright.
PALMDALE BLVD
14
VASQUEZ ROCKS COUNTY PARK
TRAIL
AGUA DULCE
ESCONDIDO CAN. RD
AGUA DULCE CAN. RD
VALLEY
PEARBLOSSOM
HWY
138
PEARBLOSSOM
PEARBLOSSOM
LITTLE ROCK
FORT TEJON
165TH ST EAST
HWY
PALMDALE
18
RD
LONGVIEW RD
SAINT ANDREWS ABBEY
BOB'S GAP RD
RD
N6
PINON HILLS
138
CREST
N4
LOS SAN
ANGELES BERNARDINO
TO VICTORVILLE
395
N E S W
DEVILS PUNCHBOWL COUNTY PARK
SAN GABRIEL MOUNTAINS
PACIFIC
TO SANTA CLARITA
14
ANTELOPE
5
210
TO LOS ANGELES
TO VICTORVILLE
15
TRAIL
TO SAN BERNARDINO

ANTELOPE VALLEY AREA
POINT OF INTEREST
PARK
AAA APPROVED HOTEL OR MOTEL
CAMPGROUND
PUBLIC GOLF COURSE
PRIVATE/SEMI-PRIVATE GOLF COURSE
FREEWAY & ACCESS RAMPS
PAVED ROAD
UNPAVED ROAD
SCALE IN MILES
0 5 10 15
MAP 2744

ANTELOPE VALLEY CALIFORNIA POPPY RESERVE *13 miles west of SR 14 on Ave. I (Lancaster Rd.) at 15101 W. Lancaster Rd. (805) 724-1180. Flower season is Mar., Apr. and May. Interpretive center open in season and for scheduled events. Entrance fee $5 per vehicle. Picnic facilities are available.* The reserve contains 1755 acres of the most consistent poppy-bearing land in California. These rolling hills provide seasonal spectacular wildflower panoramas, with 8½ miles of hiking trails. Named for the prevalence of the distinguishable California poppy, other flowers found in the reserve include the shocking pink-to-scarlet owl clover, the blue pygmy lupine, the yellow coreopsis and the red-violet filaree. The adjacent Jane S. Pinheiro Interpretive Center has won awards for its energy conservation design. It is built on a south-facing hillside and uses large windows and earth fill. This design maintains a temperate environment while taking advantage of desert sunshine. Some of the 163 paintings done by the artist for which it is named are exhibited here, as well as a video show on the poppies, a small gift shop, and water and toilet facilities (food service not available).

ANTELOPE VALLEY INDIAN MUSEUM *17 miles east of Lancaster; on Ave. M between 150th and 170th sts. (805) 942-0662. Open Oct. through May, Sat. and Sun. 11 a.m. to 4 p.m. Closed Jun. through Sept. Admission, $2; ages 6 through 12, 1$.* Completed in 1932 by artist and American Indian artifact collector H. Arden Edwards, the museum's unique Swiss chalet-style building incorporates brightly colored Indian mural painting and large granite rock formations in its design.

A later resident of the home, anthropologist Grace Oliver, expanded the collections and opened the property as an Indian museum in 1940. Oliver was dedicated to the museum for over 40 years, but in 1979 the State of California purchased the land and the museum's contents were donated to the Department of Parks and Recreation. Five rooms display items primarily representative of Indian peoples found in California, the American Southwest and the Great Basin, although artifacts are also displayed from societies in other geographic regions. Joshua Cottage features a touch table where visitors can handle various artifacts. A self-guided nature trail explores the grounds. The gift shop sells authentic American Indian arts, crafts, literature and other items.

APOLLO PARK *4 miles west of SR 14 and SR 138 at 4555 W. Ave. G, Lancaster. (805) 940-7701.* A major point of interest in this park is a test module from NASA's Apollo series. The grounds also

This Apollo test module is parked at Apollo Park.

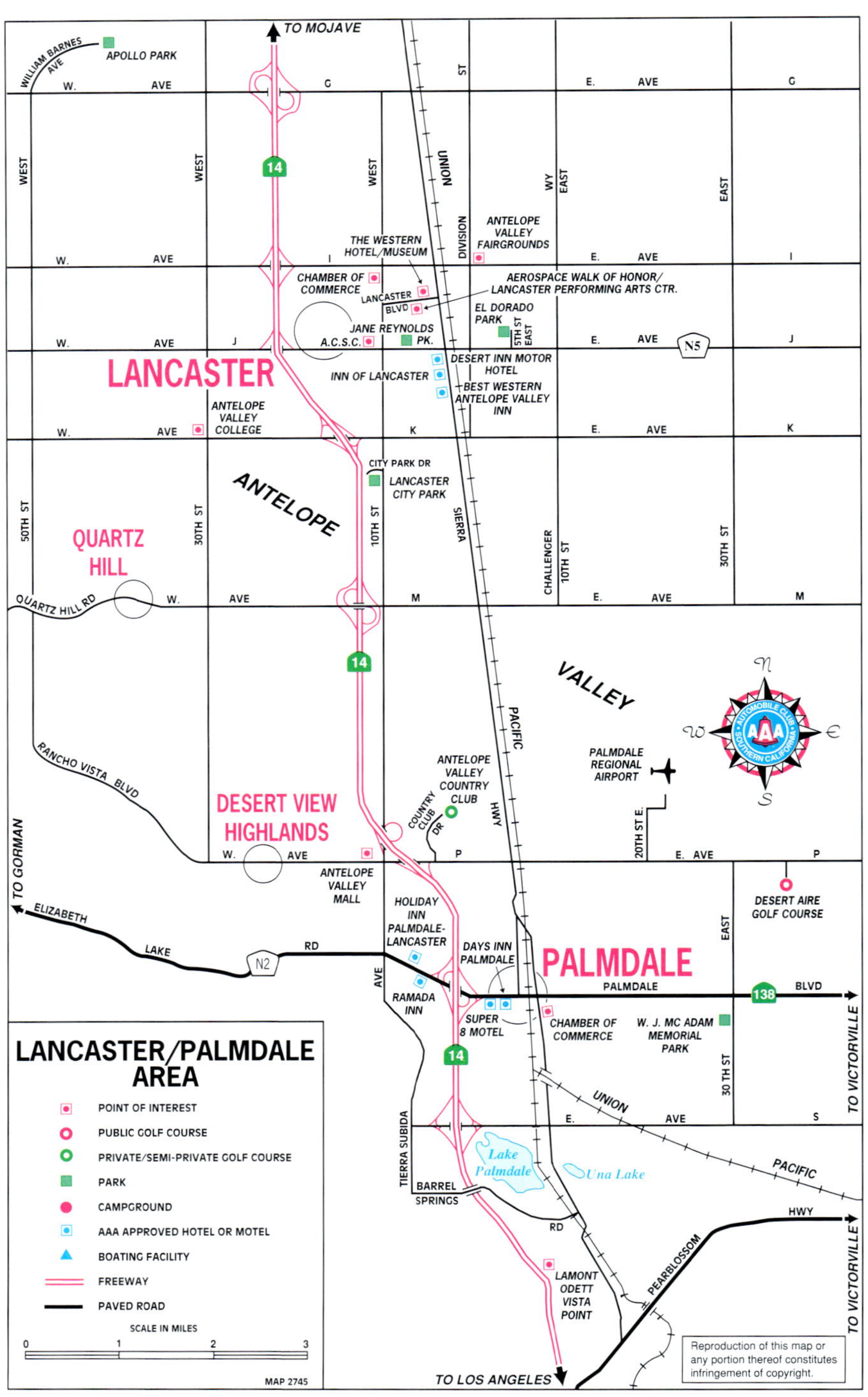
WEST MOJAVE AREA
TO MOJAVE
WILLIAM BARNES AVE
APOLLO PARK
W. AVE G
ST
E. AVE G
WEST
WEST
14
WEST
UNION
WY EAST
EAST
W. AVE I
THE WESTERN HOTEL/MUSEUM
ANTELOPE VALLEY FAIRGROUNDS
DIVISION
E. AVE I
CHAMBER OF COMMERCE
LANCASTER BLVD
AEROSPACE WALK OF HONOR/ LANCASTER PERFORMING ARTS CTR.
EL DORADO PARK
5TH ST EAST
W. AVE J
JANE REYNOLDS PK.
A.C.S.C.
E. AVE J
N5
LANCASTER
DESERT INN MOTOR HOTEL
INN OF LANCASTER
BEST WESTERN ANTELOPE VALLEY INN
W. AVE K
ANTELOPE VALLEY COLLEGE
K
E. AVE K
CITY PARK DR
LANCASTER CITY PARK
ANTELOPE
SIERRA
50TH ST
30TH ST
10TH ST
CHALLENGER
10TH ST
30TH ST
QUARTZ HILL
QUARTZ HILL RD
W. AVE M
M
E. AVE M
14
VALLEY
N
W E
S
AUTOMOBILE CLUB SOUTHERN CALIFORNIA
AAA
RANCHO VISTA BLVD
PACIFIC HWY
PALMDALE REGIONAL AIRPORT
20TH ST E.
ANTELOPE VALLEY COUNTRY CLUB
DESERT VIEW HIGHLANDS
COUNTRY CLUB DR
TO GORMAN
W. AVE P
P
E. AVE P
ANTELOPE VALLEY MALL
DESERT AIRE GOLF COURSE
ELIZABETH LAKE RD
N2
HOLIDAY INN PALMDALE-LANCASTER
DAYS INN PALMDALE
PALMDALE
EAST
AVE
PALMDALE BLVD
138
TO VICTORVILLE
RAMADA INN
CHAMBER OF COMMERCE
W. J. MC ADAM MEMORIAL PARK
SUPER 8 MOTEL
30 TH ST
14
TIERRA SUBIDA
UNION
E. AVE S
S
BARREL SPRINGS
Lake Palmdale
Una Lake
PACIFIC
RD
HWY
TO VICTORVILLE
LAMONT ODETT VISTA POINT
PEARBLOSSOM
TO LOS ANGELES
LANCASTER/PALMDALE AREA
POINT OF INTEREST
PUBLIC GOLF COURSE
PRIVATE/SEMI-PRIVATE GOLF COURSE
PARK
CAMPGROUND
AAA APPROVED HOTEL OR MOTEL
BOATING FACILITY
FREEWAY
PAVED ROAD
SCALE IN MILES
0   1   2   3
MAP 2745
Reproduction of this map or any portion thereof constitutes infringement of copyright.

offer children's play areas, three large lakes stocked with catfish and trout, covered picnic areas and paved walks throughout the park's 56 grassy acres. Bait sales, refreshment stand and rest room facilities available. An adult fishing derby is held the first Saturday in March; a children's fishing derby is on the first Saturday in May; other events are held throughout the year.

DEVIL'S PUNCHBOWL COUNTY PARK *8 miles south of Pearblossom Rd. off Co. Rd. N6 at 2800 Punchbowl Rd., Pearblossom 93553. (805) 944-2743. Open daily sunrise to sunset. Parking $3.* At the foot of the San Gabriel Mountains, up a steep, paved road, is a small canyon that underscores the awesome power of the seismic activity for which California is famous. Hidden among dense stands of juniper and piñon pine woodland are layered folds of sedimentary rock and sandstone forming the walls of this deep canyon.

It is an impressive display of the influence of three main faults on the surrounding landscape: the Pearblossom Fault, the Pinion Fault and the San Andreas Fault. A small interpretive center and a picnic area are on the rim of the "bowl," 4700 feet above sea level. Several trails lead down into the canyon and into forested areas. A ⅓-mile, self-guided nature trail is not strenuous. The loop trail is one mile and affords numerous views of the bowl.

SADDLEBACK BUTTE STATE PARK *17 miles east of Lancaster on E. Ave. J and 170th St. (805) 942-0662. $5 per vehicle entrance fee; camping, $10.* The Mojave Desert's relative flatness is broken by a 3641-foot-high, granite-capped butte which towers 1000 feet above the surrounding terrain. Joshua trees and numerous other plants indigenous to the area are found in the park's 2955 acres. Dozens of birds may be spotted here, including the golden eagle, red-

The dramatic geology of Devil's Punchbowl is partly San Andreas Fault.

The view from atop Saddleback Butte is well worth the hike.

tailed hawk, prairie falcon, Gambel's quail, owls, sparrows, wrens and swallows. Desert tortoises, rattlesnakes and lizards cohabit with coyotes, bobcats, rabbits, mice, squirrels, rats, badgers and bats. Colorful wildflowers are part of the park's spring scenery. A one-mile trail leads from the campground to the top of the peak, providing spectacular views of the surrounding terrain and the mountains to the south. A half-mile loop nature trail originates at the ranger station (see *Recreation*).

ST. ANDREW'S ABBEY *31001 Valyermo Rd., Valyermo 95563. (805) 944-1047. Ceramic shop open daily 9 a.m. to noon and 1:30 to 4 p.m.; closed major holidays. A bookstore and gift shop on the grounds is open daily 10 a.m. to noon. and 1:30 to 4 p.m.; closed major holidays.* A Benedictine retreat center at the base of the San Gabriel Mountains, the abbey is best known for its distinctive series of ceramic angel ornaments and plaques. The angels are sold in the ceramic shop.

VASQUEZ ROCKS COUNTY PARK
20 miles south of Palmdale off SR 14 at 10700 W. Escondido Rd., Agua Dulce 91350. (805) 268-0840. Open daily 8 a.m. to sunset. $3 day-use fee per vehicle. Twenty-two million years ago these intriguing rocks were on the floor of a prehistoric ocean. When the ocean dried and exposed the landscape, sporadic flooding eroded the softer formations around the rocks. Then earthquakes altered the terrain by tilting the rocks to 50-degree angles. Today, chaparral, scrub oaks, yucca and native grasses and wildflowers at once soften the landscape and intensify its harshness. Birds, lizards, snakes, coyotes and rabbits are among the animal life spotted in Vasquez Rocks. A few artifacts give evidence of early inhabitants who were later absorbed into the more dominant local Mexican

Vasquez Rocks is often used for location shots in movies and television.

population. The park is named for a bandito, Tiburcio Vasquez, who in the mid-1800s used the rocky terrain as a hideout from pursuing lawmen. The dramatic rock formations have been a popular site for filming many television shows and movies, including "Star Trek," *Bonanza, The Big Valley,* "The Charge of the Light Brigade," "Gunga Din," *Murder, She Wrote* and "The Flintstones." The park preserves 700 acres of this remarkable terrain for hiking, rock climbing, mountain biking, picnicking and camping.

THE WESTERN HOTEL/MUSEUM
557 W. Lancaster Blvd., Lancaster. (805) 723-6250. Open Tue. through Sat. 11 a.m. to 4 p.m., Sun. 1 to 4 p.m. Photographs and artifacts recall city and hotel history dating to the 1880s. Over the years the hotel hosted quilting bees, saloon fights, church socials and card parties. After falling into ruin, the structure was restored in the 1980s.

Edwards Air Force Base Area

The small community of **Boron** (population 2100) is home to two large companies, each laying claim to "world's largest" in some aspect of their operations. U.S. Borax & Chemical Company is the world's major source of borates and has the world's largest open pit mine. LUZ Engineering Corporation operates the world's largest commercial Solar Electric Generating System, northeast of town.

Windmills accent the Tehachapi Mountains west of **Mojave**, harnessing this natural power resource. The town of Mojave sits at the crossroads of SR 14 and SR 58. Most of the community's 4000 residents provide services for travelers passing through, or work at nearby Edwards Air Force Base.

California City is a residential community popular with retirees and military personnel. The planned community is home to around 6000 residents.

Rosamond, once a mining community, has blossomed into a large residential area of more than 7500 people. It sits on SR 14 at the western entrance to Edwards Air Force Base.

DESERT TORTOISE NATURAL AREA

6 miles northeast of California City via Randsburg Mojave Rd. (619/760) 384-5400. The Bureau of Land Management has established a 39½-square-mile area as a protective habitat for the endangered desert tortoise. An interpretive center describes the tortoise and other reptiles and animals found in the preserve. Closed to all motorized traffic, trails take visitors into the protected area and brochure guides explain plants, animals and other features found in the habitat.

The **Main Loop Trail** is ¼ mile long. Ten numbered stops allow for examining features of the creosote bush scrub plant community. The unpaved walkway is usually suitable for wheelchairs. Three loop trails break off from the main trail. A ⅖-mile **Plant Loop Trail** has 19 numbered stops at distinctive and significant plants. The **Animal Loop Trail** has 25 numbered stops on its ½-mile loop, describing animals, reptiles, bugs and birds typically found in the preserve. Guide brochures are not provided for the **Discovery Loop Trail**, which is 1¾ miles long.

Edwards Air Force Base

The base achieved international acclaim as a result of its involvement

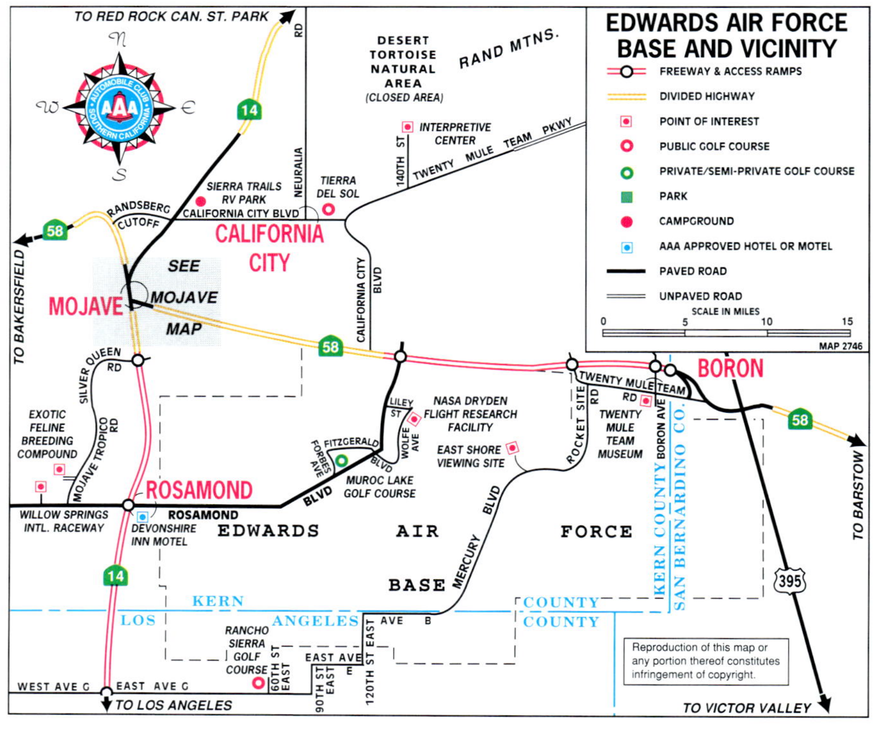

Planes at Edwards Air Force Base include (clockwise from top left) fighter trainers, a lifting body and the SR-71 Blackbird.

with the United States' space shuttle program, and is home to the Air Force Test Pilot School, which graduates about 50 test pilots annually. The 95th Air Base Wing, stationed at Edwards, is the mission support wing of the Air Force Flight Test Center.

What is now Edwards Air Force Base was originally called Muroc Bombing and Gunnery Range, established in 1933 for temporary bombing and gunnery ranges. The name Muroc dates to 1910, when area settlers reversed the spelling of their last name to obtain a post office. By 1937 the Army Air Corps had established Muroc Army Air Field, a semipermanent tent camp along the eastern shoreline of Rogers Dry Lake. During World War II the base was an important training facility for fighter and bomber crews who targeted a full-scale wooden mockup of a Japanese Mogami-class heavy cruiser built on the dry lake bed.

In 1942 Muroc was selected for the top secret testing of the Bell XP-59A "Airacomet," America's first jet aircraft. The base's excellent weather made it an ideal location for year-round light testing, and the dry lake bed provided an immense natural runway for emergency landings. These factors contributed to the installation becoming a full-time flight test facility. At Muroc in 1947, pilot Charles E. Yeager flew the Bell X-1 to a speed of Mach 1.06, exceeding for the first time ever the "speed of sound." Hundreds of experimental, military and commercial aircraft have since been tested at and over the base. Rocket engine testing also took place at Muroc, and today Edwards hosts Phillips Laboratory which develops technology for ballistic missiles and space motors.

In 1950 the base was officially renamed Edwards in honor of a test pilot who was killed in a crash of an experimental plane. A sprawling community of 8300 supports much of work that occurs at the base.

Flight Line Tours *(805) 277-3517. Tours Fri. by reservation only. Free; call for reservations.* A short video profiles aviation history at the base. A bus then transports visitors to selected sites throughout the complex while a public affairs officer identifies the various aircraft seen on the tour. The tour stops at the site of the future Air Force Flight Test Center Museum, where several historic aircraft are already on display, including a B-52 bomber.

NASA Dryden Flight Research Facility *(805) 258-3446, 258-3460 (Tour reservations and information). Tours Mon. through Fri. at 10:15 a.m. and 1:15 p.m.; reservation required; tours not offered on federal holidays and shuttle landing days. Gift shop and visitor center open from 7:45 a.m. to 3:45 p.m.* The 90-minute tour begins with a video profiling the history of space flight. A guide then escorts visitors through two hangars where aircraft may be viewed. A cafeteria also serves the public.

Space Shuttle landings *Accessible from two directions. From the south: from Lancaster north on SR 14 and exit at Ave. F, east 1 mile to Sierra Hwy., north to Ave. E, east to 140th St., north to Ave. B, then east; Ave. B becomes Mercury Blvd., which leads into the viewing area on the northeast side of Rogers Dry Lake. From the north: from SR 58 head south on Rocket Site Rd., which becomes Rich Rd. on the base; west at Mercury Blvd. to the viewing site. (805) 258-3520 (24-hour information on current space shuttle flights). East Shore Viewing Site opens 24 hours prior to landing and closes one hour prior to landing. Passes are not required.* **Currently Edwards is used as a backup landing site only.**

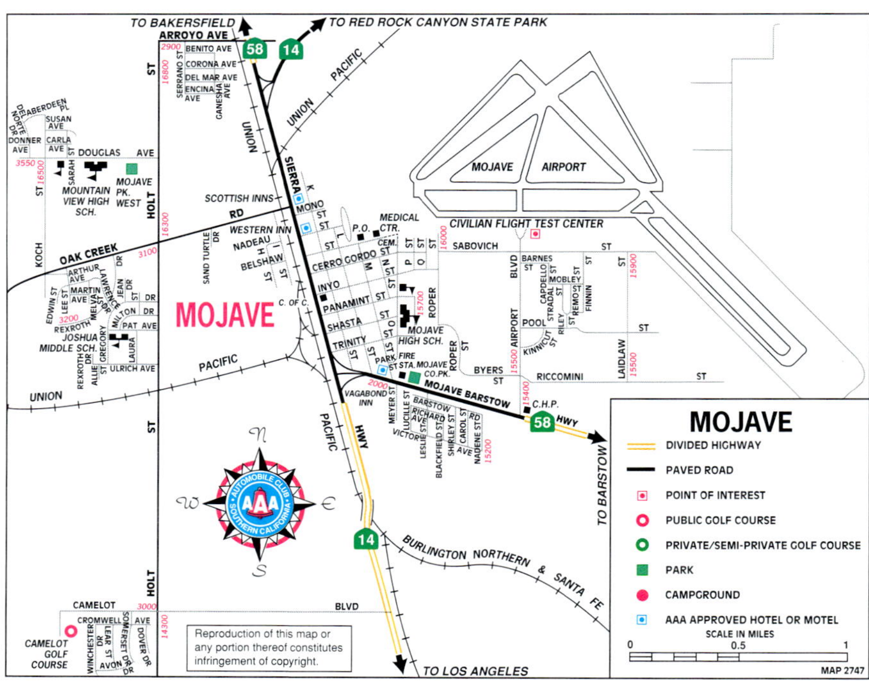

Twenty Mule Team Museum preserves lots of area history, including the story of the famous mule teams.

During shuttle landings Edwards' main gates are restricted to official business only. The public viewing site is several miles from the actual landing site but the view is unobstructed. Traffic congestion should be expected.

Spectators should be prepared to drive and park on unprepared surfaces. Food and souvenir vendors are present, and portable sanitary facilities are provided. Water supplies are very limited. Rattlesnakes may be found in the area. The following services are not available: gasoline, shelter from the sun, plumbing or electricity, and dumping facilities for recreational vehicles.

EXOTIC FELINE BREEDING COMPOUND *3½ miles west of SR 14 via Rosamond Blvd., Mojave/Tropico Rd. and Rhyolite Rd. (mailing address: HCR 1, Box 84, Rosamond 93560). (805) 256-3332. Open Thur. through Tues. 10 a.m. to 4 p.m.; last tour begins at 3:30. Donations accepted. No pets allowed.* This breeding, research and educational facility cares for up to 50 rare and exotic cats. Guided tours describe the individual felines' personalities and the species' characteristics. Both big and small cats are represented by 20 species, including leopards, tigers, cougars and ocelots.

TWENTY MULE TEAM MUSEUM *26962 Twenty Mule Team Rd., Boron 93516. (619/760) 762-5810. Open daily 10 a.m. to 4 p.m. Donation.* A renovated house from the old Baker Mine campsite contains dozens of displays profiling the area's history. Exhibits include mining equipment, a video on borate mining and the product's hundreds of uses, artifacts and photographs from the early settlement of the community, and some history on nearby Edwards Air Force Base.

WILLOW SPRINGS INTERNATIONAL RACEWAY *5 miles west of SR 14 via Rosamond Blvd. (mailing address: P.O. Box X, Rosamond 93560). (805) 256-2471. Racing Sun. Open daily.* Constructed in 1953, this 2½-mile road course has had many famous drivers roar through its nine turns at high speeds. In 1987 Michael Andretti, driving an Indy car, set a track record with an average speed of 136 miles per hour. Nigel Mansell, Rocky Moran and Davey Jones are among the well-known racers who have raced at Willow Springs, known as the fastest track in the West. Vehicles raced on the track range from Indy and Formula One to stock cars, motorcycles and midgets. An International Driving School is on the premises. Observation stands are available for spectators, and concession stands provide refreshments.

Upper Mojave Desert

Amazing natural land features are the predominant attractions in this portion of the Mojave Desert, although ancient Indians left marks of their habitation in the form of rock art, and remnants of century-old mining towns evidence man's exploitation of the land and its treasures.

The largest town in this region is Ridgecrest. Like so many towns in the American West, Ridgecrest was known by other names in its past, including Crumville and Sierra View. In 1943 it was little more than a crossroads outside the gates of the Naval base. Slow growth was the standard for the next 20 years, and today this developing city of 29,000 supports the China Lake Naval Weapons Center as well as serving as the commercial center for the area.

CHINA LAKE EXHIBIT CENTER
At east end of Blandy Rd. in the old Officers' Club building, China Lake Naval Air Weapons Station. (619/760) 939-

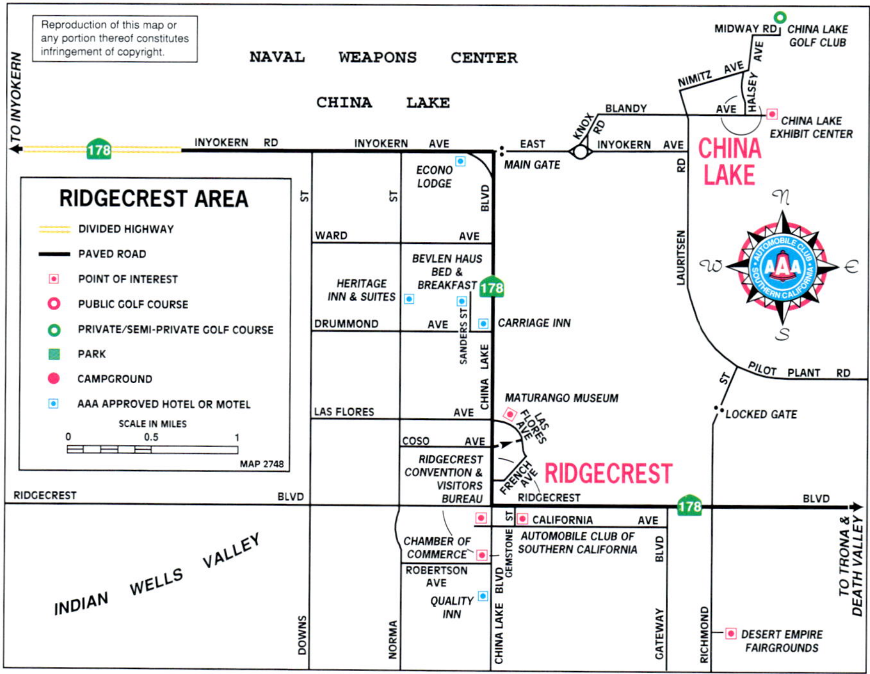

8645. Open Mon. through Fri. 7:30 a.m. to 4:30 p.m.; obtain a guest pass at the base's main gate. The Center displays items from Naval projects ranging from World War II to the Persian Gulf War. Numerous missiles, a Lunar Soft Landing Vehicle, explosive weapons and a Recoverable Test Vehicle are displayed. The center also has photographs and memorabilia from President John F. Kennedy's 1963 visit to China Lake.

FOSSIL FALLS *27 miles north of Ridgecrest via SR 178 and US 395, east via Cinder Mine Rd. (800) 847-4830. Primitive picnicking and camping. No water.* Several times during the past 100,000 years, rain and snow caused water from Owens Lake to flow in the Owens River through this narrow valley between the Coso and Sierra Nevada mountain ranges, creating a system of interconnected lakes. Evidence of these ancient lakes is seen in the region's dry lake beds. Volcanic activity as recent as 20,000 years ago sent lava through the river channel, and water erosion then polished and sculpted the formations we see today. Prehistoric people camped along the ancient rivers and lakes and hunted the mammals which populated the area. The region had become arid by 6000 B.C.—the rivers and lakes had disappeared and the inhabitants migrated to more hospitable climes. By 4000 B.C. more moderate climatic conditions had returned and a sub-group of the Shoshone people inhabited the area. Obsidian waste flakes indicate that this society made stone tools such as arrow or spear heads, knives and scrapers. Metates, smooth concave surfaces on rocks, show that they ground seeds and grain for food. Petroglyphs might have been significant in their religious practices.

See also Quick Guide box under Antelope Valley Area.

▼ *A Quick Guide to the Upper Mojave Area*

See also Quick Guide *box under Antelope Valley Area.*
Effective March 22, 1997, area code (619) will change to (760).

Police Nonemergency
(805) 371-3711

Weather   (805) 988-6610

Bus

The RATS dial-a-ride serves the City of Ridgecrest. (619/760) 375-9777. Cash fare is $1.25. Wheelchair lifts available.

Taxi

Ridgecrest Yellow Cab is based in the City of Ridgecrest; (619/760) 371-4222. Rates are regulated; the flag rate is $2.80 plus $2 per mile.

Hospitals

Ridgecrest Community Hospital
1081 N. China Lake Blvd.
Ridgecrest 93555
(619/760) 446-3551

Visitor Services

Ridgecrest Area Convention &
    Visitors Bureau
100 W. California Ave.
Ridgecrest 93555
(800) 847-4830

Automobile Club of Southern California

Ridgecrest District Office
114 S. Gemstone, Ste. A
Ridgecrest 93555
(619/760) 375-8426
Office hours: Mon. through Fri. 9 a.m. to 5 p.m.

Fossil Falls is something like a river turned to stone.

A parking area is near the top of the "falls." A path leads to an overlook of the falls, where it is possible to walk around and climb down to a sandy area at the bottom of the falls. Rock climbers like the challenge of the area's crags and smooth surfaces. Flowers provide spots of color in this intriguing, scenic spot.

MATURANGO MUSEUM *At China Lake Blvd. and 100 E. Las Flores Ave., Ridgecrest 93556. (619/760) 375-6900. Open Wed. through Sun. 10 a.m. to 5 p.m. Closed holidays. Adults, $2; seniors, military and children age 6 and over, $1. Call for tour information.* The museum, also known as Death Valley Tourist Center and Northern Mojave Visitors Center, features exhibits ranging from historic rock art and more contemporary art forms to natural and cultural objects representative of the upper Mojave Desert. The museum's Sylvia Winslow Gallery presents monthly art displays. Ancient Indian petroglyphs and other artifacts trace earlier human

Wildlife and geology displays are featured at the Maturango Museum.

An "eerie landscape" appropriately describes the Trona Pinnacles.

existence. Pioneer memorabilia, mining tools and equipment represent the impact of modern civilization on the region. Selected native mounted birds, reptiles and animals show the variety of life forms capable of surviving the desert's harsh climate. A children's section offers hands-on displays.

On weekends in spring and autumn the museum sponsors docent-led tours to Little Petroglyph Canyon on the Naval Weapons Center at China Lake. The canyon has the world's largest and best preserved concentration of petroglyphs—100,000 drawings dating back 3000 years.

PINNACLES NATIONAL NATURAL LANDMARK *20 miles east of Ridgecrest via SR 178 and dirt access road; about 7⁷⁄₁₀ miles east of its junction with Trona-Red Mountain Rd., a graded dirt road leads south from SR 178 into the pinnacles. This road is usually passable by passenger vehicles, however after rain the road may be impassable to all vehicle travel (including four-wheel-drive). Check with the Ridgecrest Area Conventions & Visitors Bureau at (800) 847-4830 for current conditions. Primitive camping; no water or other facilities are provided.*

Striking tufa spires rise out of the Searles Dry Lake basin, looking like a landscape from another world. An area roughly three miles wide by 4½ miles long has more than 500 spires, some reaching 140 feet in height. The rock formations developed between 10,000 and 100,000 years ago, when Searles Lake formed a link in a chain of interconnected lakes. The Trona Pinnacles formed under water through an unusual combination of chemical and geothermal conditions. Rich mineral runoff from surrounding geothermal sites and limited outflow from Searles Lake caused the waters to become highly concentrated carbonate brine. Underground hot springs welled up through fault line fractures on the lake bottom, introducing calcium-rich ground water that, when combined with carbonates, formed calcium carbonate deposits. Blue-green algae colonies bonded with the calcium carbonate to form the pinnacles.

At an elevation of 2000 feet, summer temperatures can reach over 120 degrees. A half-mile loop trail takes hikers around the pinnacles. Although the hike is not strenuous, closed, rubber-soled shoes with good ankle support will contribute to a more comfortable hike.

RAND MINING DISTRICT *20 miles south of Ridgecrest off US 395.* Rand Camp, a mining camp in 1896, became the community of **Randsburg**. The mining camp Osdick evolved into the community of **Red Mountain**. **Johannesburg** was established in 1896 as a planned service community for the area mining camps. Today all three towns' histories mix with the present

in historic buildings (some restored, some not), mining rigs and equipment, and an occasional "colorful character." Randsburg provides a number of antique shops, a few craft stores and a saloon where it's still possible to "wet your whistle."

RED ROCK CANYON STATE PARK *25 miles north of Mojave on SR 14 (mailing address: P.O. Box 26, Cantil 93519). (805) 942-0662. Open daily. $5 day-use fee; camping, $7-10. Facilities for primitive camping, picnicking and hiking (see* Recreation). *Interpretive programs offered in spring and autumn, including campfire programs on Fri. and Sat. and nature walks Sun. at 9 a.m.* In the high Mojave Desert near the southern end of the Sierra Nevada mountain range is an area of spectacular eroded sandstone cliffs. The rocks are representative of the Ricardo Formation, a Pleistocene Basin deposit about 6500 feet thick and consisting of white clay, red sandstone,

Erosion gives Red Rock Canyon its unusual rock formations; minerals provide the wide range of colors.

dark brown lava and pink tuff. The beds were uplifted in a manner similar to the Sierra Nevada, with gentle slopes on the west side and cliffs on the east. Water erosion created the startling sandstone formations.

The natural community of Red Rock Canyon includes dozens of plants and animals. Joshua trees, chaparral, cholla cactus, creosote and desert holly grow here. Colorful spring wildflowers include indigo bushes, Mojave asters, pink maids, scaly-stemmed sand plants and desert five spots. Among the wildlife inhabiting the park are coyotes, bats, ringtail cats, kit foxes, jack rabbits, squirrels and bobcats, in addition to such reptiles as the desert tortoise, desert iguana, and numerous lizards and snakes, including the Mojave green and sidewinder rattlers. Bird watchers have spotted golden eagles, various blackbirds and owls, quail, sparrows and wrens.

Human presence in the area is verified by Indian religious sites and grinding holes. Early pioneers discovered gold deposits, while later explorations found other minerals. The only permanent settlers were the Hagen family at Ricardo. The visitor center, on the site of the Hagen home, echoes the design of the original building. Red Rock Canyon is often used as a film location.

DEATH VALLEY AREA

eath Valley is first and foremost a place of contrasts. One of the world's hottest sections of desert is situated only a few miles from forested and often snow-covered mountain peaks. What may appear to some observers to be a barren, monotonous wasteland reveals itself to the inquiring eye to be a landscape full of remarkably diverse forms and colors. The terrain, which looks too harsh for life, is in fact the natural habitat of a wide variety of well-adapted plants and animals, including fish and birds. And man, who seems very out of place in this demanding wilderness, has in reality inhabited the valley continuously for nearly 10,000 years. The history of the Death Valley area is rich with tales of schemes by colorful, fortune-seeking individuals hoping to get rich quick—evidenced by the numerous ghost towns in the area.

The soft-sculpted sand dunes are a sharp contrast to the rugged mountains nearby.

Zabriskie Point is a favorite spot of photographers.

Artists Palette offers a veritable rainbow of colors.

Death Valley National Park preserves most of this wild land. Within the park's 3,367,628 acres are sand dunes and salt flats, valleys and mountains, mine ruins and ghost towns, scenic drives and spectacular views. Although the area was once dotted with dozens of mining camps and boom towns, today little exists in the way of modern facilities accommodating visitors. Furnace Creek, the park's headquarters, is the main tourist service area; the only other tourist facilities within the park are located at Stovepipe Wells and Scotty's Castle. A few paved highways traverse the region, but much of it is accessible only via dirt roads or hiking trails.

Just northeast of Death Valley National Park is **Beatty, Nevada**, a small town offering a variety of tourist services. The ruins of Rhyolite, a gold-mining town dating to the early 1900s, are located nearby.

The Salt Flats near Badwater are the lowest point in the Western Hemisphere.

Death Valley Area

Due to limited tourist services and extreme summer temperatures, travel in this region is best a planned activity. Reservations should be made well in advance for lodging and those campgrounds which have reservable sites.

Effective March 22, 1997, area code (619) will change to (760).

Death Valley National Park

HEADQUARTERS *Located at the Death Valley National Park Visitor Center; Death Valley National Park, Death Valley 92328. (619/760) 786-2331. Open daily 8 a.m. to 5 p.m.*

Death Valley's attraction as a tourist destination began in 1927, when a borax mining company turned its crew quarters at Furnace Creek into a resort. It proved to be very popular as a winter vacation spot, and six years later a national monument was established, preserving nearly 3000 square miles of land in Death Valley. In 1994 the monument was elevated to national park status and with the addition of 1.3 million acres, became the largest national park in the contiguous United States.

The park entrance fees are $5 per vehicle or $2 per individual entering as a pedestrian, bicyclist, motorcyclist or bus passenger. An annual pass to Death Valley costs $15. An individual planning to see several national parks or monuments during a 12-month period should obtain a Golden Eagle Passport, which provides free admission to all federal fee areas; it is available for a $25 fee. Admission is free to those holding a Golden Age Passport (available to those ages 62 and over for a one-time $10 fee) or Golden Access Passport (provided to the disabled). These passports can be obtained at fee collection stations in Death Valley.

At the park's visitor center, museum exhibits and a slide program shown every 30 minutes provide a good orientation to the natural and historic points of interest in the park. The information desk provides schedules of evening park ranger programs (given November through April) and guided walks and trips. Publications for sale include many sightseeing guides appealing to a wide variety of special interests.

Within the park, many roads, including those posted "primitive," are not maintained and should be attempted only by high-clearance four-wheel-drive vehicles. During the hot summer months, it is unwise to stray from major roads for any reason; during all seasons, sudden rainstorms can cause temporary washouts along both paved and dirt roads. Road closure signs should always be heeded. The prohibition against driving off established roads is strictly enforced.

Isn't it obvious how Mushroom Rock got its name?

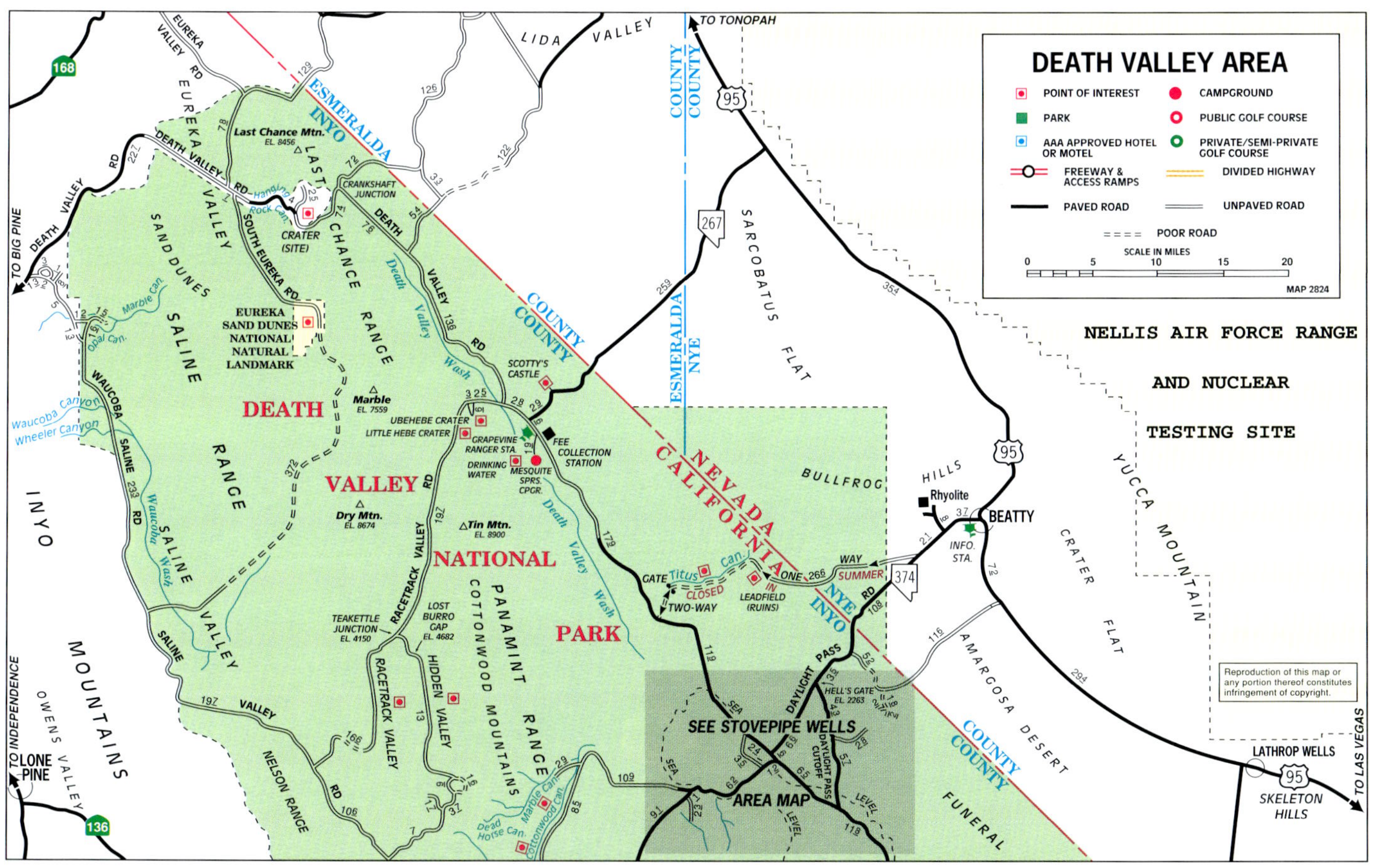
DEATH VALLEY AREA
POINT OF INTEREST
CAMPGROUND
PARK
PUBLIC GOLF COURSE
AAA APPROVED HOTEL OR MOTEL
PRIVATE/SEMI-PRIVATE GOLF COURSE
FREEWAY & ACCESS RAMPS
DIVIDED HIGHWAY
PAVED ROAD
UNPAVED ROAD
POOR ROAD
SCALE IN MILES
0 5 10 15 20
MAP 2824
NELLIS AIR FORCE RANGE
AND NUCLEAR
TESTING SITE
Reproduction of this map or any portion thereof constitutes infringement of copyright.
TO TONOPAH
LIDA VALLEY
COUNTY COUNTY
95
267
259
354
SARCOBATUS FLAT
ESMERALDA
NYE
YUCCA MOUNTAIN
CRATER FLAT
95
BULLFROG
HILLS
Rhyolite
BEATTY
37
108
21
1½
72
INFO. STA.
WAY
SUMMER
ONE-266
374
NYE
INYO
RD
116
294
AMARGOSA DESERT
LATHROP WELLS
95
SKELETON HILLS
TO LAS VEGAS
COUNTY COUNTY
FUNERAL
NEVADA
CALIFORNIA
GATE
Titus Can.
CLOSED
TWO-WAY
IN
LEADFIELD (RUINS)
11½
DAYLIGHT PASS
HELL'S GATE EL. 2263
52
3½
SEA
SEE STOVEPIPE WELLS
DAYLIGHT PASS CUTOFF
24
3½
2¾
65
LEVEL
57
2½
9½
SEA
23½
AREA MAP
LEVEL
11½
109
168
EUREKA VALLEY RD
ESMERALDA
INYO
Last Chance Mtn. EL. 8456
LAST CHANCE RANGE
129
126
122
3¾
72
54
DEATH
7½
DEATH VALLEY RD
227
Hanging Rock Can.
2½
CRATER (SITE)
CRANKSHAFT JUNCTION
TO BIG PINE
DEATH VALLEY RD
SOUTH EUREKA RD
Marble Can.
Opal Can.
SAND DUNES
1½
2½
1½
13
12
EUREKA SAND DUNES NATIONAL NATURAL LANDMARK
SALINE RANGE
Death Valley
136
RD
COUNTY COUNTY
SCOTTY'S CASTLE
3 25
28 29
DEATH
Marble EL. 7559
UBEHEBE CRATER
LITTLE HEBE CRATER
GRAPEVINE RANGER STA.
191
FEE COLLECTION STATION
DRINKING WATER
MESQUITE SPRS. CPGR.
VALLEY
372
Death Valley Wash
Wash
NATIONAL
Dry Mtn. EL. 8674
△Tin Mtn. EL. 8900
197
179
PARK
TEAKETTLE JUNCTION EL. 4150
LOST BURRO GAP EL. 4682
RACETRACK VALLEY
COTTONWOOD MOUNTAINS
PANAMINT RANGE
HIDDEN VALLEY
13
RACETRACK VALLEY RD
166
16
12
3½
Marble Can.
Cottonwood Can.
Dead Horse Can.
29
85
7
NELSON RANGE
106
197
VALLEY
WAUCOBA
SALINE 233 RD
Waucoba Canyon
Wheeler Canyon
Waucoba Wash
SALINE VALLEY
SALINE
INYO
MOUNTAINS
OWENS VALLEY
TO INDEPENDENCE
LONE PINE
136
TO LONE PINE

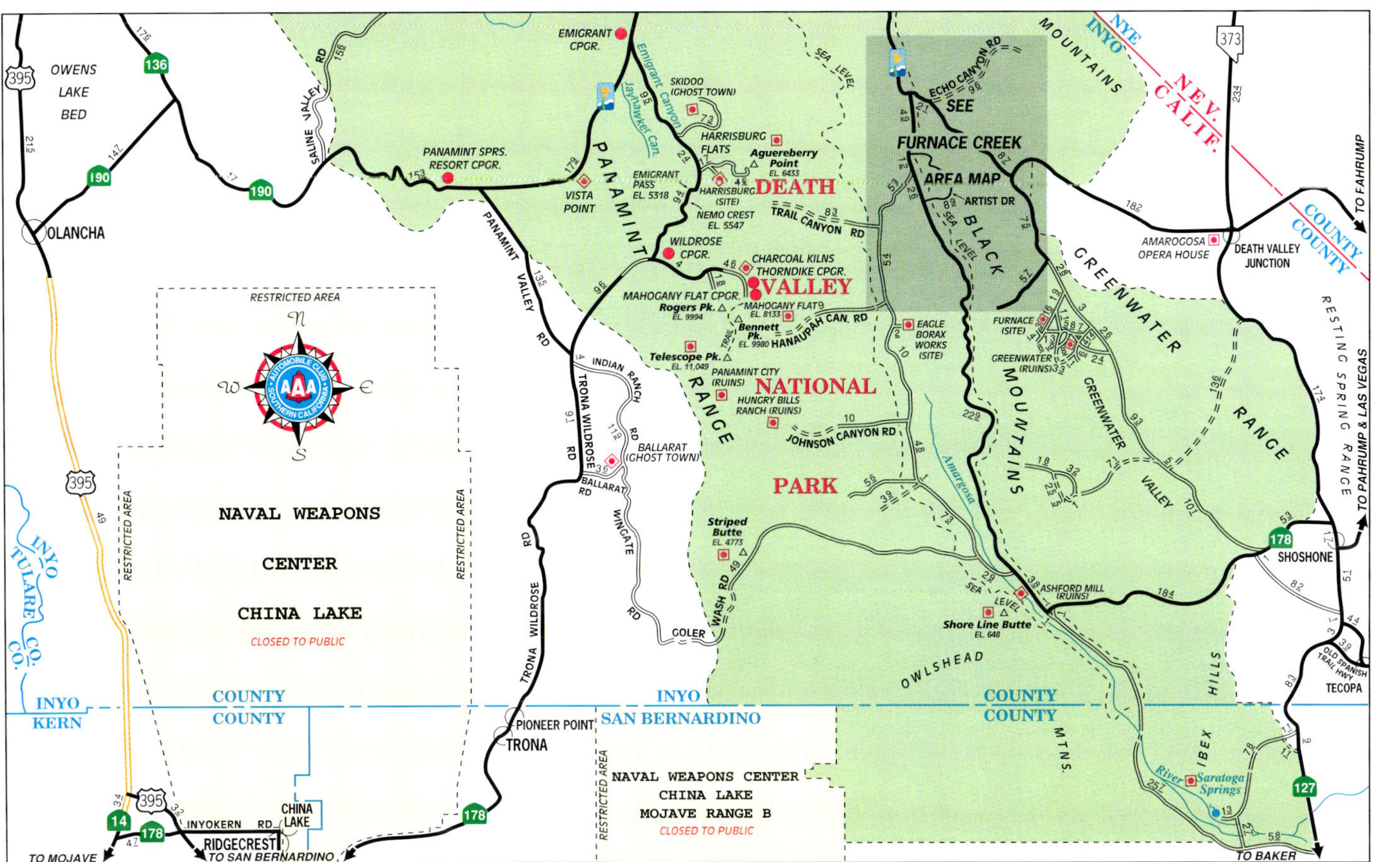
OWENS LAKE BED
136
395
215
142
190
190
OLANCHA
SALINE VALLEY RD
176
156
EMIGRANT CPGR.
Emigrant Canyon
Jayhawker Can.
PANAMINT
PANAMINT SPRS. RESORT CPGR.
SKIDOO (GHOST TOWN)
HARRISBURG FLATS
Aguereberry Point EL 6433
HARRISBURG (SITE)
DEATH
VISTA POINT
EMIGRANT PASS EL 5318
NEMO CREST EL 5547
TRAIL CANYON RD
WILDROSE CPGR.
CHARCOAL KILNS
THORNDIKE CPGR.
VALLEY
MAHOGANY FLAT CPGR.
Rogers Pk. EL 9994
MAHOGANY FLAT9 EL 8133
Bennett Pk. EL 9980
HANAUPAH CAN. RD
Telescope Pk. EL 11,049
PANAMINT CITY (RUINS)
NATIONAL
HUNGRY BILLS RANCH (RUINS)
PANAMINT VALLEY RD
INDIAN RANCH RD
TRONA WILDROSE RD
BALLARAT (GHOST TOWN)
BALLARAT RD
WINGATE RD
RANGE
PARK
JOHNSON CANYON RD
Striped Butte EL 4773
WASH RD
GOLER
RESTRICTED AREA
N E S W
NAVAL WEAPONS CENTER CHINA LAKE
CLOSED TO PUBLIC
RESTRICTED AREA
TRONA WILDROSE RD
PIONEER POINT
TRONA
INYO KERN
COUNTY COUNTY
INYO SAN BERNARDINO
COUNTY COUNTY
395
14
178
INYOKERN RD
CHINA LAKE
RIDGECREST
TO SAN BERNARDINO
TO MOJAVE
178
RESTRICTED AREA
NAVAL WEAPONS CENTER CHINA LAKE MOJAVE RANGE B
CLOSED TO PUBLIC
INYO TULARE CO. CO.
395
SEA LEVEL
ECHO CANYON RD
SEE FURNACE CREEK AREA MAP
ARTIST DR
SEA LEVEL
BLACK
NYE INYO
NEV. CALIF.
373
234
TO FAHRUMP
182
AMAROGOSA OPERA HOUSE
DEATH VALLEY JUNCTION
COUNTY COUNTY
EAGLE BORAX WORKS (SITE)
FURNACE (SITE)
GREENWATER (RUINS)
MOUNTAINS
GREENWATER
GREENWATER VALLEY
RANGE
229
Amargosa
Ashford Mill (RUINS)
Shore Line Butte EL 648
SEA LEVEL
184
OWLSHEAD
MTNS.
COUNTY COUNTY
IBEX HILLS
River
Saratoga Springs
251
RESTING SPRING RANGE
TO PAHRUMP & LAS VEGAS
174
101
136
178
SHOSHONE
OLD SPANISH TRAIL HWY
TECOPA
127
TO BAKER
93
18
71

DEATH VALLEY AREA

▼ *A Quick Guide to the Death Valley Area*

Effective March 22, 1997, area code (619) will change to (760).

Population   400

Elevation
292 ft. below sea level to 11,049 ft. above

Police Nonemergency
(619/760) 786-2331

Emergency Road Service for AAA Members

(800) AAA-HELP (in the USA and Canada)

(800) 955-4TDD (for the hearing impaired)

Newspapers

Local newspapers include the *Inyo Register*, *News-Review*, *Las Vegas Review* and the *Pahrump Valley Times*.

Radio Stations
Classical: KNPR (88.7 FM)

Bus

Limited service is provided by Greyhound to Beatty, Nev., and Ridgecrest, Calif.; phone (800) 231-2222. Las Vegas, Nev., 140 miles away, is the nearest large urban area with frequent scheduled bus service.

Train

The nearest Amtrak station is in Las Vegas, Nev., 140 miles away. Call (800) USA-RAIL for information.

Hospitals

Southern Inyo County Hospital
501 E. Locust St.
Lone Pine, CA 93545
(619/760) 876-5501

University Medical Center
1800 W. Charleston Blvd.
Las Vegas, NV 89102
(702) 383-2000

AAA Offices

California State Automobile
  Association
3312 W. Charleston Blvd.
Las Vegas, NV 89102-1892
(702) 870-9171

Automobile Club of Southern
  California
Ridgecrest District Office
114 S. Gemstone, Ste. A
Ridgecrest, CA 93555-4198
(619/760) 375-8426

Visitor Services

Tourist services available in Death Valley and the nearby town of Beatty, Nev., are summarized below. Other towns in the region offering tourist services include Ridgecrest, Trona, Shoshone and Tecopa. During summer, some facilities may close for the afternoon and open only briefly in the evening. Facilities operate year round unless otherwise indicated.

Additionally, diesel fuel is available in Pahrump, Olancha and eight miles north of Death Valley Junction on NV SR 373. Sanitary disposal stations for campers and trailers are located at Mesquite Springs, Sunset and Texas Springs campgrounds.

FURNACE CREEK RANCH

- **Park Headquarters** *(619/760) 786-2331.* Public telephone.

- **Store** *Open daily 7 a.m. to 10 p.m.* Ice and groceries.

- **Service station** *Open daily 7 a.m. to 7 p.m.* Diesel fuel, propane gas.

- Lodging; restaurants; campground; post office; coin laundry; showers; sanitary disposal station; paved, 3000-foot landing strips suitable for light planes (no aviation fuel available).

STOVEPIPE WELLS

- **Ranger Station** *(619/760) 786-2342.* Public telephone.

- **Store** *Open daily; mid-Oct. through mid-May 7 a.m. to 8 p.m., rest of year 8 a.m. to 6 p.m.* Ice, limited supplies, groceries.

- **Service station** *Open daily; mid-Oct through mid-May 7 a.m. to 8 p.m., rest of year 8 a.m. to 6 p.m.* Propane gas, white gas.

- Lodging; dining room; campground; sanitary disposal station; paved, 3000-foot landing strips suitable for light planes.

SCOTTY'S CASTLE

- **Grapevine Ranger Station** *(619/760) 786-2313.* Public telephone.

- **Service station** *Open daily 9 a.m. to 5:30 p.m.*

BEATTY, NEVADA

- **Ranger Station** *On SR 374. (702) 553-2200. Open daily 8 a.m. to 4 p.m.*

- **Service station** Diesel fuel.

AGUEREBERRY POINT *28 miles south of Stovepipe Wells via SR 190, Emigrant Canyon Rd. and 7 miles of 4x4 road.* The access road climbs 6½ miles from Emigrant Canyon to the point, named for a Basque shepherd turned prospector. From 6500 feet above the valley floor, the view encompasses much of the territory between Corkscrew Peak and Badwater. The best time to visit is in late afternoon, when the sunlight reflects the varied colors of the Funeral Mountains. Along the approach road is the site of Harrisburg, a small mining camp that existed briefly in the early 1900s before the boom days of Skidoo.

AMARGOSA OPERA HOUSE *Southeast of the park on SR 127 at Death Valley Junction. (619/760) 852-4441. Productions begin at 8:15 p.m.; mid-Oct. through the Sat. before Mother's Day on Fri., Sat. and Mon.; in May, Oct. and Dec. on Sat. only. Adults $8; ages 11 and under, $5.* Performances of ballet and pantomime, featuring many costume changes, are given by Marta Becket, a painter and dancer, in this converted movie theater.

ARTIST DRIVE *9 miles south of Furnace Creek off Badwater Rd. via a one-way paved road; vehicles or vehicle-trailer combinations in excess of 25 feet prohibited.* Oxidation has produced a rainbow of colors in the eroded clay deposits of ancient lake bed sediments. The colors are most intense during the late afternoon. Artists Palette, about halfway along the drive, is a particularly unusual mosaic of red, yellow, orange, green, violet, brown and black hues.

ASHFORD MILL RUINS *44 miles south of Furnace Creek via Badwater Rd. and a short spur road (dirt).* The fortress-thick concrete walls once housed a mill built in 1915 to process ore from a mine in the Black Mountains. Inefficient operations led to financial and legal difficulties, and the mill closed before its owners were able to realize a profit. Today only the foundations and a tailings pile remain to mark the site.

▼ *The Way to Death Valley*

Driving to Death Valley is one of those instances where the journey is as interesting as the result. From the west, SR 190 from Olancha and Panamint Springs through Towne Pass (elevation 4956 feet) is steep and narrow along some sections and is not recommended for vehicles pulling trailers. Entering from the south, the Trona-Wildrose Road from Trona through Emigrant Pass is a scenic approach to Death Valley. There is an unimproved section of road in Wildrose Canyon where vehicles and vehicle-trailer combinations in excess of 25 feet in length are prohibited; the preferred approach is to follow Panamint Valley Road north to its junction with SR 190 just east of Panamint Springs, then follow SR 190 east into Death Valley. **Note:** *Motorists towing recreational vehicles or trailers should enter Death Valley via either SR 178 at Shoshone or SR 190 at Death Valley Junction.*

BADWATER *18 miles south of Furnace Creek off Badwater Rd.* At 279.8 feet below sea level, this is the lowest point in Death Valley that is accessible by car. Two spots in the salt flats are the lowest elevations in the western hemisphere: –282 feet; they are 3⅓ and 4⅔ miles northwest of Badwater. The permanent spring-fed pool is not poisonous, although it contains very large amounts of chloride, sodium and sulfate. A soft-bodied saltwater snail, found only in the valley, shares the water with beetles and soldier fly larvae. The surrounding area may be the hottest place in the world during the summer months, when temperatures exceeding 120 degrees are typical.

The spring-fed pool near Badwater is home to snails, beetles and soldier-fly larvae.

BALLARAT GHOST TOWN *Southwest of the park off Trona-Wildrose Rd. (paved) via Ballarat Rd. (dirt).* Crumbling adobe walls and remnants of old cabins are the only remains of a town optimistically named after a famous gold center in Australia. Ballarat flourished between 1890 and the years preceding World War I as a lively supply town for prospectors working claims in the Panamint Valley region.

BORAX MUSEUM *At Furnace Creek. Exhibit building open daily 9:30 a.m. to 4:30 p.m. Free.* Large mining machinery

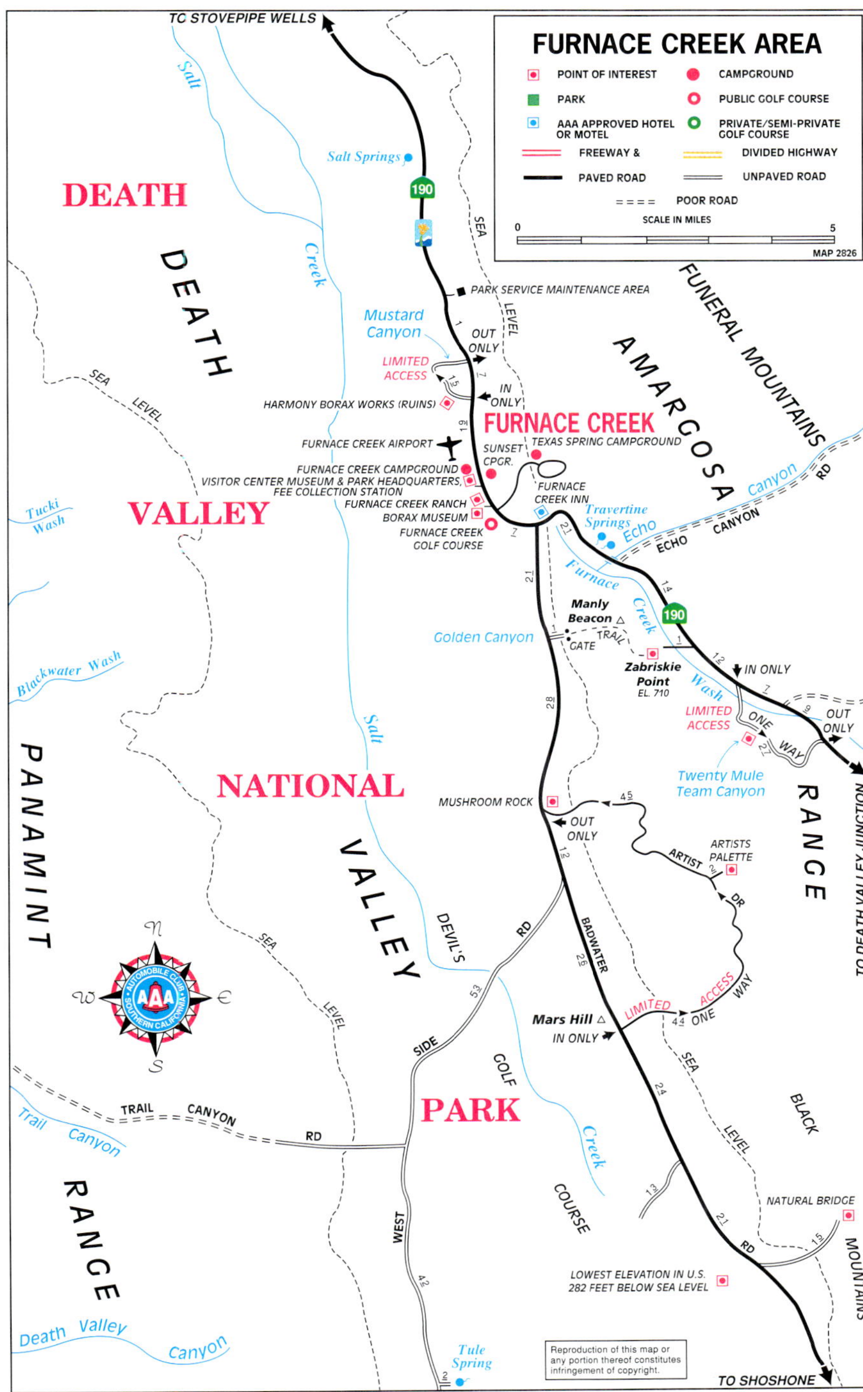

Reproduction of this map or any portion thereof constitutes infringement of copyright.

Antique mining equipment is on display at the Borax Museum.

and historical exhibits pertaining to Death Valley borax mining are on display. The main museum structure was moved from its original site in Twenty Mule Team Canyon, where it served as a boardinghouse for miners. The adjacent building is the original 20-mule-team barn, moved to Death Valley from its Mojave location.

BURNED WAGONS POINT *At Stovepipe Wells.* A historical marker just east of Stovepipe Wells Village describes a camp made here in December 1849 by a group of pioneers attempting a shortcut to the California gold fields. The travelers spent only a few days in the valley, long enough to burn their wagons (to smoke the meat of their last oxen) before heading west on foot over Towne Pass.

CHARCOAL KILNS *39 miles south of Stovepipe Wells off Emigrant Canyon Rd., 8½ miles east of Wildrose Campground.* Although they date only to 1877, these immense structures look like remnants of an ancient civilization. The 10 beehive-shaped kilns are each 30 feet in diameter and 30 feet tall. They were built to produce charcoal from the surrounding piñon pine forest for the Modoc Mine smelter, 25 miles to the west across the Panamint Valley. From the kilns a trail leads 4⅓ miles to Wildrose Peak (9064 feet), a gain of almost 3000 feet. The first 1½ miles are mostly uphill, but then the trail follows a saddle to the peak and some outstanding views of Death Valley.

CHLORIDE CITY GHOST TOWN *18 miles east of Stovepipe Wells via Daylight Pass Rd. and 7 miles of 4x4 road.* The city flourished as a silver mining center during the 1870s and again between 1905 and 1916. The inhabitants managed to build a road from Death Valley to Barstow. Now only a few shacks and foundations remain at the site. From Chloride Cliff (one mile southwest) there are extensive panoramas of the valley.

COTTONWOOD CANYON *20 miles west of Stovepipe Wells via a 4x4 road from Stovepipe Wells.* Steep canyon walls line the trail to Cottonwood

Spring. The rugged 4x4 road ends below the spring, but hikers can continue up the canyon along the shaded stream.

DANTE'S VIEW *25 miles south of Furnace Creek via SR 190 and Dante's View Rd.; vehicles or vehicle-trailer combinations in excess of 25 feet prohibited.* The spectacular view is best during the morning hours. Directly below are the Badwater area and miles of salt flats. Across the valley the sheer wall of the Panamint Mountains forms an imposing (and often snow-covered) barrier. Beyond, to the northwest, the Sierra Nevada is sometimes visible.

DEATH VALLEY BUTTES *12 miles east of Stovepipe Wells off Daylight Pass Rd.* These reddish-brown eroded hills provide an interesting contrast to the rounded sand dunes below on the valley floor and the rocky, dark-banded mountains (especially Corkscrew Peak) above.

DEVIL'S CORNFIELD *7 miles east of Stovepipe Wells on SR 190. Park at turnout and walk ¼ mile south.* Because of soil erosion, the arrowweed bushes in this area grow in individual clumps resembling strange corn shocks. The bush's name derives from the American Indians' use of the plants for arrow shafts.

DEVIL'S GOLF COURSE *13 miles south of Furnace Creek via Badwater Rd. and a graded dirt spur road.* As several ancient lakes evaporated, they left alternating layers of salt and gravel deposits on the valley floor. These layers are at least 1000 feet deep and cover an area of 200 square miles. Moisture rises to the surface from the shallow water table, carrying salt in solution. On the surface the moisture evaporates, leaving the salt

If Devil's Golf Course truly were a golf course, you'd have a devil of a time making par!

to crystallize and be sculpted into sharp ridges and spires by rain and wind. Listen to the hard crust (which is 95 percent pure table salt) expand and contract as the air temperature changes, and look for the occasional shallow water-filled depressions known as salt pools.

EAGLE BORAX WORKS SITE *20 miles south of Furnace Creek via Badwater Rd. and West Side Rd. (graded dirt).* Death Valley's first borax mill was established here in 1881. Problems with impure minerals, summer heat and competition from the Harmony Works combined to doom the enterprise after only two years. The site has been covered with soil for preservation; only small mounds remain.

ECHO CANYON *13 miles east of Furnace Creek via SR 190 and 9 miles of 4x4 road.* The canyon is cut deep into the Funeral Mountains near Furnace Creek. It is notable for some interesting and colorful geological formations and for the remains of a number of old mining camps.

EMIGRANT CANYON *18 miles southwest of Stovepipe Wells; vehicles or vehicle-trailer combinations in excess of 25 feet prohibited.* Harrisburg Flats, in the upper part of the canyon, is the remains of the ancient surface which existed before massive block faulting and folding lifted the mountains and lowered the basin that is now Death Valley.

EUREKA SAND DUNES *Located approximately 43 miles from Scotty's Castle and 50 miles from Big Pine; access from either Scotty's or Big Pine via a graded dirt road (check for current road conditions). Closed in summer.* These sand dunes, the highest in California, rise almost 700 feet from the Eureka Valley floor at the base of the Last Chance Mountain Range. This area supports about 54 species of plant life, including Eureka Valley Dune Grass, Eureka Dunes evening primrose and shining loco-weed. Cascading sand "sings," the sound resulting from vibrations during movement. Although closed to vehicles, the dunes themselves are open for hiking and playing in the sand. Hiking to the top is strenuous and three hours should be planned for the round trip. Photographers are rewarded with contrasting scenes of sand against the surrounding mountains. No drinking water is available at the dunes.

GOLDEN CANYON *3 miles south of Furnace Creek via Badwater Rd.* Late afternoon sunlight paints deep golden tones on the canyon walls, accenting the russet earth colors. American Indians used the red clay at the canyon mouth for face paint. Trails lead to three scenic areas: Red Cathedral, a large natural amphitheater; Manly Beacon, a clay pinnacle named for a pioneer hero

Manly Beacon captures his light in Golden Canyon.

Mustard Canyon, near the Harmony Borax Works Ruins, gets its coloring from salt and oxidizing iron in the clay soil.

who led a number of lost emigrants out of Death Valley in early 1850; and Zabriskie Point (see listing), offering a scenic overlook of an eroded landscape.

GREENWATER SITE *26 miles southeast of Furnace Creek via SR 190, Dante's View Rd. and 7 miles of 4x4 road.* A few foundations and a lot of rubble are all that remain of an enormous speculative fiasco. The town of Greenwater boomed after a 1905 copper discovery, thanks to exaggerated promotional campaigns, and had 1000 inhabitants, a bank, post office, stores, automobiles, telephones, two newspapers and a men's magazine. The area, however, lacked commercially useful ore, and by 1908 Greenwater was on its way to oblivion.

GROTTO CANYON *5 miles southeast of Stovepipe Wells via SR 190, a 4x4 road and trail.* A trail leads into the rugged canyon, where water erosion has carved numerous spectacular grotto formations.

HARMONY BORAX WORKS RUINS *2 miles north of Furnace Creek off SR 190 and a short spur road.* A short footpath with interpretive signs leads past the ruins of the refinery and some outlying buildings. The structures were used to process borax from 1882 to 1889. The minerals were then shipped by mule teams 165 miles over rugged desert to Mojave. A trail leads three miles northwest from the ruins across the salt flats to mounds of borax resembling haystacks. A one-way dirt road north of the works cuts through Mustard Canyon, set in a series of low clay hills colored by salt and oxidizing iron.

HIDDEN VALLEY *38 miles southwest of Scotty's Castle via Ubehebe Crater and 29 miles of graded dirt road.* This rugged and isolated area lies high on the western slope of the Cottonwood Mountains above the Racetrack. The valley is a place of great solitude; following heavy winter rains its floor is frequently transformed into a brilliant tapestry of color by spring wildflowers. A number of old mines are located in the immediate vicinity.

HUNGRY BILL'S RANCH RUINS
37 miles south of Furnace Creek via Badwater Rd., West Side Rd. (graded dirt) and Hanaupah Canyon Rd. (a 10-mile 4x4 road and unmaintained trail; check locally for current conditions). Ruins, traces of old fields and wild fruit trees remain to mark the site of an unusual desert enterprise. Swiss settlers established a farm here and grew vegetables, fruits and nuts to sell to the gold miners in Panamint City, 10 miles away. In later years the land was homesteaded by a Shoshone man named Hungry Bill, whose ancestors had lived in this area at the head of the north fork of Johnson Canyon. Trails lead from the end of the 4x4 road up both forks of the canyon, past springs and old mining sites.

JAYHAWKER CANYON *13 miles west of Stovepipe Wells off SR 190.* This canyon was one of the routes that the early pioneers took out of Death Valley in 1849. The hike up the canyon to Jayhawker Spring is about two miles.

KEANE WONDER MINE AND MILL RUINS *20 miles north of Furnace Creek via Daylight Pass Cutoff and 3 miles of graded dirt road.* Gold was discovered here in 1903, and the mine operations continued to produce profitable ore until 1916. There was another brief period of activity in the 1930s. Some mill ruins remain in the canyon; a steep one-mile trail follows the old tramway up the mountain to the mine, where there are a few old structures and some dangerous tunnels.

MAHOGANY FLAT *38 miles south of Stovepipe Wells via SR 190, Emigrant Canyon Rd., Wildrose Canyon and 4 miles of paved, graded dirt and 4x4 roads.* This is the highest point in the national park that can be reached by motor vehicle: 8133 feet. Situated in the midst of a forest of juniper and piñon pine, the area affords excellent views of the valley floor (where the temperature is often 40 degrees warmer).

MARBLE CANYON *14 miles west of Stovepipe Wells via a dirt and 4x4 road.* The narrow canyon has been cut deep into the Cottonwood Mountains by water erosion. The sheer walls are often composed of polished black limestone and in many places are etched with old Indian petroglyphs.

MOSAIC CANYON *2 miles south of Stovepipe Wells via SR 190 and a short*

These polished, multicolored rock walls are found in Mosaic Canyon.

graded dirt spur road. The road leads up a broad alluvial fan to the canyon's mouth, from which there is a sweeping view of the northern valley. A short walk into the canyon reveals patterned walls of polished, multicolored rock. Contrasts are most sharply defined around midday.

MUSHROOM ROCK *7 miles south of Furnace Creek via Badwater Rd.* This mass of old basalt has been eroded into its unusual shape by temperature extremes, water, rain and wind-blown sand and salt.

NATURAL BRIDGE *15 miles south of Furnace Creek via Badwater Rd. and a 2-mile dirt spur road. Closed in summer.* A path leads ¼ mile from the parking

Death Valley's assorted land forms include a Natural Bridge.

area into the canyon. Water rushing through cracks in weaker strata gradually undercut the rock and left a large natural bridge formation; it now looms 50 feet above the wash bed. Beyond, part of the canyon wall has been eroded into a grotto.

RACETRACK VALLEY *38 miles southwest of Scotty's Castle via Ubehebe Crater and 29 miles of graded dirt road (Racetrack Valley Rd.).* A 2½-mile-long dry mud flat in the middle of the valley is all that remains of an old lake. The flat is shaped like an oval racetrack; the outcropping at its northern end is known as The Grandstand. Rocks of varying sizes move across the lake bed, leaving long, faint tracks (straight, curved, looped or angled) in their wake. Geologists theorize that the rocks are pushed across the occasionally wet or icy surface by very high winds. The best times to find evidence of the strange migrations are at sunrise and sunset. Four-by-four roads lead to several old mines in the area.

RYAN *13 miles south of Furnace Creek via SR 190 and Dante's View Rd.* From 1914 through the 1920s Ryan was a lively, modern borax mining center. The site was closed down for economic reasons. The maintained buildings can be clearly seen from the road; however, the town is situated on private land and is not open to the public.

SALT CREEK *14 miles north of Furnace Creek via SR 190; 13 miles east of Stovepipe Wells via SR 190 and a 1-mile graded dirt spur road. Closed in summer.* A large freshwater lake covered this area as recently as 2000 years ago. Today the creek is home to a survivor from that era, the inch-long pupfish (*genus Cyprinodon*), which has successfully adapted to the heat, high salinity and intermittent lack of water in its present environment. In spring, schools of the fish, along with birds and other desert inhabitants, can be seen from the board-walk trail which parallels the creek area.

SAND DUNES *8 miles east of Stovepipe Wells via SR 190 and a short graded dirt spur road.* Sunrise, sunset and moonlit nights provide dramatic lighting for this 14-square-mile area. The changing contours, deep shadows and ripple patterns make an interesting contrast to the sharply edged mountain ranges silhouetted to the east and west. The mountain barriers, combined with opposing wind currents, prevent these large deposits of eroded quartz particles from moving cross-country. Morning visitors who look carefully will find many footprints and other traces left by nocturnal animal activities.

SARATOGA SPRINGS *83 miles south of Furnace Creek via SR 190, SR 127 and 10 miles of graded dirt and 4x4 roads.* Three all-year ponds at the southeastern corner of the park are home to one of the several varieties of pupfish. The ponds are also a seasonal habitat for countless migratory birds; coots nest in the reeds along the shore. This quiet aquatic area contrasts sharply with the dry, barren desert that surrounds it.

SCOTTY'S CASTLE *Rooms open to the public only during guided tours, which are given daily 9 a.m. to 5 p.m. Adults $8; adults with Golden Age Passport and children 6-11, $4; ages 5 and under free. Visitors can take self-guided tours of the surrounding grounds and adjacent struc-tures; an informative guide booklet is sold at the ticket booth.* Construction of this extravagant mansion in the Spanish-Moorish style began in 1924. The property, formally named Death Valley Ranch, was intended as the winter vacation residence of Albert Johnson,

Scotty's Castle is a "must see" for many visitors.

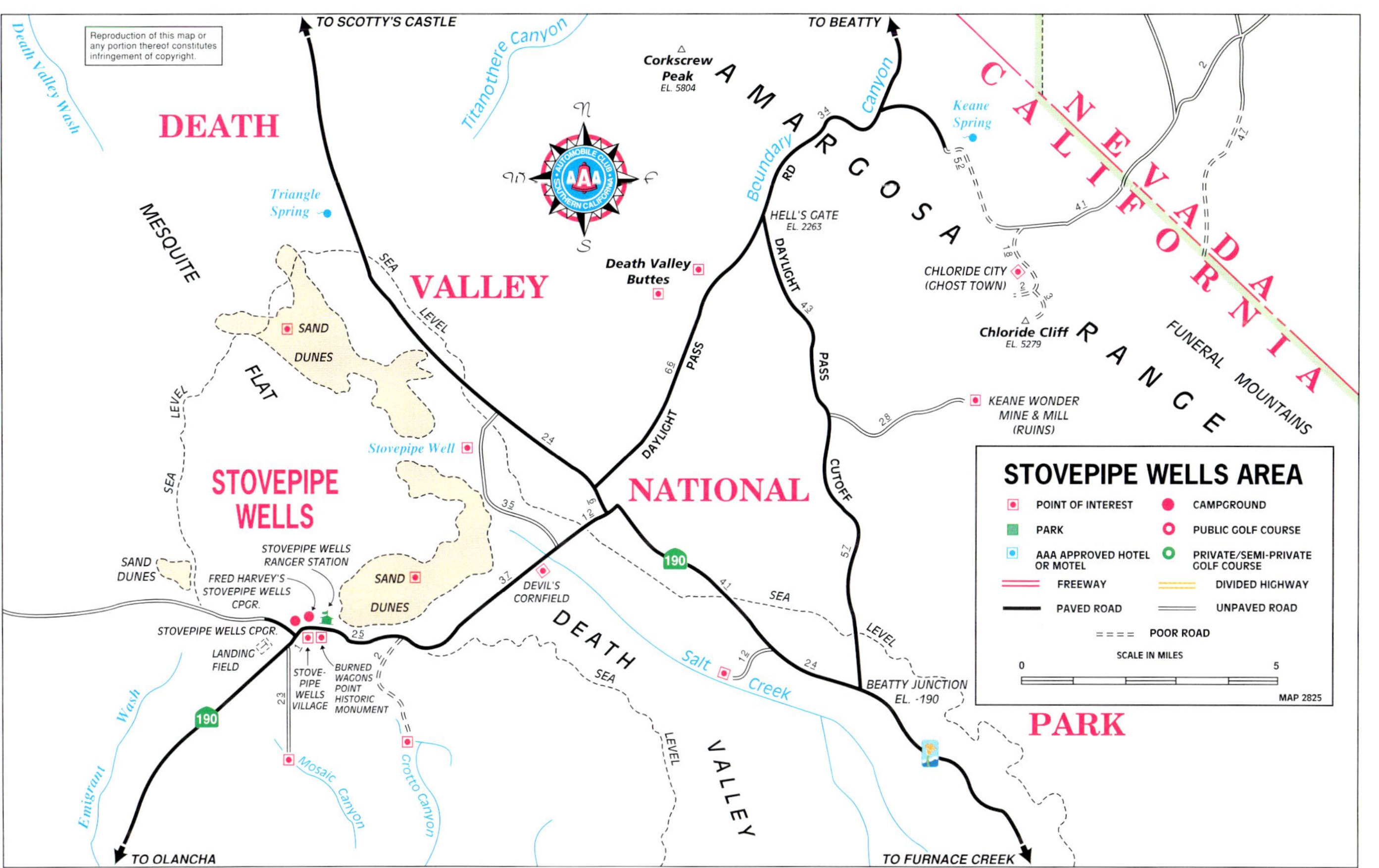
DEATH VALLEY AREA
Reproduction of this map or any portion thereof constitutes infringement of copyright.
Death Valley Wash
TO SCOTTY'S CASTLE
Titanothere Canyon
Corkscrew Peak EL 5804
AMARGOSA
Boundary RD
Canyon
TO BEATTY
Keane Spring
C A L I F O R N I A
N E V A D A
DEATH
Triangle Spring
MESQUITE
HELL'S GATE EL 2263
DAYLIGHT
CHLORIDE CITY (GHOST TOWN)
Death Valley Buttes
VALLEY
SAND DUNES
FLAT
Chloride Cliff EL 5279
RANGE
FUNERAL MOUNTAINS
SEA LEVEL
DAYLIGHT PASS
PASS
CUTOFF
KEANE WONDER MINE & MILL (RUINS)
Stovepipe Well
STOVEPIPE WELLS
NATIONAL
STOVEPIPE WELLS AREA
POINT OF INTEREST
PARK
AAA APPROVED HOTEL OR MOTEL
CAMPGROUND
PUBLIC GOLF COURSE
PRIVATE/SEMI-PRIVATE GOLF COURSE
FREEWAY
DIVIDED HIGHWAY
PAVED ROAD
UNPAVED ROAD
POOR ROAD
SCALE IN MILES
0
5
MAP 2825
SAND DUNES
STOVEPIPE WELLS RANGER STATION
FRED HARVEY'S STOVEPIPE WELLS CPGR.
STOVEPIPE WELLS CPGR.
LANDING FIELD
STOVE-PIPE WELLS VILLAGE
BURNED WAGONS POINT HISTORIC MONUMENT
SAND DUNES
DEVIL'S CORNFIELD
190
SEA LEVEL
DEATH
SEA LEVEL
Salt Creek
VALLEY
BEATTY JUNCTION EL -190
PARK
Emigrant Wash
190
Mosaic Canyon
Grotto Canyon
TO OLANCHA
TO FURNACE CREEK

a Chicago insurance millionaire. Its popular name comes from Walter Scott, a cowboy, prospector, publicity hound, prevaricator, storyteller and friend of Johnson. Scotty, whose enthusiastic flamboyance was financed by Johnson, managed to convince many that the "castle" was his personal domain. The house and outbuildings cost at least $2.5 million; work was never completed. The interior is filled with interesting, well-crafted furnishings and innovative features.

SHORE LINE BUTTE *43 miles south of Furnace Creek, visible from Badwater Rd.* West of the Ashford Mill Ruins rises a black basaltic hill marked with several horizontal bands along its flanks. This is Shore Line Butte, named for the water lines cut into it as the level of the Ice Age Lake Manly was progressively lowered by climatic changes.

SKIDOO GHOST TOWN *27 miles south of Stovepipe Wells via SR 190, Emigrant Canyon Rd. and 8 miles of 4x4 road.* Only a few scattered ruins remain at the site of a once-thriving community of 700 people. Between 1906 and 1917, gold mines in the surrounding hills were some of the few in the area that actually showed a profit. The town's residents put up a number of buildings, helped run a telegraph line across Death Valley to Rhyolite, and piped in water roughly 23 miles from a spring in the Panamint Mountains. The town acquired its name because this mileage was the same as the number in a popular saying of the era: "Twenty-Three Skidoo."

STOVEPIPE WELL *9 miles northeast of Stovepipe Wells off SR 190 and a short, graded dirt spur road.* An old, rusted hand-operated pump marks the location of a waterhole that was important to all preautomotive travelers in the valley. Old stovepipes were pounded into the sand to form walls for the well.

STRIPED BUTTE *66 miles south of Furnace Creek via Badwater Rd. and 24 miles of graded dirt and 4x4 road.* The butte rises abruptly from a level plain of granitic rubble which forms the floor of a high valley in the southern Panamints. The various bands of sediments have been thrust upward and twisted into an almost vertical direction, and thereby offer a good example of the prodigious geologic forces that have shaped the region.

TELESCOPE PEAK *44 miles south of Stovepipe Wells via SR 190, Emigrant Canyon Rd., Wildrose Canyon, and a graded dirt and 4x4 road (5 miles); 7-mile hiking trail to peak.* At 11,049 feet, this is the highest point in the park, and the views from the summit can be awesome. Both the highest (Mount Whitney) and the lowest (near Badwater) points in the contiguous United States are visible. A seven-mile hiking trail leads from Mahogany Flat through woods and across brushy and rocky terrain to the peak. Most of the path climbs moderately, but there are some steep sections near the top. Bristlecone pines, the world's oldest living trees, grow on the slopes above 10,000 feet. Hikers should carry plenty of water and should plan to climb during the late spring or fall months.

TITUS CANYON *27 miles northeast of Stovepipe Wells via SR 190, Daylight Pass Rd. and NV SR 374. Closed in summer.* The one-way route through the canyon begins seven miles east of the Nevada state line. The road crosses desert terrain, climbs via steep grades and switchbacks to a crest, then begins a long, gradual descent. West of the crest lie the rusting remnants of the town of Leadfield, which existed for only one year during the 1920s. Investors were duped by a promoter who salted some mined rubble to make it appear rich in lead ore. He published preposterous handbills showing ships full of ore navigating the dry Amargosa River through the middle of Death Valley.

Below Leadfield, Titus Canyon begins to narrow and steepen. The rock colors change from bright red and yellow hues to softer gray and russet tones. Titanic rock upthrusts are evident in the swirling stratification of the canyon walls. In the last three miles, the road passes through narrows whose sheer walls tower more than 500 feet above the canyon floor. The final section (a two-way road west of the mouth of the canyon) crosses a broad alluvial fan to its junction with the paved highway on the valley floor.

The best time to drive through the canyon is during the morning hours, when the light is behind the car. Hikers can enter from the western end and explore the narrows and beyond; the distance from the mouth to Leadfield is nine miles and the elevation gain is 3040 feet.

TWENTY MULE TEAM CANYON
5 miles southeast of Furnace Creek via SR 190 and a 3-mile, graded dirt loop road; vehicles or vehicle-trailer combinations in excess of 25 feet prohibited. The hills which form the canyon are the eroding remnants of an ancient lake bed; they audibly expand and contract as the temperature changes. One of the first frame structures in Death Valley (now the Borax Museum at Furnace Creek) was originally built here. Despite its name, the canyon never was visited by 20-mule-team borax wagons.

UBEHEBE CRATER *9 miles west of Scotty's Castle via Grapevine Ranger*

Ubehebe Crater is part of an ancient volcano.

Station. A violent volcanic explosion left this crater, which measures nearly ½-mile wide and 500 feet deep. Oxidizing ores give orange tints to the dark volcanic ash of the crater's eastern walls. A trail leads from Ubehebe ½ mile south to Little Hebe, a smaller crater whose age—perhaps 1000 years—makes it a relative infant on the geological time scale.

ZABRISKIE POINT *5 miles southeast of Furnace Creek off SR 190.* This spot, named for a borax mine superintendent, provides an excellent view of a vast area of uplifted, eroded yellow hills. These unusual contours are the remains of a lake bed whose sediments were deposited 5 to 10 million years ago. Sunrise highlights the hills in the foreground with gold tones and contrasting shadows, while the mountains across the valley subtly change from pink to blue-gray.

Beatty, Nevada Area

This town of 1900 people is nine miles from the park's border and 40 miles from the park's headquarters at Furnace Creek. Beatty offers travelers a range of services including accommodations, restaurants, campgrounds, and automotive supplies and repairs. Gambling in the local casinos is also an attraction to some visitors.

RHYOLITE *37 miles northeast of Furnace Creek via SR 190, Daylight Pass Cutoff, NV SR 374 and a 1-mile paved spur road.* The town enjoyed an incredibly prosperous period for a few years following a 1904 gold discovery in the nearby Bullfrog Hills. Tents quickly gave way to elaborate stone and wood frame buildings; two railroads were built, along with a stock exchange, hotels, an ice

Zabriskie Point provides spectacular views, especially at sunrise.

plant, opera house, churches and many other substantial structures. Nearly 6000 people lived in the modern, bustling community. The inevitable crash ended it all, and today there remain only a few imposing stone and concrete ruins and the old railroad depot. Abandoned mines dot the hillsides, and a weathered cemetery south of town is a symbolic legacy. Fences have been installed to protect the remnants of several structures from vandalism.

Annual Events

Along with the regular points of interest and recreation available throughout the year, the California desert area offers many special once-a-year affairs and sporting events. Detailed information about these events can be obtained by calling the telephone number shown in the listing or by contacting any district office of the Automobile Club of Southern California.

Effective March 22, 1997, area code (619) will change to (760).

January

BOB HOPE CHRYSLER CLASSIC GOLF TOURNAMENT *Various golf courses in the Palm Springs area. (619/760) 346-8184.* This five-day Pro-Am tournament benefits local charities. Tickets also sold through Ticketmaster.

COLORADO RIVER COUNTRY MUSIC FESTIVAL *Colorado River Country fairgrounds, Blythe. (619/760) 922-8166.* This event features three days of country music and dancing, arts and crafts booths, food vendors and a fun-fair.

PALM SPRINGS INTERNATIONAL FILM FESTIVAL *Palm Springs. (619/760) 322-2930.* More than 100 international films will be screened at this 17-day event, including world, U.S. and North American premieres.

SCORE 400 OFF-ROAD RACE *Parker. (520) 699-2174.* This three-day event includes registration of vehicles, sale of all types of automobile paraphernalia, food and crafts and culminates in a one-day, 400-mile off-road race on a course marked in the desert.

January-February

CARROT FESTIVAL *Various locations in Holtville. (619/760) 356-2923.* The ever-popular carrot is given a 10-day celebration with a parade, horse show, carrot cookoff, dance, arts and crafts show and carnival. (See separate listing.)

February

FRANK SINATRA CELEBRITY INVITATIONAL GOLF TOURNAMENT *Westin Mission Hills, Rancho Mirage. (619/760) 323-9411.* A coed field of 288 amateurs and 72 celebrities join in two days of play to benefit Desert Hospital and Barbara Sinatra Children's Center at Eisenhower Medical Center.

NATIONAL DATE FESTIVAL *Desert ExpoCentre, 46-350 Arabia St., Indio. (619/760) 863-8247.* This well-known festival offers exhibits of dates and citrus fruits, arts and crafts items, a junior livestock show, parade, an Arabian Nights Pageant, camel and ostrich races and a carnival. (See separate listing.)

SCULPTURELAND FINE ARTS FESTIVAL *57-325 Madison St., La Quinta (mailing address: P.O. Box 1566, 92253).*

In October the Old West comes alive during Calico Days.

A Fine Arts Festival is held at Sculptureland in La Quinta.

(619/760) 564-1166. The visual arts are the main focus of this three-day event, which also includes entertainment and food.

YAKULT SWALLOWS BASEBALL
Ray Croc Complex, Yuma. (520) 344-3800. This professional team from Tokyo, Japan, plays intrasquad games for three weeks as part of their spring training.

March

BALLOON FEST *Downtown Parker.* *(520) 699-3174.* Up to 60 hot air balloons float over the city in this three-day festival that includes a parade, food booths and swap meet.

CALIFORNIA MID-WINTER FAIR
Imperial County Fairgrounds, Imperial. *(619/760) 355-1181.* Ten days of festivities include motorcycle and auto races, livestock and art shows, country-western and rock concerts, a carnival, commercial exhibits such as jewelry, leather goods, clothing and accessories, and competitive exhibits of such items as home arts, photography, and arts and crafts.

DESERT DIXIELAND JAZZ FESTIVAL
Doubletree Resort Hotel, Cathedral City. *(619/760) 321-5277.* Twelve jazz bands team up for three days of music, entertainment and dancing.

LA QUINTA ARTS FESTIVAL *La Quinta Community Park, La Quinta.* *(619/760) 564-1244.* This four-day, nationally acclaimed, juried art show exhibits creations by more than 225 artists. Entertainment, food and refreshments are available.

MIDNIGHT AT THE OASIS FESTIVAL
Ray Croc Complex, Yuma. (520) 783-0071. Over 600 pre-1972 cars and trucks, rock-and-roll music and dancing, arts and crafts booths and food vendors abound during this three-day nostalgia marathon.

NABISCO DINAH SHORE LPGA GOLF TOURNAMENT *Mission Hills Country Club, Rancho Mirage. (619/760) 324-4546.* The four-day LPGA tournament showcasing the abilities of professional women golfers follows two days of celebrity Pro-Am play.

U.S. NAVY BLUE ANGELS AIR SHOW *Naval Air Facility, El Centro. (619/760) 339-2519.* Typically, the Navy's precision flying team performs following their winter training. This one-day event also features precision parachute jumping, static aircraft displays and stunt flying.

April

BORREGO SPRINGS GRAPEFRUIT FESTIVAL *Various locations, Borrego Springs. (619/760) 767-5555.* One weekend of activities includes an arts and crafts show, beef pit barbecue, all-state picnic, jazz festival, and vintage car show and run.

April-August

MAVERICKS CLASS A TEAM BASE-BALL GAMES *Maverick Stadium, 12000 Stadium Wy. at Adelanto Rd., Adelanto. (619/760) 246-6287.* Scheduled night and Sunday afternoon games are played throughout the summer against other California Class A teams.

April-September

CLASS AA BASEBALL *Sun Stadium, Sunrise Plaza Community Center, Baristo Rd. and Sunrise Wy., Palm Springs. (619/760) 323-7867.* Scheduled evening games are played April through the beginning of September between the Palm Springs Suns and other minor league teams.

May

GRUBSTAKE DAYS *Twentynine Palms Hwy, Yucca Valley. (619/760) 365-6323.* The celebration over Memorial Day weekend includes a rodeo, dancing, a parade and a carnival.

June

HUCK FINN JUBILEE *Mojave Narrows Regional Park, Victorville. (909) 387-2757.* This Father's Day weekend of activities includes a mountain man village, musical entertainment, food and craft booths, a cow-chip throwing contest, Indian dance exhibitions and more.

INNER TUBE RACES *Parker. (520) 669-3174.* Participants compete for fun and prizes in this well-known one-day float down the river.

July/August

SAN BERNARDINO COUNTY FAIR *San Bernardino County Fairgrounds, Victorville. (619/760) 951-2200.* A ten-day fair features an FFA livestock competition and auction, 4-H Club exhibits, rodeo events, art shows, sewing and baked goods exhibits and nightly entertainment.

September

FALL CONCERT SERIES *Sunrise Plaza Park, Palm Springs. (619/760) 323-8272.* Outdoor concerts featuring a variety of music are offered free each Tuesday evening in the park. Call for dates and scheduled performers.

October

BORREGO DESERT FESTIVAL *Various locations, Borrego Springs. (619/760) 767-5555.* During the last weekend in October, Borrego Springs celebrates with an arts and crafts show, parade, barbecue, chili cookoff, variety show, pancake breakfast, beauty pageant and live entertainment.

CALICO DAYS *Calico Ghost Town, Yermo. (619/760) 254-2122.* The National Gunfight Stunt Championship is staged along with a Wild West parade, a burro race and a he-man triathlon on Columbus Day weekend. Music and kids games are also available.

FESTIVAL OF THE SPRINGS *Downtown Desert Hot Springs. (619/760) 329-6403, (800) 346-3347.* Two days of activities include crafts and food booths, country music, entertainment and a chili cookoff sponsored by the International Chili Society.

LONDON BRIDGE DAYS *London Bridge and vicinity, Lake Havasu City. (520) 855-4115.* This four-day event includes a parade, concerts, dancing, a fun-fair, and arts and crafts vendors.

PIONEER DAYS *Various locations, Twentynine Palms. (619/760) 367-3445.* A rodeo, contests, entertainment, dancing and a carnival are offered to celebrate the early pioneering times in the Morongo Basin.

TWENTY MULE TEAM DAYS *Boron. (619/760) 762-5810.* During the first weekend of October, Boron hosts a parade, game booths, horseshoe pitching, a pet parade and a battle of the bands. Contests are held to select "baby beautiful" and an Honorary Mayor. Food and entertainment.

November

BRAWLEY CATTLE CALL *Various locations, Brawley. (619/760) 344-3160.* The Cattle Call's PRCA rodeo is famous throughout California. Festivities include a chuck wagon breakfast,

parade, barbecue, mariachi music, bluegrass festival and a cookoff. (See separate listing.)

COLORADO RIVER CROSSING/ BALLOON FESTIVAL *Various locations in Yuma. (520) 783-0071.* More than 50 hot air balloons, music, dancing, fireworks and an arts and crafts fair highlight this two-day event.

DEATH VALLEY ENCAMPMENT *Furnace Creek Ranch, Death Valley National Park. (619/760) 786-2331. Reservations should be made well in advance.* This five-day event commemorates the pioneer entry and crossing of Death Valley. Activities include gold-panning, painting and photography exhibits, guided hikes, pioneer costume contests, chili cookoffs, a parade featuring trail riders and wagons, and tours of the Borax Museum and other points of interest.

GOLF CART PARADE *El Paseo Dr., Palm Desert. (619/760) 346-6111.* Held on the second Sunday of the month, the parade has such traditional entries as bands and horses, as well as non-traditional entries—decorated golf carts. Festivities include parade events, food booths and entertainment.

LA QUINTA FALL FESTIVAL OF THE ARTS: JAZZART '96 *La Quinta Community Park, La Quinta. (619/760) 564-1244.* Fine wines and the finest of jazz accent a three-day show, where 125 fine artists present jewelry, ceramics, glass, handmade textiles, paintings and furniture. Food and refreshments are also available.

THE SKINS GAME *Rancho La Quinta Golf Course, Palm Desert. (619/760) 777-7755.* Four of the most celebrated golfers play for high-stakes prizes in two days of hole-by-hole competition. The Thanksgiving weekend event is preceded by a one-day tournament featuring special guest professiona_ and amateur golfers.

December

NEW YEAR'S JAZZ AT INDIAN WELLS *Stouffer Esmeralda and Hyatt Grand Champions resorts, Indian Wells. (310) 799-6055.* An international jazz festival features all forms of jazz performed by 23 bands and guest artists. The four-day event over New Year's Eve includes up to seven performance venues.

Recreation

Surprisingly, the Desert Areas can be as inviting to recreation as any less arid region. From rugged hiking to royal resort golfing, there is an abundance of enjoyable activities. For those who relax with various forms of transportation apart from automobiles, there are incredibly scenic bike trails, picturesque dunes for off-road vehicles, horseback riding—and even boating and fishing.

Effective March 22, 1997, area code (619) will change to (760).

BICYCLING

Joshua Tree National Park

Joshua Tree offers cyclists an abundance of touring opportunities. More than 80 miles of paved and 45 miles of unpaved roads provide access to one of California's most fascinating desert landscapes. Cyclists get a close-up look at the park's striking geologic curiosities, and the diverse world of plants and animals that have adapted to the desert environment.

The difficulty levels of routes in the park are as varied as the landscape. Riding can be as easy as a relaxed spin through a campground or as challenging as the six-mile, 1000-foot climb from Lost Horse Valley to Keys View.

When riding in Joshua Tree, it is important to carry water and to be aware of rising temperatures. The best times for extensive touring are in spring, fall and winter, when temperatures are mild. Also, because the desert environment is extremely fragile and easily damaged, cyclists must limit their explorations to established roads. Roads do not have shoulders and caution should be exercised.

Palm Springs

In addition to the quiet desert beauty of the Palm Springs area, attractions on or near the unusual Palm Springs Bikeway System offer something for everyone. Four public parks—Desert Highland, Ruth Hardy, Sunrise Plaza Community Center and Demuth—contain rest and recreation areas. Other points of interest include the airport and Desert Fashion Plaza, a downtown shopping mall. The excellent scenery along this system is best seen in late afternoon, when mountain shadows envelop the area in hazy twilight and temperatures drop to comfortable ranges. In spring, wildflowers are abundant.

The Palm Springs Bikeway System generally uses lightly traveled streets to provide the cyclist with routes to any point in the city and the surrounding area. The major sections of the bikeway are along Camino Real, Murray Canyon

---

Water sports are featured at Mayflower County Park in Blythe.

Drive and Toledo Avenue, Sunrise Way from Mesquite Avenue to Alejo Road, and Belardo Road between Sunny Dunes Road and Alejo Road. Several minor loops are designated within the perimeter of the system, including a section within the Tahquitz Wash; cyclists can enter at the west end of North Riverside Drive and follow the wash east as far as Cathedral Canyon Country Club. The Palm Springs Recreational Services Division has a Bicycle Touring Guide posted in their lobby; they are located at 401 S. Pavillion Way, phone (619/760) 323-8272.

A note of caution—in some places, particularly on small connecting streets, there is not enough room for safe maneuvering. Other areas of the bikeway allow up to 16 feet for use by cyclists, pedestrians or equestrians. The route is well lit for the most part, but those portions that are lighted at night also have the highest volumes of cars on the road. Traffic is especially heavy in the downtown area. Bike riders should wear something cool while riding, since temperatures often exceed 100 degrees.

GOLFING

Golf courses abound in the Southern California desert, primarily in the resort cities area. In fact, the Coachella Valley contains one of the highest concentrations of golf courses of any region in the United States.

Public, semi-private and private courses are listed by community. Public and semi-private golf course listings give general street directions from the nearest freeway. For detailed directions refer to Automobile Club of Southern California street maps. Since private courses are not open to the general public, only the telephone number is provided; contact the course directly for information about reciprocal agreements and guest play.

Information given for each course includes the name, location, mailing address, phone number and facilities available, plus yardage, par, and slope and USGA ratings (all from men's white tees). Some 9-hole courses show a slope and USGA rating that reflects play on that 9 holes plus another 9-hole course, or double play on the same course. Unless otherwise stated, each course is open daily all year. The abbreviation N/A means the information was not available. Greens fees are given for play during peak season. Many 9-hole courses list 18-hole fees because they require 18 holes of play. Some courses have senior citizen rates; call for information. Military golf courses listed in this publication show greens fees that apply to civilian guests of military personnel.

Information in this book is published as it is received from the individual courses. The publication has been made as complete as possible; however, a few courses have been intentionally omitted at the request of the operators, and some failed to respond to our request for information.

All semi-private and private courses have restrictions on public play ranging from members and guests only to liberal reciprocal agreements with members of other courses. It is impossible to list all of the restrictions for each course, so please telephone the course directly if in doubt. Reservations are advised at most courses; some country clubs require reservations months in advance.

CALIFORNIA

Apple Valley

APPLE VALLEY COUNTRY CLUB
Private
(619/760) 242-3125.

JESS RANCH GOLF CLUB Public
7 miles east of I-15 off Bear Valley Rd. at 10885 Apple Valley Rd., 92308. (619/760) 240-1800. Rates: Mon.-Fri. $13, Sat.-Sun. $18.

18-hole course. 5008 yards; par 65; 101 slope; 63.3 rating. Golf shop, professional, power carts, hand carts, rental clubs, driving range; restaurant, snack bar.

Barstow

SUN AND SKY GOLF COURSE Public
3 miles west of I-15 via Lenwood Rd. and Main St., off National Trails Hwy. at 2781 Country Club Dr., 92311. (619/760) 253-5201. Closed Dec. 25. Rates: Mon.-Fri. $6.50, Sat.-Sun. $9.50.

9-hole course. 3125 yards; par 36. Clubhouse, golf shop, professional, power carts, hand carts, rental clubs, driving range; coffee shop.

TEES AND TREES GOLF COURSE
Private (Military)
(619/760) 577-6431.

Bermuda Dunes

BERMUDA DUNES COUNTRY CLUB
Private
(619/760) 345-2771.

Blythe

BLYTHE MUNICIPAL GOLF COURSE
Public
4 miles north of I-10 off Defain Blvd. at 4708 Wells Rd., 92225. (619/760) 922-7272. Closed Dec. 25. Rates: daily $10-$17.

18-hole course. 6567 yards; par 72; 104 slope; 70.7 rating. Clubhouse, golf shop, professional, power carts, hand carts, rental clubs, driving range; coffee shop, snack bar; cocktails.

Blythe Municipal Golf Course enjoys many days of sunshine.

Borrego Springs

CLUB CIRCLE GOLF CLUB Public
10 miles northwest of SR 78 off Borrego Springs Rd. at Marker Ln. (Box 306, 92004). No phone. Rates: daily $10 for 18 holes or less.

9-hole course. 1154 yards; par 27.

DE ANZA COUNTRY CLUB Private
(619/760) 767-5105.

RAMS HILL COUNTRY CLUB Semi-Private
6 miles north of SR 78 off Yaqui Pass Rd. at 1881 Rams Hill Rd., 92004. (619/760) 767-5125. Rate includes mandatory golf cart: daily $65.

18-hole course. 6328 yards; par 72; 1125 slope; 70.7 rating. Clubhouse, locker room, golf shop, professional, power carts, rental clubs, driving range; tennis, swimming; restaurant, coffee shop; cocktails.

ROAD RUNNER CLUB Semi-Private
10 miles northeast of SR 78 off Borrego Springs Rd. at 1010 Palm Canyon Dr., 92004. (619/760) 767-5373. Rate: daily $15.

18-hole course. 2500 yards; par 54. Golf shop, hand carts, rental clubs.

Brawley

DEL RIO COUNTRY CLUB Semi-Private
1 mile east of SR 111 at 102 E. Del Rio Rd., 92227. (619/760) 344-0085. Closed Dec. 25. Rates: Mon.-Fri. $26, Sat.-Sun. $31.

18-hole course. 6001 yards; par 70; 105 slope; 67.9 rating. Clubhouse, locker room, golf shop, professional, power carts, hand cart, rental clubs, driving range; tennis; cocktails.

California City

TIERRA DEL SOL Public
7 miles north of SR 58 off California City Blvd. at 10300 N. Loop Dr., 93505.
(619/760) 373-2384. Rates: Mon.-Fri. $14, Sat.-Sun. $18.

18-hole course; 6310 yards; par 72; 121 slope; 69.9 rating. Clubhouse, golf shop, professional, power carts, hand carts, rental clubs, driving range; restaurant, coffee shop, snack bar; beer and wine.

Cathedral City

DATE PALM COUNTRY CLUB Semi-Private
½ mile north of SR 111 at 36-200 Date Palm Dr., 92234. (619/760) 328-1315. Closed Oct. Rate includes mandatory golf cart: daily $40.

18-hole course. 3083 yards; par 58; 90 slope; 54.9 rating. Clubhouse, locker room, golf shop, professional, power carts, hand carts, rental clubs; restaurant, coffee shop, snack bar; beer and wine.

DESERT PRINCESS COUNTRY CLUB AND RESORT Private
(619/760) 322-2280.

LAWRENCE WELK'S DESERT OASIS COUNTRY CLUB Semi-Private
1 mile north of SR 111 at 34567 Cathedral Canyon Dr., 92234. (619/760) 328-6571. Rates include mandatory golf cart: daily $35-85.

Three 9-hole courses. The **Lake View Course** is 3063 yards; par 36. The **Mountain View Course** is 3109 yards; par 36. The **Resort Course** is 2958 yards; par 36. Clubhouse, locker room, golf shop, professional, power carts, rental clubs, driving range; tennis; restaurant, snack bar; cocktails.

OUTDOOR RESORTS/PALM SPRINGS RV RESORT Private (Residential)
(619/760) 324-8638.

Death Valley

FURNACE CREEK GOLF CLUB Public
In Furnace Creek Ranch at SR 190, 92328.

(619/760) 786-2301. Closed Sept. Rate includes golf cart: daily $36.

18-hole course. 5891 yards; par 72; 101 slope; 66.5 rating. Golf shop, professional, power carts, hand carts, rental clubs, driving range; tennis, swimming; restaurant, coffee shop, snack bar; cocktails.

Desert Center

LAKE TAMARISK GOLF COURSE
Public
1½ miles north of I-10 off Kaiser Rd. at 26251 Parkview Dr., 92239. (619/760) 227-3203. Rate: daily $12.

9-hole course. 2934 yards; par 35. Clubhouse, power carts, hand carts.

Desert Hot Springs

DESERT CREST COUNTRY CLUB
Semi-Private
69400 S. Country Club Dr., 92241. (619/760) 329-8711. Rate: daily $7.

9-hole course. 999 yards; par 27. No facilities.

DESERT DUNES GOLF CLUB Public
2 miles north of I-10 at 18-550 Palm Dr., 92240. (619/760) 251-5370. Rates include golf cart: Mon.-Thu. $40-95, Fri.-Sun. $40-105

18-hole course. 6205 yards; par 72; 124 slope; 70.2 rating. Clubhouse, locker room, golf shop, professional, power carts, rental clubs, driving range; snack bar; beer and wine.

MISSION LAKES COUNTRY CLUB
Semi-Private
5½ miles north of I-10 off Indian Ave. at 8484 Clubhouse Blvd., 92240. (619/760) 329-8061. Closed Dec. 25. Rates include mandatory golf cart: Mon.-Fri. $55, Sat.-Sun. $65.

18-hole course. 6396 yards; par 71; 124 slope; 70.6 rating. Clubhouse, locker room, golf shop, professional,

power carts, rental clubs, driving range; tennis, swimming; restaurant, snack bar; cocktails.

SANDS MOBILE COUNTRY CLUB
Public
15500 Bubbling Wells Rd., 92240. (619/760) 329-8816. Closed mid-Sept. through Nov. 1. Rate: daily $15.

9-hole course. 1527 yards; par 3. Clubhouse, golf shop, hand carts, rental clubs; tennis, swimming.

SANDS R.V. COUNTRY CLUB Public
3½ miles north of I-10 via Palm Dr. and Dillon Rd. at 16400 Bubbling Wells Rd., 92240. (619/760) 251-1731. Rate: daily $10.

9-hole course. 2127 yards; par 32. Clubhouse, golf shop, hand carts, rental clubs, driving range; tennis, swimming.

Edwards Air Force Base

MUROC LAKE GOLF COURSE Private (Military)
(805) 277-3469.

El Centro

BROKEN SPOKE COUNTRY CLUB
Public
South of I-8 off 4th St. at 225 Wake Ave., 92243. (619/760) 353-4653. Rate: daily $8.50.

9-hole course. 1750 yards; par 31. Clubhouse, golf shop, professional, power carts, hand carts, rental clubs, driving range (night lighting); coffee shop, snack bar; beer and wine.

LAKEVIEW GOLF COURSE Public
South of I-8 at 1589 Drew Rd., 92243. (619/760) 352-6638. Rate: daily $8.

9-hole course. 2176 yards; par 33. Clubhouse, golf shop, professional, power carts, hand carts, rental clubs, driving range; swimming; snack bar; beer.

Hesperia

HESPERIA GOLF AND COUNTRY CLUB Semi-Private
7 miles east of I-15 via Main St. and I Ave. at 17970 Bangor Ave., 92345. (619/760) 244-9301. Rates: Mon.-Fri. $15; Sat., Sun. and holidays $20.

18-hole course. 6996 yards; par 72; 127 slope; 72.4 rating. Clubhouse, golf shop, power carts, hand carts, rental clubs, driving range; restaurant, snack bar; cocktails.

Holtville

BARBARA WORTH GOLF RESORT & CONVENTION CENTER Public
2 miles north of I-8 off Barbara Worth Rd. at 2050 Country Club Dr., 92250-9609. (619/760) 356-5842, 356-2806. Rates include mandatory golf cart: Mon.-Thu. $29, Fri.-Sun. $33.

18-hole course. 6302 yards; par 71; 119 slope; 70.0 rating. Clubhouse, locker room, golf shop, professional, power carts, hand carts, rental clubs, driving range; swimming; restaurant, coffee shop, snack bar; cocktails.

Indian Wells

DESERT HORIZONS COUNTRY CLUB Private
(619/760) 340-4646, 340-4651.

ELDORADO COUNTRY CLUB Private
(619/760) 346-8081.

THE GOLF RESORT AT INDIAN WELLS Public
North of SR 111 at 44-500 Indian Wells Ln., 92210. (619/760) 346-4653. Rates include golf cart: Mon.-Thu. $110, Fri.-Sun. $120.

Two 18-hole courses. The **East Course** is 6630 yards; par 72; 118 slope; 71.6 rating. The **West Course** is 6500 yards; par 72; 120 slope; 70.7 rating. Clubhouse, locker room, golf shop, professional, power carts, hand carts, rental clubs, 2 driving ranges; restaurant, coffee shop, snack bar; cocktails.

INDIAN WELLS COUNTRY CLUB Private
(619/760) 345-2561.

THE VINTAGE CLUB Private
(619/760) 862-2076.

Indio

INDIAN PALMS RESORT Semi-Private
2½ miles south of I-10 at 48630 Monroe St., 92201. (619/760) 775-4444. Rates include mandatory golf cart: daily $25-50.

Three 9-hole courses. The **Indian Palms Course** is 3178 yards; par 36. The **Mountain Palms Course** is 3187 yards; par 36. The **Royal Palms Course** is 3003 yards; par 36. Golf shop, professional, power carts, rental clubs, driving range; tennis, swimming; restaurant, snack bar; cocktails.

INDIO GOLF CLUB Public
83040 Ave. 42, 92201. (619/760) 347-9156. Rate: daily $8.

18-hole course. 3004 yards; par 54; 77 slope; 54.1 rating. Clubhouse, golf shop, professional, power carts, hand carts, rental clubs, driving range, night lighting for golf course and driving range; snack bar; beer.

OUTDOOR RESORTS MOTORCOACH RESORT AND SPA Private (Residential)
(619/760) 775-7255.

RANCHO CASA BLANCA RV RESORT AND COUNTRY CLUB Private (Residential)
(619/760) 775-7116.

Lancaster

RANCHO SIERRA GOLF CLUB Public
8½ miles east of SR 14 off Ave. G at 47205 60th St. East, 93535. (805) 946-1080. Rates: Mon.-Fri. $8, Sat.-Sun. $11.

9-hole course. 2600 yards; par 35. Clubhouse, golf shop, professional, power carts, hand carts, rental clubs, driving range (night lighting); snack bar; beer.

La Quinta

INDIAN SPRINGS COUNTRY CLUB Public
North of SR 111 at 46080 Jefferson St., 92253. (619/760) 775-3360. Rates include mandatory golf cart: Mon.-Thu. $35, Fri.-Sun. $45.

18-hole course. 6139 yards; par 71; 109 slope; 68.6 rating. Clubhouse, golf shop, professional, power carts, rental clubs, driving range; snack bar; beer.

LA QUINTA COUNTRY CLUB Private
(619/760) 546-4151.

LA QUINTA RESORT AND CLUB Semi-Private
½ mile south of SR 111 off Washington St. Mountain and Dune Courses: 50-200 Avenida Vista Bonita, 92253; Citrus Course: 50-503 Jefferson St., 92253. (619/760) 564-7610. Rates include mandatory golf cart: Mountain Course— Mon.-Thu. $195, Fri.-Sun. $210; Dunes Course—Mon.-Thu. $125, Fri.-Sun. $140; Citrus Course is private.

Three 18-hole courses (one private). The **Mountain Course** is 6300 yards; par 72; 130 slope; 71.5 rating. The **Dunes Course** is 6230 yards; par 72; 124 slope; 70.1 rating. Clubhouse, locker room, golf shop, professional, power carts, rental clubs, driving range; restaurant, snack bar; cocktails.

PALM ROYALE COUNTRY CLUB Public
1 mile north of SR 111 off Washington St. and Fred Waring Dr. at 78-259 Indigo Dr., 92253. (619/760) 345-9701. Closed in Oct. for two weeks. Rate: daily $20.

18-hole course. 2009 yards; par 54. Clubhouse, locker room, golf shop, professional, hand carts, rental clubs; restaurant; beer and wine.

PGA WEST GOLF COURSE Private
(619/760) 564-7100.

PGA WEST GOLF COURSE Public
6 miles south of I-10 off Jefferson St. at 56-150 PGA Blvd., 92253. (619/760) 564-7170. Rates include mandatory golf cart: TPC Stadium Course—Mon.-Thu. $195, Fri.-Sun. $210; Jack Nicklaus Resort Course—Mon.-Thu. $160, Fri.-Sun. $180.

Two 18-hole courses. The **TPC Stadium Course** is 6164 yards; par 72; 132 slope; 69.9 rating. The **Jack Nicklaus Resort Course** is 6037 yards; par 72; 124 slope; 69.0 rating. Clubhouse, locker room, golf shop, professional, power carts, rental clubs, driving range; tennis, swimming; restaurant, coffee shop, snack bar; cocktails.

RANCHO LA QUINTA GOLF COURSE Private
(619/760) 777-7799.

Mojave

CAMELOT GOLF COURSE Public
1 mile west of SR 14 at 3430 Camelot Blvd., 93501. (805) 824-4107. Rates: Mon.-Fri. $7, Sat.-Sun. $9.

9-hole course. 3084 yards; par 36. Clubhouse, golf shop, professional, power carts, hand carts, rental clubs, driving range; snack bar; beer.

Needles

NEEDLES MUNICIPAL GOLF COURSE Public
North of I-40 via Broadway and Bridge Rd. at 144 Marina Dr., 92363. (619/760) 326-3931. Rate: daily $18.75.

18-hole course. 6222 yards; par 70; 112 slope; 69.0 rating. Golf shop, professional, power carts, hand carts, rental clubs, driving range; restaurant, coffee shop, snack bar; cocktails.

Palmdale

ANTELOPE VALLEY COUNTRY CLUB
Private
(805) 947-3400.

DESERT AIRE GOLF COURSE Public
4 miles east of SR 14 at 3620 E. Ave. P, 93550. (805) 267-5666. Closed Dec. 25. Rates: Mon.-Fri. $8, Sat.-Sun. $9.50.

9-hole course. 3178 yards; par 36. Clubhouse, golf shop, professional, power carts, hand carts, driving range (night lighting); restaurant; beer and wine.

Palm Desert

AVONDALE GOLF CLUB Private
(619/760) 345-2727.

BIGHORN GOLF CLUB Private
(619/760) 341-4653.

CHAPARRAL COUNTRY CLUB
Private
(619/760) 340-1501.

DESERT FALLS COUNTRY CLUB
Semi-Private
3 miles west of SR 10 off Country Club Dr. at 1111 Desert Falls Pkwy., 92211. (619/760) 340-5646. Closed Oct. Rates include mandatory golf cart: Mon.-Thu. $125, Fri.-Sun. $150.

18-hole course. 6174 yards; par 72; 121 slope; 69.3 rating. Clubhouse, locker room, golf shop, professional, power carts, rental clubs, driving range; restaurant, coffee shop, snack bar; cocktails.

DESERT SPRINGS RESORT AND SPA
Semi-Private
2 miles south of I-10 off Cook St. at 74-855 Country Club Dr., 92260. (619/760) 341-1756. Rates include mandatory golf cart: Mon.-Thu. $125, Fri.-Sat. $135.

Two 18-hole courses. The **Palm Course** is 6143 yards; par 72; 114 slope; 69.0 rating. The **Valley Course** is 6063 yards; par 72; 109 slope; 68.5 rating. Clubhouse, locker room, golf shop, professional, power carts, rental clubs, driving range; restaurant, coffee shop, snack bar; cocktails.

EMERALD DESERT COUNTRY CLUB AND R.V. RESORT Public
3 miles southeast of I-10 off Monterey Ave. at 76-000 Frank Sinatra Dr., 92211. (619/760) 345-4770. Rate: daily $20.

9-hole course. 1821 yards; par 31. Clubhouse, golf shop, power carts, hand carts, rental clubs; snack bar; beer.

GOLF CENTER AT PALM DESERT
Public
1 mile north of SR 111 off Cook St. at 74-945 Sheryl Ave., 92260. (619/760) 779-1877. Rates: daily $9-12.

9-hole course. 1000 yards; par 27. Clubhouse, golf shop, professional, hand carts, rental clubs, driving range; restaurant; cocktails.

INDIAN RIDGE COUNTRY CLUB
Private
(619/760) 772-7272.

IRONWOOD COUNTRY CLUB Private
(619/760) 346-0551.

THE LAKES COUNTRY CLUB Private
(619/760) 568-4321.

MARRAKESH COUNTRY CLUB
Private
(619/760) 568-2688.

MONTEREY COUNTRY CLUB Private
(619/760) 346-1115.

OASIS COUNTRY CLUB Semi-private
1 mile southwest of I-10 off Washington St. and Country Club Dr. at 42-300 Casbah Wy., 92211. (619/760) 345-2715. Closed Oct. and Dec. 25. Rate: daily $35.

18-hole course. 3118 yards; par 60; 88 slope; 55.1 rating. Clubhouse, locker room, golf shop, professional, power carts, hand carts, rental clubs, driving range; restaurant, snack bar; cocktails.

PALM DESERT COUNTRY CLUB
Semi-Private
1½ miles southwest of I-10 via Washington St. and Fred Waring Dr. at 77-200 California Dr., 92211. (619/760) 345-2655. Closed Dec. 25. Rates include mandatory golf cart: Course 1—Mon.-Thu. $25-40, Fri.-Sun. $25-50; Course 2—daily $10.

One 18-hole course and one 9-hole course. The 18-hole **Course 1** is 6360 yards; par 72; 116 slope; 70.9 rating. The 9-hole **Course 2** is 2085 yards; par 34. Clubhouse, locker room, golf shop, professional, power carts, hand carts, driving range; restaurant, coffee shop, snack bar; cocktails.

PALM DESERT GREENS COUNTRY CLUB Private
(619/760) 346-2941.

PALM DESERT RESORT COUNTRY CLUB Public
1 mile southwest of I-10 off Washington St. at 77-333 Country Club Dr., 92211. (619/760) 345-2791. Rates: Mon.-Thu. $25-60, Fri.-Sun. $30-75.

18-hole course. 6291 yards; par 72; 112 slope; 69.2 rating. Clubhouse, locker room, golf shop, professional, power carts, rental clubs, driving range; tennis; restaurant, snack bar; cocktails.

PALM VALLEY COUNTRY CLUB
Private
(619/760) 345-2742.

PORTOLA COUNTRY CLUB Private
(619/760) 568-1592.

SANTA ROSA COUNTRY CLUB
Private
(619/760) 568-5717.

SHADOW MOUNTAIN GOLF CLUB
Private
(619/760) 346-8242.

SUN CITY PALM DESERT Semi-Private
½ mile north of I-10 off Washington St. at 38-180 Del Webb Blvd., 92211. (619/760) 772-2201. Closed Dec. 25. Rates include mandatory golf cart: daily $45-75.

18-hole course. 6162 yards; par 72; 123 slope; 70.0 rating. Clubhouse, golf shop, professional, power carts, rental clubs, driving range; restaurant, snack bar.

SUNCREST COUNTRY CLUB Semi-Private
3 miles south of I-10 off Monterey Ave. at 73-450 Country Club Dr., 92260. (619/760) 340-2467. Closed Sept. and Oct. Rate: daily $19.

9-hole course. 2250 yards; par 33. Clubhouse, golf shop, professional, power carts, hand carts, rental clubs, driving range; snack bar; beer and wine.

WOODHAVEN COUNTRY CLUB
Private
(619/760) 345-7513.

Palm Springs

CANYON COUNTRY CLUB Private
(619/760) 327-1321.

CANYON ESTATES GOLF COURSE
Private
(619/760) 327-1346.

CANYON SOUTH GOLF COURSE
Public
2 miles south of SR 111 (E. Palm Canyon Dr.) off Palm Canyon Dr. at 1097 Murray Canyon Dr., 92264. (619/760) 327-2019. Rates include mandatory golf cart: Mon.-Thu. $40, Fri.-Sun. $50.

18-hole course. 6528 yards; par 71; 109 slope; 69.6 rating. Locker room, professional, power carts, rental clubs, driving range; snack bar.

MESQUITE GOLF AND COUNTRY CLUB Public
1 mile north of SR 111 (E. Palm Canyon Dr.) at 2700 E. Mesquite Ave., 92264. (619/760) 323-9377. Rates include mandatory golf cart: Mon.-Thu. $75, Fri.-Sun. $85.

18-hole course. 6123 yards; par 72; 117 slope; 69.8 rating. Clubhouse, locker room, golf shop, professional, power carts, rental clubs, driving range; restaurant, coffee shop, snack bar; cocktails.

O'DONNELL GOLF CLUB Private
(619/760) 325-2259.

PALM SPRINGS COUNTRY CLUB Public
2½ miles southwest of I-10 via Palm Canyon and Vista Chino drs. at 2500 Whitewater Club Dr., 92262. (619/760) 323-2626. Rates include mandatory golf cart: Mon.-Thu. $40, Fri.-Sun. $50.

18-hole course. 6396 yards; par 72; 110 slope; 68.8 rating. Clubhouse, golf shop, professional, power carts, rental clubs, driving range; restaurant, snack bar; cocktails.

SEVEN LAKES COUNTRY CLUB Private
(619/760) 328-9774.

TAHQUITZ CREEK GOLF COURSE Public
1 mile northeast of SR 111 at 1885 Golf Club Dr., 92264. (619/760) 328-1005. Rates: Legend Course—Mon.-Thu. $35, Fri.-Sun. (includes mandatory golf cart) $55. Resort Course (includes mandatory golf cart)—Mon.-Thu. $75, Fri.-Sun. $85.

Two 18-hole courses. The **Legend Course** is 6452 yards; par 72; 114 slope; 69.7 rating. The **Resort Course** is 6256 yards; par 72; 116 slope; 69.2 rating. Clubhouse, golf shop, professional, power carts, hand carts, rental clubs, driving range; restaurant, coffee shop, snack bar; cocktails.

TOMMY JACOBS' BEL-AIR GREENS Public
1 mile west of SR 111 off Ramon Rd. at 1001 S. El Cielo Rd., 92264. (619/760) 322-6062. Rates: Mon.-Fri. $16, Sat.-Sun. $18.

9-hole course. 1768 yards; par 32. Clubhouse, golf shop, professional, hand carts, rental clubs, driving range (night lighting); restaurant, snack bar; cocktails.

Rancho Mirage

THE CLUB AT MORNINGSIDE Private
(619/760) 321-1555.

DESERT ISLAND GOLF AND COUNTRY CLUB Private
(619/760) 328-2111.

MISSION HILLS COUNTRY CLUB Private
(619/760) 324-7336.

MISSION HILLS NORTH GOLF COURSE Public
1½ miles west of I-5 at 70-705 Ramon Rd., 92270. (619/760) 770-9496. Closed two weeks in Nov. Rates include mandatory golf cart: Mon.-Thu. $55-120, Fri.-Sun. $60-130.

18-hole course. 6643 yards; par 72; 124 slope; 71.3 rating. Clubhouse, golf shop, professional, power carts, rental clubs, driving range; restaurant; cocktails.

RANCHO LAS PALMAS COUNTRY CLUB Private
(619/760) 862-4551.

RANCHO MIRAGE COUNTRY CLUB Semi-Private
2 miles north of SR 111 at 38-500 Bob Hope Dr., 92270. (619/760) 324-4711. Closed Oct. Rates include mandatory golf cart: Mon.-Fri. $70, Sat.-Sun. $80.

18-hole course. 5823 yards; par 70; 119 slope; 69.5 rating. Clubhouse, locker room, golf shop, professional, power carts, rental clubs, driving range; coffee shop, snack bar; cocktails.

THE SPRINGS CLUB Private
(619/760) 328-0590.

SUNRISE COUNTRY CLUB Private
(619/760) 328-1139.

TAMARISK COUNTRY CLUB Private
(619/760) 328-1090.

THUNDERBIRD COUNTRY CLUB
Private
(619/760) 328-2161.

WESTIN MISSION HILLS GOLF CLUB
Public
1½ miles south of SR 10 via Ramon Rd. and Bob Hope Dr. at 71-501 Dinah Shore Dr., 92270. (619/760) 328-3198. Rates include mandatory golf cart: Mon.-Thu. $120, Fri.-Sun. $130.

18-hole course. 6196 yards; par 70; 126 slope; 70.3 rating. Clubhouse, locker room, golf shop, professional, power carts, rental clubs, driving range; restaurant, coffee shop, snack bar; cocktails.

Ridgecrest

CHINA LAKE GOLF CLUB Public
Arrive at main gate 8 miles east of US 395 off Inyokern Rd.; 826200D, Bldg. 2606, Naval Air Weapons Station, 93555. (619/760) 939-2976. Rate: daily $12.

18-hole course. 6850 yards; par 72; 114 slope; 70.7 rating. Clubhouse, locker room, golf shop, professional, power carts, hand carts, rental clubs, driving range; snack bar; cocktails.

Thousand Palms

IVEY RANCH COUNTRY CLUB Semi-Private
3 miles southeast of I-10 off Ramon Rd. at 74-580 Varner Rd., 92270. (619/760)

343-2013. Closed Oct. Rates include mandatory golf cart: daily $20.

9-hole course. 2473 yards; par 35. Clubhouse, golf shop, professional, power carts, driving range; snack bar.

TRI-PALM ESTATES Private
(Residential)
(619/760) 343-3669.

Trona

TRONA GOLF AND SOCIAL CLUB
Public
This course failed to respond to our inquiry.

Twentynine Palms

DESERT WINDS GOLF COURSE
Private (Military)
(619/760) 830-6132.

ROADRUNNER DUNES GOLF COURSE Public
2 miles north of SR 62 off Adobe Rd. at 4733 Desert Knoll Rd., 92277. (619/760) 367-5770. Rate: daily $9.

9-hole course. 3100 yards; par 36. Clubhouse, golf shop, professional, power carts, hand carts, rental clubs, driving range; snack bar; beer.

Victorville

SPRING VALLEY LAKE COUNTRY CLUB Private
(619/760) 245-5356.

VICTORVILLE MUNICIPAL GOLF COURSE Public
East of I-15 via Palmdale Rd. and 7th St. at 14144 Green Tree Blvd., 92392. (619/760) 245-4860. Rates include mandatory golf cart: Mon.-Fri. $37; Sat., Sun. and holidays $40.

18-hole course. 6640 yards; par 72; 121 slope; 71.2 rating. Clubhouse, golf shop, professional, power carts, hand carts, rental clubs; restaurant, coffee shop; cocktails.

Yucca Valley

BLUE SKIES COUNTRY CLUB Public
North of SR 62 off Camino del Cielo at 55100 Martinez Tr., 92284. (619/760) 365-0111, (800) 877-1412. Rates: Mon.-Thu. $15, Fri.-Sun. $18.

18-hole course. 6115 yards; par 71; 108 slope; 69.8 rating. Clubhouse, professional, power carts, hand carts, rental clubs, driving range; restaurant; cocktails.

ARIZONA

Lake Havasu City

LONDON BRIDGE GOLF CLUB Semi-Private
1½ miles north of SR 95 at 2400 Club House Dr., 86405. (520) 855-2719. Rates: London Bridge Course—daily $15-55; Stone Bridge Course—daily $10-40.

Two 18-hole courses. **London Bridge Course** is 6298 yards; par 71; 120 slope; 68.9 rating. **Stone Bridge Course** is 5766 yards; par 71; 109 slope; 66.8 rating. Golf shop, professional, power carts, rental clubs, driving range; restaurant, snack bar.

HAVASU ISLAND GOLF COURSE Public
2 miles west of SR 95 at 1000 McCulloch Blvd., 86403. (520) 855-2131. Rates: daily $18-27.

18-hole course. 4312 yards; par 61; N/A slope; N/A rating. Golf shop, professional, power carts, hand carts, rental clubs, driving range; snack bar.

QUEENS BAY GOLF COURSE Public
200 yards west of SR 95 at 1477 Queens Bay, 86403. (520) 855-4777. Rates: daily $14.

9-hole course. 1600 yards; par 27. Golf shop, professional, power carts, hand carts, rental clubs; snack bar.

Yuma's Desert Hills Municipal Golf Course provides a challenging round of golf.

Parker

EMERALD CANYON GOLF COURSE
Public
*Along SR 95 at 72 Emerald Canyon Dr.,
85344. (520) 667-3366. Rates: daily
$18-35.*

18-hole course. 5903 yards; par 72;
120 slope; 68.1 rating. Golf shop,
professional, power carts, hand carts,
rental clubs; snack bar.

Yuma

**COCOPAH BEND RV & GOLF
RESORT** Public
*3½ miles south of I-8 at 6800 S. Strand,
85364. (520) 343-1663. Rates: daily
$10-18.*

18-hole course. 5251 yards; par 69;
100 slope; 65.0 rating. Golf shop,
professional, power carts, hand carts,
rental clubs, driving range; snack bar.

**DESERT HILLS MUNICIPAL GOLF
COURSE** Public
*4½ miles southwest of I-8 at 1245 Desert
Hills Dr., 85364. (520) 344-4653. Rates:
daily $8-30.*

18-hole course. 6300 yards; par 72;
113 slope; 68.8 rating. Golf club,
professional, power carts, hand carts,
rental clubs, driving range; restaurant,
snack bar.

MESA DEL SOL GOLF CLUB Public
*Along I-8 at 10583 Camino del Sol,
85367. (520) 342-1283. Rates: daily
$18-35.*

18-hole course. 6767 yards; par 72;
124 slope; 71.8 rating. Golf club,
professional, power carts, hand carts,
rental clubs, driving range; restaurant,
snack bar; cocktails.

YUMA GOLF & COUNTRY CLUB
Private
(520) 726-4210.

HIKING

Hiking trails in the Southern California
desert cover a variety of terrain—
canyons, oases, mountains, former
mining sites—and offer scenic vistas,
historic settings and typical desert flora
and fauna. Some of the most popular
trails appear as points of interest in
this book's geographical chapters.
Most of the trails listed here afford
moderate to challenging hikes. Hikers
should be sure to take along adequate
water and protection from the elements. It may also be helpful to review
the Desert Survival Tips in *California
Desert Areas.*

Antelope Valley California Poppy Reserve

*The poppy reserve's 8½ miles of trails wind
through hills that are covered with flowers
in spring. Trails are paved for handicap
access into the poppy fields. Guided nature
walks are held on weekends in spring
when the flowers are in bloom. Picnicking
is available adjacent to the visitor center.
To protect plant life visitors are asked to
stay on the established trails.*

ANTELOPE BUTTE VISTA POINT
Begins 1⅛ miles from the visitor center.
This path is a short spur off the
Antelope Loop North Trail.

**ANTELOPE NORTH & SOUTH LOOP
TRAIL** *Begins east of visitors center.*
The northern trail is 1⅗ miles long;
the southern loop is 1½ miles.

KITANEMUK VISTA POINT *Bisects the
Antelope Loop Trail east of visitors center.*
This path is 7⁄10 mile long.

**POPPY NORTH & SOUTH LOOP
TRAIL** *Begins west of visitors center.* The
trail's north section is 1 7⁄10 miles long;
the south portion is 1⅕ miles in length.

TEHACHAPI VISTA POINT *Begins ⁷⁄₁₀ miles from the visitor center.* This half-mile trail bisects the Poppy Loop Trail.

Anza-Borrego Desert State Park

Additional information about these and many other trails is available at the visitor center or by calling (619/760) 767-5311.

CACTUS LOOP TRAIL *Begins on Co. Rd. S3 just north of Tamarisk Grove Campground.* A moderately steep 1½-mile trail displays teddy bear and buckhorn cholla, and beavertail, barrel, fishhook and hedgehog cacti. At an elevation of 1500 feet, this area offers spring wildflower blossoms several weeks later than blooms in the valley.

CULP VALLEY OVERLOOK TRAIL & CALIFORNIA RIDING AND HIKING TRAIL *Culp Valley Trail starts north of Culp Valley Primitive Campground and joins the California Riding and Hiking Trail at Culp Valley Overlook.* The Culp Valley trail leads north ¼ mile. The trail then joins the California Riding and Hiking Trail and descends 2200 feet over 5½ miles to Hellhole Canyon trailhead on Co. Rd. S22 below the Montezuma Grade.

ELEPHANT TREE DISCOVERY TRAIL *Leaves from the parking lot and crosses an alluvial fan.* The easy one-mile hike passes three rare elephant trees and other plants representative of the desert. Spectacular wildflowers are common in spring. A brochure describing plants along the trail is available at the visitor center.

NARROWS EARTH TRAIL *Leaves from the south side of SR 78 at a point 4⁷⁄₁₀ miles east of Tamarisk Grove.* An easy, ⅓-mile trail provides a close-up view of the area's geology, including a canyon, fault line and an alluvial fan.

PALM CANYON NATURE TRAIL *Leaves from the campground just 1 mile from the visitor center.* This easy, three-mile round-trip hike goes to a grove of native California fan palms and a year-round stream.

YAQUI WELL NATURE TRAIL *Begins just south of Tamarisk Grove Campground.* The moderate, two-mile trail passes stands of ocotillo, mesquite and a variety of cacti on its way to Yaqui Well, where many types of birds abound. From Yaqui Well, the trail extends two miles to SR 78 near Plum Canyon.

Death Valley National Park

It is always advisable to obtain additional information about hiking trails at the visitor center at Furnace Creek. Hikers should plan to carry plenty of water and wear sturdy walking shoes when hiking anywhere in Death Valley. Some trails are closed during the warmer months.

CHARCOAL KILNS TRAIL *39 miles south of Stovepipe Wells.* The trail begins at the kilns and leads about four miles to Wildrose Peak (elevation 9064 feet), gaining almost 3000 feet in elevation. The first 1½ miles are mostly uphill, then the trail follows a saddle to the peak.

GOLDEN CANYON *3 miles south of Furnace Creek.* Beginning at the parking lot, the trail leads about ¾ mile to Red Cathedral, a natural amphitheater. This trail is signed and points out many interesting aspects of the Death Valley landscape.

HARMONY BORAX WORKS RUINS *2 miles north of Furnace Creek.* A short footpath leads past the ruins of the refinery and outlying buildings. From there a three-mile-long trail leads northwest across the salt flats to mounds of borax resembling haystacks.

MOSAIC CANYON *2 miles south of Stovepipe Wells.* A short 1½-mile trail leads into the mouth of the canyon which reveals walls of multicolored rock. Contrasts are most defined around midday.

SALT CREEK *14 miles north of Furnace Creek.* This one-mile-long boardwalk trail offers views of pupfish, birds and other desert inhabitants.

Imperial Sand Dunes Recreation Area

MESQUITE MINE OVERLOOK TRAIL *Begins at the parking lot, 3 miles north of SR 78 on G.F.O.C. Mine Rd. Open daily from 8 a.m. to 4 p.m. Rest room available at the trailhead.* A one-mile trail climbs nearly 100 feet in elevation, providing an overview of the second-largest gold mine in California. A brochure available at the trailhead describes the geology, flora and fauna visible at numbered stops on the trail.

The Mesquite Mine Overlook Trail provides a fascinating view of the desert, as well as a working gold mine.

Joshua Tree National Park

Additional information about these trails is available at the park visitor centers or by calling (619/760) 367-7511.

LOST PALMS OASIS TRAIL *Starts at Cottonwood Springs Oasis near the south entrance to the park.* A moderately strenuous four-mile hike through dry desert washes terminates at the largest oasis of the monument. This hike should *not* be attempted in hot weather because there is no shade or water available.

RYAN MOUNTAIN TRAIL *Begins at the parking area west of Sheep Pass Group Campground.* The strenuous 1½-mile hike leads to the top of 5470-foot Ryan Mountain. The panorama includes four valleys—Lost Horse, Pleasant, Queen and Hidden—and many of the tumbled rock piles for which Joshua Tree National Park is known.

Mojave National Preserve

Numerous opportunities exist for off-trail hiking in the East Mojave. Old mine roads in the New York, Castle and Providence mountains are also good hikes. A few developed trails are found in the Mid Hills area of the Providence Mountains.

AMBOY CRATER *Begins on the north side of the 285-foot high crater. Allow two*

RECREATION

to three hours for the hike. The steep hiking trail leads to the top, affording good views of the lava field, dry lake beds and other surroundings. Wildflowers provide color from late January through March.

CIMA DOME *The trail begins just north of Sunrise Rock. A four-mile, round-trip hike to Teutonia Peak takes about two hours. The trail is easy to moderate, and hikers should carry plenty of water.* The Sunrise Rock area (about six miles north of Cima) is a good place for foot exploration. From the Cima Dome lookout point, it is a rocky ¼-mile climb to the top of Teutonia Peak (elevation 5755 feet).

The area's volcanic history is evident in Cima Dome, one of many cinder cones dotting the countryside.

HOLE-IN-THE-WALL *A trail leaves from the picnic area and travels west through volcanic rock.* The descent is down metal rings as well as scrambling around and over many boulders. A second trail begins along Wild Horse Canyon Road and travels seven miles north from Hole-in-the-Wall to Mid Hills (hikers are advised to begin at Mid Hills and walk south). The path passes cactus gardens and other interesting rock formations. Backcountry camping is available at several spots on trail.

KELSO DUNES *A hike to the top and back takes approximately two hours.* The dunes can be explored on foot; they rise more than 600 feet above the desert floor. The area is closed to all vehicles.

Mount San Jacinto State Park

The park is reached by riding the Palm Springs Aerial Tramway from Valley Station in Palm Springs to Mountain Station (see the tram listing in the Resort Cities *chapter). (619/760) 327-0222 (recorded information). Long Valley Ranger Station, (909) 659-2607; San Jacinto Ranger District, (909) 659-2117. Call for additional information about hiking trails. Mule-train trips in the park are listed under Horseback Riding in this chapter.*

BACKCOUNTRY TRAILS *Accessible from the northern portions of Idyllwild.* These trails cover more than 54 miles throughout the wilderness area. A day-use permit is required and proper hiking equipment is a necessity.

DESERT VIEW LOOP TRAIL *Begins at Mountain Station of Palm Springs Aerial Tramway.* This easy two-mile walking trail passes five viewpoints overlooking the Coachella Valley.

NATURE TRAIL *Begins at Mountain Station of Palm Springs Aerial Tramway.* This ⅔-mile walk features numbered posts giving information on flora and fauna of the area.

Palm Springs

PALM SPRINGS DESERT MUSEUM *101 Museum Dr. (619/760) 325-7186. Museum Trail begins behind the museum and joins the Carl Lykken Trail at Desert Riders Overlook.* The two-mile round-trip **Museum Trail** gains 800 feet in elevation. The four-mile **Carl Lykken Trail**, named for an early Palm Springs resident, branches north to Tramway Road and south to Ramon Road near the mouth of Tahquitz Canyon. Hikers will see close-up views of cacti and other desert flora, as well as panoramic views of Palm Springs and the Coachella Valley. The trail is closed in summer.

Providence Mountains State Recreation Area

MARY BEAL NATURE STUDY TRAIL *Starts at the Mitchell Caverns Natural Preserve headquarters.* This half-mile, self-guiding loop trail ends at the parking lot. Desert plants and selected fauna are identified along the path.

Red Rock Canyon State Park

Additional information hiking in Red Rock Canyon State Park is available at the park headquarters or by calling (805) 942-0662.

DESERT VIEW NATURE TRAIL *Begins near camping area. Elevation 2700 feet.* A half-mile hike climbs 600 feet from the basin floor, with numbered stops explaining the area's geology, flora and fauna.

Saddleback Butte State Park

Additional information about this trail and other hiking in Saddleback Butte State Park is available at the park office or by calling (805) 942-0662.

JOSHUA NATURE TRAIL *Begins near the visitors center.* This easy ½-mile walk with numbered stops en route is supplemented with a printed trail guide explaining the park's flora, fauna and area geography.

SADDLEBACK PEAK TRAIL & LITTLE BUTTE TRAIL *The Saddleback Peak Trail climbs nearly 1000 feet above the desert floor's 2700 feet elevation. It intersects the Little Butte Trail, which leads to the day-use area.* The lower ⁷⁄₁₀ mile of the Saddleback Peak Trail is sandy and the climb becomes steeper. The last ³⁄₁₀ mile is quite steep and very rocky. From the top of the peak there are spectacular views of the surrounding desert and mountain ranges to the south. The Little Butte Trail, a one-mile spur, passes through a large Joshua tree forest.

Salton Sea National Wildlife Refuge

Additional information about the trail is available at the refuge headquarters or by calling (619/760) 348-5278.

ROCK HILL TRAIL *Leaves from the refuge headquarters at Sinclair and Gentry rds.* Interpretive exhibits are located near the office. Wildlife may be observed and photographed along the one-mile trail as it passes through agricultural fields and marshlands to the edge of the Salton Sea. A wildlife list is available at the office.

HORSEBACK RIDING

Riding in the desert or into nearby hills and canyons provides a close-up look at desert subtleties that might otherwise be missed. Trail guides are usually mandatory while riding in the desert. The following companies rent horses or mules; call for reservations. *Inclusion in this publication does not imply an endorsement by the Automobile Club of Southern California; listings are provided as a convenience for our readers. Rates are subject to change.*

La Quinta

RANCH OF THE 7TH RANGE *Off Ave. 58 south of PGA West Golf Course (P.O. Box 1597, La Quinta 92253). (619/760) 777-7777. Rental horses are available for $27 per hour; guide service included.* Trails lead into the foothills and canyons of the Santa Rosa Mountains. Western hoedown and barbecue.

Palm Springs

SMOKE TREE STABLES *2500 Toledo Ave., Palm Springs 92264. (619/760) 327-1372. One-hour guided rides leave daily between 8 a.m. and 5 p.m.; $25 per person. Two-hour rides to Agua Caliente Indian Reservation are offered at 8 and 10 a.m., and 2 and 4 p.m. $50 per person.*

ICE SKATING

Palm Desert

ICE CHALET *Palm Desert Town Center, 72-840 Hwy. 111, Ste. A, Palm Desert 92260. (619/760) 340-4412.* Open skating sessions Mon. from 11 a.m. to 5:30 p.m.; Tues. through Fri. from 11 a.m. to 5:30 p.m. and 7:30 to 9:30; Sat. 10 to 11:30 a.m. and 12:45 to 10 p.m.; Sun. 12 a.m. to 6 p.m. Admission is $5.25, seniors $3.75, plus $2.25 for skate rentals.

OFF-HIGHWAY-VEHICLE AREAS

Off-highway-vehicle areas in the lower desert offer exciting terrain, with hills, washes and sand dunes that challenge drivers.

Imperial Valley

Stores, repair services, restaurants and a telephone are available in Glamis. El Centro has complete support services. For further information on off-highway-vehicle use in the Imperial Valley, contact the Bureau of Land Management, El Centro Resource Area, 1661 S. 4th St., El Centro 92243. (619/760) 337-4443.

BUTTERCUP VALLEY OPEN AREA *Located at the southern end of the Algodones Dunes between I-8 and the U.S.-Mexican border.* This is a popular off-highway-vehicle area. Drivers are warned to stay clear of the border itself as that area is equipped with motion sensors for illegal activities.

IMPERIAL SAND DUNES RECRE-ATION AREA *Located between I-8 and SR 78 east of Calexico and Brawley.* This is a favorite area for off-highway-vehicle enthusiasts. (Also see the Imperial Sand Dunes Recreation Area listing in the *Imperial Valley Area* chapter.)

MAMMOTH WASH OPEN AREA *Located at the north end of Algodones Dunes and extending south 7 miles.* This is another popular off-highway-vehicle area in the Imperial Valley (watch for "Closed Area" signs).

▼ *Tips for Driving Off-Road*

In order to maintain a level of safety, the following rules and suggestions should be observed.

1. All vehicles must be registered. A license plate or "Green Sticker" must be clearly displayed on the vehicle.

2. The speed limit within 50 feet of a person, animal or campsite is 15 mph. Speeding and reckless driving are prohibited.

3. Any vehicle operating at night must have at least one lighted white headlight that enables the operator to see clearly 200 feet ahead and one lighted red taillight visible from 200 feet.

4. All vehicles must have an adequate muffler, approved brakes and spark arrester as required by the California State Vehicle Code.

5. Passengers are not allowed on OHVs.

6. Law prohibits the possession of open containers of alcoholic beverages by anyone operating or riding in or on any motorized vehicle used on public lands. Don't drink and drive.

7. A person with a suspended driver's license may not operate a vehicle in OHV areas.

8. All unlicensed drivers must complete a safety course or be supervised by an adult possessing a course certificate. Drivers under age 14 are required to complete a safety course and must be under the immediate supervision of a licensed adult. Unlicensed drivers are not permitted to drive at night.

9. Roll bars and seat belts should be used.

10. Use of an approved safety helmet is required. Protective clothing, such as gloves and boots, is recommended.

11. Carry an emergency repair kit and basic survival equipment, including ample water (one gallon per person, per day).

12. OHVs must stay out of restricted areas. This is to protect delicate plant and animal life.

13. Carry out all litter, including ashes from fires and gray water from campers and trailers.

14. Leave your itinerary and expected time of return with someone who can take action if you don't return as planned.

15. Drivers of passenger vehicles should not attempt off-road terrain.

16. When negotiating sand dunes, remember that the slip face, or eastern side, of a dune can be far steeper than the windward, or west, slope. Drivers should be careful when approaching the top of a dune because it is easy for a vehicle to become airborne while starting down the slip face.

There's lots of fun in the sun at Ocotillo Wells State Vehicular Recreation Area.

PLASTER CITY OPEN AREA *17 miles west of El Centro on Co. Rd. S80.* This area attracts cross-country vehicle users with its rolling hills and desert flats (observe posted boundaries).

Ocotillo Wells State Vehicular Recreation Area

Located north of SR 78 adjacent to the eastern edge of Anza-Borrego Desert State Park; P.O. Box 360, Borrego Springs 92004. (619/760) 767-5391. This area offers 40,000 acres of dunes, washes and hills for all types of off-highway-vehicle uses. Camping is permitted throughout the area, but no water is available. Vehicle repair shops, fuel, telephones, restaurants and groceries are available in the nearby town of Ocotillo Wells.

Stoddard Valley Off-Highway Vehicle Area *Located a short distance south of Barstow between I-15 and SR 247; Bureau of Land Management, Barstow Resource Area, 150 Coolwater Ln., Barstow 92311. (619/760) 256-8617.* This area offers rolling hills and open valley crossed by many dry washes. Primitive camping is permitted in much of the area. Motorists should avoid open mine shafts scattered throughout. Full support services are available in Barstow and Victorville.

PICNICKING

The parks listed here are within ¼ mile of a highway or major city street, or are picnic areas within a designated county or state recreation area. Each offers picnic tables and public rest rooms. Other amenities are noted.

CALIFORNIA

Barstow

CALICO GHOST TOWN REGIONAL PARK *7½ miles north on I-15, 3 miles north on Ghost Town Rd.* Hiking trail. (See *East Mojave Area.*)

Brawley

WIEST LAKE COUNTY PARK Boating, fishing, swimming. (See Water Recreation in this chapter and *Campgrounds & Trailer Parks.*)

Coachella

BAGDOUMA PARK *1 mile west of SR 111 via 52 Ave. and Douma St.* Ball field; children's play area; basketball courts; community center.

Desert Hot Springs

MISSION SPRINGS PARK *2¼ miles north of I-10 off Palm Dr.* Ball field; children's play area; jogging path.

El Centro

ADAMS PARK *On Adams Ave. between 4th and 8th sts.* Children's play area.

Indio

MILES AVENUE PARK *¾ mile southwest of SR 86 via Oasis St. and Miles Ave.* Ball field; children's play area; tennis courts.

Lancaster

APOLLO PARK *4 miles west of SR 14 and SR 138 at 4555 W Ave. G.* Children's play area; fishing; hiking trails. (See *West Mojave Area*.)

La Quinta

LAKE CAHUILLA RECREATION AREA *5 miles south of La Quinta off Madison St. and Ave. 58.* Children's play area; fishing; hiking trails; swimming. (See *Resort Cities* and Water Recreation.)

Ocotillo

AGUA CALIENTE COUNTY PARK *25⅔ miles north of I-8 on Co. Rd. S2 to the park entrance. Open Labor Day weekend to Memorial Day weekend.* Two naturally fed pools (one indoor), hiking trails, horseshoe and shuffleboard courts; children's play area.

Palm Desert

PALM DESERT CIVIC CENTER PARK *1½ miles east of SR 111 off Fred Waring Dr.* Ball field; children's play area; basketball courts, hand and racquetball courts, tennis courts, volleyball courts; rose garden; jogging trail.

Palm Springs

SUNRISE PARK *2 miles west of SR 111 off Ramon Rd.* Children's play area; basketball courts.

Twentynine Palms

KNOTT SKY PARK *South of SR 62 west of Canyon Rd.* Ball field; children's play area; hiking trails.

Lancaster's Apollo Park is popular among picnickers of both the human and feathered species.

Buckskin Mountain State Park, at Parker on the Colorado River, offers a host of facilities and recreational activities.

LUCKIE PARK *1 mile north of SR 62 via Utah Tr. and Two Mile Rd.* Ball field; children's play area; basketball courts, hand and racquetball courts, volleyball courts tennis courts; swimming.

Victorville

MOJAVE NARROWS REGIONAL PARK *4 miles east of I-15 on Bear Valley Rd., 2½ miles north on Ridgecrest and Yates rds.* Ball field; boating, fishing; hiking trails. (See *East Mojave Area* and *Annual Events*.)

Winterhaven

PICACHO STATE RECREATION AREA *26 miles north via an unpaved road.* Boating, fishing, hiking. (See *Colorado River Area*.)

Yucca Valley

ANTONE MARTIN MEMORIAL PARK (DESERT CHRIST PARK) *½ mile north of SR 62 on Sunnyslope Dr., off Mohawk Tr.* Sculpture garden.

ARIZONA

Lake Havasu City

CATTAIL COVE STATE PARK *15 miles south along SR 95.* Boating, fishing, camping, hiking. (See *Colorado River Area*.)

LAKE HAVASU STATE PARK *South of McCulloch Blvd. in Lake Havasu City along the Colorado River.* Boating, fishing, camping, hiking. (See *Colorado River Area*.)

Parker

BUCKSKIN MOUNTAIN STATE PARK *11 miles north of Parker on SR 95.* Boating, fishing, camping, hiking. (See *Colorado River Area*.)

ROCK CLIMBING

The proximity of major Southern California population centers and accessibility by paved roads make Joshua Tree National Park popular for rock climbers. Joshua Tree offers more than 3000 climbs on high-angle faces, flared chimneys and difficult jam cracks. Spring and fall bring ideal weather and temperatures, but enthusiasts scale the rocks year round. Difficulty ratings for climbing routes range from the easiest to the most difficult. Specialized equipment is necessary for many of the ascents.

Popular climbs are found in Wonderland of Rocks, Indian Cove, Hidden Valley, Real Hidden Valley and the Lost Horse area. Campgrounds are located nearby, but no water is available. Nearby communities provide showers and other facilities. Reference books on rock climbing can be purchased at the park's visitor centers.

The incredible rocks in Joshua Tree National Park offer some challenges to climbers.

TENNIS

All public tennis courts in the desert region are outdoors and most are open all year. No fees are charged nor reservations accepted unless noted in the listing. Use of the courts is on a first-come, first-play basis. Usually players are limited to one set or one hour if others are waiting.

CALIFORNIA

Borrego Springs

BORREGO SPRINGS HIGH SCHOOL *Cahuilla Rd. and Diegueño Dr. Open weekends, holidays and summer. 2* courts.

BORREGO SPRINGS TENNIS CLUB *286 Palm Canyon Dr. Fees start at $10 an hour.* 4 lighted courts.

LA CASA DEL ZORRO TENNIS CLUB *Yaqui Pass and Borrego Springs rds. Free for guests only.* 6 lighted courts for guests' use.

Brawley

MESERVE PARK *J and 2nd sts.* 3 lighted courts.

Cathedral City

EMERALD COURT RESORT *69-375 Ramon Rd.* 5 courts; $6 an hour.

PANORAMA PARK *28-905 Avenida Maravilla.* 2 courts.

2ND STREET PARK *Date Palm Dr. and Second St.* 2 lighted courts.

Coachella

BAGDOUMA PARK *Bagdad and Douma sts.* 2 lighted courts.

Desert Hot Springs

ARROYO PARK *Arroyo Dr. and Hacienda Ave.* 1 lighted court.

WARDMAN PARK *8th St. and Cactus Dr.* 2 lighted courts.

El Centro

ADAMS PARK *Adams Ave. between 4th and 8th sts.* 2 lighted courts.

Indio

INDIO HIGH SCHOOL *Clinton and Ave. 46.* 8 courts.

JACKSON PARK *Jackson St. and Date Ave.* 2 lighted courts.

MILES AVENUE PARK *Miles Ave. and Arabia St.* 1 lighted court.

NORTH JACKSON PARK *Jackson St. and Kenner Ave.* 2 courts.

Joshua Tree

SUNBURST PARK *Sunburst and Plaza sts.* 2 lighted courts.

Lancaster

EL DORADO PARK *44501 N. 5th St. East.* 1 lighted court.

JANE REYNOLDS PARK *Oldfield St. at Elm Ave.* 1 lighted court.

LANCASTER CITY PARK *43011 N. 10th St. West at Ave. L.* 8 lighted courts.

La Quinta

FRITZ BURNS PARK *52nd Ave. and Avenida Bermudas.* 8 courts, 4 lighted.

Morongo Valley

COVINGTON PARK *Covington Dr. off SR 62.* 2 courts.

Palmdale

W. J. McADAM MEMORIAL PARK *38115 30th St. East at Palmdale Blvd.* 4 lighted courts.

Palm Desert

CIVIC CENTER PARK *Fred Waring Dr. and San Pablo Ave.* 6 lighted courts.

CAHUILLA HILLS PARK *South end of Edgehill Dr.* 2 lighted courts.

COLLEGE OF THE DESERT *Fred Waring Dr. east of Monterey Ave.* 6 courts.

Palm Springs

DEMUTH PARK *4375 Mesquite Ave.* 4 lighted courts.

RUTH HARDY PARK *Tamarisk Rd. and Avenida Caballeros.* 8 courts, 3 lighted.

THE TENNIS CENTER *1300 E. Baristo Rd. (619/760) 320-0020. $12 an hour weekdays, $14 on weekends and holidays. Reservations accepted.* 9 courts, 3 lighted.

Twentynine Palms

LUCKIE PARK *Utah Tr. and Two Mile Rd.* 2 lighted courts.

Yucca Valley

HIGH DESERT PARK *South of Twentynine Palms Hwy. on Hopi Tr.* 1 court.

MACHRIS PARK *South of Twentynine Palms Hwy. off Joshua Ln.* 1 court.

ARIZONA

Lake Havasu City

LAKE HAVASU HIGH SCHOOL *2675 N. Palo Verde Rd.* 6 lighted courts.

A power boat plies the water at Wiest Lake.

Yuma

CARVER PARK *5th St. and 13th Ave.*
2 lighted courts.

DESERT SUN-CABALLERO PARK
1440 Desert Hills Dr. 9 lighted courts.

KENNEDY PARK *24th St. and Kennedy Ln.* 2 lighted courts.

WATER RECREATION

BOATING

Boating activities in the Southern California desert may sound like a contradiction, but the Coachella and Imperial valleys contain several small lakes and the Salton Sea, and the Colorado River is popular with boaters. The following listings indicate where boats can be rented and where privately owned boats can be launched or moored. Entries include each establishment's location and phone number and give additional information on rental equipment, fuel, boat repairs and other facilities and services available nearby. For additional lake descriptions, see the listings in the *Resort Cities* or *Imperial Valley Area* chapters.

FISHING

Several Coachella and Imperial Valley lakes, the Salton Sea and the Colorado River offer good year-round fishing. The freshwater lakes yield mainly bass, bluegill, catfish and crappie, with an occasional carp or trout taking the bait. The highly saline Salton Sea serves as a fishermen's mecca with its wide variety and abundant supply of fish. A California State Fishing License is required for anglers age 16 and over. All of the lakes have boat launching facilities; some have rentals as well.

LAKES

Lake Cahuilla County Park

On northeast shore of lake, 8 miles southwest of Indio via Monroe St. and Ave. 58;

c/o 58-075 Jefferson St., Thermal 92274. (619/760) 564-4712; camping reservations (800) 464-6316. Open daily. $4 day-use fee.

BOATING

$4 per-person fishing fee; $3 ages 10-15. Facilities: Launch ramp. Rentals: none. Tent and RV sites, picnic area. Boaters should beware of sudden desert winds. Gas motors are prohibited.

FISHING

Bass, bluegill, catfish, trout.

Mojave Narrows Regional Park

4 miles east of I-15 on Bear Valley Rd., 2½ miles north on Ridgecrest and Yates rds., Victorville. (714) 38-PARKS.

FISHING

Persons ages 6 and older require a county fishing permit which costs $4 per day; persons ages 16 and older need a state fishing license (available at the park). Catfish, trout.

Oxbow Lake

BOATING

PALO VERDE COUNTY PARK *2 miles southeast of Palo Verde off SR 78 (mailing address: c/o Imperial County Parks and Recreation Dept, 1002 State St., El Centro, CA 92243). (619/760) 339-4384. Open daily.* Facilities: paved ramp (free). Rentals: none. Tent and RV sites.

FISHING

Largemouth bass, catfish and rainbow trout.

Salton Sea

BOATING

BOB'S PLAYA RIVIERA *On east shore at 10-565 SR 111, North Shore 92254. (619/760) 354-1835. Open daily.* Facilities: paved ramp ($7.50), slips, boat fuel. Rentals: motorboats (2 hp). Tent and RV sites; mini-store.

DESERT SHORES TRAILER PARK *On west shore at 320 Desert Shores Dr., Desert Shores 92274. (619/760) 395-*

A youngster gets some schooling in the art of fishing at Mojave Narrows Regional Park.

5280. Open daily. Facilities: paved ramp ($4).

RED HILL MARINA *On southeast shore at 7581 Garst Rd., Calipatria 92233. (619/760) 348-2310.* Open all year. Facilities: paved ramp ($2 day-use fee). Rentals: none. Tent and RV sites, picnic area.

SALTON SEA BEACH MARINA *On west shore at 288 Coachella Ave., Salton Sea Beach 92274. (619/760) 395-5212.* Open daily. Facilities: paved ramp ($5; $2 per-person day-use fee), boat fuel. Rentals: none. Bait, groceries, ice, tent and RV sites, picnic area.

SALTON SEA STATE RECREATION AREA *On east shore at SR 111 and State Park Rd.; P.O. Box 3166, North Shore 92254; (619/760) 393-3052.* Open daily. Facilities: paved ramp ($5; $5 day-use fee), temporary mooring. Rentals: none. Bait, groceries, ice, tent and RV sites, picnic area.

FISHING

Eighteen miles of shoreline in Salton Sea State Recreation Area are available for casting, and boats can be rented from several agencies around the lake.

The Salton Sea offers great catches of sargo, tilapia, gulf croaker and the most prized species—orangemouth corvina. Sargo bite best when the water is cool, November through April, and ½- to 3- pound catches are average. Tilapia, native to Africa and the Middle East, were imported in the 1950s to control algae in the Colorado River irrigation canals; in time they migrated to the Salton Sea and adapted to its salty water. Tilapia average 1 to 2 pounds and are at their best from April through November, when the water is warm. Croaker can usually be found close to shore in the warm weather, April to October, and range from 7 to 15 inches in length. Orangemouth corvina also lurk close to shore during warm weather and in deeper water from December to March. They are the largest fish in the lake, usually ranging from 3 to 12 pounds; however, corvina as large as 36 pounds have been caught.

Because of the high amount of the mineral selenium in Salton Sea fish, the California Department of Health recommends that adult consumption should be limited to one 4-ounce portion every two weeks, or one 8-ounce portion each month. Women of child-bearing age and children under 15 years old should avoid eating any amount of Salton Sea fish.

Sunbeam Lake County Park

7 miles west of El Centro on Drew Rd.; c/o Imperial County Parks and Recreation Dept., 155 S. 11th St., Ste. C, El Centro 92243. (619/760) 352-3308. Open daily. Day-use fee $2 per vehicle for up to four persons; 50¢ per additional person.

BOATING

Facilities: paved ramp (free). Rentals: none. Snack bar (closed in winter), picnic area.

FISHING

Bass, bluegill, catfish, crappie, trout.

Wiest Lake County Park

5 miles northeast of Brawley off SR 111 and Co. Rd. S26 (Rutherford Rd.); 5351 Dietrich Rd., Brawley 92227. (619/760) 344-3712. Open daily. $2 day-use fee.

BOATING

Facilities: paved ramp (free). Rentals: none. Tent and RV sites, picnic area.

FISHING

Bass, bluegill, catfish, trout.

COLORADO RIVER

Blythe

BOATING

MAYFLOWER COUNTY PARK
*6 miles north of Blythe off US 95
(mailing address: Rt. 1, Box 190-E,
92225). (619/760) 922-4665. Open daily.*
Facilities: paved ramp ($2 day-use fee
plus $2 per person). Rentals: none.
Boat dock, tent and RV sites.

MCINTYRE PARK *8750 E. 26 Ave.,
92225. (619/760) 922-8205. Open
daily.* Facilities: paved ramp ($8 per
vehicle). Rentals: none. Boat fuel, boat
dock, groceries, ice, propane, tent and
RV sites.

RIVIERA BLYTHE MARINA *14100
Riviera Dr., 92225. (619/760) 922-5350.
Open daily.* Facilities: paved ramp ($8
day-use fee). Rentals: none. Boat fuel,
boat dock, groceries, ice, propane, bait
and tackle, tent and RV sites.

FISHING

Largemouth bass, bluegill, channel catfish, flathead catfish and striped bass.

Earp

BOATING

RIVER LAND RESORT *6 miles north
of Earp along SR 62 (mailing address:
HC-20, Box 105, 92242). (619/760) 663-
3733. Open daily.* Facilities: paved ramp
($2 day-use fee). Rentals: none. Boat
fuel, groceries, ice, bait and tackle, tent
and RV sites.

FISHING

Largemouth bass, bluegill, catfish,
crappie and trout.

Lake Havasu

BOATING

CATTAIL COVE STATE PARK *14 miles
south of Lake Havasu City off SR 95
(mailing address: Box 1990, Lake Havasu
City, AZ 86405). (520) 855-1223. Open*

All manner of water sports take place on Lake Havasu.

daily. Facilities: paved ramp ($7 day-use fee). Rentals: powerboats, rowboats. Boat fuel, bait, groceries, ice, restaurant, tent and RV sites.

CRAZY HORSE CAMPGROUND
1534 Beachcomber Blvd., Lake Havasu City, AZ 86403. (520) 855-4033. Open daily. Facilities: paved ramp ($6 day-use fee). Rentals: none. Bait, groceries, ice, tent and RV sites.

HAVASU LANDING RESORT *9 miles east of US 95 (mailing address: Havasu Lake, CA 92363). (619/760) 858-4606.* Open daily. Facilities: 3 paved ramps (fee). Rentals: none. Boat fuel, bait and tackle, groceries, ice, restaurant, casino, tent and RV sites.

ISLANDER RV RESORT *751 Beachcomber Blvd., Lake Havasu City, AZ 86403. (520) 680-2000. Open daily.* Facilities: paved ramp ($5 day-use fee plus $3 per person). Rentals: none. Groceries, ice, RV sites.

LAKE HAVASU MARINA *1100 McCulloch Blvd., Lake Havasu City, AZ 86403. (520) 855-2159. Open daily.* Facilities: paved ramp ($3 per day). Rentals: powerboats, rowboats, pontoon boats. Boat fuel, slip rentals, mechanics, bait and tackle, groceries and ice.

LAKE HAVASU STATE PARK *699 London Bridge Rd., Lake Havasu City, AZ 86406. (520) 855-2784. Open daily.* Facilities: 2 paved ramps. Rentals: none. Boat slips, tent and RV sites.

SANDPOINT MARINA & RV PARK *14 miles south of Lake Havasu City off SR 95 (mailing address: Box 1469, Lake Havasu City, AZ 86405). (520) 855-0549. Open daily.* Facilities: paved ramp ($5 day-use fee). Rentals: pontoon boats, house boats. Courtesy dock, bait and tackle, groceries, ice, tent and RV sites.

FISHING
Largemouth bass, bluegill, channel catfish and crappie.

Needles

BOATING
NEEDLES MARINA PARK *3 miles northwest of Needles off I-40 at 100 Marina Dr, 92363. (619/760) 326-2197. Open daily.* Facilities: paved ramp ($6 for visitors). Rentals: none. Boat fuel, bait, groceries, ice, snack bar, tent and RV sites.

RAINBO BEACH RESORT & MARINA *2 miles north of Needles off I-40 (mailing address: Rt. 4, Box 139, 92363). (619/760) 326-3101. Open daily.* Facilities: paved ramp ($6 for visitors). Rentals: none. Boat fuel, beverages, ice, restaurant, tent and RV sites.

FISHING
Largemouth bass, bluegill, channel catfish, rainbow trout and striped bass.

Palo Verde

BOATING
PALO VERDE OXBOW *3½ miles southeast of Palo Verde off SR 78 (mailing address: c/o BLM, 3150 Windsor Ave., Yuma, AZ 85365). (520) 317-3200. Open daily.* Facilities: paved ramp (free). Rentals: none. Tent and RV sites.

FISHING
Largemouth bass, channel catfish, crappie, flathead catfish and striped bass.

Parker

BOATING
BUCKSKIN MOUNTAIN STATE PARK *10 miles north of Parker off SR 95 (mailing address: 54751 SR 95, 85344). (520) 667-3231. Open daily.* Facilities: paved

ramp ($7 day-use fee). Rentals: none. Boat fuel, boat dock, groceries, ice, bait and tackle, restaurant, tent and RV sites.

HAVASU SPRINGS RESORT *15 miles north of Parker along SR 95 (mailing address: Rt. 2, Box 624, 85344). (520) 667-3361. Open daily.* Facilities: paved ramp. Rentals: powerboats, rowboats. Boat fuel, bait and tackle, groceries, ice, restaurant, RV sites and hotel.

LA PAZ COUNTY PARK *8 miles north of Parker off SR 95 (mailing address: 1 Park Dr., 85344). (520) 667-2069. Open daily.* Facilities: 2 paved ramps and 1 gravel ramp ($2 day-use fee). Rentals: none. Ice, tent and RV sites.

RIVER ISLAND CAMPGROUND *12 miles north of Parker along SR 95 (mailing address: 54895 SR 95, 85344). (520) 667-3386. Open daily.* Facilities: paved ramp ($7 day-use fee). Rentals: none. Tent and RV sites.

FISHING

Largemouth bass, bluegill, catfish, crappie and trout.

Parker Dam

BOATING

BIG BEND RESORT *2½ miles south of Parker Dam along SR 62 (mailing address: Box 24, 92267). (619/760) 663-3755. Open daily.* Facilities: paved ramp ($5 day-use fee). Rentals: none. Boat dock, bait and tackle, groceries, ice, tent and RV sites.

ECHO LODGE RESORT *2½ miles south of Parker Dam off SR 62 (mailing address: Box 8, 92267). (619/760) 663-4931. Open daily.* Facilities: paved ramp ($8.50 day-use fee). Rentals: none. Boat fuel, groceries, ice, bait and tackle, tent and RV sites.

RIVER LODGE RESORT *2 miles south of Parker Dam off SR 62 (mailing address: Box 57, 92267). (619/760) 663-4934. Open daily.* Facilities: paved ramp ($12.50 day-use fee). Rentals: none. Bait and tackle, groceries, ice, cafe, bar, tent and RV sites.

SUNSHINE RESORT *1 mile south of Parker Dam along SR 62 (mailing address: Box 14, 92267). (619/760) 663-3098. Open daily.* Facilities: paved ramp (free). Rentals: none. Bait and tackle, groceries, ice, tent and RV sites.

FISHING

Largemouth bass, bluegill, catfish, crappie and trout.

Topock

BOATING

GOLDEN SHORES MARINA *Intersection of I-40 and Co. Rd. 66 (mailing address: Topock, AZ 86436). (520) 768-2325. Open daily.* Facilities: paved ramp ($4.50 per water craft). Rentals: none. Boat fuel, bait, groceries, ice, restaurant and bar.

FISHING

Largemouth bass, catfish, striped bass and trout.

Winterhaven/Yuma

BOATING

HIDDEN SHORES RV VILLAGE *Northeast of Yuma via SR 95 (mailing address: Star Rt. 4, Box 40, Yuma, AZ 85365). (520) 783-1448. Open daily.* Facilities: gravel ramp ($4 per vehicle). Rentals: none. Boat fuel, bait and tackle, groceries, ice, propane, restaurant and snack bar.

PICACHO STATE RECREATION AREA *26 miles north of Winterhaven via an unpaved road (mailing address:*

Box 1207, Winterhaven, CA 92283).
(619/760) 393-3052. Open daily.
Facilities: paved ramp ($5 per launch
plus $5 day-use fee). Rentals: none.
Boat dock, tent and RV sites.

SQUAW LAKE *18½ miles northeast of
Winterhaven off Co. Rd. 24 (mailing
address: c/o BLM, 3150 Windsor Ave.,
Yuma, AZ 85365). (520) 317-3200.
Open daily.* Facilities: paved ramp (free).
Rentals: none. Tent and RV sites.

FISHING

Largemouth bass, channel catfish, crappie, flathead catfish and striped bass.

WINTER SPORTS

PALM SPRINGS NORDIC SKI CENTER
*Mount San Jacinto State Park, top of Palm
Springs Aerial Tramway, 7 miles northwest of Palm Springs; 1 Tramway Rd.,
Palm Springs 92263. (619/760) 327-
6002. The ski center is open from mid-
Nov. to mid-Apr. when there is enough
snow in the San Jacinto Mountains. Hours
Mon. through Fri. are 10:30 a.m. to 5
p.m., Sat. and Sun. 8:30 a.m. to 5 p.m.*
Rental skis, boots, poles, snowshoes
and snow boots (no rentals after 4
p.m.). Ski school.

Transportation

Take a plane, drive your car, hop aboard a bus or train. By whatever means you get to the Desert, it's more than worth the trip.

Effective March 22, 1997, area code (619) will change to (760).

AIR

Resort Cities

The Palm Springs Regional Airport serves as the major facility for Southern California desert communities and is located about 2½ miles east of downtown Palm Springs at the end of Tahquitz Canyon Way. Airlines serving the airport include Air 21, Alaska, American, America West, Delta, Northwest, Reno Air, Skywest, United/United Express and US Air Express. Many provide commuter service to other California cities. Call the airport at (619/760) 323-8161 for more information or to request a FAX of the airport arrival-departure schedule. This schedule has all of the 800 numbers of the airlines servicing the airport. Travelers may also contact any AAA Travel Agency at the Automobile Club of Southern California or the AAA airline express desk, (800) AAA-5000, to make travel arrangements.

Colorado River Area

Lake Havasu City Municipal Airport, at 5600 North Highway 95 in Lake Havasu City, is served by America West and United Express. For more information, call the airport at (520) 764-3330.

Yuma International Airport, at 2191 East 32nd Street in Yuma, is the major facility serving the southern end of the Colorado River region. The airport is primarily served by Delta's Skywest, but American Express and United Express also run flights from here. For further information call the airport at (520) 726-5882.

West Mojave

The upper desert is served by two airports. Palmdale Regional Airport, at 20th Street East and Avenue P in Palmdale, is served by United Airlines; call (805) 266-7600.

Inyokern Airport serves Ridgecrest and the Owens Valley area with American and United Airlines; call (619/760) 377-4789, 377-5844.

AUTOMOBILE

Most Southern Californians drive to destinations within the desert areas.

Resort Cities

Palm Springs lies 108 miles east of Los Angeles via I-10 and SR 111. At the northern edge of the Coachella Valley is Desert Hot Springs, a 109-mile drive from Los Angeles by way of I-10, SR 62 and Pierson Boulevard. Twenty miles southeast of Palm Springs is Indio, located near the southern junction of I-10 and SR 111. Traveling southeast from Palm Springs along SR 111, motorists pass through or near the communities of Cathedral City,

Rancho Mirage, Palm Desert, Indian Wells, La Quinta and Bermuda Dunes.

Joshua Tree Area

Extending along the western and northern edges of the Joshua Tree area, SR 62 provides access to Joshua Tree National Park and the towns of the Morongo Basin—Morongo Valley, Yucca Valley, Joshua Tree and Twentynine Palms. Entry into the monument is limited to a few paved roads; the dirt roads within the park are not recommended for passenger cars or for any vehicles during or after a rainstorm.

Pinto Basin Road, the major route through the monument, ties Twentynine Palms with I-10. South from Twentynine Palms, the 46-mile road traverses the valleys between the Hexie and Pinto mountains, dropping from the Joshua trees and high plateaus of the wetter Mojave Desert to the more arid Colorado Desert, peppered with cholla cacti, ocotillo and creosote bushes. The road passes Cottonwood Visitor Center, traverses Cottonwood Pass (2800 feet) and meets I-10 24 miles north of the Salton Sea.

The only other paved road of any length entering Joshua Tree National Park is Quail Springs Road, running more than 15 miles southeast from the town of Joshua Tree to Lost Horse Valley. At this point the road becomes known as Keys View Road and continues another five miles south to Keys View, where the road ends. From this viewpoint, a dramatic panorama encompasses the Coachella Valley, the Salton Sea and Mount San Jacinto. To the west, 11,499-foot San Gorgonio Mountain is also visible.

Three other short paved roads lead from SR 62 into the park. Indian Cove

Road, west of Twentynine Palms, runs two miles into the Indian Cove area, where nature trails and campgrounds are located. Also west of Twentynine Palms, Canyon Road barely enters the park; from the road's end, a trail leads to Fortynine Palms Oasis. Finally, from the town of Paradise Valley, between Yucca Valley and Joshua Tree, Palomar Avenue runs a short distance to Black Rock Campground.

Colorado River Area

Roughly paralleling the Colorado River is US 95. From Needles and its junction with I-40 in the north, US 95 leads south on the California side of the river to Blythe and its junction with I-10. The southward continuation of US 95 is east of the Colorado River in Arizona, beginning at Quartzsite and ending at I-8 just east of Yuma.

State routes provide alternate north-south routes on the sides of the river not served by US 95. Beginning in the northern end of the Colorado River Area, Arizona SR 95 originates at I-40 and leads south through Lake Havasu City and Parker to Quartzsite. The California side of the southern part of the region is traversed by SR 78, originating at I-10 west of Blythe, and County Route S34 to I-8 west of Winterhaven, California, and Yuma, Arizona.

Imperial Valley Area

Just south of Indio, SR 86 splits off from SR 111. These major north-south highways dissect the Imperial Valley, with SR 86 following the western shore of the Salton Sea and providing access to Desert Shores, Salton City and Westmorland, while SR 111 parallels the eastern edge of the sea, connecting the communities of Bombay Beach, Niland and Calipatria. The two highways intersect again in Brawley and continue south. SR 111 ends in Calexico on the U.S.-Mexico border, while SR 86 passes through Imperial and El Centro before stopping a few miles short of the border.

The major east-west route through the southern Imperial Valley is I-8, which runs 117 miles from San Diego to El Centro and then continues another 64 miles to Yuma, Arizona. To the north, SR 78, another east-west route, begins on the coast in Oceanside and continues east through Anza-Borrego Desert State Park to the Salton Sea. It joins SR 86 as far as Brawley and then heads east through the Algodones Dunes (formerly the Sand Hills), and eventually north along the Colorado River to Blythe.

Anza-Borrego Area

Although I-8 runs along the southern section of this area on its way from San Diego to the California-Arizona border, it only perfunctorily touches the southernmost tip of Anza-Borrego Desert State Park. Park visitors, however, have a choice of three other roads: SR 78 and County Road S22 running east-west, and County Road S2 with a northwest-southeast orientation.

County Road S22, branching off County Road S2 4½ miles west of Ranchita, offers a dramatic approach to the park as it drops several thousand feet to the desert floor. Overlooks provide views of Borrego Springs, Borrego Badlands and, on a clear day, the Salton Sea and the Chocolate Mountains to the east. SR 78 comes east from Escondido through the small towns of Ramona, Santa Ysabel and Julian to Scissors Crossing, the junction with County Road S2. From there SR 78 traverses Anza-Borrego Desert State Park and Ocotillo Wells State Vehicular Recreation Area.

County Road S2, historically known as the Great Southern Overland Stage Route, branches off SR 79 near Warner Springs and extends in a southeasterly direction, passing in and out of the park, until it leaves it altogether and joins I-8 at the town of Ocotillo.

East Mojave Area

Two interstate highways bisect the East Mojave Area, intersecting at Barstow. I-40 originates in Barstow and heads east through mostly unpopulated areas, paralleling the southern edge of the Mojave National Preserve. The major route between metropolitan Los Angeles and Las Vegas, Nevada, I-15 lies in a southwest-northeast direction and passes through Barstow and Baker.

From both interstates, secondary and unimproved roads venture into remote areas of the Mojave National Preserve. SR 247 connects the Joshua Tree area with the freeways at Barstow. From Twentynine Palms, Amboy Road leads to the National Trails Highway, which accesses I-40 and routes into the Mojave National Preserve.

West Mojave Area

US 395 bisects the West Mojave in a north-south direction from its origin in the East Mojave's Victor Valley to its continuation north along the east side of the Sierra Nevada Mountains. No communities of significant size are on its route. SR 58, the major east-west route, comes into the desert near the town of Mojave, runs along the northern edge of Edwards Air Force Base and past Boron to its terminus at Barstow and interstates 15 and 40. The majority of SR 58 is divided highway, and a section from Boron west has controlled access.

From the Santa Clarita Canyon, SR 14 descends north into the Antelope Valley until its junction with US 395 near Inyokern. The road is freeway from just south of the town of Mojave all the way down into the Los Angeles area. North of Mojave the highway is wide two lane with two sections of divided highway, one through Red Rock Canyon State Park and the other after entering Inyo County. The southern portions of the West Mojave area are connected by SR 138; SR 18 ties in Victor Valley from the East Mojave Area. The West Mojave's secondary roads tie together smaller communities. Unimproved roads reach into many old mining areas and access a few points of interest. Conditions of unpaved roads accessing remote areas should be verified prior to driving on them.

Death Valley Area

The safest route to Death Valley from the west is via SR 190 at Death Valley Junction. This is also the route recommended for motorists towing recreational vehicles or trailers. SR 190 can be picked up either from Mojave via SR 14 or from Victorville via US 395. During the hot summer months, it is unwise to stray from major roads for any reason; during all seasons, sudden rainstorms can cause temporary washouts along both paved and dirt roads. Road closure signs should always be heeded. The prohibition against driving off established roads is strictly enforced.

BUS

GREYHOUND-TRAILWAYS BUS LINES From most cities in California, Greyhound-Trailways offers service to several major destinations in the Southern California desert. Tickets are usually purchased just prior to departure; advance reservations cannot be made. For complete information, contact your local ticket office. The following bus terminals are located in the region covered by this book.

CALIFORNIA

Barstow *681 N. First Ave. in Historic Harvey House, (619/760) 256-8757*

Blythe *905 W. Rice St., (619/760) 922-5401*

Calexico *123 First St., (619/760) 357-6340*

El Centro *460 State St., (619/760) 352-6363*

Indio *45-524 Oasis St., (619/760) 347-5888*

Lancaster *44949 N. Yucca Ave., (805) 949-2827*

Palm Springs *311 N. Indian Canyon Dr., (619/760) 325-2053*

ARIZONA

Yuma *170 E. 17th Pl., (520) 783-4403*

There are also pickup points along the Salton Sea at Niland and Bombay Beach on SR 111, and at Desert Shores and Salton City on SR 86. Another stop is made in Brawley. For information on these pickup points, call the El Centro Greyhound-Trailways office.

TRAIN

Colorado River Area

The city of Yuma, Arizona, is also served by Amtrak's Sunset Limited three times a week in each direction. The Amtrak station in Yuma is located at 281 Gila Street on the north side of town.

Lodging & Restaurants

*Lodging and dining facilities in the desert range from rustic and casual to luxurious and formal, and are found in large cities, small communities and isolated settings. In addition to lodging and restaurant facilities within **California**, properties are also listed for areas adjacent to the region, including the **Arizona** communities of **Ehrenberg, Lake Havasu City, Parker** and **Yuma**.*

The lodging and restaurant properties listed in these pages have been inspected by a trained representative of the Automobile Club of Southern California. In surprise inspections, each property was found to meet AAA's extensive and detailed requirements for approval. These requirements are reflective of current industry standards and the expectations of the traveling public. Less than two-thirds of the lodging establishments open for business are listed in AAA publications.

Most listings include AAA's esteemed "diamond" rating, reflecting the overall quality of the establishment. Many factors are considered in the process of determining the diamond rating. In lodging properties, the facility is first "classified" according to its physical design—is it a motel, a hotel, a resort, an apartment, etc. Since the various types of lodging establishments offer differing amenities and facilities, rating criteria are specific for each classification. For example, a motel, which typically offers a room with convenient parking and little if any recreational or public facilities, is rated using criteria designed only for motel-type establishments—it is not compared to a hotel with its extensive public and meeting areas, or to a resort with its wide range of recreational facilities and programs. The diamonds do, however, represent standard levels of quality in all types of establishments.

There is no charge for a property to be listed in AAA publications. Many lodgings and restaurants, however, choose to advertise their AAA approval by displaying the Ⓐ emblem on the premises and using it in their advertising. These properties are especially interested in serving AAA members.

Properties are listed alphabetically under the nearest town, with lodging facilities first and restaurants second. The location is given from the center of town or from the nearest major highway.

Nearly all lodging and restaurant facilities accept credit cards as forms of payment for services rendered. The following symbols are used to identify the specific cards accepted by each property.

AE	American Express
CB	Carte Blanche
DI	Diners Club International
DS	Discover
JCB	Japan Credit Bureau
MC	MasterCard
VI	VISA

Some lodgings and restaurants listed in Auto Club publications have symbols indicating that they are accessible to individuals with disabilities. The criteria used in qualifying these listings are consistent with, but do not represent the full scope of, the Americans with Disabilities Act of 1990. AAA does not evaluate recreational facilities, banquet rooms or convention and meeting facilities for accessibility. Individuals with disabilities are urged to phone ahead to fully understand an establishment's facilities and accessibility.

In accommodations, a ♿ indicates that at least one fully accessible guest room exists and that an individual with mobility impairments will be able to park and enter the building, register, and use at least one food and beverage outlet. For restaurants, the symbol indicates that parking, dining rooms and rest rooms are accessible.

The ⚏ in a lodging listing means that the following elements are provided: closed captioned decoders; text telephones; visual notification for fire alarms, incoming phone calls and door knocks; and phone amplification devices.

Lodging

The following accommodations classifications may appear in this book.

Bed & Breakfast—Usually a small establishment emphasizing personal attention. Individually decorated guest rooms provide an at-home feeling but may lack some amenities. Usually owner-operated with a common room or parlor where guests and owners can interact during evening and breakfast hours. May have shared bathrooms. A continental or full hot breakfast is included in the room rate.

Complex—A combination of two or more kinds of lodgings.

Cottage—Individual bungalow, cabin or villa, usually containing one rental unit equipped for housekeeping. May have a separate living room and bedroom(s). Parking is usually at each unit.

Country Inn—Similar in definition to a bed and breakfast. Offers a dining room reflecting the ambience of the inn. At a minimum, breakfast and dinner are served.

Hotel—A multistory building usually including a coffee shop, dining room, lounge, room service, convenience shops, valet, laundry and full banquet/meeting facilities. Parking may be limited.

Lodge—Typically two or more stories with all facilities in one building. Located in vacation, ski, fishing areas, etc. Usually has food and beverage service. Adequate on-premises parking.

Motel—Usually one or two stories; food service, if any, consists of a limited facility or snack bar. Often has a pool or playground. Ample parking, usually adjacent to guest room.

Motor Inn—Usually two or three stories, but may be a high-rise. Generally has recreation facilities, food service and ample parking. May have limited banquet/meeting facilities.

Apartment—Usually four or more stories with at least half the units equipped for housekeeping. Often in a vacation destination area. Units typically provide a full kitchen, living room and one or more bedrooms, but may be studio-type rooms with kitchen equipment in an alcove. May require minimum stay and/or offer discounts for longer stays. This classification may also modify any of the other lodging types.

Condominium—A destination property located in a resort area. Guest units consist of a bedroom, living room and kitchen. Kitchens are separate from bedrooms and are equipped with a stove, oven or microwave, refrigerator, cooking utensils and table settings for the maximum number of people occupying the unit. Linens and maid service are provided at least twice weekly. This classification may also modify any of the other lodging types.

Historic—Accommodations in restored, pre-1930 structures, reflecting the ambience of yesteryear and the surrounding region. Rooms may lack some modern amenities and have shared baths. Usually owner-operated and provides food service. Parking is usually available. This classification may also modify any of the other lodging types.

Resort—May be a destination in itself. Has a vacation atmosphere offering extensive recreational facilities for such specific interests as golf, tennis, fishing, etc. Rates may include meals under American or Modified American plans. This classification may also modify any of the other lodging types.

Suite—Units have one or more bedrooms and a living room, which may or may not be closed off from the bedrooms. This classification may also modify any of the other lodging types.

A property's **diamond rating** is not based on the room rate or any one specific aspect of its facilities or operations. Many factors are considered in calculating the rating, and certain minimum standards must be met in all inspection categories. If a property fails approval in just one category, it is not

listed in Club publications. The inspection categories include housekeeping, maintenance, service, furnishings and decor. Guest comments received by AAA may also be reviewed in a property's approval/rating process.

These criteria apply to all properties listed in this publication:

- Clean and well-maintained facilities
- Hospitable staff
- Adequate parking
- A well-kept appearance
- Good quality bedding and comfortable beds with adequate illumination
- Comfortable furnishings and decor
- Smoke detectors
- Adequate towels and supplies
- At least one comfortable easy chair with adequate illumination
- A desk or other writing surface with adequate illumination

Lodging ratings range from one to five diamonds and are defined below:

♦—Good but unpretentious. Establishments are functional. Clean and comfortable rooms must meet the basic needs of privacy and cleanliness.

♦ ♦—Shows noticeable enhancements in decor and/or quality of furnishings over those at the one-diamond level. May be recently constructed or an older property. Targets the needs of a budget-oriented traveler.

♦ ♦ ♦—Offers a degree of sophistication with additional amenities, services and facilities. There is a marked upgrade in services and comfort.

♦ ♦ ♦ ♦—Excellent properties displaying high levels of service and hospitality, and offering a wide variety of amenities and upscale facilities, inside the room, on the grounds and in the common areas.

♦♦♦♦♦—Renowned for an exceptionally high degree of service, attractive and luxurious facilities and many extra amenities. Guest services are executed and presented in a flawless manner. Guests are pampered by a very professional, attentive staff. The property's facilities and operations set standards in hospitality and service.

The Diamond ratings shown in this publication are based on inspections done in 1995-96. Occasionally a property is listed without a rating, as when an establishment is under construction or renovations are in progress and a rating cannot be determined. A few bed and breakfast inns do not meet AAA standards for approval, but are listed as a convenience.

Room rates shown in the listings are provided by each establishment's management for publication by the Auto Club. **All rates are subject to change.** During special events or holiday periods rates may exceed those published and special discounts or savings programs may not be honored. High-season rates are always shown; off-season rates are listed if they are substantially lower than the rest of the year. Rates are for typical rooms, not special units, and do not include taxes.

Many properties make special and discounted rates available exclusively to AAA members. Two publications list these rates: The AAA *TourBook*, published annually, offers two additional rate options—*Guaranteed Rates*, meaning the management has agreed to honor the published rates for AAA members; and *AAA Special Value Rates*, which gives AAA members at least 10 percent off the published rates. The monthly *Member $aver*, published by the Automobile Club of Southern California, lists many short-term rates and packages. Both publications are available at no charge to members through Auto Club offices.

Some properties offer discounts to senior citizens, or special rate periods such as weekly or monthly rentals. Inquiries as to the availability of any special discounts should be made at the time of registration. Typically, a property will allow a guest to take advantage of only one discount during the stay (i.e., a guest staying at a property offering both the *AAA Special Value Rates* and senior discount may choose only one of the two savings plans).

Each rate line gives the dates for which the rates are valid, and the rates for one person (abbreviated 1P), two persons with one bed (2P/1B), two persons with two beds (2P/2B) and the rate for each extra person (XP) not included in the family rate. Figures following these abbreviations are the price(s) for the specified room and occupants. Most rates listed are European plan, which means that no meals are included in the rate. Some lodgings' rates include breakfast [BP] or continental breakfast [CP]. A few properties offer the American Plan [AP], which includes three meals, or a Modified American Plan [MAP] which offers two meals, usually breakfast and dinner.

All baths have a combination tub and shower bath unless noted otherwise. Since nearly all establishments have air conditioning, telephones and color TV, only the absence of any of these items is noted in the listing. Check-in time is shown only if it is after 3 p.m.; check-out time is shown only if it is before 10 a.m. Service charges are not shown unless they are $1 or more, or at least 5 percent of the room rate. The pet acceptance policy is stated in the listing except where it varies within the

> *Palm Springs Ordinance 11.60 prohibits hotels from permitting persons under age 18 to occupy a room unless accompanied by a parent or other specified responsible adult. Reservations are strongly advised to assure availability of suitable accommodations in this popular resort area.*

establishment, and then no mention of pets is made (the prospective guest should call ahead to discuss specific requirements). By U.S. and Canada law, pet restrictions do not apply to guide dogs. A heated pool is heated when it is reasonable to expect use of a pool. Outdoor pools may not open in winter.

Reservations are always advisable in resort areas and may be the only way to assure obtaining the desired type of accommodations. Deposits are almost always required. Should someone need to cancel a reservation, it is helpful to be aware of the amount of notice required to receive a refund of the deposit.

Many properties welcome children in the same room with their parents at no additional charge; individual listings indicate if there is an age limit. There may be charges for additional equipment, such as roll-aways or cribs. Some properties offer a discount for guests ages 60 and older, but travelers should be aware that the Senior Discount cannot usually be taken in conjunction with or in addition to other discounts.

Fire warning and protection equipment are indicated by the symbols Ⓓ (all guest rooms have smoke detectors) and Ⓢ (all guest rooms have sprinklers). Many properties have reserved rooms for nonsmokers; the availability of these rooms is shown with the ⊗ symbol in the listing. If this kind of room is desired, it should be requested both upon making the reservation and at registration.

Restaurants

Restaurants listed in this publication have been found to be consistently good dining establishments. In metropolitan areas, where many restaurants are above average, AAA selects some of those known for the superiority of their food, service and atmosphere and also those offering a selection of quality food at moderate prices (including some cafeterias and family restaurants). In smaller communities the restaurants considered to be the best in the area may be listed.

The type of cuisine featured at a restaurant is used as a means of classification for restaurants. There are listings for Steakhouses and Continental cuisine as well as a range of ethnic foods, such as Chinese, Japanese, Italian and yes, American. Special menu types, such as early bird, a la carte, children's or Sunday Brunch, are also listed. In most cases something about each restaurant's atmosphere and appropriate attire is indicated. The availability of alcoholic beverages is shown, as well as entertainment and dancing.

Price ranges are for an average, complete meal without alcoholic beverage. Taxes and tips are not included.

Restaurant ratings are applied to two categories of operational style—full-service eating establishments, and self-service, family dining operations such as cafeterias or buffets.

♦—Good but unpretentious dishes. Table settings are usually simple and may include paper place mats and napkins. Alcoholic beverage service, if any, may be limited to beer and wine. Usually informal with an atmosphere conducive to family dining.

♦ ♦—More extensive menus representing more complex food preparation and, usually, a wider variety of alcoholic beverages. The atmosphere is appealing and suitable for either family or adult dining. Service may be casual, but host or hostess seating can be expected. Table settings may include tablecloths and cloth napkins.

♦ ♦ ♦—Extensive or specialized menus and more complex cuisine preparation requiring a professional chef contribute to either a formal dining experience or a special family meal. Cloth table linens, above-average quality table settings, a skilled service staff and an inviting decor should all be provided. Generally, the wine list includes representatives of the best domestic and foreign wine-producing regions.

♦ ♦ ♦ ♦—An appealing ambience is often enhanced by fresh flowers and fine furnishings. The overall sophistication and formal atmosphere visually create a dining experience more for adults than for families. A wine steward presents an extensive list of the best wines. A smartly attired, highly skilled staff is capable of describing how any dish is prepared. Elegant silverware, china and correct glassware are typical. The menu includes creative dishes prepared from fresh ingredients by a chef who frequently has international training. Eye-appealing desserts are offered at tableside.

♦ ♦ ♦ ♦ ♦—A world-class operation with even more luxury and sophistication than four-diamond restaurants. A proportionally large staff, expert in preparing tableside delicacies, provides flawless service. Tables are set with impeccable linens, silver and crystal glassware.

CALIFORNIA

Effective March 22, 1997, portions of area code (619) will change to area code (760).

Baker

LODGING

BUN BOY MOTEL ⓐⓐⓐ ♦ Motor Inn
At jct I-15 & SR 127; Box 130, 92309.
(619/760) 733-4363.

Fri-Sat	1P	$ 40	2P/1B	$ 49	2P/2B	$ 53
Sun-Thu	1P	$ 30	2P/1B	$ 39	2P/2B	$ 43

XP $10; discount for children ages 12 and under. Credit card deposit required. Senior discount. 1 story; exterior corridors. 20 rooms. Shower baths, cable TV, free movies. Small pets only. AE, DI, DS, MC, VI. 24-hr restaurant; $6-12; cocktails. Ⓓ ⊘

Barstow

LODGINGS

BARSTOW INN ⊛ ♦ Motel

⅛ mile west of I-15; from I-15 & westbound I-40, E Main St exits; 1261 E Main St, 92311. (619/760) 256-7581.

| All Year | 1P $ 22- 35 | 2P/1B $ 28- 40 | 2P/2B $ 33- 45 |

XP $5; discounts for children. Credit card guarantee required. Weekly rates. Senior discount. 2 stories; exterior corridors. 33 rooms; 10 kitchens, $5 extra, no utensils. Cable TV, free movies, radios; some refrigerators. Small pool. Small pets only, in smokers' rooms. AE, CB, DI, DS, JCB, MC, VI. Ⓓ ⊘

BARSTOW-SUPER 8 MOTEL ⊛ ♦ ♦ Motel

³⁄₁₀ mile west of I-15 off Main St, south to 170 Coolwater Ln, 92311. (619/760) 256-8443; FAX (619/760) 256-0997.

| All Year | 1P $ 50 | 2P/1B $ 50 | 2P/2B $ 50 |

XP $5; children ages 12 and under stay free. Reservation deposit required. 1 story; exterior corridors. 51 rooms. Cable TV, pay movies, coffee makers. Pool. Pets, $3. AE, CB, DI, DS, JCB, MC, VI. Restaurant nearby. Ⓓ ⊘

BEST WESTERN DESERT VILLA MOTEL ⊛ ♦ ♦ ♦ Motel

Adjacent to I-40, westbound exit Main St, eastbound exit Montara; ½ mi east of I-15 at 1984 E Main St, 92311. (619/760) 256-1781; FAX (619/760) 256-9265.

| All Year | 1P $ 62- 76 | 2P/1B $ 64- 78 | 2P/2B $ 67- 80 |

XP $5; children ages 12 and under stay free. Credit card guarantee required. Senior discount. 2 stories; exterior corridors. 95 rooms. Cable TV, free movies, coffee makers; fee for microwaves & refrigerators; some whirlpools. Pool, whirlpool. Coin laundry. No pets. AE, CB, DI, DS, JCB, MC, VI. Dining room, 5-8 pm, in summer 5-9 pm; $7-9; cocktails. Ⓓ ⊘

ECONO LODGE ⊛ ♦ Motel

⅛ mile west of I-15; from I-15 & westbound I-40, E Main St exits; 1230 E Main St, 92311. (619/760) 256-2133.

| 6/15-9/15 | 1P $ 28- 50 | 2P/1B $ 33- 60 | 2P/2B $ 35- 75 |
| 9/16-6/14 | 1P $ 25- 40 | 2P/1B $ 29- 55 | 2P/2B $ 29- 60 |

XP $5. Credit card guarantee required. Weekly rates. 2 stories; exterior corridors. 51 rooms; 2 kitchens, no utensils. Cable TV, coffee makers, refrigerators; some air conditioning, phones, shower baths. Heated pool. Pets, $5. AE, CB, DI, DS, MC, VI. Ⓓ ⊘

GATEWAY MOTEL ⊛ ♦ Motel

Just east of I-15; from I-15 & westbound I-40, E Main St exits; 1630 E Main St, 92311. (619/760) 256-8931.

| All Year | 1P $ 22- 35 | 2P/1B $ 28- 40 | 2P/2B $ 32- 52 |

XP $5; discount for children. Reservation deposit required. Weekly rates. Senior discount. 2 stories; exterior corridors. 33 rooms. Modest rooms. Cable TV, free movies. Pool. Small pets only, in smokers' rooms. AE, DI, DS, MC, VI. Coffee shop nearby. D ⊘

GOOD NITE INN 🔺 ♦ Motel
8 miles south on I-15; 2551 Commerce Pkwy, 92311.
(619/760) 253-2121; FAX (619/760) 253-2088.

All Year	1P $ 31- 52	2P/1B $ 37- 52	2P/2B $ 42

XP $6; children ages 18 and under stay free. Credit card guarantee required. Across freeway from factory outlet shopping mall. 3 stories; exterior corridors. 110 rooms. Cable TV; fee for VCPs. Heated pool, whirlpool, exercise room. Small pets only. Coin laundry. AE, CB, DI, DS, MC, VI. Restaurant nearby. D S ⊘

HOLIDAY INN 🔺 ♦ ♦ ♦ Motor Inn
⁹⁄₁₀ mile west of I-15; from I-15 & westbound I-40, E Main St exits; 1511 E Main St, 92311.
(619/760) 256-5573; FAX (619/760) 256-5917.

All Year	1P $ 68	2P/1B $ 68	2P/2B $ 68

XP $6. Credit card guarantee required. Weekly and monthly rates. 3 stories; interior corridors. Nicely landscaped pool area. 148 rooms. Cable TV, free movies. Heated pool, whirlpool. No pets. Meeting rooms. AE, CB, DI, DS, JCB MC, VI. Restaurant, 6 am-10 pm; $7-13; cocktails. D S ⊘

HOLIDAY INN EXPRESS ♦ ♦ ♦ Motel
⅛ mile northeast of I-15, exit west Main St; 1861 W Main St, 92311.
(619/760) 256-1300; FAX (619/760) 256-6807.

All Year [CP]	1P $ 67- 75	2P/1B $ 67- 75	2P/2B $ 67- 75

XP $10; children ages 18 and under stay free. Credit card guarantee required. 3 stories; interior corridors. 65 rooms. Cable TV, free movies, VCPs, coffee makers; some microwaves, refrigerators, shower baths. Small pool. Coin laundry. No pets. AE, CB, DI, DS, JCB, MC, VI. Restaurant nearby. D S ⊘

STARDUST INN 🔺 ♦ Motel
1⅛ miles west of I-15; from I-15 & westbound I-40, E Main St exits; 901 E Main St, 92311.
(619/760) 256-7116; FAX (619/760) 256-6417.

All Year	1P $ 24- 28	2P/1B $ 28- 35	2P/2B $ 35- 45

XP $3; children ages 10 and under stay free. Reservation deposit required. Weekly rates. 2 stories; exterior corridors. 24 rooms; 6 kitchens, no utensils. Cable TV, free movies; some refrigerators. Small pool. Small pets only, $3. AE, DI, DS, MC, VI. D ⊘

RESTAURANT

IDLE SPURS STEAK HOUSE 🔺 ♦ ♦ Steak House
North of town, on SR 58, 3 miles west of jct I-15 at 690 Hwy 58, 92311.
(619/760) 256-3888.

Lunch $7-11; dinner $12-20. Open Mon-Fri 11 am-9:30 pm, Fri to 10:30 pm; Sat 4-10:30 pm; Sun 4-9 pm. Closed 1/1, Thanksgiving & 12/25. Casual attire. Attractive western decor. Features prime rib, steak and seafood. Cocktails & lounge. AE, DS, MC, VI. ⊘

Blythe

LODGINGS

BEST WESTERN SAHARA MOTEL AAA ◆◆ Motel
Just north of I-10, Lovekin Bl exit; 825 Hobsonway, 92225.
(619/760) 922-7105; FAX (619/760) 922-5836.

1/20-2/10 [CP]	1P	$ 75- 95	2P/1B	$ 75-110	2P/2B	$ 75-110
2/11-1/19 [CP]	1P	$ 44- 54	2P/1B	$ 49- 60	2P/2B	$ 52- 62

XP $5; children ages 12 and under stay free. Credit card guarantee required. Senior discount. Palm-shaded grounds. 1 story; exterior corridors. 47 rooms. Coffee makers, microwaves, refrigerators, cable TV, VCPs, free movies. Pool, whirlpool. Pets. AE, CB, DI, DS, MC, VI. Coffee shop nearby. Ⓓ ⊘

BEST WESTERN TROPICS MOTOR HOTEL AAA ◆◆ Motel
From I-10 exit Intake Bl, 1 block north, then ⅓ mile west; 9274 E Hobsonway, 92225.
(619/760) 922-5101; FAX (619/760) 921-2610.

1/10-2/10	1P	$ 52	2P/1B	$ 56	2P/2B	$ 62
2/11-1/9	1P	$ 48	2P/1B	$ 52	2P/2B	$ 58

XP $4; children ages 16 and under stay free. Reservation deposit required. Weekly rates. Senior discount. 2 stories; exterior corridors. 56 rooms. Cable TV, free movies; some microwaves, refrigerators, shower baths. Pool, whirlpool. Pets, $20 deposit required. AE, CB, DI, DS, JCB, MC, VI. Coffee shop nearby. Ⓓ ⊘

BLYTHE TRAVELODGE AAA ◆◆ Motel
Just northwest of I-10, exit Lovekin Bl; 850 W Hobsonway, 92225.
(619/760) 922-515; FAX (619/760) 922-8422.

1/19-2/10	1P	$ 60- 70	2P/1B	$ 60- 70	2P/2B	$ 70- 80
2/11-1/18	1P	$ 39	2P/1B	$ 42- 44	2P/2B	$ 46- 48

XP $3; children ages 17 and under stay free. Reservation deposit required. Weekly rates. 1-2 stories; exterior corridors. 50 rooms. Coffee makers, free movies, refrigerators, cable TV; some microwaves, shower baths. Pool. No pets. AE, CB, DI, DS, JCB, MC, VI. Restaurant nearby. Ⓓ ⊘

COMFORT INN AAA ◆◆ Motel
Just north of I-10, exit Lovekin Bl; 903 W Hobsonway, 92225.
(619/760) 922-4146; FAX (619/760) 922-8481.

1/21-2/10 [CP]	1P	$ 65	2P/1B	$ 75- 85	2P/2B	$ 75- 85
2/11-1/20 [CP]	1P	$ 45- 54	2P/1B	$ 49- 59	2P/2B	$ 55- 62

XP $5; children ages 18 and under stay free. Reservation deposit required. Senior discount. 1-2 stories; exterior corridors. 48 rooms. Cable TV, free movies, refrigerators; some microwaves. Pool, whirlpool. Small pets, in smokers rooms only. AE, CB, DI, DS, MC, VI. Restaurant nearby. Ⓓ ⊘

COMFORT SUITES AAA ◆◆◆ Motel
⅓ mile northwest of I-10, exit 7th St; 545 E Hobsonway, 92225.
(619/760) 922-9209; FAX (619/760) 922-0427.

| 1/15-2/15 [CP] | 1P $ 79 | 2P/1B $ 89 | 2P/2B $109 |
| 2/16-1/14 [CP] | 1P $ 59- 69 | 2P/1B $ 69- 79 | 2P/2B $ 79- 89 |

XP $8-10; children ages 12 and under stay free. Reservation deposit required. Senior discount. 2 stories; exterior corridors. 67 rooms. Microwaves, refrigerators, cable TV, VCPs. Pool, whirlpool. Coin laundry. No pets. Meeting rooms. AE, CB, DI, DS, JCB, MC, VI. Ⓓ Ⓢ ⊘

HAMPTON INN ⊛   ◆ ◆ ◆ Motel
Just northwest of I-10, exit Lovekin Bl; 900 W Hobsonway, 92225.
(619/760) 922-9000; FAX (619/760) 922-9011.

| 1/15-3/31 [CP] | 1P $ 75- 95 | 2P/1B $ 75-110 | 2P/2B $ 75-110 |
| 4/1-1/14 [CP] | 1P $ 60- 79 | 2P/1B $ 60- 79 | 2P/2B $ 69 |

Credit card guarantee required. 2 stories; exterior corridors. 59 rooms; 4 suites. Microwaves, refrigerators, cable TV, free movies, VCPs, data ports. Pool, exercise room. Pets in designated rooms. AE, CB, DI, DS, MC, VI. Restaurant nearby. Ⓓ Ⓢ ⊘

HOLIDAY INN EXPRESS   ◆ ◆ Motel
Adjacent to south side of I-10, exit Lovekin Bl; 600 W Donlon St, 92225.
(619/760) 921-2300; FAX (619/760) 921-2307.

| 1/16-2/10 [CP] | 1P $ 79- 89 | 2P/1B $ 79- 99 | 2P/2B $ 89-109 |
| 2/11-1/15 [CP] | 1P $ 50- 60 | 2P/1B $ 55- 65 | 2P/2B $ 60- 70 |

XP $8-10; children ages 12 and under stay free. Reservation deposit required. Weekly & monthly rates. Senior discount. 2 stories; exterior corridors. 66 rooms. Cable TV, free movies, data ports; fee for VCPs; some microwaves, refrigerators, whirlpools. Heated indoor pool, whirlpool. Coin laundry. Pets, $10. Meeting rooms. AE, CB, DI, DS, JCB, MC, VI. Restaurant nearby. Ⓓ Ⓢ ⊘

Borrego Springs

LODGINGS

LA CASA DEL ZORRO RESORT HOTEL ⊛   ◆ ◆ ◆ ◆ Resort Complex
5½ miles southeast on Co Rd S3 at jct Yaqui Pass & Borrego Springs rds; Box 127, 92004.
(619/760) 767-5323; FAX (619/760) 767-4782.

| 5/16-10/15 | 1P $ 75-325 | 2P/1B $ 75-325 | 2P/2B $ 75-325 |
| 10/16-5/15 | 1P $ 90-505 | 2P/1B $ 90-505 | 2P/2B $ 90-505 |

XP $10; children ages 12 and under stay free. Check in 4 pm. 2-night minimum stay weekends. Reservation deposit required; 3-day refund notice. Weekly rates. Senior discount. Long established resort on several acres of attractive, tree-shaded & open grounds. Beautifully appointed rooms, suites & villas, many with wood-burning fireplace. 1-2 stories; exterior corridors. 77 rooms; 2- to 4-bedroom casitas, $200-495 in season; 32 efficiencies; 1 kitchen. Coffee makers, cable TV, free movies; fee for VCPs; some refrigerators, microwaves, honor bars. 3 heated pools, whirlpools, putting green, 6 lighted tennis courts; rental bicycles; fee for massage. No pets. Conference facilities. AE, CB, DI, DS, MC, VI. Cocktail lounge; Dining Room, see separate listing. Ⓓ ⊘

PALM CANYON RESORT △△△   ◆ ◆ ◆ Motor Inn
½ mile west on Co Rd S22 at 221 Palm Canyon Dr; Box 956, 92004.
(619/760) 767-5341; FAX (619/760) 767-4073.

6/1-10/31	1P	$ 55- 95	2P/1B	$ 55- 95	2P/2B $ 55- 95
11/1-5/31	1P	$ 75-150	2P/1B	$ 75-150	2P/2B $ 75-150

XP $10; children ages 12 and under stay free. Check in 4 pm. Reservation deposit required; 3-day refund notice. Spacious grounds; Western atmosphere. 2 stories; exterior corridors. 60 rooms; 1 2-bedroom unit. Cable TV, coffee makers; fee for VCPs; some microwaves, refrigerators. Heated pool, whirlpool. Coin laundry. No pets. Meeting rooms. AE, CB, DI, DS, MC, VI. Restaurant; 1/1-4/30 7 am-10 pm; 5/1-12/31 11 am-5 pm; $6-12; cocktails. Ⓓ ⊗

RESTAURANTS

CROSSWINDS RESTAURANT   ◆ American
On Hwy 22, 4 miles east of traffic circle, at airport; 1816 Palm Canyon, 92004.
(619/760) 767-4646.

Lunch $5-12; dinner $5-15. Open 11 am-9 pm. Casual attire. Local restaurant, views of airplanes landing and taking off. Menu includes steak, seafood and buffalo dishes. Carryout, a la carte. Cocktails & lounge. AE, MC, VI. ⊗

LA CASA DEL ZORRO RESORT HOTEL DINING ROOM   ◆ ◆ ◆ American
3845 Yaqui Pass, 92004.
(619/760) 767-5323.

Lunch $7-11; dinner $15-29. Open 7 am-2 & 5-10 pm. Reservations suggested. Semiformal attire. Attractive dining in an early California atmosphere. Cocktails & lounge. AE, CB, DI, DS, MC, VI. ⊗

Brawley

LODGINGS

BRAWLEY INN △△△   ◆ ◆ ◆ Motel
On SR 86 at 575 Main St, 92227.
(619/760) 344-1199; FAX (619/760) 344-2251.

5/1-8/31 [CP]	1P	$ 59	2P/1B	$ 59	2P/2B $ 59
9/1-4/30 [CP]	1P	$ 65	2P/1B	$ 65	2P/2B $ 65

XP $10; children ages 17 and under stay free. Credit card guarantee required. Senior discount. 2 stories; exterior corridors. 87 rooms; 8 minisuites, $80-100; presidential suite, $150-200. Cable TV, free movies; some refrigerators, microwaves. Heated pool, whirlpool. Guest laundry. No pets. Meeting rooms. AE, CB, DI, DS, MC, VI. Restaurant nearby. Ⓓ Ⓢ ⊗

TOWN HOUSE LODGE △△△   ◆ ◆ Motel
At jct SR 78 & 86; 135 Main St, 92227.
Phone & FAX (619/760) 344-5120.

All year	1P	$ 45	2P/1B	$ 49	2P/2B $ 50

XP $3. Reservation deposit required. Weekly rates. Senior discount. Comfortable, compact rooms. 2 stories; exterior corridors. 39 rooms. Cable TV, free movies, VCPs, refrigerators, microwaves, coffee makers, data ports. Small pool. Small pets only. AE, CB, DI, DS, JCB, MC, VI. Ⓓ ⊘

Calexico

LODGING

HOLLIE'S FIESTA MOTEL ⒶⒶ　　　　　　　　　　　　　　　◆ Motor Inn
On SR 111, ¾ mile north of Mexican border at 801 Imperial Av, 92231.
(619/760) 357-3271; FAX (619/760) 357-7975.

| All Year | 1P $ 41 | 2P/1B $ 47 | 2P/2B $ 47 |

XP $6; children ages 11 and under stay free. Credit card guarantee required. Weekly and monthly rates. Senior discount. 2 stories; interior corridors. 60 rooms. Cable TV, free movies. Pool. No pets. AE, CB, DI, DS, MC, VI. Dining room, restaurant; 6 am-10 pm; $7-14; cocktails. Ⓓ ⊘

Calipatria

LODGING

CALIPATRIA INN ⒶⒶ　　　　　　　　　　　　　　　◆ ◆ ◆ Motel
½ mile north on SR 111; Box 30, 92231.
(619/760) 348-7348.

| All Year [CP] | 1P $ 48 | 2P/1B $ 52 | 2P/2B $ 52 |

XP $5; children ages 12 and under stay free. Reservation deposit required. Monthly rates. Senior discount. 1-2 stories; exterior corridors. 40 rooms; 1 2-bedroom unit; 1-bedroom suites with efficiency, $88; large room with whirlpool, $79-100. Cable TV, free movies, data ports; some refrigerators, microwaves. Heated pool, whirlpool. Small pets only, $10 deposit required. AE, DS, MC, VI. Ⓓ Ⓢ ⊘

Cathedral City

LODGINGS

CATHEDRAL CITY TRAVELODGE ⒶⒶ　　　　　　　　　　◆ ◆ Motel
2 miles west at 67-495 Hwy 111, 92234.
(619/760) 328-2616; FAX (619/760) 328-0577.

Fri-Sat 2/1-5/31	1P $ 60- 71	2P/1B $ 60- 71	2P/2B $ 60- 71
Fri-Sat 6/1-9/30	1P $ 40- 45	2P/1B $ 45- 50	2P/2B $ 45- 50
Fri-Sat 10/1-1/31	1P $ 47- 52	2P/1B $ 52- 57	2P/2B $ 52- 57
Sun-Thu	1P $ 30- 48	2P/1B $ 35- 53	2P/2B $ 35- 53

XP $5; children ages 17 and under stay free. Credit card guarantee required. Nicely decorated rooms. Across the street from Camelot Amusement Park. 2 stories; interior corridors. 43 rooms. Cable TV, free movies. Heated pool, whirlpool. No pets. AE, CB, DI, MC, VI. Restaurant nearby. Ⓓ ⊘

DAYS INN SUITES ⒶⒶⒶ ♦♦ Motel

On Hwy 111 at 69-151 E Palm Canyon Dr, 92234.
(619/760) 324-5939; FAX (619/760) 324-3034.

1/1-1/14 & 2/1-5/31 [CP]	1P $ 74-119	2P/1B $ 84-119	2P/2B $ 99-169
1/15-1/31 & 10/1-12/31 [CP]	1P $ 72-102	2P/1B $ 72-102	2P/2B $ 92-122
6/1-9/30 [CP]	1P $ 52- 72	2P/1B $ 52- 72	2P/2B $ 52- 92

XP $10; children ages 16 and under stay free. Credit card guarantee required. Senior discount. 3 stories; exterior corridors. 97 rooms; 1- & 2-bedroom suites with kitchen; 2-bedroom/2-bath units with parlor & kitchen, $84-147 for up to 4 persons. Coffee makers, cable TV, free & pay movies. Heated pool, whirlpool. Airport transportation. Coin laundry. Small pets only. Meeting rooms. AE, CB, DI, DS, MC, VI. Complimentary barbecue Wed evenings. Ⓓ ⊘

DOUBLETREE RESORT AT DESERT PRINCESS
COUNTRY CLUB ⒶⒶⒶ ♦♦♦ Resort Complex

3 miles east of Hwy 111 at Landau & 67-967 Vista Chino, 92234; Box 1644, Palm Springs 92263.
(619/760) 322-7000; FAX (619/760) 322-6853.

1/6-4/28	1P $130	2P/1B $130	2P/2B $130
4/29-6/16 & 9/30-1/5	1P $105	2P/1B $105	2P/2B $105
6/17-9/29	1P $ 75	2P/1B $ 75	2P/2B $ 75

XP $15; children ages 18 and under stay free. Reservation deposit required; 3-day refund notice. Weekly & monthly rates. Spacious grounds. Nicely furnished rooms with patio or balcony. 4 stories; interior corridors. 289 rooms. Refrigerators, cable TV, free & pay movies, safes. Heated pool, whirlpools, rental bicycles. Fee for: 27 holes golf, racquetball court, 10 tennis courts (5 lighted), health club, massage. Airport transportation. Small pets only, $100 deposit required. Meeting rooms. AE, CB, DI, DS, JCB, MC, VI. Dining room; 6:30 am-10 pm, Fri & Sat to 11 pm; $8-12; cocktails. Ⓓ Ⓢ ⊘

Death Valley National Park

LODGINGS

FURNACE CREEK INN ⒶⒶⒶ ♦♦♦♦ Resort Hotel

On SR 190; 1 mile south of visitor center; SR 190, Box 1, 92328.
(619/760) 786-2345; FAX (619/760) 786-9945.

5/13-10/16	1P $170-210	2P/1B $170-210	2P/2B $170-210
10/17-5/12	1P $235-275	2P/1B $275-275	2P/2B $275-275

XP $14; children ages 5 and under stay free. Check in 4 pm. Reservation deposit required. Senior discount. Historic hotel, opened in 1927. Picturesque location overlooking Death Valley. Palm-shaded terrace grounds. A variety of rooms from small and cozy to large, nicely decorated. 3-4 stories; interior/exterior corridors. 66 rooms. Refrigerators, cable TV; some shower baths. Heated pool, saunas, 4 lighted tennis courts, exercise room. Fee for 18 holes golf, horseback riding.

No pets. AE, CB, DI, DS, MC, VI. Dining room (see separate listing), restaurant; 7-9 am, noon-1:30 & 6-10 pm; $15-35; cocktails & lounge; Sun brunch 11 am-2 pm; afternoon tea; entertainment. ⓓ ⓢ ⊘

FURNACE CREEK RANCH ⒶⒶ   Nonrated Resort Complex
On SR 190; 1 mile south of visitor center; SR 190, Box 1, 92328.
(619/760) 786-2345; FAX (619/760) 786-9945.
All year   1P $ 80-120   2P/1B $ 80-120   2P/2B $ 80-120
XP $14; children ages 18 and under stay free. Check in 4 pm. Reservation deposit required. Senior discount. On spacious grounds. Contemporary motel-type units and cabins. 2 stories; interior/exterior corridors. 224 rooms; 27 cabins. Pay movies; some shower baths, refrigerators, cable TV. Heated pool, 2 lighted tennis courts, playground, Borax Museum, general store, gas station, 3020-ft landing strip for light aircraft (unicom 122.8). Fee for: 18 holes golf, hayrides, carriage rides, horseback riding. Guest laundry. No pets. AE, CB, DI, DS, MC, VI. Restaurant, cafeteria, coffee shop; 6 am-10 pm; $8-20; cocktails. ⓓ ⊘

STOVEPIPE WELLS   Nonrated Motor Inn
On SR 190, 24 miles northwest of the visitor center; SR 190, 92328.
(619/760) 786-2387; FAX (619/760) 786-2389.
All year   1P ...   2P/1B ...   2P/2B $ 53- 76
XP $10; children ages 12 and under stay free. Reservation deposit required. Located just west of the Sand Dunes. Water in some rooms unsuitable for drinking. Modest to large, nicely furnished rooms. 1 story; exterior corridors. 83 rooms. Some shower baths, refrigerators; no phones, TVs. Heated pool. Service station, general store, landing strip for light aircraft. Pets, $20 deposit required. AE, DS, MC, VI. Restaurant; 7 am-2 & 5:30-9 pm; in summer 7 am-10 & 7-10 pm; $10-20; cocktails. ⓓ ⊘

RESTAURANT

THE DINING ROOM AT FURNACE CREEK INN   ♦♦♦ American
On SR 190, 1 mile south of visitor center, 92328.
(619/760) 786-2345.

Lunch $8-14; dinner $35. Open daily 7-9 am, noon-1:30 & 6-10 pm. Reservations required. Semiformal attire. Elegant dining with formal service. 5-course dinners with a nice variety of entrees. Salad, sandwiches & entrees available at lunch. Sun brunch. Cocktails & lounge. AE, DI, DS, MC, VI. Smoking outside only. ⊘

Desert Hot Springs

LODGINGS

DESERT HOT SPRINGS SPA HOTEL ⒶⒶ   ♦♦♦ Motor Inn
1 mile north at 10805 Palm Dr, 92240.
(619/760) 329-6000; FAX (619/760) 329-6915.
6/1-9/30   1P $ 29- 49   2P/1B $ 39- 49   2P/2B $ 45- 59
10/1-12/23   1P $ 45- 59   2P/1B $ 49- 59   2P/2B $ 55- 65
12/24-5/31   1P $ 49- 89   2P/1B $ 49- 89   2P/2B $ 59- 99

XP $6; children ages 11 and under stay free. Credit card guarantee required; 3-day refund notice; cancellation fee. Package plans. Senior discount. Popular spa facility open to the public. 2 stories; exterior corridors. 50 rooms. Cable TV; rental refrigerators. Wading pool, saunas, 4 hot natural mineral water pools, 4 mineral water whirlpools. Fee for massage. No pets. AE, CB, DI, DS, MC, VI. Dining room & coffee shop; 7 am-11 pm; $9-15; cocktails. Ⓓ

LINDA VISTA LODGE ⏧　　　　　　　　　　　　　　　　◆ Motel
⅛ mile east of Palm Dr at 67-200 Hacienda Dr, 92240.
(619/760) 329-6401; FAX (619/760) 251-2873.

4/1-5/31 &						
10/1-11/30	1P	$ 40- 48	2P/1B	$ 40- 48	2P/2B	$ 40- 48
6/1-9/30	1P	$ 39- 45	2P/1B	$ 39- 45	2P/2B	$ 39- 45
12/1-3/31	1P	$ 40- 55	2P/1B	$ 40- 55	2P/2B	$ 40- 55

XP $7; children ages 3 and under stay free. Reservation deposit required; 7-day refund notice. Weekly & monthly rates. 2 stories; exterior corridors. 40 rooms; 1 2-bedroom unit; 29 kitchens; some smaller rooms. Cable TV; some shower baths, refrigerators. Sauna, hot mineral water pool, 2 indoor & 1 outdoor mineral water whirlpools. No pets. AE, MC, VI. Ⓓ

SAM'S FAMILY SPA MOTEL　　　　　　　　　　　　　　　◆ Motel
4½ miles east of Palm Dr at 70-875 Dillon Rd, 92241.
(619/760) 329-6457; FAX (619/760) 329-8267.

All Year	1P	…	2P/1B	$ 55- 72	2P/2B	$ 72- 92

XP $7. 2-night minimum stay weekends. Reservation deposit required. Weekly & monthly rates. Extensive grounds including park area with large lake where guests may observe & feed ducks, birds & other fowl. Park area has picnic tables & barbecues available to the public. 2 stories; interior corridors. 13 rooms; 1 2-bedroom unit; 5 kitchens. Cable TV, refrigerators; some shower baths; no phones. Heated pool, wading pool, sauna, 2 natural hot mineral water whirlpools & 2 natural hot mineral pools, playground. Coin laundry. No pets. Meeting rooms. Dining 11/1-5/31, 7 am-2 pm; closed Mon-Tue. Ⓓ

STARDUST MOTEL ⏧　　　　　　　　　　　　　　　　　　◆ Motel
½ mile north, just east of Palm Dr at 66-634 5th St, 92240.
(619/760) 329-5443.

5/16-6/30 &						
10/1-11/30	1P	$ 40- 42	2P/1B	$ 40- 42	2P/2B	$ 45- 47
7/1-9/30	1P	$ 37- 39	2P/1B	$ 37- 39	2P/2B	$ 40- 42
12/1-5/15	1P	$ 43- 45	2P/1B	$ 43- 45	2P/2B	$ 47- 49

XP $7. Reservation deposit required; cancellation fee. Weekly & monthly rates. Modestly furnished rooms. Located in quiet residential area. 2 stories; exterior corridors. 16 rooms; 12 kitchens, $9-15 extra. Cable TV; some shower baths, refrigerators; no phones. Heated pool; hot mineral water whirlpool. Pets. MC, VI. Ⓓ ⊘

Room rates are subject to change.

TRAVELLERS REPOSE BED & BREAKFAST   ♦ ♦ Bed & Breakfast
From I-10, 4½ miles north to Pierson Bl, ½ mile east to First St, north to 66-920 First St;
Box 655, 92240.
(619/760) 329-9584.

9/1-6/30 [BP]   1P $ 59- 79   2P/1B $ 65- 85   2P/2B ...

Children ages 6 and under stay free. Closed Jul & Aug. 2-night minimum stay holiday weekends. Credit card guarantee required; 10-day refund notice. Victorian-style home in quiet residential area. Some rooms have antique or country-style furnishings, views of San Gorgonio and Mount San Jacinto. 2 stories; interior corridors. 3 rooms. No phones, TVs. Whirlpool. No pets. Complimentary beverages. Smoking outside only. Ⓓ

El Centro

LODGINGS

BARBARA WORTH GOLF RESORT &
CONVENTION CENTER ⨀   ♦ ♦ ♦ Resort Motor Inn
9 miles east of El Centro; 2³⁄₁₀ miles west of Holtville; from I-8, take Bowker Rd 2 miles
north, then 3 miles east on Co Rd S80; 2050 Country Club Dr, 92250.
(619/760) 536-2806; FAX (619/760) 356-4653.

All year   1P $ 52   2P/1B $ 58   2P/2B $ 58

XP $6; children ages 13 and under stay free. Reservation deposit required; 3-day refund notice. Weekly & monthly rates available. Quiet, restful setting. Large, nicely furnished rooms, most overlooking the golf course. 2 stories; interior/exterior corridors. 103 rooms; 4 suites with kitchen. Cable TV, free movies. 2 heated pools, whirlpool, playground, putting green. Fee for 18 holes golf. Valet parking. Coin laundry. Small pets only. Conference facilities. Dining room; cocktail lounge; Restaurant, see separate listing. AE, CB, DI, DS, JCB, MC, VI. Ⓓ ⊗

BEST WESTERN JOHN JAY INN ⨀   ♦ ♦ ♦ Motel
Adjacent to I-8, exit Fourth St; 2352 S Fourth St, 92243.
(619/760) 337-8677; FAX (619/760) 337-8693.

All year [CP]   1P $ 52   2P/1B $ 54   2P/2B $ 58

XP $6. Reservation deposit required; 3-day refund notice. 3 stories; interior corridors. 58 rooms. Cable TV, coin laundry; some refrigerators. Pool, sauna, whirlpool. Coin laundry. No pets. AE, DI, DS, MC, VI. Ⓓ

BRUNNER'S ⨀   ♦ ♦ Motor Inn
1 mile north of I-8, exit Imperial Av; 215 N Imperial Av, 92243.
Phone & FAX (619/760) 352-6431.

All year   1P $ 46- 53   2P/1B $ 49- 55   2P/2B $ 49- 52

XP $3. Credit card guarantee required. Weekly & monthly rates. Senior discount. Wide variety of nicely decorated rooms. 1-2 stories; exterior corridors. 88 rooms; 20 1-bedroom apartments, $70-80 for 2 persons. Coffee makers, refrigerators, microwaves, cable TV, free movies, VCPs, data ports. Pool, whirlpool, exercise room. Coin laundry. Pets. AE, CB, DI, DS, MC, VI. Restaurant, coffee shop; 5 am-10 pm; $5-23; cocktails. Ⓓ ⊘

EXECUTIVE INN OF EL CENTRO ⓐⓐ ◆ Motel
Downtown 6 blocks east of Imperial Av at 725 State St, 92243.
(619/760) 352-8500.

| All year | 1P $ 27 | 2P/1B $ 35 | 2P/2B $ 40 |

XP $2. 2 stories; exterior corridors. 42 rooms; 2 suites with kitchen; 5 efficiencies. Cable TV; some refrigerators. Pool. Coin laundry. Small pets only. MC, VI. Ⓓ

LAGUNA INN ⓐⓐ ◆ Motel
Just northwest of I-8, exit Imperial Av; 2030 Cottonwood Cir, 92243.
(619/760) 353-7750; FAX (619/760) 353-7755.

| 6/1-8/31 [CP] | 1P $ 40 | 2P/1B $ 44 | 2P/2B $ 49 |
| 9/1-5/31 [CP] | 1P $ 48 | 2P/1B $ 48 | 2P/2B $ 54 |

XP $5. 2 stories, exterior corridors. 27 rooms; 4 1-bedroom suites with efficiency, $58. Refrigerators, microwaves, cable TV, free movies. Whirlpool. Small pets only. Restaurant nearby. AE, CB, DI, DS, MC, VI. Ⓓ ⊘

RAMADA INN ⓐⓐ ◆ ◆ ◆ Motor Inn
Adjacent to I-8, exit Imperial Av. 1455 Ocotillo Dr, 92243.
(619/760) 352-5152; FAX (619/760) 337-1567.

| All Year | 1P $ 44 | 2P/1B $ 48 | 2P/2B $ 52 |

XP $6; children ages 18 and under stay free. Credit card guarantee required. Monthly rates available. Senior discount. 2 stories; interior corridors. 148 rooms. Cable TV, free & pay movies, data ports; some microwaves, refrigerators. Heated pool, wading pool, exercise room. Coin laundry. Small pets only. Restaurant; 24 hours; $6-9; cocktails. AE, CB, DI, DS, JCB, MC. Ⓓ ⊘

TRAVELODGE-EL DORADO ⓐⓐ ◆ Motel
From I-8, 1½ miles north on Imperial Av, just east on SR 86; 1464 Adams Av, 92243.
(619/760) 352-7333.

| All Year [CP] | 1P $ 36 | 2P/1B $ 41 | 2P/2B $ 45 |

XP $4; children ages 12 and under stay free. Credit card guarantee required. Weekly rates. 2 stories; exterior corridors. 73 rooms; 6 efficiencies. Cable TV, free movies; some shower baths, refrigerators, VCPs. Pool. Daytime airport transportation. Pets. AE, CB, DI, DS, MC, VI. Restaurant nearby. Ⓓ ⊘

VACATION INN ⓐⓐ ◆ ◆ Motor Inn
Adjacent to I-8, exit Imperial Av; 2015 Cottonwood Cir, 92243.
(619/760) 352-9523; FAX (619/760) 353-7620.

| All year | 1P $ 49 | 2P/1B $ 49 | 2P/2B $ 54 |

XP $5; children ages 17 and under stay free. Reservation deposit required. Weekly & monthly rates. Senior discount. 2 stories; exterior corridors. 189 rooms; 18 efficiencies. Cable TV, free movies, data ports; some refrigerators. 2 heated pools, whirlpools. Coin laundry. Pets, $25. Meeting rooms. AE, CB, DI, DS, MC, VI. Restaurant; 5:30 am-10 pm; Sun from 7 am; $10-16; cocktails. Ⓓ ⊘

RESTAURANTS

BARBARA WORTH GOLF RESORT RESTAURANT   ♦ ♦ ♦ American
At Barbara Worth Golf Resort, 2050 Country Club Dr, 92250.
(619/760) 356-2806.

Lunch $5-9; dinner $10-18. Open 6 am-10 pm. Fri seafood buffet, 5-9 pm; Sat prime rib buffet, 5-10 pm. Closed 12/25. Reservations accepted. Casual attire. Attractive restaurant with view of golf course. Sun brunch. Cocktails & lounge. AE, CB, DI, DS, MC, VI. ⊘

GRASSO'S ITALIAN RESTAURANT   ♦ Italian
½ mile west of Imperial Av at 1902 W Main St, 92243.
(619/760) 352-4635.

$11-20. Open 5:30-10 pm. Closed Mon, Tue & major holidays. Very casual atmosphere. A small, unpretentious restaurant serving a selection of pasta, pizza, veal & a few steak & chicken entrees. Children's menu, a la carte. Beer & wine. AE, MC, VI. Smoking outside only. ⊘

Hesperia

LODGINGS

DAYS INN ⊛   ♦ ♦ Motel
Just east of I-15, exit Bear Valley Rd; 14865 Bear Valley Rd, 92345.
(619/760) 948-0500; FAX (619/760) 956-8645.

All Year [CP]   1P $ 39- 69   2P/1B $ 45- 69   2P/2B $ 45- 69

XP $5; children ages 12 and under stay free. Credit card guarantee required. Weekly & monthly rates. ½ mile east of Victor Valley Mall. 2 stories; exterior corridors. 24 rooms; 3 2-bedroom units. Refrigerators, cable TV, free movies; some whirlpools. Indoor whirlpool. Coin laundry. Small pets only. Restaurant nearby. AE, CB, DI, DS, MC, VI. Ⓓ Ⓢ ⊘

SUPER 8 MOTEL ⊛   ♦ ♦ Motel
Just southeast of I-15, exit Bear Valley Rd; 12033 Oakwood Av, 92345.
(619/760) 949-3231; FAX (619/760) 949-0237.

All Year   1P $ 40- 50   2P/1B $ 42- 55   2P/2B $ 42- 60

XP $4; children ages 11 and under stay free. Reservation deposit required. Across freeway from Victor Valley Mall. 2 stories; exterior corridors. 72 rooms. Cable TV, free movies; some refrigerators, whirlpools. Pool, whirlpool. No pets. AE, DI, DS, MC, VI. Ⓓ Ⓢ ⊘

RESTAURANT

PAGANO'S RESTAURANT ⊛   ♦ ♦ Italian
Just east of I-15, exit Bear Valley Rd; 14747 Bear Valley Rd, 92345.
(619/760) 948-4880.

Lunch $6-9; dinner $9-18. Open Wed-Fri 11:30 am-2:30 pm & 5-10 pm, Sat-Sun 5-10 pm. Closed Mon, Tue, Thanksgiving & 12/25. Reservations suggested.

Casual attire. Charming restaurant featuring a nice selection of well-prepared Italian cuisine. Beer & wine. AE, DS, MC, VI. Smoking outside only. ⊗

Imperial

LODGING

BEST WESTERN IMPERIAL VALLEY INN ⊛   ♦ ♦ Motor Inn
On SR 86, 2½ miles north of El Centro; 1093 Airport Bl, 92251.
(619/760) 355-4500; FAX (619/760) 355-8645.

7/1-8/31	1P $ 42- 75	2P/1B $ 48- 75	2P/2B $ 52
9/1-6/30	1P $ 44- 77	2P/1B $ 50- 77	2P/2B $ 54

XP $6. Credit card guarantee required. Next to Imperial County Airport. 2 stories; exterior corridors. 90 rooms; 10 suites, $77. Cable TV, free movies, data ports; some microwaves, refrigerators. Pool, sauna, whirlpool, exercise room. Coin laundry. Small pets only. AE, CB, DI, DS, MC, VI. Restaurant; 11 am-10 pm; $7-12; cocktails. Ⓓ ⊗

Indian Wells

LODGINGS

HYATT GRAND CHAMPIONS RESORT ⊛   ♦ ♦ ♦ ♦ Resort Hotel
On SR 111 at 44-600 Indian Wells Ln, 92210.
(619/760) 341-1000; FAX (619/760) 568-2236.

2/1-4/30	1P $270- 365	2P/1B $270- 365	2P/2B $270- 365
5/1-5/31	1P $219- 285	2P/1B $219- 285	2P/2B $219- 285
6/1-9/15	1P $125- 189	2P/1B $125- 189	2P/2B $125- 189
9/16-1/31	1P $199- 265	2P/1B $199- 265	2P/2B $199- 265

XP $25; children ages 18 and under stay free. Check in 4 pm. Reservation deposit required; cancellation fee. 5 stories; interior/exterior corridors. 336 rooms; 20 1- & 2-bedroom villas with fireplace, whirlpool & butler service, $350-950. Spacious, beautifully landscaped grounds. Large, attractively decorated rooms with step-down parlor area & patio or balcony. Cable TV, free & pay movies, refrigerators, coffee makers, data ports. 4 heated pools, saunas, steam room, whirlpools, exercise room, volleyball court, playground, children's program. Fee for: 36 holes golf; 12 tennis courts, 8 lighted (2 clay, 2 grass). Pay valet parking. Valet laundry. No pets. Business center, meeting rooms. AE, CB, DI, DS, JCB, MC, VI. Dining room & restaurant; 6:30 am-10 pm; $10-25; cocktails; entertainment. Ⓓ Ⓢ ⊗

INDIAN WELLS RESORT HOTEL ⊛   ♦ ♦ ♦ Hotel
76-661 Hwy 111, 92210.
(619/760) 345-6466; FAX (619/760) 772-5083.

2/1-4/27	1P $149- 264	2P/1B $149- 264	2P/2B $149- 264
4/28-7/6 &			
9/29-1/31	1P $ 89- 184	2P/1B $ 89- 184	2P/2B $ 89- 184
7/7-9/28	1P $ 65- 124	2P/1B $ 65- 124	2P/2B $ 65- 124

9/29-7/6 XP $15; children ages 12 and under stay free. Credit card guarantee required. Monthly rates. Attractive hotel adjoining Indian Wells Country Club. Many rooms with view of golf course. 3 stories; interior corridors. 151 rooms; 2-room suites, $189-309. Cable TV, pay movies, honor bars, safes, data ports. Heated pool, whirlpool, 2 tennis courts, exercise room. Fee for 36 holes golf. Valet parking. Fee for airport transportation. No pets. Meeting rooms. AE, CB, DI, DS, JCB, MC, VI. Dining room; 6:30 am-2 & 5-10 pm, Fri & Sat to 10:30 pm; $14-25; cocktails. Ⓓ Ⓢ ⊘

RENAISSANCE ESMERALDA RESORT ⊛   ♦ ♦ ♦ ♦ Resort Hotel
On SR 111 at 44-400 Indian Wells Ln, 92210.
(619/760) 773-4444; FAX (619/760) 346-9308.

1/1-1/31	1P	$310- 410	2P/1B	$310-410	2P/2B $310- 410
2/1-5/31	1P	$300- 400	2P/1B	$300- 400	2P/2B $300- 400
6/1-9/27	1P	$150- 210	2P/1B	$150- 210	2P/2B $150- 210
9/28-12/31	1P	$240- 320	2P/1B	$240- 320	2P/2B $240- 320

XP $25; children ages 18 and under stay free. Reservation deposit required; 3-day refund notice. Large lobby with contemporary decor. Unique staircase leads down to restaurant & pool area. Waterfalls, 3 large heated pools and sand beach are located in center of beautifully landscaped grounds. 7 stories; interior corridors. 560 rooms. Cable TV, free & pay movies, honor bars, data ports; some refrigerators, whirlpools. 3 large heated pools & sand beach, saunas, steam room, whirlpools, health club, basketball court, croquet court, sand volleyball court; rental bicycles. Fee for: 36 holes golf; 7 tennis courts, 2 lighted; massage; valet parking; airport transportation. Coin laundry. No pets. Business center, meeting rooms, secretarial services. AE, CB, DI, DS, JCB, MC, VI. 24-hour room service. Dining room, restaurant; 6 am-11 pm; $13-30; cocktails; entertainment. Sirocco, see separate listing. Ⓓ Ⓢ ⊘

RESTAURANTS

DON DIEGO'S   ♦ ♦ Mexican
At Cook St in the Village Shopping Center. 74-969 Hwy 111, 92210.
(619/760) 340-5588.

Lunch $5-8; dinner $8-17. Open 11 am-9 pm; Fri & Sat to 10 pm; Sun 10 am-9 pm. Closed Thanksgiving & 12/25. Reservations suggested. Casual attire. Colorfully decorated restaurant. Children's menu, Sun brunch 10 am-2:30 pm. Cocktails. AE, DI, DS, MC, VI. Smoking outside only. ⊘

SIROCCO   ♦ ♦ ♦ Mediterranean
In Renaissance Esmeralda Resort, 44-400 Indian Wells Ln, 92210.
(619/760) 773-4444.

Lunch $10-14; dinner $18-40. Open Tue-Sat 6-10 pm, Wed-Sat also 11:30 am-1 pm. Closed Sun, Mon & 6/15-9/1. Reservations suggested. Valet parking. Casual attire. Mediterranean cuisine served in an elegant but relaxed atmosphere. A la carte. Cocktails AE, CB, DI, DS, JCB, MC, VI. ⊘

Indio

LODGINGS

BEST WESTERN DATE TREE MOTOR HOTEL ⊛   ♦ ♦ ♦ Motel
½ mile south of I-10, westbound exit Monroe St, eastbound exit Indio Bl. 81-909 Indio Bl, 92201.
Phone & FAX (619/760) 347-3421.

1/16-4/5 [CP]	1P $ 49- 79	2P/1B $ 59- 89	2P/2B $ 64- 98
4/6-10/2 [CP]	1P $ 44- 54	2P/1B $ 49- 59	2P/2B $ 54- 64
10/3-1/15 [CP]	1P $ 49- 59	2P/1B $ 54- 69	2P/2B $ 56- 69

XP $6-10; children ages 18 and under stay free. Credit card guarantee required. Continental breakfast plan available. Weekly & monthly rates. Senior discount. Nicely furnished rooms. Large pool area. Grounds landscaped in palm & fruit trees with attractive cactus beds. 120 rooms; 3 2-bedroom units; 3 efficiencies. Refrigerators, cable TV, free movies, data ports; fee for VCPs; some shower baths, whirlpools, microwaves. Heated pool, whirlpool, playground. Coin laundry. Pets, $50 deposit required. AE, CB, DI, DS, JCB, MC, VI. Restaurant nearby. Ⓓ ⊘

COMFORT INN ⊛   Nonrated Motel
½ mile south of I-10, exit Monroe St; 43-505 Monroe St, 92201.
(619/760) 347-4044; FAX (619/760) 347-1287.

| 6/1-10/31 | 1P $ 44- 49 | 2P/1B $ 49- 59 | 2P/2B $ 54- 64 |
| 11/1-5/31 | 1P $ 49- 64 | 2P/1B $ 59- 79 | 2P/2B $ 59- 99 |

XP $6; children ages 18 and under stay free. Reservation deposit required. Senior discount. 2 stories; interior corridors. 63 rooms. Cable TV, free movies, refrigerators. Heated pool, whirlpool. AE, CB, DI, DS, JCB, MC, VI. Coffee shop nearby. Ⓓ ⊘

PALM SHADOW INN ⊛   ♦ ♦ Motel
⅛ mile east of Jefferson Av. 80-761 Hwy 111, 92201.
(619/760) 347-3476; FAX (619/760) 342-8333.

1/1-5/31	1P $ 69	2P/1B $ 97	2P/2B $129
6/1-9/14	1P $ 49	2P/1B $ 59	2P/2B $ 69
9/15-12/31	1P $ 59	2P/1B $ 79	2P/2B $ 97

XP $15; children ages 6 and under stay free. Reservation deposit required. Weekly & monthly rates. Senior discount. Nicely furnished rooms. Large pool and lawn area. 1 story; exterior corridors. 18 rooms; $10-15 extra for efficiency. Cable TV, refrigerators, data ports, in-room fax machine & office supplies (extra charge); fee for VCPs; some coffee makers, microwaves, shower baths. Heated pool, whirlpool, croquet, horseshoe pit, shuffleboard court, barbecue. Pets, $5 daily. AE, DI, DS, MC, VI. Restaurant nearby. Ⓓ ⊘

ROYAL PLAZA INN ⊛   ♦ ♦ Motor Inn
On SR 111, ⅔ mile east of Monroe St at 82-347 Hwy 111, 92201.
(619/760) 347-0911; FAX (619/760) 347-8644.

2/1-5/31	1P $ 59- 89	2P/1B $ 69- 89	2P/2B $ 69- 89
6/1-10/31	1P $ 52- 59	2P/1B $ 52- 59	2P/2B $ 52- 69
11/1-1/31	1P $ 59- 79	2P/1B $ 59- 79	2P/2B $ 59- 79

Credit card guarantee required; 3-day refund notice. Weekly rates. Located 1 block west of Riverside County Government complex & Desert ExpoCentre. 2 stories; interior corridors. 99 rooms. Cable TV; some refrigerators. Heated pool, whirlpool, shuffleboard courts. Coin laundry. Pets. Meeting rooms. AE, DI, DS, MC, VI. Restaurant; 5 am-10 pm, Fri & Sat to 11 pm; $8-23; cocktails. ⒹⒹ ⊘

Lancaster

LODGINGS

BEST WESTERN ANTELOPE VALLEY INN ⊛   ◆◆◆ Motor Inn
2³⁄₁₀ miles east of SR 14 & 138, exit Av J; 44055 N Sierra Hwy, 93534.
Phone & FAX (805) 948-4651.

All Year	1P $ 59- 69	2P/1B $ 65- 75	2P/2B $ 65- 75

XP $6. Credit card guarantee required. Monthly rates. Large landscaped courtyard. 3 stories; interior/exterior corridors. 148 rooms. Cable TV, free & pay movies, data ports; some shower baths, refrigerators, microwaves. Heated pool, whirlpool. Valet laundry. Pets, $25. Conference facilities. AE, CB, DI, DS, MC, VI. Coffee shop; 5 am-11 pm, Fri & Sat 6 am-midnight; $10-20; Desert Rose, see separate listing. Ⓓ ⊘

DESERT INN MOTOR HOTEL ⊛   ◆◆ Motor Inn
2 miles east of SR 14 & 138, exit Av J; 44219 N Sierra Hwy, 93534.
(805) 942-8401; FAX (805) 942-8950.

All Year	1P $ 62- 75	2P/1B $ 67- 80	2P/2B $ 68- 80

XP $2. Reservation deposit required. Weekly rates. Senior discount. Nicely landscaped grounds. 1-2 stories; exterior corridors. 144 rooms; 2 2-bedroom units; 25 kitchens. Refrigerators, coffee makers, cable TV, free movies, data ports; some shower baths, microwaves. 2 heated pools, wading pool, sauna, whirlpool, racquetball courts, exercise room. Fee for massage. Valet laundry. Pets, $25 deposit required. Business center, conference facilities. AE, CB, DI, MC, VI. Coffee shop; 5:30 am-10 pm; $7-15; cocktails; entertainment. Granada Room, see separate listing. Ⓓ ⊘

INN OF LANCASTER   ◆◆◆ Motel
2 miles east of SR 14 & 138, exit Av J; 44131 N Sierra Hwy, 93534.
(805) 945-8771; FAX (805) 948-3355.

All Year [CP]	1P $ 54- 62	2P/1B $ 54- 62	2P/2B $ 60- 68

XP $4; children ages 18 and under stay free. Credit card guarantee required. 2 stories; exterior corridors. 103 rooms. Refrigerators, microwaves, coffee makers, cable TV, free movies, safes, data ports; some VCPs. Heated pool, whirlpool, exercise room. Valet laundry. No pets. AE, CB, DI, DS, MC, VI. Tue night complimentary barbecue. Ⓓ ⊘

RESTAURANTS

CASA DE MIGUEL   ◆◆ Mexican
2 miles east of SR 14 & 138, exit Av J; 44245 N Sierra Hwy, 93534.
(805) 948-0793.

Lunch $5-8; dinner $7-13. Open Mon-Sat 11 am-10 pm; Fri & Sat to 11 pm; Sun 10 am-10 pm. Closed Thanksgiving and 12/25. Attractive Mexican decor. Nice selection of Mexican entrees; also hamburgers, shrimp & steak. A la carte, children's menu, carryout, Sun brunch. Cocktails & lounge. AE, DI, DS, MC, VI. ⊗

DESERT ROSE   ♦ ♦ Steakhouse
At Best Western Antelope Valley Inn, 44055 N Sierra Hwy, 93534.
(805) 948-4651.

Dinner $10-20. Open Mon-Sat 5-10 pm. Closed Sun. Casual attire. Chicken, lamb, salads, seafood, steaks & prime rib. Children's menu, salad bar, carryout. Cocktails & lounge. Entertainment. AE, CB, DI, DS, JCB, MC, VI. Smoke-free premises. ⊗

DOWNTOWN BISTRO & CAFE   ♦ ♦ American
Just east of 10th St W at 858 W Lancaster Bl, 93534.
(805) 948-2253.

Lunch $5-10; dinner $7-14. Open 7:30 am-2:30 & 5-8:30 pm; Fri to 9:30 pm; Sat 8:30 am-2:30 & 5-9:30 pm; Sun 8:30 am-2:30 & 5-8:30 pm. Closed Mon, one week in summer and major holidays. Reservations suggested. Casual attire. Sandwiches, salads, chicken, lamb, duck, pasta, steak & fresh seafood. Fresh breads prepared & baked on premises. Children's menu, Sun brunch, health conscious menu, carryout. Cocktails. AE, MC, VI. Smoking outside only. ⊗

GRANADA ROOM   ♦ ♦ American
At Desert Inn Motor Hotel, 44219 N Sierra Hwy, 93534.
(805) 942-8401.

$11-20. Open 11:30 am-2 & 5-9:30 pm; Fri & Sat to 10 pm; Sun 10 am-2 & 5-9:30 pm. Closed Mon and 12/25. Semiformal atmosphere. Attractive dining room with a nice selection of entrees. A la carte, Sun brunch. Cocktails & lounge. Entertainment. AE, CB, DI, MC, VI. ⊗

La Quinta

LODGING

TWO ANGELS INN   Nonrated Bed & Breakfast
4 miles south of I-10, exit Washington St; south to 47th Av, left to 78-120 Caleo Bay Dr, 92253.
(909) 882-0826.

All Year	1P $195-340	2P/1B $185-350	2P/2B $185-350

Reservation deposit required; 14-day refund notice. Replica of a French chateau with Old World decor & furnishings. Private patio & balcony overlooking the lake. 2 stories; interior corridors. 11 rooms. Cable TV, free movies, data ports; some shower baths, whirlpools. Heated pool, whirlpool; instruction in meditation, rowing & yoga available. No pets. AE, MC, VI. Afternoon & evening refreshments. Smoking outside only; roll-in showers. ⊗

Room rates may increase during special events.

RESTAURANTS

CUNARD'S
♦ ♦ ♦ ♦ Continental

From SR 111, 2½ mile south on Washington St, ½ mile west on 52nd Av, just north at 78-045 Calle Cadiz, 92253.
(619/760) 564-4443.

Dinner $25-50; minimum charge $16. Open 9/1-6/1, 5-10 pm. Closed 1/1 & 12/25. Reservations suggested. Semiformal attire. Built within a large 1930s villa. Located on extensive, landscaped grounds. A la carte. Cocktails & lounge. AE, DI, MC, VI. Smoking outside only. ⊘

LA QUINTA CLIFFHOUSE
♦ ♦ ♦ American

Just west of Washington St at 78-250 Hwy 111, 92253.
(619/760) 360-5991.

Lunch $6-12; dinner $15-26. Open daily 5-9:30 pm; Fri & Sat to 10 pm; 11/1-5/1, 11:30 am-2 & 5-9:30 pm. Closed 12/25. Valet parking. Casual attire. Located on a bluff with a mountain view. Beautifully landscaped terraces with plants & a waterfall. Sun brunch (11/1-5/31, 10 am-2 pm), a la carte, children's menu, early bird specials. Cocktails & lounge. AE, DI, MC, VI. Smoking outside only. ⊘

LA QUINTA GARDEN CAFE
♦ ♦ ♦ Italian

4 miles south of Hwy 111 via Washington St; 78-073 Calle Barcelona, 92253.
(619/760) 564-0169.

Dinner $15-25. Open 10/1-5/29, Tue-Sun 4:30-9:30 pm. Closed Mon. Reservations suggested. Valet parking. Casual attire. Light opera & Broadway music by strolling singers. Some early bird specials $11.95, children's menu. Cocktails & lounge. AE, CB, DI, DS, MC, VI. ⊘

Mojave

LODGINGS

SCOTTISH INNS ⚙
♦ ♦ Motel

On SR 14 at 16352 Sierra Hwy, 93501.
(805) 824-9317; FAX (805) 824-9393.

All Year　　　　1P $ 35- 45　　　2P/1B $ 42- 50　　　2P/2B $ 40- 55

XP $5. Reservation deposit required. Weekly rates. Senior discount. 2 stories; exterior corridors. 25 rooms. Refrigerators, microwaves, cable TV, free movies. Small pool, whirlpool. Small pets only, $5; $10 deposit required. AE, CB, DI, DS, MC, VI. Ⓓ ⊘

VAGABOND INN ⚙
♦ Motel

Just east of SR 14, 2145 Hwy 58, 93501.
(805) 824-2463; FAX (805) 824-9508.

All Year [CP]　　　1P $ 31- 45　　　2P/1B $ 36　　　　2P/2B $ 45

XP $5; children ages 18 and under stay free. Credit card guarantee required. Senior discount. 2 stories, exterior corridors. 33 rooms. Cable TV, free movies. Pool. Pets. AE, CB, DI, DS, MC, VI. Ⓓ ⊘

WESTERN INN ⊛   ◆ ◆ Motor Inn
On SR 14 at 16200 Sierra Hwy, 93501.
(805) 824-3601; FAX (805) 824-3605.

| All Year | 1P $ 33- 40 | 2P/1B $ 38- 45 | 2P/2B $ 38- 45 |

XP $5. Reservation deposit required. Senior discount. 2 stories; exterior corridors. 51 rooms. Cable TV, free movies; some microwaves, refrigerators. Pool, whirlpool. No pets. Coffee shop; 7 am-10 pm; $6-9; beer only. AE, DI, DS, MC, VI. Ⓓ Ⓢ ⊘

Needles

LODGINGS

BEST WESTERN COLORADO RIVER INN ⊛   ◆ ◆ ◆ Motel
⅓ mile east of I-40, W Broadway/River Rd exit; 2371 W Broadway, 92363.
(619/760) 326-4552; FAX (619/760) 326-4562.

4/2-5/31 & 10/1-10/31	1P $ 55- 60	2P/1B $ 55- 60	2P/2B $ 55
6/1-9/30	1P $ 60- 65	2P/1B $ 60- 65	2P/2B $ 60
11/1-4/1	1P $ 50	2P/1B $ 50	2P/2B $ 55

XP $5; children ages 12 and under stay free. Reservation deposit required. Weekly & monthly rates. Senior discount. 2 stories; exterior corridors. 63 rooms. Cable TV, free movies; some microwaves, refrigerators. Heated indoor pool, sauna, whirlpool. Coin laundry. Small pets only. AC, CB, DI, DS, JCB, MC, VI. Restaurant nearby. Ⓓ Ⓢ ⊘

DAYS INN ⊛   ◆ ◆ ◆ Motel
Adjacent to I-40, W Broadway/River Rd exit; 1111 Pashard St, 92363.
(619/760) 326-5660; FAX (619/760) 326-4002.

| 4/1-10/31 | 1P $ 55 | 2P/1B $ 65 | 2P/2B $ 65 |
| 11/1-3/31 | 1P $ 45 | 2P/1B $ 50 | 2P/2B $ 50 |

XP $5; children ages 10 and under stay free. Reservation deposit required. Weekly & monthly rates. Senior discount. 2 stories; exterior corridors. 60 rooms. Cable TV, free movies; some microwaves, refrigerators. Pool, sauna, indoor whirlpool. Coin laundry. Small pets only. AE, CB, DI, DS, MC, VI. Restaurant nearby. Ⓓ Ⓢ ⊘

IMPERIAL 400 MOTOR INN ⊛   ◆ Motel
From I-40 eastbound exit J St, westbound exit E Broadway; 644 Broadway, 92363.
(619/760) 326-2145.

| All year | 1P $ 20- 26 | 2P/1B $ 24- 29 | 2P/2B $ 29 |

XP $4. Reservation deposit required. Weekly & monthly rates. 2 stories; exterior corridors. 31 rooms. Cable TV, refrigerators. Pool. Small pets only. AE, DS, MC, VI. Restaurant nearby. Ⓓ ⊘

RIVER VALLEY MOTOR LODGE ⊛   ◆ Motel
1 mile northwest on I-40 business loop; from I-40 westbound exit J St, eastbound exit W Broadway; 1707 W Broadway, 92363.
(619/760) 326-3839.

| All year | 1P $ 21- 27 | 2P/1B $ 22- 32 | 2P/2B $ 26- 35 |

XP $3; discounts for children ages 12 and under. Reservation deposit required. Weekly & monthly rates. Senior discount. 1 story; exterior corridors. 27 rooms. Cable TV, free movies, refrigerators; some microwaves. Pool. Pets, $5. AE, CB, DI, DS, JCB, MC, VI. Ⓓ ⊘

SUPER 8 MOTEL OF NEEDLES ◆ ◆ Motel
Adjacent to I-40 exit US 95, E Broadway; 1102 E Broadway, 92363.
(619/760) 326-4501; FAX (619/760) 326-2054.

Fri-Sat 4/1-9/30 [CP]	1P $ 45	2P/1B $ 50	2P/2B $ 55
Sun-Thu 4/1-9/30 & 10/1-3/31	1P $ 35	2P/1B $ 40	2P/2B $ 45

XP $5; children ages 12 and under stay free. Credit card guarantee required. Senior discount. 2 stories; exterior corridors. 30 rooms. Cable TV. Pool. Guest laundry. Pets, $20 deposit required. AE, DS, MC, VI. Ⓓ ⊘

TRAVELERS INN ⓐⓐⓐ ◆ ◆ Motel
Adjacent to I-40, exit J St; 1195 3rd St Hill, 92363.
(619/760) 326-4900; FAX (619/760) 326-4980.

All year	1P $ 30	2P/1B $ 37	2P/2B $ 37

XP $4; children ages 11 and under stay free. Reservation deposit required. Senior discount. 3 stories; exterior corridors. 117 rooms; 3 1-bedroom suites, $57.95 for 2 persons. Cable TV, free movies; some refrigerators. Heated pool, whirlpool. Coin laundry. No pets. Meeting rooms. AE, CB, DI, DS, MC, VI. Ⓓ Ⓢ ⊘

Nipton

LODGING

HOTEL NIPTON Nonrated Bed & Breakfast
72 Nipton Rd; HCR #1, Box 357, 92364.
(619/760) 856-2335.

All Year [CP]	1P ...	2P/1B $ 50	2P/2B $ 50

XP $10. Reservation deposit required, 2-day refund notice; 10% cancellation fee. 4 rooms with 2 shared baths. Early 1900, renovated adobe hotel is located in the Mojave National Preserve. Continental breakfast served in the hotel parlor. Whirlpool. No pets. DS, MC, VI. Smoking permitted outside only. ⊘

Palmdale

LODGINGS

DAYS INN PALMDALE ⓐⓐⓐ ◆ ◆ ◆ Motel
Just east of SR 14, Hwy 138/Palmdale Bl exit at 130 E Palmdale Bl, 93550.
(805) 273-1400; FAX (805) 272-9473.

All Year	1P $ 34- 42	2P/1B $ 39- 42	2P/2B $ 44

XP $5; children ages 16 and under stay free. Credit card guarantee required. 2 stories; exterior corridors. 75 rooms. Cable TV, free movies; some refrigerators, microwaves, VCPs. Pool, whirlpool. No pets. Meeting rooms. AE, CB, DI, DS, VI. Coffee shop nearby. Ⓓ ⊘

HOLIDAY INN PALMDALE-LANCASTER   ♦ ♦ Motor Inn
Palmdale Hwy & SR 14 at 38630 5th St W, 93551.
(805) 947-8055; FAX (805) 947-9957.

All Year [BP]	1P	$ 75	2P/1B	$ 85	2P/2B	$ 85

XP $10; children ages 12 and under stay free. Credit card guarantee required. Monthly rates. 5 stories; interior corridors. 153 rooms; 8 suites, $98-135. Cable TV, pay movies, data ports; fee for refrigerators, microwaves, VCPs. Heated pool, whirlpool, exercise room; health club privileges. Valet laundry. Small pets only, $15 refundable deposit. Conference facilities. AE, CB, DI, DS, JCB, MC, VI. Restaurant; 6 am-1 pm & 5-10 pm; $7-12; cocktails. Ⓓ Ⓢ ⊗

RAMADA INN Ⓐ   ♦ ♦ Motor Inn
Adjacent to SR 14; exit Palmdale Bl; 300 W Palmdale Bl, 93551.
(805) 273-1200; FAX (805) 947-9593.

All Year [BP]	1P	$ 55	2P/1B	$ 60	2P/2B	$ 65

XP $5. Credit card guarantee required. Weekly & monthly rates. Senior discount. 4 stories; interior corridors. 135 rooms. Cable TV, free movies; some VCPs, coffee makers, refrigerators, microwaves. Pool, whirlpool, exercise room. Coin laundry. No pets. Conference facilities. AE, CB, DI, DS, MC, VI. Restaurant; 6 am-1 & 5-9 pm; $8-12; cocktails; entertainment. Ⓓ ⊗

SUPER 8 MOTEL Ⓐ   ♦ ♦ Motel
Adjacent to jct SR 14 & 138; exit Palmdale Bl; 200 W Palmdale Bl, 93550.
(805) 273-8000; FAX (805) 266-4521.

All Year	1P	$ 32	2P/1B	$ 35	2P/2B	$ 40

XP $3; children ages 12 and under stay free. Credit card guarantee required. Weekly rates. Continental breakfast plan available. 2 stories; interior corridors. 94 rooms. Cable TV, free movies; fee for VCPs; some refrigerators. Heated pool, whirlpool. No pets. AE, CB, DI, DS, MC, VI. Restaurant nearby. Ⓓ ⊗

RESTAURANT

MR B'S RESTAURANT   ♦ ♦ American
19½ miles east via Palmdale Bl, 1³⁄₁₀ miles north via 170th St E in the Lake Los Angeles area; 93544.
(805) 264-2169.

Dinner $5-10. Open Wed-Sun 5-9 pm; Fri & Sat to 10 pm; Sun 4-9 pm. Closed Mon, Tue & 12/25. Reservations suggested on weekends. Selection of steak, seafood, chicken, pasta and prime rib. Children's menu, carryout. Cocktails & lounge. AE, CB, DI, DS, MC, VI. ⊗

Palm Desert

LODGINGS

CASA LARREA RESORT Ⓐ   ♦ ♦ Motel
2 blocks south of Hwy 111, between San Luis Rey & Portola Av at 73-771 Larrea St, 92260.
(619/760) 568-0311; FAX (619/760) 776-1082.

6/1-9/30 [CP]	1P	$ 50- 80	2P/1B	$ 50- 80	2P/2B	$ 50- 80
10/1-5/31 [CP]	1P	$ 64-104	2P/1B	$ 64-104	2P/2B	$ 64-104

XP $11. Reservation deposit required; 7-day refund notice; cancellation fee. Weekly & monthly rates. Located in a quiet residential area. All rooms have private patios. Tastefully decorated rooms. 1 story; exterior corridors. 11 rooms; 8 kitchens. Refrigerators, microwaves; some efficiencies, coffee makers, VCPs. Heated pool, whirlpool. Pets, $100 deposit required. DS, MC, VI. Ⓓ ⊘

DESERT PATCH INN ◆ ◆ Motel
3 blocks south of Hwy 111, between San Luis Rey & Portola Av at 73-758 Shadow Mountain Dr, 92260.
(619/760) 346-9161; FAX (619/760) 776-9661.

6/1-7/31 & 9/1-9/30 [CP]	1P	$ 47- 72	2P/1B	$ 47- 72	2P/2B	$ 47- 72
10/1-5/31 [CP]	1P	$ 54- 94	2P/1B	$ 54- 94	2P/2B	$ 54- 94

XP $10-20. Closed Aug. 2-night minimum stay weekends. Reservation deposit required; 7-day refund notice; cancellation fee. Weekly & monthly rates. Beautifully landscaped grounds. Located in a quiet residential area. Nicely furnished rooms. 1 story; exterior corridors. 14 rooms; 10 kitchens; some suites with kitchen, living room & bedroom; 3 smaller rooms. Cable TV, refrigerators; some shower baths; some coffee makers, microwaves, VCPs. Heated pool, whirlpool, putting green, shuffleboard courts. Pets, $25 deposit required. AE, DS, MC, VI. Ⓓ

EMBASSY SUITES HOTEL Ⓐ ◆ ◆ ◆ Suite Motor Inn
1½ miles east at 74-700 Hwy 111, 92260.
(619/760) 340-6600; FAX (619/760) 340-9519.

1/1-4/27 [BP]	1P	$159-219	2P/1B	$159-219	2P/2B	$159-219
4/28-6/22 & 9/21-12/31 [BP]	1P	$109-159	2P/1B	$109-159	2P/2B	$109-159
6/23-9/20 [BP]	1P	$ 69-125	2P/1B	$ 69-125	2P/2B	$ 69-125

XP $15; children ages 12 and under stay free. Check in 4 pm. Reservation deposit required; 3-day refund notice. Monthly rates. Spanish-style exterior. Nicely landscaped courtyard. 3 stories; exterior corridors. 198 rooms. Cable TV, free & pay movies, refrigerators, coffee makers; some microwaves. Heated pool, whirlpool, 6 lighted tennis courts, putting green, exercise room. Fee for airport transportation. Coin laundry. No pets. Secretarial services, meeting rooms. AE, CB, DI, DS, MC, VI. Complimentary evening beverages. Restaurant; 11:30 am-2:30 and 5-10 pm; $12-20; cocktails. Ⓓ Ⓢ ⊘ ▨

HOLIDAY INN EXPRESS-PALM DESERT Ⓐ ◆ ◆ ◆ Motel
1½ miles east at 74-675 Hwy 111, 92260.
Phone & FAX (619/760) 340-4303.

1/1-4/15 [CP]	1P	$ 89-149	2P/1B	$ 89-149	2P/2B	$ 89-149
4/16-5/31 [CP]	1P	$ 75- 99	2P/1B	$ 75- 99	2P/2B	$ 75- 99
6/1-9/30 [CP]	1P	$ 39- 79	2P/1B	$ 39- 79	2P/2B	$ 39- 79
10/1-12/31 [CP]	1P	$ 59- 89	2P/1B	$ 59- 89	2P/2B	$ 59- 89

Reservation deposit required. Senior discount. Attractive Southwest decor. 3 stories; interior corridors. 129 rooms; rooms with 1 and 2 beds; 2-bedded rooms somewhat crowded. Cable TV, free & pay movies, coffee makers, data ports; some refrigerators. Coin laundry. Heated pool, whirlpool, exercise room, tennis court, 2 lighted shuffleboard courts. Area transportation and to Betty Ford Center. No pets. Meeting rooms. AE, CB, DI, DS, MC, VI. Restaurant nearby. Ⓓ Ⓢ ⊘

THE INN AT DEEP CANYON   ♦ ♦ Motel
Just south of SR 111 via Deep Canyon Rd at 74470 Arbonia Tr, 92260.
(619/760) 346-8061; FAX (619/760) 341-9120.

6/1-6/30 &					
9/16-12/15	1P $ 49	2P/1B $ 69	2P/2B $ 89
7/1-9/15	1P $ 39	2P/1B $ 59	2P/2B $ 69
12/16-5/31	1P $ 59	2P/1B $ 79	2P/2B $ 99

Children ages 12 and under stay free. Credit card guarantee required; 3-day refund notice. Weekly & monthly rates. 2 stories; exterior corridors. 31 rooms; 15 efficiencies; 3 2-bedroom units. Refrigerators, cable TV; some shower baths. Heated pool, whirlpool. Pets, $50 deposit required. AE, DS, MC, VI. Ⓓ ⊘

INTERNATIONAL LODGE ⏣   ♦ ♦ ♦ Apartment Motel
½ block south of Hwy 111 via Panorama Dr at 74-380 El Camino, 92260.
(619/760) 346-6161; FAX (619/760) 568-0563.

5/16-7/7 &					
8/31-12/20	1P $ 65	2P/1B $ 65	2P/2B $ 65
7/8-8/30	1P $ 50	2P/1B $ 50	2P/2B $ 50
12/21-5/15	1P $ 95	2P/1B $ 95	2P/2B $ 95

XP $10; children ages 3 and under stay free. Credit card guarantee required. Weekly & monthly rates. Located in a quiet residential area. Spacious, individually decorated rooms. 2 stories; exterior corridors. 49 rooms. Cable TV, efficiencies; some shower baths, cable TV, radios. 2 heated pools, whirlpool. Coin laundry. No pets. AE, DS, MC, VI. Ⓓ ⊘

MARRIOTT'S DESERT SPRINGS RESORT & SPA ⏣   ♦ ♦ ♦ ♦ Resort Hotel
1½ miles north of Hwy 111 via Cook St at 74-855 Country Club Dr, 92260.
(619/760) 341-2211; FAX (619/760) 341-1872.

1/1-5/26	1P ...	2P/1B $245	2P/2B $245
5/27-9/16	1P ...	2P/1B $110	2P/2B $110
9/17-12/31	1P ...	2P/1B $165	2P/2B $165

Check in 4 pm. Credit card guarantee required; 10-day refund notice; cancellation fee. Package plans. Tropically landscaped grounds. 8-story atrium lobby built around cascading pools & indoor & outdoor series of manmade lakes. Mountain view. Extensive recreational, shopping & dining facilities. 8 stories; interior/exterior corridors. 884 rooms. Honor bars, cable TV, free & pay movies, safes, data ports; some whirlpools. 5 heated pools, saunas, whirlpools, boccie ball, basketball, volleyball, croquet & badminton courts. Fee for: 36 holes golf, 18-hole putting course, putting green, 21 tennis courts (8 lighted), health club, massage. Pay valet parking. Valet laundry. No pets. Secretarial services; business center, conference facilities. AE, CB, DI, DS, MC, VI. 2 dining rooms, 3 restaurants & coffee shop; 6:30 am-11 pm; $8-25; cocktails & lounge; entertainment. Ⓓ Ⓢ ⊘

SHADOW MOUNTAIN RESORT & RACQUET CLUB ⊛   ♦♦♦ Resort Motor Inn
½ mile south of Hwy 111 at 45-750 San Luis Rey, 92260.
(619/760) 346-6123; FAX (619/760) 346-6518.

Fri-Sat						
5/23-9/25 [EP]	1P	...	2P/1B	$ 85-115	2P/2B	$ 85-115
Sun-Thu						
5/23-9/25 [EP]	1P	...	2P/1B	$ 59- 69	2P/2B	$ 59- 69
2/1-4/12 [CP]	1P	...	2P/1B	$143-189	2P/2B	$143-189
4/13-5/22 &						
9/26-1/31 [CP]	1P	...	2P/1B	$110-147	2P/2B	$110-147

XP $15; children ages 12 and under stay free. Reservation deposit required; 3- to 7-day refund notice; cancellation fee. Weekly & monthly rates. Package plans. Breakfast plan available with studio units. Rooms, studios, 1- to 3-bedroom apartments & villas. Gated tennis resort. 2 stories; exterior corridors. 100 rooms; 40 kitchens, 60 efficiencies. Coffee makers, microwaves, cable TV; fee for VCPs; some shower baths. 4 heated pools, saunas, whirlpools, 16 tennis courts (6 lighted), paddle tennis, basketball & volleyball courts, exercise room, massage; rental bicycles. Coin laundry. No pets. Meeting rooms. AE, DI, MC, VI. Restaurant; 12/26-7/9 & weekends 9/1-12/25, 7:30 am-2:30 pm; closed 7/10-8/31; cocktails. Designated smoking area. Ⓓ ⊘

TRAVELERS INN ⊛   ♦♦♦ Motel
1 block east of Fred Waring Dr at 72-322 Hwy 111, 92260.
(619/760) 341-9100; FAX (619/760) 773-3515.

Sun-Thu 2/1-6/1 [CP]	1P	$ 85	2P/1B	$ 85	2P/2B	$ 85
Fri-Sat 2/1-6/1 [CP]	1P	$ 95	2P/1B	$ 95	2P/2B	$ 95
6/2-10/10 [CP]	1P	$ 48	2P/1B	$ 54	2P/2B	$ 54
10/11-1/31 [CP]	1P	$ 75	2P/1B	$ 75	2P/2B	$ 75

XP $7; children ages 11 and under stay free. Reservation deposit required. Senior discount. Centrally located in area with many large shopping centers & restaurants. Large guest rooms. 3 stories; interior corridors. 112 rooms. Cable TV, free movies; many patios or balconies; some refrigerators. Heated pool, whirlpool, putting green. Valet laundry. No pets. Meeting rooms. AE, CB, DI, DS, MC, VI. Ⓓ Ⓢ ⊘

TRES PALMAS BED & BREAKFAST   ♦♦♦ Bed & Breakfast
1 block south of El Paseo, 1 block east of SR 74; 73-135 Tumbleweed Ln; Box 2115, 92260.
(619/760) 773-9858; FAX (619/760) 776-9159.

7/1-9/30 [CP]	1P	$ 60-100	2P/1B	$ 60-100	2P/2B	...
10/1-6/30 [CP]	1P	$100-160	2P/1B	$100-160	2P/2B	...

XP $20. 2-night minimum stay weekends. Reservation deposit required; 7-day refund notice. Weekly & monthly rates. Located in residential area, within walking distance of El Paseo area. Southwest decor and architecture. 1 story; interior corridors. 4 rooms. Cable TV; no phones. Heated pool, whirlpool. No pets. MC, VI. Smoking outside only. Ⓓ ⊘

VACATION INN ⓐⓐ   ♦ ♦ Motel
1½ miles east at 74-715 Hwy 111, 92260.
(619/760) 340-4441; FAX (619/760) 773-9413.

4/15-5/31 &					
9/15-12/28	1P $ 75	2P/1B $ 75	2P/2B $ 75
6/1-9/14	1P $ 50	2P/1B $ 50	2P/2B $ 50
12/29-4/14	1P $ 93	2P/1B $ 93	2P/2B $ 93

XP $10; children ages 16 and under stay free. Credit card guarantee required. Senior discount. 3 stories; exterior corridors. 130 rooms. Balconies or patios, efficiencies, refrigerators, coffee makers, safes, cable TV, free & pay movies; some microwaves. Coin laundry. Heated pool, whirlpool, putting green, 2 tennis courts, exercise room. Small pets only, $25 deposit required. Meeting rooms. AE, CB, DI, DS, JCB, MC, VI. Ⓓ Ⓢ ⊘

RESTAURANTS

CASUELAS CAFE   ♦ ♦ Mexican
Between San Luis Rey & Larkspur at 73-703 Hwy 111, 92260.
(619/760) 568-0011.

Lunch & dinner $6-10. Open Sun-Fri 10 am-10 pm, Sat 8 am-11 pm. Closed Thanksgiving & 12/25. Casual attire. Popular Mexican restaurant. Heated and mist-cooled year-round patio dining. A la carte. Cocktails & lounge. AE, CB, DI, DS, MC, VI. ⊘

CEDAR CREEK INN   ♦ ♦ American
1 block south of Hwy 111 at 73-445 El Paseo and San Pablo, 92260.
(619/760) 340-1236.

Lunch $7-12; dinner $14-20. Open 11 am-9 pm. Reservations suggested. Casual attire. Attractive restaurant featuring a nice selection of salads, sandwiches, entrees & a large selection of homemade desserts. Patio dining available. Children's menu, Sun brunch. Cocktails & lounge. AE, MC, VI. ⊘

CLUB 74   ♦ ♦ ♦ Continental
1 block south of Hwy 111 at 73-061 El Paseo, 92260.
(619/760) 568-2782.

Lunch $7-14; dinner $16-25. Open 8/1-7/1, Mon-Sat 11:30 am-2:30 & 5:30-10 pm; Sun 5:30-10 pm. Closed Thanksgiving & 12/25. Reservations suggested. Semiformal attire. Located on the 2nd floor; rooftop patio dining available. Intimate dining atmosphere. A la carte. Cocktails. AE, DI, DS, MC, VI. ⊘

CUISTOT   ♦ ♦ ♦ French
1 block south of Hwy 111 at 73-111 El Paseo, 92260.
(619/760) 340-1000.

Lunch $10-15; dinner $18-29. Open 9/8-8/1 Tue-Sun, 11:30 am-2:30 & 6-10 pm, Sun 6-10 pm. Closed Mon and 8/2-9/7. Reservations suggested. Casual attire. Located in the Galleria Centre. Large desserts made fresh at restaurant. A la carte. Cocktails. Smoking outside only. AE, DI, MC, VI. ⊘

LG'S STEAK HOUSE
◆ ◆ ◆ Steakhouse

At El Paseo and SR 111, 74-225 Hwy 111, 92260.
(619/760) 779-9799.

Dinner $18-50. Open 5-10 pm. Reservations suggested. Valet parking. Casual attire. Southwestern decor. Dining in pueblo-style landmark building. Entrees include steak, chicken & seafood. A la carte. Cocktails & lounge. AE, DI, DS, MC, VI. ⊘

MAYO'S ON EL PASEO
◆ ◆ ◆ Continental

79-990 El Paseo, 92260.
(619/760) 346-2284.

Dinner $14-28. Open daily 5:30-10 pm; in summer call for hours. Closed major holidays. Casual attire. Contemporary, intimate atmosphere. Very good food & service. Interesting neon art work. Cocktails. AE, DI, MC, VI. ⊘

RISTORANTE MAMMA GINA
◆ ◆ ◆ Italian

1 block south of Hwy 111 at 73-705 El Paseo, 92260.
(619/760) 568-9898.

Lunch $8-15; dinner $16-28. Open 9/1-7/5, 11:30 am-2 & 5:15-10:30 pm; Sun 5:15-10 pm. Closed 7/6-8/31 and major holidays. Reservations suggested. Casual attire. Northern Italian cuisine featuring homemade pasta, chicken & veal specialties. A la carte. Cocktails. AE, DI, MC, VI. Smoking outside only. ⊘

Palm Springs

LODGINGS

Palm Springs Ordinance 11.60 prohibits hotels from permitting persons under age 18 to occupy a room unless accompanied by a parent or other specified responsible adult. Reservations are strongly advised to assure availability of suitable accommodations in this popular resort area.

AMERICAN HOTEL ⓐⓐ
◆ Motel

1 mile south at 1200 S Palm Canyon Dr, 92264.
(619/760) 320-4399.

7/8-9/30	1P	$ 30	2P/1B	$ 30- 38	2P/2B	$ 38- 46
10/1-7/7	1P	...	2P/1B	$ 38- 48	2P/2B	$ 44- 54

XP $5-6; children ages 10 and under stay free. Senior discount. 2 stories; exterior corridors. 15 rooms; 7 kitchens, $10 extra. Shower baths, cable TV. Heated pool. Airport transportation. No pets. AE, MC, VI. Ⓓ ⊘

A SUNBEAM INN
◆ Apartment Motel

1¼ miles north; 1¼ block east of Palm Canyon Dr at 291 Camino Monte Vista, 92262.
(619/760) 323-3812.

| 6/11-10/14 | 1P ... | 2P/1B $ 35- 49 | 2P/2B $ 35- 49 |
| 10/15-6/10 | 1P ... | 2P/1B $ 49- 75 | 2P/2B $ 49- 75 |

XP $10; children ages 14 and under stay free. Reservation deposit required; 7-day refund notice; cancellation fee. Weekly & monthly rates. 2 stories; exterior corridors. 15 rooms; 2 2-bedroom kitchen apts, $110; 7 1-bedroom kitchen apts. Cable TV, refrigerators; some microwaves, shower baths. Heated pool. Small pets only. AE, MC, VI. Ⓓ

BEST WESTERN INN AT PALM SPRINGS ⒶⒶⒶ   ♦♦♦ Motel

1½ miles south at jct E Palm Canyon Dr; 1633 S Palm Canyon Dr, 92264.
Phone & FAX (619/760) 325-9177.

7/6-9/30 [CP]	1P ...	2P/1B $ 39- 78	2P/2B $ 48- 78
10/1-12/24 [CP]	1P ...	2P/1B $ 49- 98	2P/2B $ 58- 98
12/25-7/5 [CP]	1P ...	2P/1B $ 69-118	2P/2B $ 78-118

XP $10; children ages 12 and under stay free. Reservation deposit required. Weekly & monthly rates. 2-3 stories; exterior corridors. 72 rooms; kitchen unit on 2 levels for up to 6 people, $250-300, depending on season. Cable TV, refrigerators, data ports; some microwaves. Heated pool, whirlpool. Valet laundry. No pets. AE, CB, DI, DS, JCB, MC, VI. Ⓓ ⊘

BEST WESTERN LAS BRISAS HOTEL ⒶⒶⒶ   ♦♦♦ Motel

¼ mile south at 222 S Indian Canyon Dr, 92262.
(619/760) 325-4372; FAX (619/760) 320-1371.

1/1-5/31 [BP]	1P $ 99-129	2P/1B $ 99-129	2P/2B $ 99-129
6/1-7/3 &			
10/1-12/31 [BP]	1P $ 56-109	2P/1B $ 56-109	2P/2B $ 56-109
7/4-9/30 [BP]	1P $ 49- 99	2P/1B $ 49- 99	2P/2B $ 49- 99

XP $10. 2-night minimum stay weekends. Reservation deposit required. Attractive garden setting. Nicely furnished rooms. 3 stories; exterior corridors. 90 rooms. Refrigerators, coffee makers, cable TV; some whirlpools. Heated pool, whirlpool. Coin laundry. No pets. Meeting rooms. AE, CB, DI, DS, MC, VI. Cocktails & lounge. Ⓓ Ⓢ ⊘

CASA CODY COUNTRY INN   ♦♦ Historic Motel

2 blocks west of Palm Canyon Dr, 1 block south of Tahquitz Canyon Wy at 175 S Cahuilla Rd, 92262.
(619/760) 320-9346; FAX (619/760) 325-8610.

5/1-7/4 &			
10/2-12/19 [CP]	1P $ 65- 99	2P/1B $ 65- 99	2P/2B $125-175
7/5-10/1 [CP]	1P $ 49- 69	2P/1B $ 49- 69	2P/2B $ 60-115
12/20-4/30 [CP]	1P $ 69-115	2P/1B $ 69-115	2P/2B $135-185

XP $10; children ages 12 and under stay free. Reservation deposit required; 3-day refund notice; cancellation fee. Weekly & monthly rates. Restored historic inn on attractive grounds. Quiet location. Exterior corridors. 26 rooms; studios & 1- & 2-bedroom villas, many with wood-burning fireplace; also 2 smaller units; 15 efficiencies, 6 kitchens. Some cable TV, VCPs, air conditioning, phones. 2 heated pools, whirlpool. Small pets only, $10. AE, CB, DI, DS, MC, VI. Ⓓ

COURTYARD BY MARRIOTT   ◆ ◆ ◆ Motor Inn
1 mile east of Indian Canyon Dr at 1300 Tahquitz Canyon Wy, 92262.
(619/760) 322-6100; FAX (619/760) 322-6091.

Fri-Sat 1/1-6/1	1P	$149	2P/1B	$149	2P/2B	$149
Sun-Thu 1/1-6/1	1P	$ 99	2P/1B	$ 99	2P/2B	$ 99
Fri-Sat 6/2-12/31	1P	$ 64- 94	2P/1B	$ 64- 94	2P/2B	$ 64- 94
Sun-Thu 6/2-12/31	1P	$ 49- 64	2P/1B	$ 49- 64	2P/2B	$ 49- 64

Children ages 17 and under stay free. Check in 4 pm. Credit card guarantee
required. Weekly & monthly rates. Nicely landscaped interior courtyard. 3 stories;
interior corridors. 149 rooms. Cable TV, free & pay movies, coffee makers, data
ports; some refrigerators. Heated pool, whirlpool, exercise room. Airport transportation. Coin laundry. No pets. Meeting rooms. AE, DI, DS, MC, VI. Dining
room; 6:30-10:30 am; Sat & Sun 7 am-noon; Sun-Thu room service 5-10 pm only;
cocktails. Ⓓ Ⓢ ⊘

DESERT HILLS APT. HOTEL ⒶⒶ   ◆ ◆ ◆ Apartment Motel
½ mile west of Palm Canyon Dr at 601 W Arenas Rd, 92262.
(619/760) 325-2777; FAX (619/760) 325-6423.

4/22-6/15 & 9/15-12/15 [CP]	1P	...	2P/1B	$ 65-140	2P/2B	$ 60-115
6/16-9/14 [CP]	1P	...	2P/1B	$ 60-135	2P/2B	$ 55- 95
12/16-4/21 [CP]	1P	...	2P/1B	$ 70-155	2P/2B	$ 65-125

XP $10. Reservation deposit required; 5-day refund notice. Monthly rates.
Spacious, attractively furnished rooms. 1 story; exterior corridors. 14 rooms;
2-bedroom/2-bath unit with kitchen and wood-burning fireplace, $120-150.
Refrigerators, microwaves, coffee makers, cable TV; 11 kitchens, VCPs; some
shower baths. Heated pool, whirlpool, bicycles. Valet laundry. No pets. AE, DS,
MC, VI. Ⓓ ⊘

EL RANCHO LODGE ⒶⒶ   ◆ ◆ Motel
2 miles southeast at 1330 E Palm Canyon Dr, 92264.
(619/760) 327-1339.

6/1-9/30 [CP]	1P	...	2P/1B	$ 40- 55	2P/2B	$ 40- 55
10/1-5/31 [CP]	1P	...	2P/1B	$ 61- 80	2P/2B	$ 61- 80

XP $20. Credit card guarantee required; 7-day refund notice; cancellation fee.
Monthly rates. 1 story; exterior corridors. 19 rooms; 6 efficiencies; 9 kitchens.
Refrigerators, cable TV; some shower baths. Heated pool, whirlpool. Coin laun-
dry. No pets. AE, DS, MC, VI. Ⓓ

ESTRELLA INN AT PALM SPRINGS ⒶⒶ   ◆ ◆ ◆ Complex
1 block west of SR 111, Palm Canyon Dr, 415 S Belardo Rd, 92262.
(619/760) 320-4117; FAX (619/760) 323-3303.

1/1-5/31 [CP]	1P	$150-325	2P/1B	$150-325	2P/2B	$ 150-325
6/1-6/30 & 9/16-12/31 [CP]	1P	$ 95-250	2P/1B	$ 95-250	2P/2B	$ 95-250
7/1-9/15 [CP]	1P	$ 79-150	2P/1B	$ 79-150	2P/2B	$ 79-150

XP $20. Reservation deposit required; 3-day refund notice. Weekly & monthly rates. Senior discount. Restored and redecorated hotel built in the late 1930s. Grounds landscaped with palms, citrus trees and colorful flowers. 1-2 stories; interior/exterior corridors. 64 rooms; 8 2-bedroom units; 4 cottages with private outdoor whirlpool; 12 efficiencies; 18 kitchens. Some coffee makers, microwaves, radios, phones, air conditioning, shower baths. 3 pools (2 heated), whirlpools, shuffleboard court, volleyball court. Barbecues. Coin laundry. Small pets only, $20 daily. Meeting rooms. AE, CB, DI, MC, VI. ⒟ ⊘

FOUR SEASONS APARTMENT HOTEL ⒶⒶⒶ   ♦ ♦ ♦ ♦ Apartment Motel
5 blocks west of Palm Canyon Dr at 290 San Jacinto Dr & Baristo Dr, 92262.
Phone & FAX (619/760) 325-6427.

2/1-3/31	1P	$105-135	2P/1B	...	2P/2B $105-135
4/1-5/31 & 12/16-1/31	1P	$100-125	2P/1B	...	2P/2B $100-125
6/1-9/30	1P	$ 60- 85	2P/1B	...	2P/2B $ 60- 85
10/1-12/15	1P	$ 85-110	2P/1B	...	2P/2B $ 85-110

XP $15. Reservation deposit required; 14-day refund notice, cancellation fee. Monthly rates. Located in quiet residential area. Exterior corridors. 11 rooms; spacious, beautifully decorated 1-bedroom suites with kitchen; also 1 2-bedroom unit with gas fireplace, $125-165; 1 smaller unit. Cable TV, refrigerators; some kitchens, microwaves. Heated pool, whirlpool, bicycles. Valet laundry. No pets. MC, VI. ⒟ ⊘

HAMPTON INN   ♦ ♦ ♦ Motel
1½ miles north at 2000 Palm Canyon Dr, 92262.
(619/760) 320-0555; FAX (619/760) 320-2261.

5/27-9/13 [CP]	1P	$ 49- 59	2P/1B	$ 49- 59	2P/2B	$ 49- 59
9/14-12/20 [CP]	1P	$ 54- 64	2P/1B	$ 59- 69	2P/2B	$ 59- 69
12/21-5/26 [CP]	1P	$ 74- 84	2P/1B	$ 78- 89	2P/2B	$ 78

Credit card guarantee required. 2 stories; exterior corridors. 96 rooms. Cable TV, free movies, data ports; some refrigerators. Heated pool, whirlpool. No pets. Meeting rooms. AE, CB, DI, DS, MC, VI. Light menu served poolside 3-7 pm, from 11 am in season; restaurant nearby. ⒟ Ⓢ ⊘

HOLIDAY INN PALM MOUNTAIN RESORT ⒶⒶⒶ   ♦ ♦ ♦ Motor Inn
1 block west of Palm Canyon Dr at 155 S Belardo, 92262.
(619/760) 325-1301; FAX (619/760) 323-8937.

1/15-4/30	1P	$109-135	2P/1B	$109-135	2P/2B $109-135
5/1-5/31 & 9/16-1/14	1P	$ 89-119	2P/1B	$ 89-119	2P/2B $ 89-119
6/1-9/15	1P	$ 59- 91	2P/1B	$ 59- 91	2P/2B $ 59- 91

XP $10; children ages 18 and under stay free. Reservation deposit required. Senior discount. 2-3 stories; exterior corridors. 122 rooms; 4 efficiencies. Refrigerators, microwaves, coffee makers, cable TV, pay movies, data ports; many patios or balconies; some shower baths, whirlpools. Heated pool, whirlpool. Coin laundry. No pets. AE, CB, DI, DS, JCB, MC, VI. Restaurant; 7-10 am, 11:30-2 pm & 5-10 pm; $10-20; cocktails & lounge; entertainment. ⒟ ⊘

HOTEL CALIFORNIA ♦ ♦ Motel
1½ mile south of Tahquitz Canyon at 424 E Palm Canyon Dr, 92254.
(619/760) 322-8855.

5/1-7/4 &					
10/1-12/23	1P ...	2P/1B	$ 50- 85	2P/2B	$ 50- 85
7/5-9/30	1P ...	2P/1B	$ 45- 75	2P/2B	$ 45- 75
12/24-4/30	1P ...	2P/1B	$ 52- 89	2P/2B	$ 59- 95

XP $10. Reservation deposit required; 3-day refund notice. Weekly & monthly rates. 2 stories; exterior corridors. 8 rooms. Efficiencies, shower baths, cable TV. Heated pool. Coin laundry. Small pets only, $20 deposit required. AE, MC, VI. Ⓓ

HYATT REGENCY SUITES PALM SPRINGS ⒶⒶ ♦ ♦ ♦ Suite Hotel
285 N Palm Canyon Dr, 92262.
(619/760) 322-9000; FAX (619/760) 322-6009.

6/1-9/15	1P ...	2P/1B	$109-145	2P/2B	$109-145
9/16-12/22	1P ...	2P/1B	$165-195	2P/2B	$165-195
12/23-5/31	1P ...	2P/1B	$205-249	2P/2B	$205-249

XP $25; children ages 18 and under stay free. Reservation deposit required. Adjacent to Desert Fashion Plaza. 6 stories; interior corridors. 192 rooms; 1-bedroom units with living room & balcony; 5 2-bedroom suites, $225-425. Cable TV, free & pay movies, coffee makers, honor bars; some whirlpools. Heated pool, whirlpool, exercise room. Valet parking. Airport transportation. Valet laundry. Small pets only, $25. Meeting rooms, secretarial services. AE, CB, DI, DS, JCB, MC, VI. Restaurant; 7 am-10 pm, Fri & Sat to midnight; $10-21; cocktails; entertainment, Thu-Sat live entertainment. Ⓓ Ⓢ ⊘

INGLESIDE INN ⒶⒶ ♦ ♦ ♦ Hotel
1 block west of Palm Canyon Dr at 200 W Ramon Rd, 92264.
(619/760) 325-0946; FAX (619/760) 325-0710.

Fri & Sat					
7/1-9/30 [CP]	1P $ 72-289	2P/1B	$ 72-289	2P/2B	$ 72-289
Sun-Thu					
7/1-9/30 [CP]	1P $ 62-250	2P/1B	$ 62-250	2P/2B	$ 62-250
6/1-6/30 [CP]	1P $ 86-338	2P/1B	$ 86-338	2P/2B	$ 86-338
10/1-5/31 [CP]	1P $ 95-385	2P/1B	$ 95-385	2P/2B	$ 95-385

XP $20. Reservation deposit required. Weekly & monthly rates. Each room or villa contains beautifully restored antiques. Many rooms with wood-burning fireplace; some with private patio. 1-2 stories; exterior corridors. 29 rooms; 2 2-bedroom units. Refrigerators, coffee makers, whirlpools, cable TV; some VCPs. Heated pool, whirlpool, croquet lawn. Airport transportation. No pets. Meeting rooms. AE, DI, DS, MC, VI. Melvyn's, see separate listing. Ⓓ

KORAKIA PENSIONE Nonrated Bed & Breakfast
257 S Patencio Rd, 92262.
(619/760) 864-6411.

9/1-7/31 [CP]	1P ...	2P/1B	$ 79-169	2P/2B	$129-169

XP $30. Closed Aug. 2 pm check in; noon check out. 2-night minimum stay on weekends. Reservation deposit required; 14-day refund notice. Lower rates available

7/5-7/31. Restored 1920s Moroccan villa at the foot of Mt San Jacinto, 4 blocks from downtown. Rooms furnished with antiques. Winston Churchill was once a guest at this home. 11 rooms and 5 bungalows, each with private bath. Refrigerators; some fireplaces, kitchens. 2 pools, ping pong table; hiking trails nearby. Pets allowed in some rooms. Expanded continental breakfast served in the guest room or on the patio; full breakfast Sun. Smoking permitted in the courtyard only. ⊗

LA MANCHA PRIVATE VILLAS & COURT CLUB ⊛   Nonrated Resort Complex
Under major renovation. ¾ mile east of Indian Canyon Dr via Alejo Rd; 444 Avenida Caballeros; Box 340, 92262.
(619/760) 323-1773; FAX (619/760) 323-5928.

All year	1P …		2P/1B $130-695	2P/2B …

XP $25; children ages 12 and under stay free. Reservation deposit required; 3-day refund notice; cancellation fee. Weekly & monthly rates. Spacious, beautifully furnished 1- to 3-bedroom villas, some with private pool and/or whirlpool. Some villas have washer & dryer. 2 stories; exterior corridors. 69 rooms; 10 2-bedroom units; 14 3-bedroom units; 54 kitchens. Cable TV, coffee makers, microwaves, refrigerators, safes, pay movies; fee for VCPs. Heated pool, saunas, whirlpool, massage, putting green, 2 lighted paddle courts, croquet courts, exercise room, table tennis. Fee for 7 tennis courts (4 lighted), bicycles. Airport transportation. No pets. AE, DS, MC, VI. Dining room, open to public by reservation only; 7:30 am-2:30 & 5:30-10 pm; cocktails. Ⓓ **(See ad below.)**

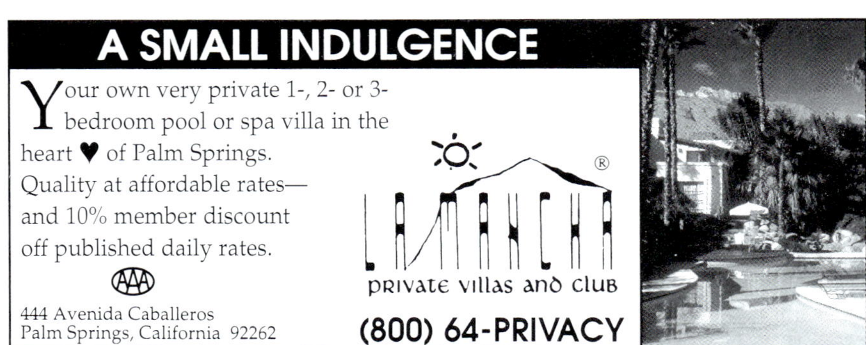

ORCHID TREE INN   ♦ ♦ ♦ Complex
1 block west of S Palm Canyon Dr at 261 S Belardo Rd, 92262.
(619/760) 325-2791; FAX (619/760) 325-3855.

6/1-7/5 &				
10/1-10/31 [EP]	1P $ 75-230	2P/1B $ 75-230	2P/2B $ 75-230
7/6-9/30 [EP]	1P $ 60-200	2P/1B $ 60-200	2P/2B $ 60-200
11/1-5/31 [CP]	1P $ 95-290	2P/1B $ 95-290	2P/2B $ 95-290

XP $15. Reservation deposit required; 7-day refund notice. Weekly & monthly rates. Nicely landscaped grounds & garden areas. 1-2 stories; exterior corridors. 36 rooms; 30 kitchen units, $10 extra. Coffee makers, cable TV; fee for VCPs;

some shower baths, refrigerators, whirlpools. 2 heated pools, whirlpool. Valet laundry. No pets. AE, MC, VI. Ⓓ ⊘ **(See ad below.)**

PALM COURT INN   Nonrated Motor Inn

Under major renovation. 1½ miles north of downtown on SR 111; 1983 N Palm Canyon Dr, 92262.
(619/760) 416-2333.

1/1-4/30	1P	$ 49- 79	2P/1B	$ 49- 79	2P/2B $ 59- 89
5/1-9/30	1P	$ 39	2P/1B	$ 39	2P/2B $ 39
10/1-12/31	1P	$ 39	2P/1B	$ 39	2P/2B $ 49

XP $8; children ages 16 and under stay free. Reservation deposit required. Continental breakfast plan available. Weekly rates. Senior discount. 1-2 stories; exterior corridors. 80 rooms. Cable TV. Heated pool, wading pool, whirlpool. No pets. Meeting rooms. AE, CB, DI, DS, MC, VI. ⊘

PALM SPRINGS HILTON RESORT   ♦ ♦ ♦ Hotel

1 block east of Indian Canyon Dr at 400 E Tahquitz Canyon Wy, 92262.
(619/760) 320-6868; FAX (619/760) 320-2126.

6/1-7/4 & 9/1-12/27	1P ...		2P/1B $110- 165	2P/2B	$110- 165
7/5-8/31	1P ...		2P/1B $ 70- 90	2P/2B	$ 70- 90
12/28-5/31	1P ...		2P/1B $165- 225	2P/2B	$165- 225

Credit card guarantee required; 3-day refund notice. Package plans. Attractively landscaped courtyard & pool area. Balconies or patios. 3 stories; interior corridors. 260 rooms. Cable TV, free & pay movies, honor bars, data ports; some coffee makers, refrigerators. Heated pool, saunas, whirlpools, exercise room, video game room. Fee for 6 lighted tennis courts, health club, massage, bicycles. Pay valet parking. Airport transportation. Valet laundry. Pets, $300 deposit required. Meeting rooms; secretarial services. AE, CB, DI, DS, MC, VI. 2 dining rooms; 6 am-11 pm; $9-30; cocktails; entertainment. Ⓓ Ⓢ ⊘

AAA members must identify themselves upon making reservations and at registration to receive special and discounted rates.

PALM SPRINGS MARQUIS CROWNE PLAZA RESORT & SUITES ⊛   ♦♦♦ Hotel
½ block south of Tahquitz Canyon Wy; 150 S Indian Canyon Dr, 92262.
(619/760) 322-2121; FAX (619/760) 322-2380.

1/4-5/31	1P	$169-257	2P/1B	$169-257	2P/2B $169-257
9/14-1/3	1P	$133-216	2P/1B	$133-216	2P/2B $133-216
6/1-9/13	1P	$ 89-163	2P/1B	$ 89-163	2P/2B $ 89-163

XP $20. Check in 4 pm. Credit card guarantee required. Weekly & monthly rates. Package plans. Senior discount. Spacious rooms & 1- & 2-bedroom suites. Patios or balconies. 3 stories; interior corridors. 264 rooms; 101 kitchens (utensils extra charge), refrigerators. Coffee makers, cable TV, pay movies, safes, data ports. 2 heated pools, wading pool, whirlpools, exercise room, game room, Kid's Camp (winter). Fee for 2 lighted tennis courts, massage. Pay valet parking. Airport transportation. Valet laundry. No pets. Business center, meeting rooms; secretarial services. AE, CB, DI, DS, JCB, MC, VI. Dining room & restaurant; 6:30 am-10:30 pm; $7-25; cocktails. Ⓓ Ⓢ ⊘

PALM SPRINGS RIVIERA RESORT ⊛   ♦♦♦ Hotel
1½ miles north at 1600 N Indian Canyon Dr, 92262.
(619/760) 327-8311; FAX (619/760) 327-4323.

2/1-5/31	1P	$129	2P/1B	$129	2P/2B $129
6/1-8/1	1P	$ 69	2P/1B	$ 69	2P/2B $ 69
9/1-1/31	1P	$ 99	2P/1B	$ 99	2P/2B $ 99

XP $20; children ages 12 and under stay free. Closed Aug. Reservation deposit required; cancellation fee. Package plans. 2-3 stories; interior corridors. 480 rooms. Refrigerators, cable TV, pay movies, data ports; some whirlpools. 2 heated pools, wading pool, whirlpools, exercise room, basketball and volleyball courts. Fee for 9 tennis courts (5 lighted), lighted putting course. Valet parking. Airport transportation. Valet laundry. Pets, $200 deposit required. Business center, meeting rooms. AE, DS, MC, VI. Ⓓ Ⓢ ⊘

PLACE IN THE SUN   ♦♦♦ Apartment Motel
3½ blocks east of Palm Canyon Dr via Mesquite Av & Random Rd; 754 San Lorenzo Rd, 92264.
Phone & FAX (619/760) 325-0254.

6/2-12/15	1P	$ 60- 90	2P/1B	$ 60- 90	2P/2B $ 60- 90
12/16-6/1	1P	$ 69-109	2P/1B	$ 69-109	2P/2B $ 69-109

XP $12; discount for children. Reservation deposit required. Weekly & monthly rates. Patios. Attractive grounds with many fruit trees. 1 story; exterior corridors. 16 rooms; studio & 1-bedroom apartments; 14 kitchens, 2 efficiencies. Cable TV, coffee makers, microwaves, refrigerators; some radios. Heated pool, whirlpool, putting green. Coin laundry. Small pets only, $10. MC, VI. Ⓓ ⊘

QUALITY INN ⊛   ♦♦♦ Motel
2¼ miles southeast at 1269 E Palm Canyon Dr, 92264.
(619/760) 323-2775; FAX (619/760) 323-4234.

6/1-12/23	1P	$ 39- 99	2P/1B	$ 39- 99	2P/2B $ 49- 99
12/24-5/31	1P	$ 59-129	2P/1B	$ 59-129	2P/2B $ 69-139

XP $10; children ages 18 and under stay free. Credit card guarantee required. Senior discount. Spacious grounds. 2 stories; exterior corridors. 145 rooms; 1-bedroom suites, 12/26-5/31, $119-169; 6/1-12/25, $79-89. Cable TV, pay movies, coffee makers; some refrigerators, microwaves. Heated pool, wading pool, whirlpool. Coin laundry. Small pets only. Meeting rooms. AE, CB, DI, DS, MC, VI. Restaurant nearby. Ⓓ ⊘

RAMADA RESORT INN & CONFERENCE CENTER ⒶⒶⒶ   ♦ ♦ ♦ Motor Inn
Formerly Shilo Inns Sunrise Resort. 2½ miles southeast at 1800 E Palm Canyon Dr, 92264.
(619/760) 323-1711; FAX (619/760) 327-6941.

6/1-9/30	1P	$ 49- 99	2P/1B	$ 49-109	2P/2B	$ 49-109
10/1-12/22	1P	$ 59- 99	2P/1B	$ 59- 99	2P/2B	$ 59- 99
12/23-5/31	1P	$ 79-149	2P/1B	$ 79-149	2P/2B	$ 79-149

XP $15; children ages 18 and under stay free. Reservation deposit required. Weekly & monthly rates. Senior discount. 3 stories; interior/exterior corridors. 255 rooms; 2 2-bedroom units. Cable TV, pay movies, coffee makers, refrigerators; fee for microwaves; some safes. Heated pool, saunas, whirlpools, exercise room. Coin laundry. Small pets only, $50 deposit required. Meeting rooms; secretarial services. AE, CB, DI, DS, MC, VI. Restaurant, coffee shop; 6:30 am-1 am; $10-26; cocktail lounge. Ⓓ ⊘

ROYAL SUN HOTEL ⒶⒶⒶ   ♦ ♦ Motel
1½ miles southeast at 1700 S Palm Canyon Dr, 92264.
(619/760) 327-1564; FAX (619/760) 323-9092.

1/1-5/31 [CP]	1P	$ 79- 89	2P/1B	$ 79- 89	2P/2B	$ 89- 99
6/1-9/30 [CP]	1P	$ 49- 59	2P/1B	$ 49- 59	2P/2B	$ 59- 69
10/1-12/31 [CP]	1P	$ 59- 69	2P/1B	$ 59- 69	2P/2B	$ 69- 79

XP $6; children ages 12 and under stay free. Credit card guarantee required. Weekly & monthly rates. Senior discount. Balconies or patios. 3 stories; exterior corridors. 66 rooms; luxury level rooms; 2 efficiencies. Coffee makers, cable TV; fee for microwaves; some refrigerators, safes. Heated pool, sauna, whirlpool. Coin laundry. Small pets only, $10. AE, DS, MC, VI. Restaurant nearby. Ⓓ ⊘

SHILO INN   ♦ ♦ Motel
1½ miles north at 1875 N Palm Canyon Dr, 92262.
(619/760) 320-7676; FAX (619/760) 320-9543.

Fri & Sat					
1/1-5/31 [CP]	1P	$110-139	2P/1B	$110-139	2P/2B	$110-139
Sun-Thu					
1/1-5/31 [CP]	1P	$ 95-115	2P/1B	$ 95-115	2P/2B	$ 95-115
6/1-12/31 [CP]	1P	$ 62- 88	2P/1B	$ 62- 88	2P/2B	$ 62- 88

XP $12; children ages 12 and under stay free. Credit card guarantee required. Weekly & monthly rates. Senior discount. Nicely landscaped grounds. Patios or balconies. 124 rooms; 4 kitchen units, $20 extra. Refrigerators, microwaves, cable TV, free movies. 2 heated pools, sauna, whirlpools, exercise room. Airport transportation. Coin laundry. No pets. Meeting rooms. AE, DI, DS, JCB, MC, VI. Restaurant nearby. Ⓓ Ⓢ ⊘

LODGING & RESTAURANTS

SPA HOTEL & CASINO RESORT & MINERAL SPRINGS (AAA)   ♦ ♦ ♦ Hotel
100 N Indian Canyon Dr at Tahquitz Canyon Wy, 92262.
(619/760) 325-1461; FAX (619/760) 325-5635.

6/16-9/14	1P ...	2P/1B $ 69- 94	2P/2B $ 69- 94
9/15-12/26	1P ...	2P/1B $114-144	2P/2B $114-144
12/27-6/15	1P ...	2P/1B $159-199	2P/2B $159-199

XP $15-25. Check in 4 pm. Reservation deposit required; 3-day refund notice. Weekly & monthly rates. 5 stories; interior corridors. 230 rooms; 15 efficiencies. Cable TV, pay movies, coffee makers, honor bars, data ports; fee for refrigerators; some whirlpools. Heated pool, outdoor hot mineral pool, hot mineral whirlpool, health spa. Valet parking. Airport transportation. Valet laundry. No pets. Meeting rooms. AE, CB, DI, DS, MC, VI. 2 restaurants; 7 am-10 pm; $10-19; cocktails & lounge; indoor & outdoor dining Fri & Sat to 11 pm; 24-hr room service; entertainment. (D) ⊘

SUPER 8 LODGE (AAA)   ♦ Motel
1½ miles north at 1900 N Palm Canyon Dr, 92262.
(619/760) 322-3757; FAX (619/760) 323-5290.

7/1-9/30 [CP]	1P $ 50	2P/1B $ 56	2P/2B $ 60
10/1-6/30 [CP]	1P $ 56	2P/1B $ 66	2P/2B $ 70

XP $5; children ages 18 and under stay free. Credit card guarantee required. Senior discount. 2 stories; exterior corridors. 61 rooms; executive parlor rooms $75-85. Refrigerators, cable TV, data ports. Heated pool, whirlpool. Coin laundry. No pets. AE, CB, DI, DS, MC, VI. Restaurant nearby. (D) (S) ⊘

TRAVELODGE-PALM SPRINGS (AAA)   ♦ ♦ Motel
1½ miles south of Tahquitz Canyon Wy at 333 E Palm Canyon Dr, 92264.
(619/760) 327-1211; FAX (619/760) 320-4672.

6/13-9/1	1P ...	2P/1B $ 35- 45	2P/2B $ 43- 55
9/2-12/23	1P ...	2P/1B $ 45- 60	2P/2B $ 55- 65
12/24-6/12	1P ...	2P/1B $ 59- 75	2P/2B $ 69- 85

XP $10; children ages 18 and under stay free. Reservation deposit required. Weekly rates. Large rooms with balcony or patio. 2 stories; exterior corridors. 157 rooms. Cable TV, free movies, coffee makers; fee for refrigerators, microwaves; some shower baths, radios. 2 heated pools, whirlpool, volleyball court, badminton, shuffleboard court. Coin laundry. No pets. AE, DI, DS, MC, VI. Restaurant nearby. (D) ⊘

VAGABOND INN (AAA)   ♦ ♦ ♦ Motel
1½ miles south at jct E Palm Canyon Dr; 1699 S Palm Canyon Dr, 92264.
(619/760) 325-7211; FAX (619/760) 322-9269.

6/2-6/15	1P $ 49- 85	2P/1B $ 49- 85	2P/2B $ 53- 89
6/16-9/26	1P $ 39- 49	2P/1B $ 39- 49	2P/2B $ 44- 54
9/27-12/24	1P $ 49- 65	2P/1B $ 49- 65	2P/2B $ 54- 69
12/25-6/1	1P $ 66- 85	2P/1B $ 66- 85	2P/2B $ 71- 89

XP $3-6. 3-night minimum stay holidays. Credit card guarantee required; 3-day refund notice. Monthly rates. 3 stories; exterior corridors. 120 rooms; 1 2-

bedroom unit. Cable TV, coffee makers; some refrigerators. Heated pool, saunas, whirlpool. No pets. Meeting rooms. AE, CB, DI, DS, JCB, MC, VI. Coffee shop; 7 am-3 pm. D ⊘

VILLA ROSA INN ♦♦ Motel
2 miles southeast on Palm Canyon Dr, 1½ blocks north at 1577 S Indian Tr, 92264. (619/760) 327-5915.

6/1-7/31 & 9/1-9/30 [CP]	1P	$ 45- 89	2P/1B	$ 45- 89	2P/2B	...
10/1-5/31 [CP]	1P	$ 65-110	2P/1B	$ 65-110	2P/2B	...

Open 9/1-7/31. 2-night minimum stay weekends. Reservation deposit required; 3-day refund notice. Weekly & monthly rates. Tastefully decorated rooms. Quiet, garden setting. 1 story; exterior corridors. 6 rooms; 2 1-bedroom suites with kitchen, $85-110 for 2 persons. Cable TV; some shower baths, microwaves, VCPs. Heated pool. No pets. AE, MC, VI. Restaurant nearby. Smoking outside only. D ⊘

VILLA ROYALE BED & BREAKFAST INN ♦♦ Country Inn
2 miles southeast on Palm Canyon Dr, then 1 block north at 1620 S Indian Tr, 92264. (619/760) 327-2314; FAX (619/760) 322-3794.

7/7-9/30 [CP]	1P	$ 60-150	2P/1B	$ 60-150	2P/2B	$ 60-150
10/1-7/6 [CP]	1P	$ 65-295	2P/1B	$ 65-295	2P/2B	$ 65-295

XP $25. 2-night minimum stay weekends. Reservation deposit required; 10-day refund notice. Monthly rates available. Senior discount. Old World ambiance. Nicely landscaped courtyards and individually decorated rooms and suites. 1 story; exterior corridors. 31 rooms; 4 2-bedroom units; 8 efficiencies, 7 kitchens. Cable TV; some shower baths, coffee makers, microwaves, fireplace, private outdoor whirlpool. 2 heated pools, whirlpool. No pets. AE, DI, MC, VI. Restaurant; 11:30 am-2 and 5:30-10 pm; closed Mon and 6/1-10/1; $13-22; cocktail lounge. D ⊘

VILLE ORLEANS RESORT HOTEL ♦♦ Motel
1½ miles north of downtown, just east of Indian Canyon Dr; 269 Chuckwalla Rd, 92262. (619/760) 864-6200; FAX (619/760) 864-6208.

6/1-8/31	1P	...	2P/1B	$ 59-165	2P/2B	$ 95-115
9/1-5/31	1P	...	2P/1B	$ 69-225	2P/2B	$115-135

XP $15; children ages 5 and under stay free. Reservation deposit required; 3-day refund notice. Weekly & monthly rates. Senior discount. 1-2 stories; exterior corridors. 14 rooms; 1 2-bedroom unit; 2-bedroom/2-bath suite, $165-225; 8 kitchens. Coffee makers, refrigerators, safes, cable TV, VCPs; some shower baths. Heated pool, whirlpool. Video library. Small pets only, $10. AE, MC, VI. Designated smoking area. D ⊘

WYNDHAM PALM SPRINGS ♦♦♦ Hotel
3 blocks east of Indian Canyon Dr at 888 E Tahquitz Canyon Wy, 92262. (619/760) 322-6000; FAX (619/760) 322-5351.

1/5-7/5	1P	$120	2P/1B	$130	2P/2B	$130
7/6-10/2	1P	$ 70	2P/1B	$ 80	2P/2B	$ 80
10/3-1/4	1P	$110	2P/1B	$120	2P/2B	$120

XP $25. Reservation deposit required; 3-day refund notice. Package plans. 5 stories; interior corridors. 410 rooms. Coffee makers, cable TV, pay movies, data ports; some rental refrigerators. Heated pool, wading pool, sauna, whirlpools, exercise room. Fee for massage. Airport transportation. Valet laundry. Small pets only, $25 nonrefundable deposit. Meeting rooms; business center. AE, CB, DI, DS, JCB, MC, VI. Dining room, restaurant; 6:30 am-11 pm; $8-21; cocktails; entertainment. Ⓓ Ⓢ ⊘

RESTAURANTS

BANDUCCI'S BIT OF ITALY ⬟   ♦ ♦ Italian
1 mile south at 1260 S Palm Canyon Dr, 92264.
(619/760) 325-2537.

Dinner $8-16. Open 5 pm-11. Closed Thanksgiving. Reservations suggested in season. Valet parking. Casual attire. Popular, long established restaurant. Informal decor & service. Indoor & outdoor patio dining. Cocktails & lounge; piano bar Wed-Sun. AE, DI, DS, MC, VI. ⊘

BILLY REED'S RESTAURANT ⬟   ♦ ♦ American
1½ miles north at 1800 N Palm Canyon Dr, 92262.
(619/760) 325-1946.

Lunch $6-13; dinner $8-19. Open 7 am-10:45 pm. Closed 12/25. Casual attire. Popular restaurant featuring a large selection of salads, sandwiches & entrees. Victorian decor. Children's menu; early bird specials; carryout. Cocktails & lounge; entertainment. AE, DI, DS, MC, VI. ⊘

CEDAR CREEK INN   ♦ ♦ ♦ American
1 mile south at 1555 S Palm Canyon Dr, 92264.
(619/760) 325-7300.

Lunch $7-13; dinner $16-20. Open 11 am-10 pm. Closed major holidays. Reservations suggested. Casual attire. Very attractive restaurant featuring a large selection of salads, sandwiches, entrees & homemade desserts. Sun brunch, carryout. Cocktails & lounge; entertainment. AE, MC, VI. ⊘

LAS CASUELAS   ♦ Mexican
Downtown; 368 N Palm Canyon Dr, 92262.
(619/760) 325-3213.

Lunch & dinner $6-12. Open 10 am-9 pm, Fri & Sat to 10 pm. Closed Thanksgiving & 12/25. Reservations suggested. Small, long established restaurant located in center of town. Children's menu, a la carte, carryout. Beer & wine. AE, DI, MC, VI. ⊘

LAS CASUELAS TERRAZA ⬟   ♦ Mexican
Downtown at 222 S Palm Canyon Dr, 92262.
(619/760) 325-2794.

Lunch $7-9; dinner $7-14. Open 11 am-10 pm; Sun from 10 am. Closed Thanksgiving & 12/25. Reservations suggested weekends. Casual attire. Popular restaurant. Indoor & patio dining. Children's menu, carryout. Cocktails & lounge; entertainment. AE, DI, DS, MC, VI. ⊘

LE VALLAURIS ◆◆◆◆ French
3 blocks west of Palm Canyon Dr at 385 W Tahquitz Canyon Wy, 92262.
(619/760) 325-5059.

Lunch $4-14; dinner $25-32. Open 11:30 am-3 & 5:30-11 pm. Reservations suggested. Valet parking. Semiformal attire. Fine dining in a beautifully decorated restaurant and tree-shaded patio. A la carte, Sun brunch 11:30 am-2 pm. Cocktails & lounge. AE, CB, DI, DS, MC, VI. ⊘

LYONS ENGLISH GRILLE ◆◆ American
At 233 E Palm Canyon Dr, 1½ miles south of Tahquitz Canyon Wy, 92264.
(619/760) 327-1551.

Dinner $13-20. Open 10/2-6/30; 4:30-10:30 pm. Reservations suggested. Valet parking. Casual attire. Children's menu, early bird specials, carryout. Cocktails. AE, DI, MC, VI. ⊘

MELVYN'S ◆◆◆ Continental
At Ingleside Inn, 200 W Ramon Rd, 92264.
(619/760) 325-2323.

Lunch $9-15; dinner $21-31. Open Mon-Fri noon-3 & 6-11:30 pm, Sat 11 am-3 & 6-11:30 pm; Sun 9 am-3 & 6-11:30 pm. Reservations suggested. Valet parking. Casual attire. Garden setting; enclosed patio dining. Sat brunch 11 am-3 pm, Sun brunch 9 am-3 pm. Cocktails & lounge; entertainment. AE, DI, DS, MC, VI. Smoking outside only. ⊘

OTANI-A GARDEN RESTAURANT ◆◆◆ Japanese
3 blocks east of Indian Canyon Dr; across from convention center at 266 Avenida Caballeros, 92262.
(619/760) 327-6700.

Lunch $6-10; dinner $10-24. Open 11:30 am-2 & 6-9:30 pm; Sat 5-9:30 pm; Sun 11 am-2 & 5-9:30 pm. Reservations suggested. Casual attire. Tempura, sushi, yakatori and teppan-yaki dining areas. A la carte, carryout, children's menu, Sun brunch; early dining specials Jun-Nov. Cocktails & lounge. AE, DI, JCB, MC, VI. Smoking outside only. ⊘

ROCK GARDEN CAFE ◆ American
777 S Palm Canyon Dr, 92262.
(619/760) 327-8840.

Lunch $3-7, dinner $8-16. Open 7 am-midnight. Casual attire. Family restaurant. Patio seating available. Pasta, beef, fish and chicken entrees; also, salads, sandwiches and breakfast served all day. Bakery and small gift shop. A la carte, children's menu, senior's menu, health conscious menu. Cocktails & lounge; live entertainment Wed-Sat. AE, CB, DI, DS, MC, VI. ⊘

SIAMESE GOURMET RESTAURANT ◆◆ Thai
5 miles southeast in Rimrock Shopping Center; 4711 E Palm Canyon Dr & Gene Autry Tr, 92264.
(619/760) 328-0057.

Lunch $5-10; dinner $8-16. Open 11:30 am-2:30 and 5 to 10 pm, Sun from 5 pm. Reservations suggested. Casual attire. Small restaurant serving nice selection of Thai cuisine. A la carte; early bird specials; carryout. Beer & wine. AE, DI, DS, MC, VI. Smoking outside only. ⊘

Rancho Mirage

LODGINGS

MARRIOTT'S RANCHO LAS PALMAS RESORT　　　　◆◆◆◆ Resort Hotel
¼ mile north of Hwy 111 at 41-000 Bob Hope Dr, 92270.
(619/760) 568-2727; FAX (619/760) 568-5845.

5/29-9/16	1P	$ 99	2P/1B	$ 99	2P/2B	$ 99
9/17-12/30	1P	$149	2P/1B	$149	2P/2B	$149
12/31-5/28	1P	$245	2P/1B	$245	2P/2B	$245

XP $10; children ages 16 and under stay free. Check in 4 pm. Credit card guarantee required. Senior discount. Early California-Spanish ambiance. Public areas & most guest rooms have view of golf course fairways, lakes & pools. Beautifully landscaped. 2 stories; exterior corridors. 450 rooms. Balcony or patio, honor bars, cable TV, free & pay movies, data ports; some refrigerators. 2 heated pools, whirlpools, putting green, 3 clay courts, exercise room, children's program, playground. Fee for: 27 holes golf, 25 tennis courts (8 lighted), bicycles, massage. Coin laundry. Fee for airport transportation. Small pets only. Business center, conference facilities, secretarial services. AE, CB, DI, DS, JCB, MC, VI. Dining room, 2 restaurants, coffee shop; 6:30 am-11 pm, 6/1-8/31 to 10 pm; $8-30; cocktails; entertainment. Ⓓ ⊘

THE RITZ-CARLTON, RANCHO MIRAGE ⊕　　　　◆◆◆◆ Resort Hotel
½ mile south of SR 111 at 68-900 Frank Sinatra Dr, 92270.
(619/760) 321-8282; FAX (619/760) 321-6928.

5/26-9/11	1P	$ 99-175	2P/1B	$119-195	2P/1B	$119-195
9/12-12/28	1P	$175-285	2P/1B	$195-305	2P/2B	$195-305
12/29-5/25	1P	$275-435	2P/1B	$295-445	2P/2B	$295-445

XP $25; children ages 18 and under stay free. Reservation deposit required; 7-day refund notice. Continental breakfast plan available. Hilltop location. Elegantly decorated public facilities & guest rooms. 3 stories; interior corridors. 239 rooms. Cable TV, free & pay movies, honor bars; fee for VCPs. Heated pool; whirlpool; putting green; exercise room; children's program; playground; basketball, volleyball & croquet courts. Fee for: 10 lighted tennis courts, health club, massage. Valet parking. Valet laundry. No pets. Business center, meeting rooms, secretarial services. AE, CB, DI, DS, JCB, MC, VI. 2 restaurants; 7 am-10 pm; $12-30; cocktails; dress code for dinner; 24-hr room service; afternoon tea; The Dining Room, see separate listing. Ⓓ Ⓢ ⊘

THE WESTIN MISSION HILLS RESORT ⊕　　　　◆◆◆◆ Resort Hotel
2 miles southwest of I-10, exit Bob Hope Dr to 71-333 Dinah Shore Dr, 92270.
(619/760) 328-5955; FAX (619/760) 321-2955.

1/1-4/30	1P	$249-390	2P/1B	$249-390	2P/2B	$249-390
5/1-6/11 &						
9/11-12/31	1P	$199-320	2P/1B	$199-320	2P/2B	$199-320
6/12-9/10	1P	$109-250	2P/1B	$109-250	2P/2B	$109-250

XP $25; children ages 18 and under stay free. Check in 4 pm. Reservation deposit required; 7-day refund notice; $4 service charge. Package plans. Attractively landscaped grounds, interesting use of water, greenery and contemporary sculptures. Attractive Moroccan architecture, spacious rooms. 2 stories; exterior corridors. 512 rooms; deluxe suites available. Patio or balcony, cable TV, pay movies, honor bars, coffee makers, safes, data ports. 3 large heated pools, water slide, whirlpools, steam rooms, exercise room, children's program, volleyball & croquet, soccer and softball fields. Fee for: 36 holes golf, 7 lighted tennis courts, bicycles, massage. Valet laundry. Small pets only. Business center, conference facilities, secretarial services. AE, CB, DI, DS, JCB, MC, VI. Dining room, restaurant; 6 am-10 pm; $11-24; cocktails; 24-hr room service. D S ⊘

RESTAURANTS

THE BEACH HOUSE   ♦ ♦ American
70-115 Hwy 111, 92270.
(619/760) 328-6585.

Dinner $15-22. Open Mon-Thu 4:30-10 pm, Fri-Sat 5-10 pm; Sun 10 am-2:30 & 5-10 pm. Closed Thanksgiving and 12/25. Reservations suggested. Valet parking. Casual attire. Large selection of fish, fowl and beef. Excellent selection of early dining specials. Patio dining. Children's menu, early bird specials, Sun brunch, carryout. Cocktails & lounge. AE, DI, DS, MC, VI. ⊘

CONTINENTAL CAFE   ♦ ♦ Continental
In Rancho Las Palmas Shopping Center; 42-490 Bob Hope Dr, 92270.
(619/760) 346-7113.

Lunch $7-9; dinner $14-24. Open 11:30 am-2:30 & 5:30-9:30 pm. Reservations suggested in season. Casual attire. Bistro ambience. Friendly service & patio seating. A la carte. AE, DI, DS, MC, VI. ⊘

THE DINING ROOM   ♦ ♦ ♦ ♦ French
At the Ritz-Carlton, Rancho Mirage; 68-900 Frank Sinatra Dr, 92270.
(619/760) 321-8282.

Dinner $37-54. Open 9/6-7/5, 6-10 pm; Fri-Sat to 10:30 pm. Closed Mon, Tue. Reservations suggested. Valet parking. Semiformal attire. Dining in formal elegance. A la carte, prix fixe. Cocktails. AE, CB, DI, DS, JCB, MC, VI. Smoking outside only. ⊘

KOBE JAPANESE STEAK HOUSE   ♦ ♦ Japanese
1 block east of Frank Sinatra Dr at 69-838 Hwy 111, 92270.
(619/760) 324-1717.

Dinner $13-26. Open 5:30-10 pm; Fri & Sat to 11; Sun 5-10 pm. Closed Thanksgiving. Reservations suggested. Valet parking. Casual attire. Tepan-yaki food preparation & sushi bar; lively atmosphere. A la carte, children's menu, early bird specials. Cocktails & lounge. AE, CB, DI, MC, VI. ⊘

LAS CASUELAS NUEVAS   ♦ ♦ Mexican
70-050 Hwy 111, 92270.
(619/760) 328-8844.

Lunch $4-9; dinner $10-15. Open 11 am-9:30 pm; Fri-Sat to 10 pm; Sun 10 am-9:30 pm. Closed Thanksgiving & 12/25. Reservations suggested weekends. Casual attire. Colorfully decorated dining room & mist-cooled outdoor patio. Mariachi music Fri-Sun evenings and Sun brunch. Children's menu, a la carte, carryout, Sun brunch. Cocktails & lounge. AE, DI, DS, MC, VI. ⊗

LORD FLETCHER INN   ♦ ♦ American
1 mile west at 70-385 Hwy 111, 92270.
(619/760) 328-1161.

Dinner $17-22. Open 9/1-7/2, Tue-Sat 5:30-10 pm; Fri-Sat to 11 pm. Closed Sun, Mon, Thanksgiving & 12/251. Reservations suggested. Valet parking. Fine English fare served in Old English atmosphere. A la carte, children's menu. Cocktails. MC, VI. Smoking outside only. ⊗

WALLY'S DESERT TURTLE   ♦ ♦ ♦ ♦ Continental
71-775 Hwy 111, 92270.
(619/760) 568-9321.

Dinner $25-40. Open 9/28-6/5, daily 6:30-10 pm, Fri-Sat to 10:30 pm; 11/1-5/1 lunch served Fri 11:30 am-2 pm. Reservations suggested. Valet parking. Semi-formal attire. Elegant decor & gracious service. A la carte. Cocktails & lounge. AE, MC, VI. ⊗

Randsburg

LODGING

THE COTTAGE HOTEL BED AND BREAKFAST   ♦ ♦ Historic Bed & Breakfast
130 Butte Av; Box D, 93554.
(619/760) 374-2285; FAX (619/760) 374-2132.

All Year	1P $ 50- 55	2P/1B $ 60- 65	2P/2B ...

Check in 4 pm. Reservation deposit required. Located in a historical mining district. 1 story; interior corridors. 5 rooms; 4 bed & breakfast rooms; 1 housekeeping cottage with kitchen, $60 for 2 persons, $10 each additional person. Rooms individually decorated in period themes. Cable TV; some shower baths; no phones. Whirlpool. No pets. Antique & gift shop. AE, DS, MC, VI. Dinner available by prior arrangement. Sundown refreshments. Designated smoking area. Ⓓ Ⓢ ⊗

Ridgecrest

LODGINGS

BEVLEN HAUS BED & BREAKFAST   Nonrated Bed & Breakfast
809 N Sanders St, 93555.
(619/760) 375-1988.

All Year 1P $ 45 2P/1B $ 55- 65 2P/2B …

Check in 3 pm. Reservation deposit required; 1-day refund notice. Rambling ranch house located near town center has antique kitchen fixtures and sitting room furnishings. 3 guest rooms, each with private bath. In-room air cooling. Whirlpool. Alcoholic beverages not permitted in rooms. Full breakfast is served in the dining room. AE, DS, MC, VI.

CARRIAGE INN ⊛   ◆ ◆ ◆ Motor Inn
On SR 178 & US 395 business route; 901 N China Lake Bl & Drummond Av, 93555.
(619/760) 446-7910; FAX (619/760) 446-6408.

All Year 1P $ 80- 85 2P/1B $ 90- 95 2P/2B $ 90- 95

XP $10; children ages 12 and under stay free. Credit card guarantee required. Senior discount 2 stories; exterior corridors. 163 rooms. Cable TV, free & pay movies, coffee makers; some rental refrigerators & microwaves. Heated pool, whirlpool, sauna, exercise room. Valet laundry. No pets. Conference facilities. AE, CB, DI, DS, MC, VI. Restaurant; 6 am-10 pm; $6-13; cocktails. Ⓓ ⊗

ECONO LODGE ⊛   ◆ ◆ Motel
1 block west of China Lake Bl at 201 Inyokern Rd, 93555.
(619/760) 446-2551; FAX (619/760) 446-5740.

Fri-Sat 1P $ 35 2P/1B $ 35 2P/2B $ 39
Sun-Thu 1P $ 44 2P/1B $ 46 2P/2B $ 50

XP $2; children ages 16 and under stay free. Reservation deposit required. Weekly rates. Continental breakfast plan available. 2 stories; exterior corridors. 54 rooms. Cable TV, free movies, refrigerators; fee for microwaves. Small pets only. AE, CB, DI, DS, JCB, MC, VI. Ⓓ ⊗

HERITAGE INN & SUITES ⊛   ◆ ◆ ◆ Motor Inn
Just north of Drummond Av at 1050 N Norma, 93555.
(619/760) 446-6543; FAX (619/760) 446-2884.

All Year [BP] 1P $ 80- 100 2P/1B $ 80- 100 2P/1B $ 80- 100

XP $5; children ages 18 and under stay free. Credit card guarantee required. Monthly rates. 2 stories; interior corridors. 170 rooms; 89 efficiencies. Cable TV, free & pay movies, coffee makers, microwaves, refrigerators, data ports; fee for VCPs; some whirlpools. 2 heated pools, whirlpools, exercise room. Coin laundry. Pets. Conference facilities, PC. AE, CB, DI, DS, MC, VI. Restaurant; 5:30-11 am & 5-10 pm, Sat & Sun 7 am-noon & 5-10 pm; $10-16; cocktails & lounge. Ⓓ ⊗

QUALITY INN ⊛   ◆ ◆ Motel
½ mile south of Ridgecrest Bl on US 395 business route; 507 S China Lake Bl, 93555.
(619/760) 375-9731; FAX (619/760) 375-6484.

All Year 1P $ 41- 45 2P/1B $ 41- 52 2P/2B $ 42- 50

XP $5; children ages 17 and under stay free. Credit card guarantee required. Weekly rates. Senior discount. 2 stories, exterior corridors. 85 rooms; 14 units with microwave, coffee makers and recliners, $49. Cable TV, free movies, refrigerators; fee for microwaves. Pool. Valet laundry. Small pets, in designated rooms only. AE, CB, DI, DS, MC, VI. Restaurant nearby. Ⓓ ⊗

Rosamond

LODGING

DEVONSHIRE INN MOTEL ⨀ ♦♦ Motel
Just east of SR 14, exit Edwards/Rosamond; 2076 Rosamond Bl; Box 2080, 93560.
(805) 256-3454; FAX (805) 256-9205.

| All Year [CP] | 1P $ 52 | 2P/1B $ 52 | 2P/2B $ 62 |

Credit card guarantee required; children ages 18 and under stay free. Senior discount. 2 stories; exterior corridors. 30 rooms; 2 suites, $73. Cable TV, free movies, refrigerators. Small heated pool, whirlpool. Coin laundry. Small pets only. AE, DI, DS, MC, VI. Ⓓ ⊘

Thousand Palms

LODGING

TRAVELERS INN ⨀ ♦♦ Motel
Adjacent to I-10, exit Ramon Rd; 72-215 Varner Rd, 92276.
(619/760) 343-1381; FAX (619/760) 343-3082.

6/1-10/31	1P $ 34	2P/1B $ 41	2P/2B $ 41
11/1-12/15	1P $ 36	2P/1B $ 43	2P/2B $ 43
12/16-5/31	1P $ 38	2P/1B $ 45	2P/2B $ 45

XP $4; children ages 11 and under stay free. Reservation deposit required. Senior discount. Convenient to freeway. 3 stories; exterior corridors. 114 rooms. Cable TV, free movies. Heated pool, whirlpool. No pets. AE, CB, DI, DS, MC, VI. Ⓓ Ⓢ ⊘

Twentynine Palms

LODGINGS

BEST WESTERN GARDENS MOTEL ⨀ ♦♦♦ Motel
1½ miles west on SR 62 at 71-487 Twentynine Palms Hwy, 92277.
(619/760) 367-9141; FAX (619/760) 367-2584.

| All year | 1P $ 62-110 | 2P/1B $ 66-110 | 2P/2B $ 68-110 |

XP $4. Credit card guarantee. Senior discount. Nicely furnished rooms. 1-2 stories; interior/exterior corridors. 84 rooms; 12 1-bedroom units with efficiency, $84-140. Cable TV, pay movies; some coffee makers, refrigerators, microwaves, whirlpools. Heated pool, whirlpool. No pets. AE, DI, DS, JCB, MC, VI. Ⓓ ⊘

CIRCLE 'C' ♦♦ Motel
1½ miles west on SR 62, 1 block north at 6340 El Rey Av, 92277.
(619/760) 367-7615; FAX (619/760) 361-0247.

| All year [CP] | 1P $ 70 | 2P/1B $ 85 | 2P/2B $ 85 |

XP $10; discount for children. Reservation deposit required; cancellation fee. Spacious, exceptionally well-maintained rooms with a residential feeling. Nicely landscaped pool area. 1 story; exterior corridors. 11 rooms. Kitchens, cable TV, free movies, VCPs. Heated pool, whirlpool. Small pets with prior approval. AE, CB, DI, DS, JCB, MC, VI. Ⓓ ⊘

HOMESTEAD INN BED & BREAKFAST Ⓐ ♦♦ Bed & Breakfast
1 mile north of Hwy 62 via Adobe Rd, ½ mile east to 74153 Two Mile Rd, 92277.
(619/760) 367-0030; FAX (619/760) 367-1108.

9/1-7/5 [BP]   1P $ 85- 95   2P/1B $ 85- 95   2P/2B …

2-night minimum stay weekends. Reservation deposit required; 3-day refund notice holiday weekends. Weekly & monthly rates. Senior discount. Historic home built in 1928. Located in a quiet residential desert location. Friendly, homelike atmosphere. Gazebo with whirlpool, rock fountain and cactus garden. Interior corridors. 5 rooms; 2 rooms with sitting area, private patio & whirlpool bathtub, $125-150. Radios; some coffee makers, refrigerators, whirlpools, TVs; no in-room phones. Whirlpool, bicycles, horseshoe pit. Fee for massage, horseback riding. Meeting rooms No pets. AE, DS, MC, VI. Beer & wine only. Complimentary evening desserts & beverages. Smoke-free premises. Ⓓ ⊘

THE K-B RANCHOTEL BED & BREAKFAST   Nonrated Bed & Breakfast
6048 Noels Knoll Rd, 92277.
(619/760) 367-3353; FAX (619/760) 367-1554.

All Year   1P $ 45   2P/1B $ 55   2P/2B …

XP $10. Closed 6/28-9/15, except by arrangement. Check in from 5 to 8 pm. Reservation deposit required; 7-day refund notice. Quiet hours are from 10 pm to 6 am. Large, historic adobe homestead built in 1935, situated on 5 acres of high desert. Decorated with many original furnishings, the house also features 6 fireplaces, a walled courtyard with a fishpond, a sun deck and two cactus gardens on the grounds. 2 rooms, each with private bath and fireplace. Pets by prior arrangement, $15 deposit required. Continental breakfast served in the dining area. Afternoon snack consists of house specialties, such as homemade salsa and chips or mesquite-smoked turkey. Smoking permitted in common areas.

TOWER HOMESTEAD BED AND BREAKFAST   Nonrated Bed & Breakfast
Amboy and Mojave rds; Box C141, 92277.
(619/760) 367-7936.

All Year   1P $ 55   2P/1B $ 65   2P/2B …

Reservation deposit required; 7-day refund notice. Built in 1932 from a dismantled 100-year old Pasadena house, the structure is part of a 160-acre homestead and contains desert flagstone patios and fireplace, pine paneling, functional antiques and desert landscaping. 2 bedrooms, each with living room, fireplace, bath and TV. Spa. No pets. Barbecue facilities. Full breakfast served in the dining area or on the patio. Smoking permitted.

Victorville

LODGINGS

BEST WESTERN-GREEN TREE INN Ⓐ   ♦♦♦ Motor Inn
East side of I-15, SR 18W, Palmdale Rd exit; 14173 Green Tree Bl, 92392.
(619/760) 245-3461; FAX (619/760) 245-7745.
All Year   1P $ 52- 80   2P/1B $ 56- 80   2P/2B $ 56- 80

XP $6. Reservation deposit required. Senior discount. Many rooms overlook a shaded lawn area & golf course; some smaller rooms facing the parking lot. 2-3 stories; exterior corridors. 168 rooms; 72 1-bedroom suites with coffee maker, refrigerator & microwave or cooking surface. Cable TV, pay movies; some whirlpools. Heated pool, wading pool, indoor whirlpool. No pets. Meeting rooms. AE, CB, DI, DS, MC, VI. Dining room & coffee shop; 24 hrs; $6-15; cocktails; entertainment. Ⓓ ⊘

BUDGET INN ⊛   ♦ Motel
From I-15, exit SR 18W, Palmdale Rd, 2 blocks west, then ½ block north to 14153 Kentwood Bl, 92392.
(619/760) 241-8010; FAX (619/760) 245-8970.

All Year	1P $ 30- 32	2P/1B $ 32- 36	2P/2B $ 36- 42

XP $5. Reservation deposit required; 3-day refund notice. 2 stories; exterior corridors. 40 rooms. Cable TV, free movies, refrigerators. Small pets only, $10 deposit required. AE, CB, DI, DS, MC, VI. Restaurant nearby. Ⓓ Ⓢ ⊘

HOLIDAY INN ⊛   ♦ ♦ ♦ Hotel
1 block west of I-15, exit SR 18W to 15494 Palmdale Rd, 92392.
(619/760) 245-6565; FAX (619/760) 245-6649.

All Year	1P $ 70	2P/1B $ 76	2P/2B $ 76

XP $6; children ages 12 and under stay free. Credit card guarantee required. Senior discount. 6 stories; interior corridors. 162 rooms. Cable TV, free & pay movies. Pool. Coin laundry. Pets, $25 deposit. Meeting rooms. AE, CB, DI, DS, MC, VI. Dining room & coffee shop; 6 am-10 pm; $6-16; cocktails; entertainment. Ⓓ ⊘

RED ROOF INN   ♦ ♦ ♦ Motel
East side of I-15, between Bear Valley Rd and Palmdale Rd exits; 13409 Mariposa Rd, 92392.
(619/760) 241-1577; FAX (619/760) 241-3627.

All Year	1P $ 36- 38	2P/1B $ 41- 43	2P/2B $ 47- 53

XP $7; children ages 18 and under stay free. 3 stories; exterior corridors. 94 rooms; 14 1-bedroom suites with living room. Cable TV, free movies, data ports; some microwaves, refrigerators. Pool, whirlpools. Small pets only. AE, CB, DI, DS, MC, VI. Ⓓ Ⓢ ⊘

RESTAURANT

CASK 'N' CLEAVER   ♦ American
From I-15, exit SR 18, Palmdale Rd, 1 block west, then 3 blocks south to 13885 Park Av, 92392.
(619/760) 241-7318.

Dinner $11-20. Open 5-9 pm; Fri & Sat to 10 pm; Sun 4:30-9 pm. Closed 1/1, 7/4, Thanksgiving & 12/25. Casual dining. Features a selection of steaks, prime rib, seafood & chicken. Children's menu, salad bar. Cocktails & lounge. AE, DS, MC, VI. Smoking outside only. ⊘

Be sure to read the introduction to Lodging & Restaurants.

Yucca Valley

LODGINGS

DESERT VIEW MOTEL ⊛   ♦ ♦ Motel
Just east of SR 247 and SR 62, south on Airway Av to 57471 Primrose Dr, 92284.
(619/760) 365-9706; FAX (619/760) 365-6021.
All year [CP]   1P $ 40- 43   2P/1B $ 43- 49   2P/2B $ 46- 53
XP $5. 2-night minimum stay weekends. Credit card guarantee required. Exterior corridors. 14 rooms. Cable TV, free movies, coffee makers; some shower baths, refrigerators. Pool. No pets. AE, CB, DI, DS, MC, VI. Ⓓ ⊗

OASIS OF EDEN INN & SUITES ⊛   ♦ ♦ ♦ Motel
1 mile west of jct SR 62 and SR 247 at Twentynine Palms Hwy, 92284.
(619/760) 365-6321; FAX (619/760) 365-9592.
6/2-9/30 [CP]   1P $ 44   2P/1B $ 55   2P/2B $ 55
10/1-6/1 [CP]   1P $ 45   2P/1B $ 65   2P/2B $ 65
XP $5. Reservation deposit required. Weekly & monthly rates. Senior discount. 2 stories, exterior corridors. Rooms imaginatively and attractively decorated, some theme rooms. 39 rooms; spa rooms, $107; 4 rooms decorated in special themes, $86; 6 efficiencies, whirlpools. Cable TV, free movies; fee for microwaves, refrigerators, VCPs. Heated pool, whirlpool. Small pets only, $10; $25 deposit required. AE, CB, DI, DS, MC, VI. Restaurant nearby. Ⓓ ⊗

RESTAURANT

STEPHANO'S GIARDINO ITALIAN RESTAURANT   ♦ Italian
2 miles west of jct SR 62 and SR 247, at 55509 Twentynine Palms Hwy, 92284.
(619/760) 228-3118.
Lunch $5-16; dinner $6-18. Open 11 am-3 & 5-10:30 pm, Fri & Sat 1-11:30 pm, Sun 4-10:30 pm. Closed Thanksgiving and 12/25. Reservations suggested. Casual attire. Small charming restaurant serving traditionally prepared Italian dishes. Children's menu, carryout. Cocktails. AE, DI, DS, MC, VI. Smoking outside only.

ARIZONA

Ehrenberg

LODGING

BEST WESTERN FLYING J MOTEL ⊛   ♦ ♦ Motor Inn
Adjacent to I-10, exit 1, ½ mile east of the Colorado River at Flying J Travel Plaza; Box 801, 85334.
(520) 923-9711; FAX (520) 923-8335.
All year [CP]   1P $ 45- 50   2P/1B $ 50- 55   2P/2B $ 55- 60
XP $5; children ages 18 and under stay free. Credit card guarantee required. Senior discount. 2 stories; interior corridors. 86 rooms. Free movies, VCPs; some

microwaves, refrigerators. Heated pool, whirlpool. Coin laundry. Pets. Meeting rooms. AE, CB, DI, DS, MC, VI. Restaurant; 24 hrs; $6-11; wine & beer. Ⓓ ⊗

Lake Havasu City

LODGINGS

BEST WESTERN LAKE PLACE INN Ⓐ   ◆ ◆ Motel
1 mile east of SR 95 via Swanson Av; 31 Wing's Loop, 86403.
(520) 855-2146; FAX (520) 855-3148.

All year	1P	$ 48- 76	2P/1B	$ 50- 76	2P/2B	$ 55- 89

XP $6; children ages 12 and under stay free. Credit card guarantee required. Weekly & monthly rates. Senior discount. Large units. Desert-landscaped courtyard. 1-2 stories; exterior corridors. 40 rooms. Coffee makers, cable TV. Heated pool. Pets, $6. AE, DI, DS, MC, VI. Restaurant nearby. Ⓓ ⊗

HAVASU TRAVELODGE Ⓐ   ◆ ◆ Motel
1 mile north of London Bridge; 480 London Bridge Rd, 86403.
(520) 680-9202; FAX (520) 680-1511.

Fri-Sat						
2/1-11/30 [EP]	1P	$ 45- 50	2P/1B	$ 55- 60	2P/2B	$ 55- 60
Sun-Thu						
2/1-11/30 [CP]	1P	$ 40- 50	2P/1B	$ 50- 55	2P/2B	$ 50- 55
12/1-1/31 [CP]	1P	$ 35- 40	2P/1B	$ 40- 45	2P/2B	$ 40- 45

XP $5; children ages 12 and under stay free. Reservation deposit required; 7-day refund notice, 30-day notice for Spring Break & Oct. Weekly & monthly rates. Senior discount. Near Windsor Beach State Park. 2 stories; interior corridors. 40 rooms; 1 2-bedroom unit; suites, $75-100. Cable TV, free movies, data ports; some kitchens; fee for microwaves, refrigerators. Indoor whirlpool. No pets. AE, CB, DI, DS, MC, VI. Restaurant nearby. Ⓓ Ⓢ ⊗

HIDDEN PALMS Ⓐ   ◆ ◆ Motel
1 mile east of London Bridge on SR 95, just south at 2100 Swanson Av, 86403.
(520) 855-7144; FAX (520) 855-2620.

Fri-Sat	1P	$ 70- 80	2P/1B	$ 70- 80	2P/2B	$ 70- 80
Sun-Thu	1P	$ 60- 70	2P/1B	$ 60- 70	2P/2B	$ 60- 70

XP $10; children ages 12 and under stay free. Reservation deposit required; 3-day refund notice; cancellation fee imposed. Weekly & monthly rates. 2 stories; exterior corridors. 22 rooms. Coffee makers, kitchens, microwaves, refrigerators, cable TV. Heated pool. Coin laundry. No pets. MC, VI. Restaurant nearby. Ⓓ ⊗

HOLIDAY INN   ◆ ◆ Motor Inn
½ mile north of London Bridge at 245 London Bridge Rd, 86403.
(520) 855-4071; FAX (520) 855-2379.

Fri-Sat 2/1-11/30	1P	$ 70	2P/1B	$ 70	2P/2B	$ 70
Sun-Thu 2/1-11/30	1P	$ 55	2P/1B	$ 55	2P/2B	$ 55
12/1-1/31	1P	$ 50	2P/1B	$ 50	2P/2B	$ 50

XP $8; children ages 18 and under stay free. Credit card guarantee required. Weekly & monthly rates. Senior discount. Many units with balconies. 4 stories; interior/exterior corridors. 162 rooms. Cable TV, free & pay movies, refrigerators, data ports; fee for microwaves. TVs with video game systems. Heated pool, whirlpool. Coin laundry. Small pets only. Conference facilities, secretarial services. AE, CB, DI, DS, JCB, MC, VI. Dining room; 6 am-2 & 5-10 pm; $5-14; cocktails; entertainment. Ⓓ ⊘

HOWARD JOHNSON LODGE & SUITES ⒶⒶⒶ ♦ ♦ ♦ Motel
⅙ mile north of London Bridge at 335 London Bridge Rd, 86403.
(520) 453-4656; FAX (520) 680-4551.

2/1-9/30 [CP]	1P	$ 60	2P/1B	$ 60	2P/2B	$ 65
10/1-10/31 [CP]	1P	$ 70	2P/1B	$ 75	2P/2B	$ 80
11/1-1/31 [CP]	1P	$ 55	2P/1B	$ 55	2P/2B	$ 60

XP $5; children ages 18 and under stay free. Reservation deposit required; 14-day refund notice. Weekly & monthly rates. Senior discount. Some units with balcony & view of lake. 2 stories; interior corridors. 46 rooms; suites, $60-93. Free movies, cable TV; some microwaves, refrigerators. Whirlpool, small heated indoor pool. Coin laundry. No pets. AE, CB, DI, DS, MC, VI. Restaurant nearby. Ⓓ Ⓢ ⊘

INN AT TAMARISK ⒶⒶⒶ ♦ ♦ Motel
4⅕ miles north of London Bridge at 3101 London Bridge Rd, 86404.
(520) 764-3033; FAX (520) 764-3046.

All year	1P	$ 43-115	2P/1B	$ 43-115	2P/2B	$ 43-115

XP $8; children ages 12 and under stay free. Reservation deposit required. Weekly & monthly rates. Senior discount. Tastefully furnished. 2 stories; exterior corridors. 17 rooms; some 1- and 2-bedroom suites, some have lake view; 5 2-bedroom units; 9 kitchens. Coffee makers, refrigerators, shower baths, cable TV; some microwaves, radios. Pool, horseshoe pit, shuffleboard. Coin laundry. No pets. AE, CB, DI, DS, MC, VI. Ⓓ ⊘

ISLAND INN HOTEL ⒶⒶⒶ ♦ ♦ ♦ Motor Inn
½ mile southwest of SR 95, over London Bridge; 1300 W McCulloch Bl, 86403.
(520) 680-0606; FAX (520) 680-4218.

All year	1P	$ 65- 85	2P/1B	$ 65- 85	2P/2B	$ 65- 85

XP $8; children ages 16 and under stay free. Credit card guarantee required; 3-day refund notice. Weekly & monthly rates. ½ mile from London Bridge & Island Fashion Mall shops. Many rooms with balcony. 4 stories; interior corridors. 116 rooms. Cable TV, data ports; some microwaves; fee for refrigerators. Heated pool, whirlpool. Coin laundry. Airport transportation. Small pets only, $10. Conference facilities; meeting rooms. AE, CB, DI, DS, MC, VI. Ⓓ Ⓢ ⊘

LAKE HAVASU CITY SUPER 8 ♦ Motel
Just west of SR 95, exit Palo Verde; 305 London Bridge Rd, 86403.
(520) 855-8844; FAX (520) 855-7132.

Fri-Sat	1P	$ 42- 53	2P/1B	$ 46- 57	2P/2B	$ 52- 63
Sun-Thu	1P	$ 36- 39	2P/2B	$ 38- 41	2P/2B	$ 43- 46

Credit card guarantee required. Monthly rates. Some lakeview units. ½ mile from London Bridge & English Village. 3 stories; no elevator; interior corridors. 60 rooms. Heated pool, whirlpool. Small pets only, $25 deposit required per pet. AE, CB, DI, DS, JCB, MC, VI. Dining room nearby. Ⓓ ⊘

SANDS VACATION RESORT   ♦ ♦ Suite Motel
1 mile east of SR 95, just north of McCulloch Bl; 2040 Mesquite Av, 86403.
(520) 855-1388; FAX (520) 453-1802.

| All year | 1P $ 50-130 | 2P/1B $ 50-130 | 2P/2B $ 50- 130 |

XP $10; children ages 12 and under stay free. Reservation deposit required. Weekly & monthly rates. Package plans. All suites nicely furnished and decorated. 2 stories. 42 rooms; 6 2-bedroom units, $99-230 for up to 4 persons, $10 per extra person. Coffee makers, kitchens, microwaves, refrigerators, cable TV, VCPs. Heated pool, 1 lighted tennis court, horseshoes, shuffleboard, boccie courts. Coin laundry. No pets. AE, CB, DI, DS, MC, VI. Ⓓ

RESTAURANTS

CITY OF LONDON ARMS PUB & RESTAURANT ⊛   ♦ ♦ American
422 English Village, 86403.
(520) 855-8782.

Lunch $5-8; dinner $8-15. Open 7 am-9 pm, Fri & Sat to 10 pm. Fee for parking. Casual attire. Nice variety of English & American appetizers, entrees & ale. English high tea served daily. Children's menu, early bird specials, senior's menu, health-conscious menu, carryout. Cocktails & lounge. ⊘

KRYSTAL'S FINE DINING ⊛   ♦ ♦ Steak & Seafood
Just east of London Bridge Rd at 460 El Camino Wy, 86403.
(520) 453-2999.

Dinner $10-20. Open daily 4-10 pm. Closed 12/25. Reservations suggested. Casual attire. Extensive variety of seafood and limited meat selections. Early bird specials. Cocktails & lounge. MC, VI. ⊘

MONTANA STEAK HOUSE   ♦ American
4 miles south of London Bridge, just north of SR 95 & Oro Grande at 3301 Maricopa Av, 96403.
(520) 855-3736.

Dinner $10-20. Open Wed-Sun 3:30-9:30 pm. Closed Mon, Tue, Thanksgiving & 12/25. Reservations suggested. Casual attire. Casual family atmosphere. Good selection of steak, seafood & chicken. Steak is the house specialty. Early bird specials. Cocktails. AE, MC, VI. ⊘

SHUGRUE'S   ♦ ♦ American
1425 McCulloch Bl, 86403.
(520) 453-1400.

Dinner $10-24. Open daily 11 am-3 & 5-10 pm, Sun from 10 am. Closed 12/25. Casual attire. Overlooks channel to Lake Havasu & London Bridge. Pastries &

breads baked on premises. Fresh seafood daily. Sushi available Thu evening. Children's menu, carryout. Cocktails & lounge. AE, MC, VI.

VERSAILLES RISTORANTE   ◆ ◆ ◆ French
Just east of SR 95 between Smoketree & Mulberry sts at 357 S Lake Havasu Av, 86403. (520) 855-4800.

Dinner $18-25. Open Tue-Sun 5-10 pm. Closed Mon, 1/1 & 12/25. Reservations suggested. Casual attire. Wonderful selection of French & Italian dishes. Frog legs, escargot & other appetizers. Fine dining with lake view. Cocktails & lounge. AE, MC, VI. ⊗

Parker

LODGING

HOLIDAY KASBAH ⌘   ◆ Motel
½ mile west of SR 95 at 604 California Av, 85344. (520) 669-2133; FAX (520) 669-6676.

Fri-Sat [CP]	1P	$ 45	2P/1B	$ 55	2P/2B	$ 63
Sun-Thu [CP]	1P	$ 39	2P/1B	$ 42	2P/2B	$ 45

XP $7; children ages 7 and under stay free. Reservation deposit required. Senior discount. Modest, unpretentious rooms. 2 stories; exterior corridors. 40 rooms. Refrigerators, pay movies; some microwaves. Coin laundry. Pets, $5. AE, DI, DS, MC, VI. ⒟ ⊗

Yuma

LODGINGS

BEST WESTERN CHILTON INN ⌘   ◆ ◆ ◆ Motor Inn
On I-8 business loop, 2½ miles south of jct SR 95; 300 E 32nd St, 85364. (520) 344-1050; FAX (520) 344-4877.

1/1-3/31 [BP]	1P	$ 59- 79	2P/1B	$ 59- 79	2P/2B	$ 79
4/1-12/31 [BP]	1P	$ 59- 70	2P/1B	$ 59- 70	2P/2B	$ 65

XP $5; children ages 18 and under stay free. Credit card guarantee required. Senior discount. 2 stories; exterior corridors. 121 rooms. Cable TV, free movies, refrigerators, data ports. Heated pool, wading pool, whirlpool. Airport transportation. Coin laundry. Small pets only. Meeting rooms. AE, CB, DI, DS, JCB, MC, VI. Restaurant; 6-10 am & 5-10 pm; $6-12; cocktails. ⒟ ⊗

BEST WESTERN CORONADO ⌘   ◆ ◆ ◆ Motor Inn
On I-8 business loop; from I-8, east bound exit 4th Av, ½ mile south; westbound exit 1 (Giss Pkwy), ½ mile west; 233 4th Av, 85364. (520) 783-4453; FAX (520) 782-7487.

1/1-4/15 [CP]	1P	$ 57- 62	2P/2B	$ 57- 75	2P/2B	$ 79- 99
4/16-12/31 [CP]	1P	$ 45- 50	2P/2B	$ 50- 55	2P/2B	$ 57- 79

XP $5; children ages 12 and under stay free. Credit card guarantee required. Weekly & monthly rates. Long-established motel with a variety of accommodations from cozy to spacious, nicely furnished rooms. 1-2 stories; exterior corridors. 86 rooms; 32 2-bedroom units; 7 kitchens, $10 extra. Refrigerators, cable TV, VCPs, data ports; some microwaves, whirlpools, shower baths. 2 pools (1 heated), whirlpool. Coin laundry. Small pets only. Meeting rooms. AE, CB, DI, DS, JCB, MC, VI. Restaurant; 6 am-2 am; $5-13; cocktails. Ⓓ ⊗

BEST WESTERN INNSUITES HOTEL & SUITES ⒶⒶⒶ ♦ ♦ ♦ Motel
Just northeast of I-8 at jct SR 95 (16th St); 1450 Castle Dome Av, 85365.
(520) 783-8341; FAX (520) 783-1349.

1/5-4/10 & 8/31-9/1 [BP]	1P $ 69- 89	2P/1B $ 74- 99	2P/2B $ 74- 99
4/11-8/30 & 9/2-1/4 [CP]	1P $ 59- 69	2P/2B $ 64- 84	2P/2B $ 69- 89

XP $5; children ages 18 and under stay free. Credit card guarantee required. Senior discount. A variety of rooms & suites decorated in a Southwest motif. 2-3 stories; exterior corridors. 166 rooms; 80 efficiencies. Coffee makers, microwaves, refrigerators, cable TV, free & pay movies; some whirlpools. Heated pool, whirlpool, 2 lighted tennis courts, exercise room, playground. Coin laundry. Pets, $25 deposit required. Meeting rooms. AE, CB, DI, DS, MC, VI. Complimentary evening beverages. Small restaurant; 6 am-2 & 6-10 pm; $8-15; wine & beer. Ⓓ ⧄ ⊗

DAYS INN ⒶⒶⒶ ♦ ♦ Motel
On US 95 (16th St), just east of I-8 at 1671 E 16th St, 85365.
Phone & FAX (520) 329-7790.

1/1-4/15 [CP]	1P $ 59- 74	2P/2B $ 69- 79	2P/2B $ 79
4/16-9/15 [CP]	1P $ 39- 49	2P/2B $ 49- 54	2B/2B $ 59- 64
9/16-12/31[CP]	1P $ 49- 59	2P/2B $ 54- 64	2B/2B $ 69

XP $5; children ages 12 and under stay free. Credit card guarantee required. Senior discount. 2 stories; exterior corridors. 65 rooms; 4 rooms with whirlpool tub, $69-89. Cable TV, free movies, refrigerators, data ports; some shower baths. Small pool, whirlpool. Coin laundry. No pets. AE, CB, DI, DS, JCB, MC, VI. Restaurant nearby. Ⓓ Ⓢ Ⓓ ♿ Roll-in showers.

HOLIDAY INN EXPRESS ⒶⒶⒶ ♦ ♦ Motel
On I-8 business loop, 2 miles south of jct US 95 (32nd St); 3181 S 4th Av, 85364.
(520) 344-1420. FAX (520) 341-0158.

1/1-4/30 [CP]	1P $ 69- 79	2P/1B $ 75- 85	2P/2B $ 75- 85
5/1-12/31 [CP]	1P $ 55- 65	2P/1B $ 61- 71	2P/2B $ 61- 71

XP $6; children ages 18 and under stay free. Credit card guarantee required. Weekly rates. Senior discount. Across from shopping centers. 2 stories; exterior corridors. 120 rooms. Coffee makers, microwaves, refrigerators, cable TV, free & pay movies, data ports. Heated pool, whirlpool. Coin laundry. Small pets only. Meeting rooms. AE, CB, DI, DS, JCB, MC, VI. Complimentary evening beverages Mon-Sat. Restaurant nearby. Ⓓ ⊗

LA FUENTE INN ⒶⒶⒶ ♦ ♦ ♦ Motel
On US 95 (16th St), just east of I-8; 1513 E 16th St, 85365.
(520) 329-1814; FAX (520) 343-2671.

| 1/1-5/1 [CP] | 1P | $ 76- 96 | 2P/1B | $ 76- 96 | 2P/2B | $ 76- 96 |
| 6/1-12/31 [CP] | 1P | $ 66- 86 | 2P/1B | $ 66- 86 | 2P/2B | $ 66- 86 |

XP $10; children ages 12 and under stay free. Credit card guarantee required. Attractive grounds with large pool surrounded by grass, shrubs and many trees. Nicely furnished rooms & 1-bedroom suites. 2 stories; exterior corridors. 96 rooms. Coffee makers, refrigerators, cable TV, free movies, data ports; some microwaves; fee for VCPs. Heated pool, whirlpool, exercise room. Airport transportation. Coin laundry. No pets. AE, DI, DS, MC, VI. Complimentary evening beverages. Restaurant nearby. Ⓓ Ⓢ ⊘

RADISSON SUITES INN YUMA ⒶⒶⒶ　　　　　　◆ ◆ ◆ Suite Motel

On I-8 business loop, 1½ miles south of jct US 95; 2600 S 4th Av, 85364. (520) 726-4830; FAX (520) 341-1152.

| 1/1-4/30 [CP] | 1P | $ 89 | 2P/2B | $ 89 | 2P/2B | $ 99 |
| 5/1-12/31 [CP] | 1P | $ 72 | 2P/1B | $ 72 | 2P/2B | $ 82 |

XP $10; children ages 16 and under stay free. Credit card guarantee required. Weekly rates. Senior discount. All units are 1-bedroom suites with wet bar. 3 stories; exterior corridors. 164 rooms. Coffee makers, microwaves, refrigerators, cable TV, free & pay movies, data ports; fee for VCPs. Heated pool, whirlpool. Coin laundry. Small pets only. Meeting rooms. AE, CB, DI, DS, JCB, MC, VI. Complimentary evening beverages, 5-7 pm. Ⓓ Ⓢ ⊘

SHILO INN HOTEL　　　　　　　　　　　　◆ ◆ ◆ Motor Inn

Just northeast of I-8 at jct SR 95 (16th St) at 1550 S Castle Dome Av, 85365. (520) 782-9511; FAX (520) 783-1538.

| All year [BP] | 1P | $ 79- 135 | 2P/1B | $ 79- 135 | 2P/2B | $ 89- 135 |

XP $12; children ages 12 and under stay free. Credit card guarantee required. Weekly & monthly rates. Senior discount. A contemporary, full-service hotel on nicely landscaped grounds. 4 stories; interior corridors. 134 rooms; 15 kitchens. Cable TV, free movies, refrigerators; fee for VCPs; some microwaves. Heated pool, sauna, steam room, whirlpool, exercise room. Airport transportation. Coin laundry. Pets, $7. Conference facilities. AE, CB, DI, DS, JCB, MC, VI. Restaurant; 6 am-10 pm; $9-17; cocktails. Ⓓ Ⓢ ⊘

YUMA CABANA MOTEL ⒶⒶⒶ　　　　　　　　◆ ◆ Motel

On I-8 business loop, ⅜ mile south of jct US 95; 2151 S 4th Av, 85364. (520) 783-8311; FAX (520) 783-1126.

1/1-2/28	1P	$ 60- 72	2P/1B	$ 65- 77	2P/2B	$ 76- 88
3/1-3/31 & 12/1-12/31	1P	$ 45- 60	2P/1B	$ 50- 65	2P/2B	$ 55- 70
4/1-11/30	1P	$ 30- 40	2P/1B	$ 35- 50	2P/2B	$ 40- 55

XP $5; children ages 15 and under stay free. Credit card guarantee required; 3-day refund notice. 2 stories; interior corridors. 63 rooms; 4 1-bedroom efficiencies & 7 rooms with kitchen, $12 extra. Coffee makers, cable TV, free movies, shower baths, data ports; fee for microwaves, refrigerators; some balconies. Heated pool, shuffleboard. Coin laundry. No pets. AE, CB, DI, DS, MC, VI. Restaurant nearby. Ⓓ ⊘

LODGING & RESTAURANTS

YUMA 4TH AVE TRAVELODGE Ⓐ   ♦ ♦ Motel
On I-8 business loop, ½ mile south of jct US 95; 2050 S 4th Av, 85364.
(520) 782-3831; FAX (520) 783-4616.

2/1-2/28	1P	$ 62	2P/1B	$ 72	2P/2B $ 82
3/1-3/31 &					
12/1-1/31	1P	$ 42	2P/1B	$ 52	2P/2B $ 62
4/1-11/30	1P	$ 32	2P/1B	$ 42	2P/2B $ 52

XP $5; children ages 16 and under stay free. Credit card guarantee required. Weekly rates. Senior discount. Small picnic area with barbecue and tables. 2 stories; exterior corridors. 48 rooms; 3 rooms with kitchen & 4 2-room units, $5 extra. Coffee makers, cable TV, free movies; some shower baths, refrigerators. Heated pool. Coin laundry. No pets. AE, CB, DI, DS, JCB, MC, VI. Coffee shop nearby. Ⓓ ⊘

YUMA SUPER 8 MOTEL   ♦ ♦ Motel
Just west of I-8, exit US 95/16th St; 1688 S Riley Av, 85364.
(520) 782-2000; FAX (520) 782-6657.

1/1-3/31	1P	$ 53	2P/1B	$ 56	2P/2B $ 61
4/1-10/1	1P	$ 49	2P/1B	$ 52	2P/2B $ 57
10/2-12/31	1P	$ 51	2P/1B	$ 54	2P/2B $ 59

XP $3; children ages 12 and under stay free. Credit card guarantee required. 3 stories; interior corridors. 82 rooms. Cable TV, free movies, data ports; some microwaves, refrigerators. Heated pool, whirlpool. Coin laundry. Pets, $5. AE, CB, DI, DS, JCB, MC, VI. Restaurant nearby. Ⓓ Ⓢ ⊘

RESTAURANTS

EL PAPPAGALLO MEXICAN RESTAURANT   ♦ Mexican
Just north of 16th St (SR 95); 1½ miles west of I-8 business loop; 1401 S Av B, 85364.
(520) 343-9451.

Lunch $4-8; dinner $8-12. Open daily 11 am-9 pm, Fri & Sat to 9:30 pm. Closed Thanksgiving & 12/25. Casual attire. A small, casual restaurant. Family recipes used in food preparation. Carryout. Cocktails. AE, CB, DI, DS, JCB, MC, VI. ⊘

THE GARDEN CAFE   ♦ American
Downtown, just east of I-8 business loop (4th Av), adjacent to Arizona Historical Society Museum; 250 Madison Av, 85364.
(520) 783-1491.

Lunch $5-8. Open 10/1-6/30, Tue-Fri 9 am-2:30 pm, Sat & Sun from 8 am; breakfast served to 11 am. Closed Mon & major holidays. No air conditioning. Casual attire. Delightful dining in a terraced, outdoor tree-shaded patio area in building complex that dates to 1887. Nice variety of salads, sandwiches, soups, quiche & desserts. Sun brunch. AE, MC, VI.

MANDARIN PALACE   ♦ ♦ ♦ Chinese
On I-8 business loop, 2⅝ miles southeast of jct US 95; 350 E 32nd St, 85364.
(520) 344-2805.

Lunch $6-8; dinner $8-20. Open daily 11 am-10 pm, Fri & Sat to 11 pm. Lunch buffet Mon-Fri 11 am-2 pm. Casual attire. Mandarin & Szechuan cuisine; complete dinners $12-$13.50. Limited selection of American entrees. Early bird specials, carryout, a la carte. Cocktails & lounge. AE, DI, MC, VI. ⊘

Campgrounds & Trailer Parks

Desert, mountain and lakeside camping can all be enjoyed in the California desert. Campgrounds range from remote, primitive sites suitable for tents to privately operated recreational vehicle resorts offering a wide range of on-site amenities and activities.

Effective March 22, 1997, area code (619) will change to (760).

Listings are alphabetical by city, or national or state park or recreation area. Fees shown are usually for two people, plus a recreational vehicle. Any charge for each additional person in indicated by "XP" and the dollar amount. **All camping fees are subject to change.** Electricity, water and sewer hookups are indicated by the letters E, W and S; some campgrounds also have hookups for telephones (phones) and cable TV. Unless otherwise noted, campgrounds are open all year. Most campgrounds provide running water and hot showers, so only the absence of these is noted. Tables and barbecues or fire rings are also generally provided at all but the most primitive campgrounds. The private campgrounds listed have been inspected by Automobile Club representatives and meet current AAA quality standards. The 🅰🅰 symbol preceding a listing identifies that establishment as a AAA Official Appointment; it indicates that the campground has expressed a particular interest in serving AAA members. A detailed list of public and private campgrounds can also be found in the ACSC *Central and Southern California Camping* map.

Reservations

State campsite reservations can be made through DESTINET reservations company (campground listings indicate when DESTINET can be used). Otherwise, reservations can usually be made with the campground directly or, in some cases, reservations may not be accepted. Automobile Club members can make reservations for private campgrounds that accept them through any Auto Club office. In many cases reservations are accepted only during a campground's peak season. If this is the case, campsites are available on a first-come, first-served basis during the remainder of their open period.

When calling DESTINET for state park campground reservations, the caller is first asked to make selections on a touch-tone phone (a caller using a rotary dial phone should stay on the line until connected to a reservation agent). The caller receives recorded instructions for indicating the following information regarding the reservation request: family or group campsite; the first four letters of the name of the state park; type of site (tent, motor home or trailer); arrival date; and number of nights desired. The recording responds with information on availability; if space is available the caller remains on the line to be connected with a reservation agent.

DESTINET

- Per reservation, nonrefundable reservation fee $6.75; cancellation fee $6.

- Reservations can be made between eight weeks and 24 hours before date of arrival. There is an eight-day cancellation notice.

- *By phone*: Charge reservations to an American Express, VISA, MasterCard or Discover number by calling (800) 444-7275 daily from 8 a.m. to 5 p.m.

The TDD number for hearing-impaired users is (800) 284-7275.

- *By mail*: Send a check, money order or credit card number with the reservation request and mail at least 10 days and no earlier than nine weeks in advance to DESTINET CA, P.O. Box 85705, San Diego, CA 92186-5705.

CALIFORNIA

Adelanto

ADELANTO RV PARK ⒶⒶ
½ mile west of US 395 at 11301 Air Base Rd, 92301.
(619/760) 246-7775.

$18 for 2; XP $2. Credit card guarantee required; 3-day refund notice. Weekly & monthly rates. 4 acres. 73 RV spaces; 73 EWS. Desert location. Disposal station, flush toilets, cable TV hookups, 50 amps. Pool, whirlpool, recreation room. Coin laundry. Small pets only. Propane and groceries. MC, VI. (Private)

GOLDEN POND RV PARK
On US 395, ½ mile north of junction SR 18; 14530 Hwy 395, 92392.
(619/760) 245-5879.

$16-18 for 2; XP $2. Weekly & monthly rates. Open & shaded sites. El 2800. 20 acres. 74 RV spaces; 74 EW, 42 S. Disposal station, flush toilets, 30 amps, air conditioning & heaters ($2 ea). Recreation room, fishing pond. Coin laundry. Pets. Propane. (Private)

Anza-Borrego Desert State Park

AGUA CALIENTE COUNTY PARK
1 mile southwest of Agua Caliente Springs off Co Rd S2; 5201 Ruffin Rd, San Diego 92123-1699.
(619) 565-3600.

Closed Jun through Aug. $10-14. 29 tent spaces, 117 tent/RV spaces (40-ft maximum RV length); 55 EWS, 50 EW. Flush toilets. Therapy pools. (County)

PARK HEADQUARTERS
Via SR 78 & co rds S2, S3 and S22 on Palm Canyon Dr; Box 299, Borrego Springs 92004.
(619/760) 767-5311.

Although a number of designated campgrounds are found throughout the park, it is permissible to camp practically anywhere. The only restrictions are that vehicles should park no more than a car's length from the road, and no camp should be established within 200 yards of a water source (animals stay away if humans are too close). Ground fires are prohibited in the park. All primitive camp areas have no designated campsites. Unless DESTINET is specified in the listing, all campgrounds are on a first-come, first-served basis. (Also see the park listing in the *Anza-Borrego Area* chapter.)

Arroyo Salado *16 miles east of Borrego Springs off Co Rd S22.*
No fee. 20 tent/RV spaces. No water or toilets. Pets. (State)

Blair Valley *11 miles northwest of Agua Caliente County Park on Co Rd S2.*
No fee. El 2500 ft. 20 tent/RV spaces. No water or toilets. Pets. (State)

Borrego Palm Canyon *2½ miles west of Borrego Springs off Co Rd S22 and Palm Canyon Dr.*
$14-18 per night. 30-night maximum stay. DESTINET. Unlimited private camping. 117 tent/RV spaces (31-ft maximum RV length); 48 EWS. Flush toilets. Nature trails, horseback riding. Visitor center. Coin laundry. Pets, $1. 24-hr attendant. Propane, groceries. Hospital in Brawley, 65 miles. Wheelchair accessible. (State)

Bow Willow *11½ miles southeast of Agua Caliente County Park off Co Rd S2.*
$7-9. 16 tent/RV spaces (24-ft maximum RV length). Pit toilets. Pets, $1. (State)

Culp Valley *8 miles west of Borrego Springs off Co Rd S22.*
No fee. El 3400. 20 tent/RV spaces. No water or toilets. Pets. (State)

Fish Creek *12 miles south of Ocotillo Wells off Split Mountain Rd.*
No fee. 7 tent/RV spaces. No water or toilets. (State)

Mountain Palm Springs *10½ miles southeast of Agua Caliente Park off Co Rd S2.*
No fee. 10 tent/RV spaces. No water or toilets. Pets. (State)

Tamarisk Grove *11 miles south of Borrego Springs on Co Rd S3.*
$14. 30-night maximum stay. DESTINET. Backcountry camping along 500 miles of primitive roads. 25 tent/RV spaces (21-foot maximum RV length). Piped water, flush toilets, no showers. Nature trails. Pets, $1. Propane, groceries. 24-hr attendant. Hospital in Brawley, 55 miles. Wheelchair accessible. (State)

Vern Whitaker Horse Camp *7 miles north of Borrego Springs.*
$16. DESTINET. 10 tent/RV spaces (30-ft maximum RV length). Flush toilets. Pets, $1. Horse camp. (State)

Yaqui Pass *8 miles south of Borrego Springs on Co Rd S3.*
No fee. Open tent sites. No water or toilets. Pets. (State)

Yaqui Well *11 miles south of Borrego Springs off Co Rd S3.*
No fee. 12 tent/RV spaces. No water; pit toilets. Pets. (State)

VALLECITO COUNTY PARK
4 miles northwest of Agua Caliente Springs on Co Rd S2; 5201 Ruffin Rd, San Diego 92123-1699.
(619) 565-3600.

Closed Jun through Aug. $8. 50 tent/RV spaces (35-ft maximum RV length). Flush toilets. Pets, $1. (County)

Barstow

BARSTOW/CALICO KOA CAMPGROUND
7 miles northeast; adjacent to I-15, exit Ghost Town Rd; Box 967, Yermo 92398.
(619/760) 254-2311.

$16-23 for 2; XP $2.50. Reservation deposit required. In desert area. Many shaded sites. 8 acres. 17 tent sites, 61 RV spaces; 61 EW, 16 S. Disposal station; flush toilets, 50 amps ($2). Pool, recreation room, playground. Coin laundry. Pets. Groceries, propane. DS, MC, VI. (Private)

CALICO GHOST TOWN REGIONAL PARK
11 miles northeast off I-15; Box 638, Yermo 92398.
(619/760) 254-2122.

$9. Reservations. 287 tent/RV sites; 45 EWS. Disposal station; flush toilets. Pets. (County)

DESERT SPRINGS RV PARK
1 mile south of I-15, 1¼ miles north of I-40; from I-15 exit Ghost Town Rd, from I-40 exit Daggett; Box 396, Daggett 92327.
(619/760) 254-2000.

$10-18 for 2; XP $2. Weekly & monthly rates. Open sites, many pull-thru. Tree-shaded picnic area around fishing pond. 10 acres. 10 tent sites, 52 RV spaces; 52 EWS. Disposal station; phone hookups; flush toilets. Pool, fishing pond. Coin laundry. Pets. (Private)

OWL CANYON CAMPGROUND
Exit I-15 or I-40 at E Main St; west to Yucca St RR Bridge following Ft Irwin Rd to Fossil Bed Rd, right on Rainbow Basin Rd; c/o BLM Barstow Resource Area, 150 Coolwater Ln, 92311.
(619/760) 256-3591.

$4. 14-night maximum stay. Adjacent to Rainbow Basin Geological Area. 40 acres. 31 tent/RV sites. No showers, vault toilets. Pets. 24-hr attendant. Hospital in town. (BLM)

Blythe

COON HOLLOW
15 miles west on I-10, 12 miles south on Wiley's Well Rd; c/o BLM, 400 S Farrell Dr, Ste B-205, Palm Springs 92262.
(619/760) 251-0692.

No fee. 14-night maximum stay. 29 tent/RV sites. No showers, no drinking water. Rock hounding areas. Hospital in town. (BLM)

MAYFLOWER PARK
7 miles northeast of Blythe via US 95 and 6th Av to 4980 Colorado River Rd; Rt 1, Box 190E, 92225.
(619/760) 922-4665.

$10-12 for 4. 14-night maximum stay 4/1-10/1. Monthly rates 10/1-3/31. On the Colorado River. Grass sites, some tree-shaded. 30 acres. 150 tent/RV spaces. 150 EW. Disposal station, flush toilets. Boat ramp. Pets, $1. Hospital in town. (County)

McINTYRE PARK
7 miles south on Intake Bl; 8750 E 26th Av, 92225.
(619/760) 922-8205.

$16-19 for 2; XP $4. Weekly & monthly rates. On the Colorado River. Grass sites. 21 acres. 60 tent sites, 145 tent/RV spaces; 145 EW. Disposal station, flush toilets, showers. Swimming, fishing, boat ramp. No pets. Propane, groceries. (Private)

RIVIERA RV RESORT AND MARINA
2½ miles east off I-10 at 14100 Riviera Dr, 92225.
(619/760) 922-5350; FAX (619/760) 922-6540.

$15-25 for 2; XP $4. 6 pm check in. Reservation deposit required; 14-day refund notice; cancellation fee. Weekly & monthly rates. On Colorado River. 27 acres. 50 tent sites, 235 RV spaces. Disposal station, phone & cable TV hookups. Heated pool, whirlpool, boat ramp, marina, fishing. Coin laundry. Pets. Groceries, propane. AE, DI, DS, MC, VI. (Private)

WILEY'S WELL
15 miles west on I-10, 9 miles south on Wiley's Well Rd; c/o BLM, 400 S Farrell Dr, Ste B-205, Palm Springs 92262.
(619/760) 323-4421.

No fee. 14-night maximum stay. 200 acres. 15 tent/RV spaces. No showers, no drinking water. Rock hounding area. Hospital in town. (BLM)

Bombay Beach

FOUNTAIN OF YOUTH SPA ⦿
14 miles northwest of Niland via SR 111 and Hot Mineral Spa Rd at 10249 Coachella Canal Rd, Dept A, 92257.
(619/760) 354-1340; FAX (619/760) 354-1558.

10/1-3/31 $13-20 for 2; 4/1-9/30 $11-17 for 2; XP $2. Weekly & monthly rates. Open sites in desert area, some with view of Salton Sea. 75 acres. 930 tent/RV spaces; 630 EWS. Disposal station, flush toilets, air conditioning (50¢), 30 amps, cable TV hookups. 2 heated pools, sauna, whirlpools, 2 hot mineral pools, recreation room, exercise room, social program 9/15-3/15, massage (fee). Coin laundry. Pets. Groceries, propane. Snack bar. (Private)

Borrego Springs

PALM CANYON RESORT RV PARK ⦿
221 Palm Canyon Dr; Box 956, 92004.
(619/760) 767-5341; FAX (619/760) 767-4073.

6/1-10/31 $18; 11/1-5/31 $21. Reservation deposit required; 3-day refund notice; cancellation fee. Weekly & monthly rates. Open sites, mostly pull-thru. Motel units also available. 14 acres. 131 RV spaces; 131 EWS. Flush toilets, showers, cable TV hookups, tables. Heated pool, whirlpool. Coin laundry. Pets. Groceries. AE, CB, DI, DS, MC, VI. Restaurant and lounge. (Private)

Brawley

WIEST LAKE COUNTY PARK
5 miles northeast off Rutherford Rd; c/o Imperial County Parks & Recreation, 155 S 11th St, Ste C, El Centro 92243-2851.
(619/760) 344-3712.

$7. 28 tent/RV sites (45-foot maximum RV length); 23 EW. Disposal station, flush toilets. Fishing, swimming (in season). Pets. (County)

Cathedral City

OUTDOOR RESORTS/PALM SPRINGS
2 miles north at 69-411 Ramon Rd, 92234.
(619/760) 324-4005; FAX (619/760) 321-9952.

6/1-9/30 $30-35 for 2, 10/1-5/31 $37.50-47.50 for 2; XP $1. Reservation deposit required; 3-day refund notice; cancellation fee. Weekly & monthly rates. Beautifully landscaped grounds. Grass sites with concrete pads. Many sites located adjacent to golf course. 135 acres. 400 RV spaces; 400 EWS. Flush toilets, cable TV hookups; limited facilities in summer. 8 heated pools, saunas, whirlpools, 14 lighted tennis courts, recreational program; fee for putting green and 27 holes golf. Coin laundry. Pets, $1. Beauty shop, groceries and restaurant in season. MC, VI. (Private)

Death Valley National Park

HEADQUARTERS AT FURNACE CREEK
Via SR 178 and SR 190; Death Valley 92328.
(619/760) 786-2331.

Emigrant *9 miles southwest of Stovepipe Wells Village off SR 190.*
No fee. Closed Nov through Apr. El 2100. 10 tent/RV spaces. Piped water, flush toilets. (NP)

Furnace Creek *1 mile north of Furnace Creek Ranch off SR 190.*
$10. 14-night maximum stay. DESTINET. 30 acres. 33 tent sites, 103 tent/RV spaces. Disposal station, flush toilets. Horseback riding. Pets. Hospital in Lone Pine, 100 miles. (NP)

Mahogany Flat *38 miles south of Stovepipe Wells Village off Trona-Wildrose Rd.*
No fee. Closed Dec through Mar. 30-night maximum stay. El 8200. 10 tent/RV spaces. No showers or drinking water; pit toilets. Pets allowed. Hospital in Ridgecrest, 70 miles. (NP)

Mesquite Spring *5 miles south of Scotty's Castle on Grapevine Rd.*
$6. 30-night maximum stay. 2 acres. 30 RV spaces. Disposal station, flush toilets, no showers. Pets. Hospital in Tonopah, NV, 90 miles. (NP)

Stovepipe Wells *At north end of Stovepipe Wells Village.*
$4. Closed May through Sep. $6 per night. 30-night maximum stay. 200 tent/RV spaces. Disposal station, flush toilets, no showers. Hospital in Lone Pine, 78 miles. Pets. (NP)

CAMPGROUNDS & TRAILER PARKS

Sunset *¼ mile east of Furnace Creek Ranch.*

$6. Closed May through Sep. 30-night maximum stay. 1000 tent/RV spaces. Disposal station, flush toilets, no showers. Pets. Hospital in Lone Pine, 100 miles. (NP)

Texas Spring *¼ mile east of Furnace Creek Ranch off SR 190.*

$6. Closed May through Sep. 30-night maximum stay. 10 acres. 36 tent sites, 60 tent/RV spaces. Disposal station, flush toilets, no showers. Pets. Hospital in Lone Pine, 100 miles. (NP)

Thorndike *37 miles south of Stovepipe Wells Village off Trona-Wildrose Rd.*

No fee. Closed Nov through Mar. Well-shaded sites in a secluded canyon. El 7500. 8 tent/RV spaces. No water; pit toilets. Pets. (NP)

Wildrose *30 miles southeast of Stovepipe Wells Village off Trona-Wildrose Rd.*

No fee. 30-night maximum stay. El 4100. 30 tent/RV spaces. No drinking water in winter, no showers; pit toilets. Pets. Hospital in Ridgecrest, 63 miles. (NP)

PANAMINT SPRINGS RESORT CAMPGROUND
30 miles west of Stovepipe Wells on SR 190; Box 395, Ridgecrest 93556.
(702) 482-7680; FAX (702) 482-7682.

$8-15 for 2; XP $1-3. Reservation deposit required. Open & shaded sites. 14 motel units available. 40 tent/RV spaces, 12 RV spaces. 12 ES, 52 W. Flush toilets, 30 amps. Pets, $2. Propane, groceries. AE, MC, VI. Restaurant 6:30 am-10 pm, in winter 7 am-9 pm. (Private)

Desert Center

CORN SPRINGS
8 miles east on I-10, 6 miles south on Corn Springs Rd; c/o BLM, 400 S Farrell Dr, Ste B-205, Palm Springs 92262.
(619/760) 323-4421.

$4 per night. 14-night maximum stay. In a natural palm oasis. 50 acres. 27 tent/RV spaces. Cold showers, pit toilets. Hospital in Indio, 50 miles. (BLM)

Desert Hot Springs

SAM'S FAMILY SPA ⊛
4½ miles east of Palm Dr at 70-875 Dillon Rd, 92241.
(619/760) 329-6457; FAX (619/760) 329-8267.

$33 for 2; XP $6. Weekly & monthly rates. Extensive grounds including park area with large lake where guests may observe & feed ducks, birds & other fowl. Park area has picnic tables & barbecues. Available to public for day use. 40 acres. 225 RV spaces; 225 EWS. Flush toilets. Heated pool, wading pool, sauna, 2 natural mineral pools, 2 natural hot mineral whirlpools, exercise room, recreation room, playground. Coin laundry. Pets allowed. Groceries. Restaurant 11/1-5/31; 7 am-2 pm; closed Mon & Tue. (Private)

SKY VALLEY PARK EAST

5 miles north of I-10, exit Palm Dr; 74-711 Dillon Rd, 92241.
(619/760) 329-2909; FAX (619/760) 329-9473.

$31 for 2; XP $2. Check out 1 pm. Reservation deposit required. Weekly & monthly rates. 12 acres. 330 RV spaces; 330 EWS. Dump station, flush toilets, phone & cable TV hookups. 2 heated pools, saunas, whirlpools, 2 tennis courts, exercise room, recreation program, full-time activities director. Coin laundry. Small pets only, 1 per site. MC, VI. (Private)

SKY VALLEY PARK WEST

5 miles north of I-10, exit Palm Dr; 74-565 Dillon Rd, 92241.
(619/760) 329-7415; FAX (619/760) 329-9473.

$28 for 2; XP $2. Check out 1 pm. Reservation deposit required. Weekly & monthly rates. 200 acres. 284 RV spaces; 284 EWS. Dump station, flush toilets, phone & cable TV hookups. 2 heated pools, saunas, whirlpools, 2 tennis courts, recreation program, full-time activities director. Coin laundry. Small pets only, 1 per site. MC, VI. Restaurant Oct-May. (Private)

TAMARISK RV PARK

3½ miles east of Palm Dr, ½ mile south of Dillon at 18025 Langlois Rd, 92241.
Phone & FAX (619/760) 329-7943.

$15-17 for 4. Weekly & monthly rates. Quiet desert location. Tree-shaded sites. 10 acres. 98 RV spaces; 98 EWS. Flush toilets, phone & cable TV hookups. Heated indoor pool, whirlpool, recreation room, horseshoe pit, shuffleboard courts, volleyball court. Coin laundry. MC, VI. (Private)

El Centro

BUTTERCUP

40 miles east of El Centro on I-8; c/o BLM, 1661 S 4th St, 92243.
(619/760) 337-4400.

No fee. 180 tent/RV spaces. No water, vault toilets. Pets. (BLM)

COUNTRY LIFE RV PARK

3½ miles southeast at 375 E Ross Rd, 92243.
(619/760) 353-1040; FAX (619/760) 353-1948.

$15-18.50 for 2. Reservation deposit required; 5-day refund notice. Weekly & monthly rates. Many grass-covered pull-thru sites in rural area. 10 acres. 6 tent sites, 175 RV spaces; 175 EWS. Disposal station, flush toilets. Heated pool, recreation room. Coin laundry. Pets. Propane, groceries. MC, VI. (Private)

DESERT TRAILS RV PARK ⒶⒶⒶ

225 Wake Av, 92243.
(619/760) 352-7275; FAX (619/760) 352-7474.

$20 for 2. Check out 10 am. Reservation deposit required; cancellation fee. Weekly & monthly rates. Nicely landscaped with many tree-shaded sites. 64 acres. 404 RV spaces; 404 EW, 387 S. Flush toilets, phone & cable TV hookups,

50 amps. Heated pool, whirlpool, recreation room, 9-hole executive golf course, driving range. Coin laundry. Small pets only. (Private)

MIDWAY
40 miles east of El Centro on I-8, 2 miles west on Gray's Well Rd; c/o BLM, 1661 S 4th St, 92243.
(619/760) 337-4400.

No fee. 80 tent/RV spaces. No water, vault toilets. Pets. (BLM)

RIO BEND RV RESORT RANCH
7 miles west on I-8, south to 1589 Drew Rd, 92243.
(619/760) 352-7061; FAX (619/760) 352-0055.

RV spaces $21 for 2; tent sites $13; XP $2. Reservation cancellation fee. Weekly & monthly rates. In a quiet rural location. 40 acres. 20 tent sites, 270 RV spaces; 270 EW, 228 S. Flush toilets, phone & cable TV hookups, 50 amps. Heated pool, whirlpool, fishing, putting green, shuffleboard court, recreation room, 9 holes golf (fee). Coin laundry. Pets. Propane, groceries. MC, VI. (Private)

SUNBEAM LAKE RV RESORT
7 miles west on I-8, ½ mile north on Drew Rd; 1716 W Sunbeam Lake Dr, 92243.
(619/760) 352-7154.

$20 for 2; XP $2. Reservation deposit required; 30-day refund notice; cancellation fee. Weekly & monthly rates. Open sites, some pull-thru. 35 acres. 309 RV spaces; 309 EWS. Disposal station, flush toilets, phone & cable TV hookups, 50 amps. Heated pool, whirlpool, boat ramp, fishing, kayaks (fee), rental paddleboats. Coin laundry. Pets. MC, VI. (Private)

VACATION INN RV PARK
Adjacent to I-8, exit Imperial Av; 2015 Cottonwood Cir, 92243.
(619/760) 352-9523.

$17 for 4; XP $1. Credit card guarantee required. Weekly & monthly rates. 1 acre. 31 RV spaces; 31 EWS. Flush toilets, phone & cable TV hookups. 2 heated pools, whirlpools. Propane, coin laundry. Pets. AE, CB, DI, DS, MC, VI. Restaurant & lounge. (Private)

Glamis

GECKO
6½ miles west of Glamis on SR 78, then 3 miles south on Gecko Rd; c/o BLM, 1661 S 4th St, 92243.
(619/760) 337-4400.

No fee. 120 tent/RV spaces. No water; vault toilets. (BLM)

ROADRUNNER
6½ miles west of Glamis on SR 78, then 5½ miles south on Gecko Rd; c/o BLM, 1661 S 4th St, 92243.
(619/760) 337-4400.

No fee. 80 tent/RV spaces. No water; vault toilets. (BLM)

Holtville

HEBER DUNES COUNTY PARK
6½ miles south, off SR 111 on Heber Rd; 121 W 5th St, 92250.
(619/760) 339-4384.

No fee. Open tent/RV spaces. Flush toilets. Pets. (County)

Indio

FIESTA RV PARK ⓐⓐⓐ
3 miles south of I-10, eastbound exit Jefferson south to SR 111, then 1 mile east; westbound exit Auto Center Dr, west to SR 111, then 3 miles east; 46-421 Madison St, 92201.
(619/760) 342-2345; FAX (619/760) 342-2712.

$20-25 for 2; XP $2. Reservation deposit required. Weekly & monthly rates. Spacious sites, paired with grass and concrete patio area. Many sites have shade trees. Mountain views from many sites. 17 acres. 200 RV spaces. Disposal station, flush toilets, phone & cable TV hookups. 3 heated pools, saunas, whirlpools, billiard tables, horseshoe pit, shuffleboard, putting green, recreation program. Coin laundry. Pets. MC, VI. (Private)

OUTDOOR RESORTS-MOTORCOACH RESORT & SPA
Just south of SR 111, just east of Jefferson; 80-394 48th Av, 92201.
(619/760) 775-7255; FAX (619/760) 347-0825.

$35 for 4; XP $5. Class A or C motor homes only, 25-ft minimum. Reservation deposit required; 30-day refund notice; $25 cancellation fee. Monthly rates. Desert setting. Extensive grassy areas, fountains & pools. Resort surrounds golf course. 66 acres. 212 RV spaces. Flush toilets, phone & cable TV hookups. Putting green, heated pool, saunas, whirlpools, 2 lighted tennis courts, 9 holes golf (fee). Coin laundry. Pets. MC, VI. (Private)

Joshua Tree National Park

HEADQUARTERS
74485 National Park Dr, Twentynine Palms 92277.
(619/760) 367-7511.

Camping within the park is on a first-come, first-served basis, except for Black Rock Canyon campground. During spring and fall campgrounds typically fill early in the day. A 14-day camping limit is in effect Oct 2 through May 31, and a 30-day limit exists Jun 1 through Oct 1. Water is available only at Black Rock Canyon and Cottonwood campgrounds. Visitors must bring their own firewood. Pets must be leashed at all times and are prohibited on trails and farther than 100 yards from roads and campgrounds. (Also see the park listing in the *Joshua Tree Area* chapter.)

Belle *9 miles south of Twentynine Palms on Utah Tr & Pinto Basin Rd.*
(619/760) 367-7511.

No fee. 17 tent/RV spaces. No water or showers. Hospital in Joshua Tree, 21 miles. (NP)

Black Rock Canyon *5 miles southeast of Yucca Valley on Joshua Ln.*
$10. DESTINET. 80 acres. 100 tent/RV spaces (35-foot maximum RV length). Disposal station, flush toilets, no showers. Nature trails. Visitor center. Hospital in Joshua Tree, 14 miles. (NP)

Cottonwood Springs A & B Loops *32 miles northeast of Indio off I-10 via Cottonwood Springs Rd.*
$8. B Loop section of the park is open 10/1-6/1. 62 tent/RV spaces. Disposal station, flush toilets, no showers. Hospital in Indio, 25 miles. (NP)

Hidden Valley *14 miles south of Joshua Tree via main park road.*
No fee. 3 acres. 39 tent/RV spaces. No water, pit toilets. Hospital in Joshua Tree, 18 miles. (NP)

Indian Cove *8 miles southwest of Twentynine Palms on Indian Cove Rd.*
No fee. 107 tent/RV spaces. No water, pit toilets. Hospital in Joshua Tree, 12 miles. (NP)

Jumbo Rocks *11 miles south of Twentynine Palms on Utah Tr.*
No fee. 125 tent/RV spaces. No water, pit toilets. Hospital in Joshua Tree, 26 miles. (NP)

Ryan *16 miles southwest of Joshua Tree via Park Bl.*
No fee. 4 acres. 29 tent/RV spaces. No water, pit toilets. Hospital in Joshua Tree, 20 miles. (NP)

White Tank *11 miles south of Twentynine Palms via Utah Tr.*
No fee. 15 tent/RV spaces. No water, pit toilets. Hospital in Joshua Tree, 31 miles. (NP)

La Quinta

LAKE CAHUILLA RECREATION AREA
6 miles southwest of La Quinta via Monroe St; Box 3507, Riverside 92519.
(619/760) 564-4712; camping reservations (800) 284-7275.

$12-16. DESTINET. 158 tent/RV spaces (30-ft maximum RV length); 60 EW. Disposal station, flush toilets. Swimming ($1), fishing, children's playground. Pets, $2. (County)

Mojave

SIERRA TRAILS RV PARK ⓐⓐⓐ
6 miles northeast of Mojave; 21282 Hwy 14, 93501.
(619/760) 373-4950.

$15 for 2; XP $2. Tents, vans & cars, $10. Monthly rates. Shaded sites. Some pull-thru sites. El 2700. 5 acres. 18 RV spaces, 8 tent/RV spaces; 26 E, 17 S. Flush toilets, air conditioning & electric heaters ($1 ea). Heated pool (5/1-9/30), recreation room. Coin laundry. Pets, $1. (Private)

If your plans change, don't forget to cancel your reservations.

Mojave National Preserve

AFTON CANYON

35 miles northeast of Barstow off I-15 on Afton Rd; c/o 150 Coolwater Ln, Barstow 92311.
(619/760) 256-3591.

$4. 14-night maximum stay. In scenic Afton Canyon. 25 acres. 22 tent/RV sites, 22 W. No showers; pit toilets. Wildlife observation. 24-hr attendant. Hospital in town. (BLM)

PARK SERVICE OFFICE

Via I-40 and I-15, 40 miles northeast of Barstow in Baker; Mojave Desert Information Center, Box 241, Baker 92309.
(619/760) 733-4040.

Hole-in-the-Wall *25½ miles northwest of Essex off I-40 via Essex and Black Canyon rds.*
$10. El 4200. 20 acres. 37 tent/RV spaces (50-ft maximum RV length). Disposal station, no showers, pit toilets. Hospital in Needles. (NP)

Mid Hills *35½ miles northwest of Essex off I-40 via Essex and Black Canyon rds.*
$5. 14-night maximum stay. El 5600. 40 acres. 26 tent/RV spaces (25-ft maximum RV length). No showers, pit toilets. (NP)

Needles

MOABI REGIONAL PARK

11 miles southeast of Needles off I-40; Park Moabi Rd, 92363.
(619/760) 326-3831.

$10-15. Reservations. 647 tent/RV spaces; 11 EW, 131 EWS. Disposal station, flush toilets. Swimming, fishing, playground. Pets, $1. (County)

NEEDLES KOA

Just off I-40; westbound exit Needles Hwy, ½ mile north then 1 mile west on National Trails Hwy; eastbound use Needles Hwy Cut Off exit, 1 block northwest then ½ mile southeast on National Trails Hwy; 5400 National Trails Hwy; Rt 4, Box 175, 92363.
(619/760) 326-4207.

$17.95-22.95 for 2; XP $2. Reservation deposit required; 3-day refund notice. Open & some shaded sites in desert area. 12 acres. 94 tent/RV spaces; 94 EW, 63 S. Flush toilets, 30-50 amps. Pool, playground, recreation room. Coin laundry. Pets. Propane, groceries. MC, VI. Snack bar. (Private)

NEEDLES MARINA PARK

From I-40, J St exit to W Broadway, ⅘ mile west to Needles Hwy then ½ mile east; 100 Marina Dr, 92363.
(619/760) 326-2197.

$23-25 for 3; XP $3-6. Check in 6 pm in summer. Reservation deposit required; 14-day refund notice; cancellation fee. Weekly & monthly rates in winter. On the Colorado River next to municipal golf course. Some sites with shade trees. 33 acres. 85 tent/RV spaces, 102 RV spaces. Flush toilets, air conditioning ($2.50), 50 amps. Pool, whirlpool, boat ramp, playground, recreation room, gas, marina (fee), fishing, water-skiing. Coin laundry. Pets. Groceries. MC, VI. (Private)

CAMPGROUNDS & TRAILER PARKS

RIVER ROAD RESORT
½ mile north of Needles via W Broadway/River Rd exit off I-40; Rt 4, Box 99, 92363.
(619/760) 326-3423.

$16 for 2; XP $2. Reservation deposit required. Weekly rates. On the Colorado River. 4 acres. 4 tent sites, 26 RV spaces. Flush toilets, 35 amps. Boat ramp, dock, fishing. Coin laundry. Pets (maximum 2). MC, VI. (Private)

Ocotillo Wells State Vehicular Recreation Area

HEADQUARTERS
North of SR 78 on the eastern edge of Anza-Borrego Desert State Park at 5172 Hwy 78; Box 360, Borrego Springs 92204.
(619/760) 767-5391.

No fee. Primitive camping on a first-come, first-served basis. 30-night minimum stay. 40,000 acres. 500 tent sites. Disposal station, flush toilets, no showers, no drinking water. Hospital in Brawley, 46 miles. (State)

Palo Verde

PALO VERDE COUNTY PARK
3 miles south on SR 78; c/o Imperial County Property Services, 1002 State St, El Centro 92243.
(619/760) 339-4384.

No fee. 25 tent/RV spaces (45-ft maximum RV length). Flush toilets. Fishing. Pets. (County)

WALTER'S CAMPES
35 miles south of Blythe on SR 78 at Walter's Camp Rd; Box 31, 92266.
(619/760) 854-3322.

$10-17. 5-month maximum stay. 64 tent/RV spaces, 50 RV spaces (40-foot maximum RV length); 50 EW. Disposal station, flush toilets. Swimming, hunting, fishing, water-skiing, boat ramp (fee). Coin laundry. Groceries. Hospital in Blythe, 35 miles. Lounge, snack bar. (Public)

Parker Dam

BLACK MEADOW LANDING RESORT
9½ miles west of Parker Dam on Lake Havasu; Box 98, 92267.
(619/760) 663-4901.

$6-25 for 2; XP $4. 50 tent sites; 400 tent/RV spaces. Disposal station, flush toilets. 9 holes golf, swimming, boat ramp, playground, recreation room, fishing, water-skiing. Coin laundry. Groceries, propane. 24-hr attendant. Hospital in town. Lounge, snack bar. (BLM)

Providence Mountains State Recreation Area

HEADQUARTERS
16 miles northwest of Essex off I-40; Box 1, Essex 92332.
(805) 942-0662.

$12. El 4300. 6 tent/RV sites (27-ft maximum RV length). Flush toilets. Pets, $1. (State)

Red Rock Canyon State Park

HEADQUARTERS
Exit SR 14 at Abbott Dr; Box 26, Cantil 93519.
(805) 942-0662.

$7. El 2600. 10,384 acres. Primitive campground. 50 tent/RV spaces (30-foot maximum RV length). Disposal station, pit toilets. Nature trails. Pets, $1. Hospital in Mojave, 25 miles. (State)

Saddleback Butte State Park

HEADQUARTERS
17 miles east of Lancaster on E Av J and 170th St; 1051 W Av M, Ste 201, Lancaster 93534.
(805) 942-0662.

$10. 2955 acres. 50 tent/RV spaces (30-foot maximum RV length). Disposal station, pit toilets, no showers. Nature trails. Visitor center. Hospital in town, 17 miles. (State)

Salton Sea National Wildlife Refuge

RED HILL MARINA COUNTY PARK
8½ miles southwest off SR 111 and Sinclair Rd; 7581 Garst Rd, Calipatria 92233.
(619/760) 348-2310.

$7. 200 tent sites, 40 RV sites; 40 EW (45-ft maximum RV length). Flush toilets. Fishing. Pets. (County)

Salton Sea State Recreation Area

HEADQUARTERS
10½ miles southeast of Mecca off SR 111; Box 3666, North Shore 92254.
(619/760) 393-3052.

Camping at the recreation area, with the exception of the improved campsites at Headquarters, are on a first-come, first-served basis. Seniors 62 and over get a $2 discount. Elevation is 220 feet below sea level. Pet dogs permitted at all campgrounds, $1. (Also see the Salton Sea listing in the *Imperial Valley Area* chapter.)

Bombay Beach *18 miles northwest of Niland off SR 111.*
$7. 200 tent/RV spaces. Chemical toilets. Swimming, fishing. (State)

Corvina Beach *13½ miles southeast of Mecca off SR 111.*
$7. 500 tent/RV spaces. Chemical toilets. Swimming, fishing. (State)

Headquarters *10½ miles southeast of Mecca off SR 111; Box 3666, North Shore 92254.*
(619/760) 393-3052.
10/1-5/31 $12-16. 30-night maximum stay. Some primitive sites. 17,900 acres. 150 tent/RV spaces (35-ft maximum RV length). Disposal station, flush & pit toi-

lets. Swimming, boat ramp (fee), nature trails, boating, water-skiing, fishing. Visitor center. Hospital in Indio. (State)

Mecca Beach *12 miles southeast of Mecca off SR 111.*
$12. 110 tent/RV spaces (30-ft maximum RV length). Flush toilets. Swimming, fishing. (State)

Salt Creek Primitive Area *17 miles southeast of Mecca off SR 111.*
$7. 100 tent/RV spaces. No water, chemical toilets. Swimming, fishing. (State)

Twentynine Palms

KNOTT SKY PARK
South of SR 62, west of Canyon Rd; Box 995, 92277.
(619/760) 367-9669.

$10.70-16.16. Reservations. El 2000 ft. 1-acre tent area accommodates 100 single tents or 50 group tents; 38 tent/RV spaces (40-ft maximum RV length); 24 EWS, 14 EW. Disposal station, flush toilets. Playground. Pets. (County)

29 PALMS RV RESORT ⊛
From SR 62, 2 miles north via Adobe Rd, ½ mile east on Amboy Rd to 4949 Desert Knoll Av, 92777.
(619/760) 367-3320.

$19-22 for 2; XP $5. Reservation deposit required; 30-day refund notice. Weekly and monthly rates. Open, pull-thru sites; some on 8th fairway of Roadrunner Dunes Golf Course. 20 acres. 197 RV spaces; 197 EWS. Flush toilets. Sauna, whirlpool, heated pool covered in winter, recreation room, exercise room, shuffleboard, horseshoes, 1 tennis court, 9 holes golf (fee). Coin laundry. Pets. Propane. MC, VI. (Private)

Victorville

MOJAVE NARROWS REGIONAL PARK
4 miles east of I-15 on Bear Valley Rd, 2½ miles north on Ridgecrest and Yates rds; Box 361, 92392.
(619/760) 245-2226.

$9. El 2700. 47 tent/RV spaces, 38 RV spaces; 38 EWS. Disposal station, flush toilets. Fishing, playground, horseback riding. Pets, $1. Horse camp. (County)

VICTORVILLE KOA
2 miles north, adjacent to I-15; northbound Stoddard Wells Rd exit, southbound 2nd Stoddard Wells exit; 16530 Stoddard Wells Rd, 92392.
(619/760) 245-6867.

$18.50 for 2; XP $2. Reservation deposit required. Weekly & monthly rates. Located in a wooded area next to the Mojave River. 8 Kamping Kabins, $28. El 3000. 10 acres. 136 tent/RV spaces; 116 E ($2), 136 W, 86 S ($2). Disposal station, flush toilets, 30 amps. Pool, playground, recreation room. Coin laundry. Pets. Propane, groceries. AE, MC, VI. (Private)

Winterhaven

(See also Yuma, Arizona.)

PICACHO STATE RECREATION AREA
25 miles north on Picacho Rd, on the Colorado River; Box 1207, 92283.
(619/760) 393-3052.

$7 per night. 45-night maximum stay. 7000 acres. 59 tent/RV spaces. Narrow, winding dirt roads. Primitive campground. Pit toilets. Water-skiing, fishing, boat ramp. Pets, $1. 24-hour attendant. Hospital in Yuma, Ariz, 25 miles. (State)

RIVER'S EDGE RV RESORT
Off I-8, eastbound take first Winterhaven exit, westbound exit Winterhaven Dr, ½ mile east on frontage rd; 2999 Winterhaven Dr, 92283.
(619/760) 572-5105; FAX (619/760) 572-5640.

$20 for 2; XP $2. Reservation deposit required; 3-day refund notice; cancellation fee. On the Colorado River, 1 mile west of Yuma, Ariz. 50 acres. 494 RV spaces; 494 EWS. Flush toilets, cable TV hookups. Pool, whirlpool, swimming, boat ramp, recreation room, horseshoe pit, shuffleboard court, fishing. Coin laundry. Small pets only. Propane, groceries. MC, VI. (Private)

ARIZONA

Lake Havasu City

CATTAIL COVE STATE PARK
17 miles south on SR 95; Box 1990, 86405.
(520) 855-1223.

$3-14. 120 tent/RV spaces; 40 RV spaces; 40 EWS. El 200. Disposal station, flush toilets. Beach, swimming, boat ramp, fishing, water-skiing, boat rentals. Coin laundry. Propane, groceries. Hospital in town. (State)

LAKE HAVASU STATE PARK
Junction of SR 95 & London Bridge Rd, west on London Bridge Rd, then 2½ miles to park entrance; 1801 Hwy 95, 86406.
(520) 855-7851.

$3-14. 25 tent sites; 50 tent/RV spaces. 11,000 acres. Flush toilets. Beach, swimming, boat ramp. 24-hr attendant. Hospital in town. (State)

SANDPOINT MARINA & RV PARK
12 miles south on SR 95, sign reads Cattail Cove/Sandpoint/Lake Havasu State Park; Box 1469, 86405-1469.
(520) 855-1223; FAX (520) 855-3008.

$22 for 2; XP $3. Reservation deposit required; 30-day refund notice. Weekly & monthly rates. Adjacent to Lake Havasu. Shaded sites & cabanas. 175 RV spaces; 175 EWS. 6 acres. Disposal station, flush toilets. Cable TV hookups, air conditioning ($4). Beach, swimming, boat ramp, dock, marina, playground, recreation room, fishing, boating, house & pontoon boats. Coin laundry. Pets, leash & cleanup required. Propane, groceries. MC, VI. (Private)

Parker

BIG BEND RESORT CONCESSION
3 miles south of Parker Dam, CA; Box 24, Parker Dam, CA 92267. (619/760) 663-3755.

$12.50-18 for 2; XP $3-5. 245 tent/RV spaces (60-ft maximum RV length); 135 ES, 161 W. 42 acres. Air conditioning & heaters ($3 ea). Disposal station, flush toilets. Beach, swimming, boat ramp, dock, boating, fishing. Coin laundry. Groceries, propane. Lounge, snack bar. (BLM)

BUCKSKIN MOUNTAIN STATE PARK
11 miles north at 54751 SR 95, on the Colorado River; Box BA, Parker, AZ 85344. (520) 667-3231.

$3-20 per night. 83 tent/RV spaces; 48 EW. 1676 acres. 21 cabanas with electric & water hookups. Disposal station, flush toilets. Playground, beach, swimming, boat ramp, boat rentals, fishing, hiking trails. Groceries. Hospital in town. (State)

Buckskin Mountain River Island Unit
12 miles north at 54751 SR 95, on the Colorado River; Box BA, Parker, AZ 85344. (520) 667-3386.

$5-20 per night. 15-night maximum stay. 22 tent/RV spaces; 22 E, $1. Disposal station, flush toilets. Boating, fishing, hiking trails. 24-hour attendant. Hospital in town. (State)

CROSSROADS
8 miles north of Parker on the California side; Parker Dam Rd, Parker Dam, CA 92267. (520) 855-8017.

No fee. 8 tent/RV sites. Vault toilets, no showers. Beach, wading pool, swimming. 24-hour attendant. Hospital in town. (BLM)

ECHO LODGE RESORT CONCESSION
11 miles north of Parker on California side; Parker Dam Rd, Parker, AZ 85344. (619/760) 663-4931.

$16-23. 150 tent/RV spaces. Disposal station, flush toilets, showers. Swimming, fishing, boating, boat ramp, dock, beach, wading pool. Coin laundry. Groceries. 24-hour attendant. Lounge. (BLM)

EMERALD COVE CAMPGROUND RESORT CONCESSION
3 miles north of Parker on California side; Parker Dam Rd, Parker, AZ 85344. (619/760) 663-3737.

$16-23. 450 tent/RV spaces. Disposal station, flush toilets. Swimming, beach, pool, boat ramp, fishing. Coin laundry. Groceries. Lounge, club house. 24-hr attendant. (BLM)

EMPIRE LANDING

10 miles north of Parker on California side; Parker Dam Rd, 92242.
(520) 855-8017.

$8. 20 acres. 26 tent sites, 50 RV spaces (35-ft maximum RV length). Disposal station, flush toilets, cold showers. Swimming, fishing, hiking trails. Pets allowed except weekends of Memorial Day, July 4th & Labor Day. Hospital in town. (BLM)

HAVASU SPRINGS RESORT CONCESSION

17 miles north of Parker on AZ SR 95; Rt 2, Box 624, 85344.
(520) 667-3361.

$20-22. On southern shore of Lake Havasu. 90 tent/RV spaces. Disposal station, flush toilets, showers. Beach, swimming, boat ramp, marina, fishing, boat rentals. Coin laundry. Groceries. 24-hour attendant. Lounge. (BLM)

LA PAZ COUNTY PARK

8 miles north of Parker off AZ SR 95; 1 Park Dr, 85344.
(520) 667-2069.

$8-12 for 2. 160 acres. 99 RV sites; 99 W; 99 E, $5. Dry camp area on 1 mile of beachfront. Other county parks are Bouse Community Park & Centennial Park. Disposal station ($5), flush toilets. Golf, swimming, 1 tennis court, volleyball, horseshoes, boating, water-skiing. Pets. Hospital in town. (County)

RIO DEL COLORADO RESORT CONCESSION

7 miles north of Parker on California side; Parker Dam Rd, Parker, AZ 85344.
(619/760) 663-3636.

$16-23. 50 tent/RV spaces. Flush toilets; no showers. Beach, swimming, boat ramp, dock, boating, fishing. Coin laundry. 24-hour attendant. Lounge. (BLM)

RIVER LAND RESORT CONCESSION

6 miles north of Parker on California side; Parker Dam Rd, Parker, AZ 85344.
(619/760) 663-3733.

$12-18. 58 tent/RV spaces. Disposal station, flush toilets. Beach, swimming, boat ramp, dock, recreation room, boating, fishing. Coin laundry. Groceries. 24-hr attendant. (BLM)

RIVER LODGE RESORT CONCESSION

16 miles north of Parker on California side; Parker Dam Rd, Parker, AZ 85344.
(619/760) 663-4934.

$15. 350 tent/RV spaces. Disposal station, flush toilets. Beach, swimming, boat ramp, dock, boating, fishing. Groceries. 24-hour attendant. (BLM)

SUNSHINE RESORT CONCESSION

14 miles north of Parker on California side; Parker Dam Rd, Parker, AZ 85344.
(619/760) 663-3098.

$15. 34 tent/RV spaces. Disposal station, flush toilets. Beach, swimming, boat ramp, dock, boating, fishing. Coin laundry. Groceries. 24-hour attendant. (BLM)

Yuma

(See also Winterhaven, California.)

ARABY ACRES TRAVEL PARK

5 miles east on I-8, exit Araby Rd, ⅙ mile southeast; 6649 E Hwy 80, 85365.
(520) 342-2999; FAX (520) 341-1049.

9/1-6/1 $24 per night for 2; 6/2-8/31 $20 per night for 2; XP $2. Age restrictions may apply. Reservation deposit required; 7-day refund notice. Weekly & monthly rates. 23 acres. 258 spaces, 80 RV spaces; 80 EWS. Flush toilets; cable TV & phone hookups, 60 amps. Putting green, 2 heated pools, whirlpools, recreation room, exercise room, horseshoe pits, lighted shuffleboard courts. Coin laundry. Small pets only. Propane. (Private)

BONITA MESA RV RESORT

9½ miles east on north side of I-8, Fortuna Rd exit 12, then 1½ miles west to 9400 N Frontage Rd, 85365.
(520) 342-2999; FAX (520) 342-4614.

$22 for 2; XP $2. Reservation deposit required; 30-day refund notice; cancellation fee. Weekly & monthly rates. 30 acres. 550 RV spaces; 550 EWS. Flush toilets, phone & cable TV hookups, 50 amps. Heated pool, whirlpool, recreation room, exercise room, horseshoe pits, shuffleboard courts, billiard room. Coin laundry. Pets. (Private)

COCOPAH BEND RV RESORT

From business loop 8, 3⅘ miles west on 8th St, then 1⅘ miles north on Hope, Riverside Dr and Strand Av; 6800 S Strand Av, 85364.
(520) 343-9300; FAX (520) 343-0699.

$17.50-22.50 for 2; XP $2. Age restrictions may apply. Reservation deposit required; 30-day refund notice; cancellation fee. Weekly, monthly and seasonal rates. 160 acres. 806 spaces; 600 RV spaces, 600 EWS. Large RV resort located in a quiet, rural location. Extensive recreational facilities. Flush toilets, phone & cable TV hookups, 50 amps. Heated pool, whirlpool, 1 lighted tennis court, recreation room, exercise room, horseshoe pits, lighted shuffleboard courts, fishing, 18 holes golf (fee). Coin laundry. Pets. DS, MC, VI. Snack bar. (Private)

HIDDEN SHORES RV VILLAGE

25 miles northeast of Yuma via Imperial Co Rd S24; Star Rt 4, Box 40, 85365.
(520) 783-1448.

$12 for 2. 5-month stay limit. 284 tent/RV spaces, 70 RV spaces (40-ft maximum RV length); 284 EW. Disposal station, flush toilets. Swimming, boating, boat ramp, fishing. Coin laundry. Groceries, propane. Hospital in town. (BLM)

IMPERIAL DAM LONG TERM VISITOR AREA (CALIFORNIA)

24 miles north via Imperial Co Rd S24; exit I-8 at Winterhaven, CA exit.
(520) 726-6300.

9/15-4/15 $50. Closed 4/16-9/14; limited facilities in winter. Weekly rates. 3200 acres. 2000 tent/RV spaces; 4 W. Disposal station, cold showers, flush toilets. Pets. 24-hr attendant. Hospital in town. (BLM)

SENATOR WASH RECREATION SITE

18½ miles northeast of Yuma off Imperial Co Rd S24 via Senator Wash Rd; 2555 E Gila Ridge Rd, Yuma, AZ 85365.
(520) 317-3200.

No fee. Open sites. Disposal station, flush toilets. Swimming, fishing. Pets. (BLM)

SHANGRI-LA RV PARK RESORT

10 miles east of Yuma on north side of I-8, Fortuna Rd exit 12, then ½ mile west; 10498 N Frontage Rd, 85365.
(520) 342-9123.

$15 for 2; XP $1. Reservation deposit required; cancellation fee. Weekly, monthly & seasonal rates. 16 acres. 303 RV spaces; 303 EWS; air conditioning $1. Flush toilets, 30 amps. Whirlpool, recreation room, horseshoe pit, shuffleboard court. Coin laundry. Small pets only. Propane. (Private)

SQUAW LAKE CAMPGROUND

29 miles north of AZ SR 95 via Imperial Dam Rd & Imperial Co Rd S24, on California side of river; 2555 E Gila Ridge Rd, Yuma, AZ 85365.
(520) 726-6300.

$5 per night. 115 tent/RV sites (30-foot maximum RV length). Cold showers, flush toilets. Beach, swimming, fishing, boating, hiking trail. Pets. (BLM)

WESTWIND RV & GOLF RESORT

10 miles east of Yuma on south side of I-8, Fortuna Rd exit 12, then 1 mile west; 9797 E Hwy 80, 85365.
(520) 342-2992; FAX (520) 342-4251.

9/1-4/30 $20 for 2; 5/1-8/31 $15 for 2; XP $3. Limited facilities 5/1-8/31. Reservation deposit required; 30-day refund notice. Weekly, monthly & seasonal rates. 72 acres. 920 RV spaces; 706 EWS. Phone & cable TV hookups, flush toilets. Heated pool, whirlpool, golf driving range, recreation room, exercise room, horseshoe pits, lighted shuffleboard court, Sat night dances in season, 9 holes golf (fee). Coin laundry. Small pets only. MC, VI. (Private)

WINDHAVEN RV PARK ⨁

6 miles southeast of Yuma off I-8; 6580 E Hwy 80, 85365.
(520) 726-0284; FAX (520) 726-6622.

9/15-4/15 $15-22 for 2; 4/16-9/14 $12-14.95 for 2; XP $3. Reservation deposit required; 5-day refund notice. Weekly, monthly & seasonal rates. 10 acres. 111 RV spaces, 20 tent/RV spaces; 131 EWS. Some pull-thru sites. RV parts & supplies available. Flush toilets, 50 amps, phone & cable TV hookups. Heated pool, whirlpool, billiard room, exercise room, horseshoe pit, shuffleboard court. Coin laundry. Pets. Propane. MC, VI. (Private)

Index

This index contains listings for points of interest, cities, activities, events and recreational sites.

Index to Advertisers

Acknowledgements

Writer ....Bryan Wilhite

Contributing Writers ...Robert Saunders
George Yago III
Kristine Miller

Cartographer ....Edward Davis

Graphic Artist ....Virginia Matijevac

Cover Design.................Michael C. Lee

Editor............................Kristine Miller

page 2: *Algodones Dunes*

page 3: *Date palms, Indio*

Photography by Todd Masinter, except as noted:

pages 30, 33, 36 ......Auto Club Archives

page 126 ....Mark Jorgensen/
Anza-Borrego Desert State Park

page 198.................Calico Ghost Town
Regional Park